Catalogue of the
Ethiopic Manuscript Imaging Project

Ethiopic Manuscript Imaging Project

Ethiopic Manuscripts, Texts, and Studies

Series Editor
Steve Delamarter

Published Volumes

EMTS 1. Getatchew Haile, Melaku Terefe, Roger M. Rundell, Daniel Alemu, and Steve Delamarter. *Catalogue of the Ethiopic Manuscript Imaging Project: Volume 1, Codices 1–105, Magic Scrolls 1–134.*

EMTS 2. Steve Delamarter, and Melaku Terefe. *Ethiopian Scribal Practice 1: Plates for the Catalogue of the Ethiopic Manuscript Imaging Project* (Companion to EMIP Catalogue 1).

EMTS 3. Veronika Six, Steve Delamarter, Melaku Terefe, Getatchew Haile, Jeremy R. Brown, and Erik C. Young. *Catalogue of the Ethiopic Manuscript Imaging Project: Volume 2: Codices 106–200, Magic Scrolls 135–284.*

Forthcoming volumes

EMTS 4. *Ethiopian Scribal Practice 2: Plates for the Catalogue of the Ethiopic Manuscript Imaging Project* (Companion to EMIP Catalogue 2).

EMTS 5. *Catalogue of the Ethiopic Manuscript Imaging Project: Volume 3, Codices 201—300.*

EMTS 6. *Ethiopian Scribal Practice 3: Plates for the Catalogue of the Ethiopic Manuscript Imaging Project* (Companion to EMIP Catalogue 3).

EMTS 7. *Catalogue of the Ethiopic Manuscript Imaging Project: Volume 4, Codices 301—400 and Magic Scrolls 285ff.*

EMTS 8. *Ethiopian Scribal Practice 4: Plates for the Catalogue of the Ethiopic Manuscript Imaging Project* (Companion to EMIP Catalogue 4).

EMTS 9. *Catalogue of the Ethiopic Manuscript Imaging Project: Volume 5, Codices 401—500.*

EMTS 10. *Ethiopian Scribal Practice 5: Plates for the Catalogue of the Ethiopic Manuscript Imaging Project* (Companion to EMIP Catalogue 5).

EMTS 11. *Catalogue of the Ethiopic Manuscript Imaging Project: Volume 6, Codices 501–600, Arabic Manuscripts from Harar.*

EMTS 12. *Ethiopian Scribal Practice 6: Plates for the Catalogue of the Ethiopic Manuscript Imaging Project* (Companion to EMIP Catalogue 6).

EMTS 14. *Ethiopian Scribal Practice 7: Plates for the Catalogue of the Ethiopic Manuscript Imaging Project* (Companion to EMIP Catalogue 7).

Catalogue of the Ethiopic Manuscript Imaging Project

Volume 7–Codices 601–654:
The Meseret Sebhat Le-Ab Collection
of Mekane Yesus Seminary, Addis Ababa

Kesis Melaku Terefe, Steve Delamarter,
and Jeremy R. Brown

With a foreword by Richard Pankhurst and contributions from
Loren Bliese, Meheretab Bereke, Walda Estifanos,
Ted Erho, and Ralph Lee

◈PICKWICK *Publications* · Eugene, Oregon

CATALOGUE OF THE ETHIOPIC MANUSCRIPT IMAGING PROJECT

Volume 7, Codices 601–654: The Meseret Sebhat Le-ab Collection of Mekane Yesus Seminary, Addis Ababa

Ethiopic Manuscripts, Texts, and Studies 13

Copyright © 2011 Steve Delamarter. All rights reserved. Except for brief quotations in critical publications or reviews, no part of this book may be reproduced in any manner without prior written permission from the publisher. Write: Permissions, Wipf and Stock Publishers, 199 W. 8th Ave., Suite 3, Eugene, OR 97401.

Pickwick Publications
A Division of Wipf and Stock Publishers
199 W. 8th Ave., Suite 3
Eugene, OR 97401
www.wipfandstock.com

ISBN13: 978-1-61097-412-7

Cataloging-in-Publication data:

Delamarter, Steve.
    Catalogue of the Ethiopic Manuscripts in the Meseret Sebhat Le-Ab collection of Mekane Yesus Seminary, Addis Ababa / Steve Delamarter, Melaku Terefe, and Jeremy R. Brown.

    p. ; cm. —Includes bibliographies, references, and indexes.

Ethiopic Manuscripts, Texts, and Studies 13

ISBN 13: 978-1-61097-412-7

    1. Codicology. 2. Manuscripts—Ethiopic—Catalogs. 3. Scribes—Ethiopian. 4. Scribes—Africa. I. Terefe, Melaku. II. Title. III. Series.

BS4.5 E75 v. 13

Manufactured in the U.S.A.

Cover art: MYS 21, f. 1r: Saint Yared sings and dances before the King.

Aläqa Meseret Sebhat Le-Ab (1926–1998)

Contents

Series Foreword / xiii
Abbreviations / xv
Foreword: Ethiopian Manuscripts and Their Preservation / xix
    by Richard Pankhurst
Preface / xxiii
    by Steve Delamarter
Introduction to the Collection / xxvii
    by Steve Delamarter
Aläqa *Meseret Sebhat Le-Ab: A Biography / xxxi*
    by Loren Bliese, Mehret-Ab Bereke, and Walda Estifanos
The Dəgg^{w}a of St Yared and the Musical Manuscripts in the Collection / lvii
    by Ralph Lee
The Textual Character of Jubilees in Mekane Yesus Seminary 54 / lxv
    By Ted M. Erho

Catalogue of the Manuscripts / 1
    by *Kesis* Melaku Terefe, Jeremy Brown and Steve Delamarter

List of the Manuscripts by MYS shelf mark / 219
List of Dated or Datable Manuscripts by Date / 225
List of Undated Manuscripts by Date / 227
Bibliography / 229
Index of Worksin the Codices / 239
Index of Names and Places / 245
Index of Miniatures / 247
Index of Scribal Practices / 249

Contents of the Companion, Plates Volume, *Ethiopian Scribal Practice 7*

Codicology and Scribal Practice in the Mekane Yesus Collection
    by Sara Vulgan and Steve Delamarter
Scribal Intervention in the Mekane Yesus Collection
    by Jeremy Brown
Illuminated Manuscripts in the Mekane Yesus Collection
    by Marilyn Heldman

Series Foreword

The series *Ethiopic Manuscripts, Texts, and Studies* offers, in the first place, catalogues of the Ethiopic Manuscript Imaging Project whose purpose it is to digitize and catalogue collections of Ethiopic manuscripts in North America and around the world. Beyond this, though, the series offers a venue for monographs, revised dissertations, and texts that explore the rich historical, literary, and artistic traditions of Ethiopia and the Ethiopian Orthodox Church.

The series has particular interest in Ethiopic manuscripts and the scribal practices in evidence within them. This includes analytical studies of particular manuscripts or particular scribal practices and illuminations. Moreover, the interest extends to synthetic studies that explore the developments of scribal and artistic practice across time or those that probe the interconnections between common elements in manuscripts, scribal practices, scribal education, and community ideology.

Steve Delamarter, series editor

Abbreviations

AbbCat	Abbadie, Antoine d'. *Catalogue raisonné de manuscrits éthiopiens appartenant à Antoine d'Abbadie*. Paris, 1859.
AE	Annales d'Éthiopie
AF	Äthiopistische Forschungen
Apocryphes	Basset, René. *Les Apocryphes éthiopiens traduits en français. I–XI*. Paris: Bibliotheque de la Haute Science, 1893–1909
AṢZ	*Ammestu Ṣawatewa Zemawočč*, አምስቱ፡ ጸዋትው፡ ዜማዎች፡፡ እነርሱም፤ ፩ኛ – ጾም፡ ድጓ፤ ፪ኛ – ምዕራፍ፤ ፫ኛ – ዚቅ፤ መዝሙር፤ አስመ፡ ለዓለም፤ ፬ኛ – ዝማሬ፤ ፭ኛ – ምዋሥዕት፡፡ Addis Ababa: Bərhanənna Sälam Press, 1965 EC
BBB	Bonner Biblische Beiträge
BL	Stefan Strelcyn. *Catalogue of Ethiopian Manuscripts in the British Library Acquired since the Year 1877*. London: British Museum, 1978
BVTA	August Dillmann. *Biblia Veteris Testamenti Aethiopica*. Leipzig: Fr. Chr. Guil. Vogelii, 1853
CSCO	Corpus Scriptorum Christianorum Orientalium (Louvain, 1930–)
DChr	*August Dillmann*. Chrestomathia Aethiopica (Leipzig 1866). Second edition, edited and corrected by Enno Littmann (Leipzig 1941)
DChr	August Dillmann. *Chrestomathia Aethiopica*. Leipzig: Weigel, 1866. 2nd edition, edited and corrected by Enno Littmann. Berlin: Akademie, 1941
DAP	August Dillmann. *Annotationes in Pentateuchos*. Leipzig: Fr. Chr. Guil. Vogelii, 1853
DM	ድርሳነ፡ ሚካኤል፡ ወድርሳነ፡ ሩፋኤል፡፡ መልክአ፡ ሚካኤል፡ ወመልክአ፡ ሩፋኤል፡፡ ዘአገተም፡ ተስፋ፡ ገብረ፡ ሥላሴ፡ ዘብሔረ፡ ቡልጋ፡፡ = *Dərsanä Mikaʾel wä-Dərsanä Rufaʾel. Mälkəʾa Mikaʾel wä-Mälkəʾa Rufaʾel.* Addis Ababa: Täsfa, 1940 EC
EA	*Encyclopaedia Aethiopica* (Hamburg 2003–)
EC	Ethiopian Calendar, seven to eight years behind AD
EMML	Getatchew Haile and William F. Macomber, *A Catalogue of Ethiopian Manuscripts Microfilmed for the Ethiopian*

	Manuscript Microfilm Library, Addis Ababa and for the Hill Monastic Manuscript Library, Collegeville. Collegeville: Hill Museum and Manuscript Library, 1973–
EMIP	Ethiopic Manuscript Imaging Project (Portland, Oregon)
EMTS	Ethiopic Manuscripts, Texts, and Studies (Eugene, OR, 2009–)
JA	*Journal asiatique (*Paris, 1822–)
JES	*Journal of Ethiopian Studies* (Addis Ababa, 1963–)
JSS	*Journal of Semitic Studies* (Manchester, 1956–)
JSSSup	Journal of Semitic Studies Supplement (Oxford, 1993–)
Lincei	Stefan Strelcyn. *Catalogue des manuscrits éthiopiens de l'Accademia Nazionale dei Lincei: Fonds Conti Rossini et Fonds Caetani 209, 375, 376, 377, 378.* Rome: Accademia Nazionale dei Lincei, 1976
Liturgy	Daoud, Marcos, and H. E. Blatta Marsie Hazen. *The Liturgy of the Ethiopian Church.* Cairo: Egyptian Book Press, 1959.
MD59	መዝሙር፡ ዘዳዊት፡ = *Mäzmur zä- Dawit.* Addis Ababa: Bərhanənna Sälam Press, 1959 EC
MD59	መዝሙር፡ ዳዊት፡ = *Mäzmurä Dawit.* Addis Ababa: Bəhanənna Sälam Press, 1959 EC
Me_erāf	Velat, Bernard. *Me_erāf.Commun del'office divin éthiopien pour toute l'année.* PO 34 (1966) I–XV and 1–413. Paris: Firmin-Didot, 1966
MG59	ሰባቱ፡ ኪዳናት።፡ ቅዳሴ፡ ማርያም፡ መልክእ፡ ጉባኤ።፡ = *Säbattu Kidanat. Qəddase Maryam Mälkə'a Guba'e.* Addis Ababa: Täsfa Press, 1959 EC
MQ51	መጽሐፉ፡ ቅዳሴ።፡ በግዕዝና፡ ብአማርኛ።፡ = *Mäṣḥäfä Qəddase. Bä-Gə_əzənna bä-Amarəñña.* Addis Ababa: Täsfa Press, 1951 EC
NF	Neue Folge
Notice	Carlo Conti Rossini. "Notice sur les manuscrits éthiopiens de la collection d'Abbadie." *JA* 10.15 (1912) 551–78 [I]; 20 (1913) 5–72, 449–94 [II]; 11.2 (1913) 5–64 [III]; 5 (1915) 189–238, 447–93 [IV]; reprinted. Paris, 1914
NS	New Series
Or	*Orientalia* (Rome)
OC	*Oriens Christianus* (Wiesbaden, 1901–)
PL	Pietas Liturgica (Mainz)
PO	Patrologia Orientalis (Paris, 1907–)
SA	Scriptores Aethiopici (within CSCO)
SBL	Society of Biblical Literature

Textes	Lifchitz, D bor ah, and Sylvain Gr ba ut. *Textes éthiopiens magico-religieux*. Paris: Institut d'ethnologie, 1940.
TM89	*Tä'amrä Maryam*. Addis Ababa: Tənśa'e zä-guba'e, 1989 EC
VOHD	Verzeichnis der orientalischen Handschriften in Deutschland, Volumes 20.1–6 (Stuttgart, 1973–1999)
ZDMG	*Zeitschrift der deutschen morgenländischen Gesellschaft* (Leipzig, Wiesbaden, Stuttgart, 1847–)

Foreword

Ethiopian Manuscripts and their Preservation

Richard Pankhurst

Ethiopia is fortunate–and unusual in Africa–in possessing both a long-established written language and a rich literary heritage. The country was likewise well endowed with an abundance of cattle, sheep and goats from whose skins a seemingly limitless number of manuscripts could be fashioned.

Innumerable Ethiopian manuscripts have been produced over the last half millennium or so in many parts of the country–the oldest dating from perhaps the twelfth or thirteenth centuries, or even earlier. Such texts, written for the most part in Ethiopia's age-old Semitic language Gəʻəz–but also in modern Amharic–are important not only for the understanding of the country's own history, culture and religion, but also more broadly for that of the Christian Orient as a whole.

Many manuscripts warrant scholarly study, primarily for their texts– as their authors and/or scribes intended, but other volumes are also of great interest for their calligraphy (or style of hand-writing), illumination and binding.

Ethiopian classical texts cover a wide range of themes, both religious and secular. These include theology and biblical studies, but also subjects as distinct from one another as literature, history and chronology, government, law, geography and mathematics–traditionally needed to determine the date of Easter and other religious festivals; also medicine, and music. Study of the latter was facilitated by the existence of Ethiopian musical notation, neatly placed above the words to be sung,

Much information about the past is also preserved in manuscript marginalia (i.e. otherwise blank or unoccupied pages usually at the beginning and/or the end of a bound text). These pages in not a few instances record such data as royal charters; purchase and sale of land; inventories of church and monastic property, including books; tax records; and marriage contracts.

Manuscript illuminations can also be historically instructive. Representation of biblical or other religious themes often reflect what the artist actually saw, rather than the supposed realities of biblical times, and thus provide valuable glimpses of such important artifacts as agricultural tools and weapons, houses and clothing, crowns, jewelry, hairstyles, and horse, mule and other decorations.

Manuscript bindings may similarly be of historical interest in that that they are in many cases enlivened by the insertion of pieces of colorful silk or other imported cloth. The presence of such material would testify to its availability at the period of binding–and may thus throw light on the international commerce of the time, as well as on the trade routes through which it was probably procured.

The dating of Ethiopian manuscripts often poses problems. In some cases a scribe may record–either in the text or in marginalia –the date of the manuscript's composition, or may note the monarch in whose reign it was produced, or even in what year of that reign. In other cases reliance must be paid to other evidence. This may include the manuscript's calligraphy, the character of its illumination - perhaps even the kind of paints employed; the type of cloth used in the binding, if any–and finally the manuscript's general appearance–whether its text and binding seem "fresh" and "new", or "worn" and "faded" etc.

Manuscripts (unlike printed books) are copied out by hand–and in many cases written out from memory. Every manuscript, whatever its text, is therefore unique. A manuscript library must therefore collect manuscripts in multiple copies–to establish the earliest or most original version, as well as to trace how its text and/or illuminations changed or evolved over time.

Many Ethiopian manuscripts have been lost, damaged or destroyed in the course of time, some as a result of fire or excessive exposure to rain, some through the depredations of insects or rodents, and some as a result of war, and looting.

The preservation of Ethiopia's surviving manuscripts is a matter of national importance, in which friends of Ethiopia and of scholarship can, and must, contribute. Manuscripts should at the same time be catalogued and digitized or microfilmed.

Pioneering efforts in the field of Ethiopian microfilming were carried out in the Lake Tana area after the close of World War II by Professor Ernst Hammerschmidt of the University of Hamburg, Subsequent microfilming, much of it directed by Professor Getatchew Haile, was organized on a considerably larger scale by the Ethiopian Manuscript Microfilm Library (EMML), in collaboration with the Monastic Manuscript Microfilm Library of St John's Abbey and University in Collegeville, Minnesota, whose published microfilm catalogue currently runs to ten volumes.

The initiative in recording Ethiopian manuscripts–by digitization rather than microfilming–has more recently passed to the Ethiopic Manuscript Imaging Project (EMIP) In the past few years, EMIP has located and digitized more than 8,500 manuscripts. The largest of their projects has been the digitization of 5,749 items in the Archives and Manuscripts Department of the Institute of Ethiopian Studies, also in Addis Ababa, with the support of the British Library's Endangered Archives Programme.

The microfilming, or more recently digitization, of manuscripts is essential both to preserve them for posterity and to extend and facilitate their study. In this latter connection it should be emphasized that digitization can enlarge and enhance a reader's view of a manuscript, and thus contribute greatly to the comparative study of more than one volume, as Professor Delamarter has shown in several recent scholarly studies.

We are indebted to the Mekane Yesus Seminary in Addis Ababa for preserving the small, but interesting collection of 54 manuscripts here catalogued. Special thanks should go to its scholarly Librarian, *Aläqa* Meseret Sebhat Le-ab, who collected these works between 1977 and 1980.

We are all no less grateful to the dedication of Professor Stephen Delamarter, and to his Ethiopic Manusript Imaging Project team from George Fox University in Portland, Oregon, who have expertly digitized this collection, as well as the considerably larger one at the Institute of Ethiopian Studies.

Preface

Steve Delamarter

It was Dr. Loren Bliese who first told me about the collection of manuscripts at the Mekane Yesus Seminary library in Addis Ababa. Dr. Bliese was a former president of the seminary and worked with the United Bible Society in Ethiopia on translation projects for several languages, most notably the Afar language, on which Bliese had written his doctoral dissertation. We met by chance at the regional Society of Biblical Literature Meeting which was held in early May, 2009, at Pacific Lutheran University in Tacoma, Washington. Based on his experience with the phenomenon of seemingly-spontaneous poetic composition in cultural gatherings in Ethiopia, he presented a paper analyzing the chiastic structures of an Old Testament book. I presented a paper on the marking of the midpoint of Ethiopian Psalters. We discovered that we were both working in Ethiopia (Dr. Bliese for many decades; I for just a few years) and that we lived within about 75 miles of one another. A few weeks later I visited him at his home and we talked about things Ethiopian. It was at this time he told me the fascinating story of *Aläqa* Meseret Sebhat Le-ab and of his remarkable collection of manuscripts there at the Mekane Yesus Seminary in Addis Ababa.

Within a couple of weeks I had contacted *Ato* Meheret-Ab Bereke, librarian at Mekane Yesus Seminary and, with their permission, made arrangements to digitize the collection. This was accomplished by me and *Ato* Kaleab Demeke on July 2–4, 2009 in the seminary's computer lab. We were assisted throughout by *Ato* Waktola Walda Michael from the library staff.

Almost as we were shooting the manuscripts, my friend, *Ato* Demeke Berhane, head of manuscripts at the Institute of Ethiopian Studies, helped to devise a handlist of the manuscripts. I began to think of people we might ask to help with the process of cataloguing and describing the collection.

About this same time, another friend, Dr. Tim Teusink, a medical doctor working in Addis, introduced me to Dr. Ralph Lee. After his undergraduate work at Cambridge, Ralph had earned a PhD from the University of Strathclyde, Glasgow, Scotland, in Chemical Engineering. He and his wife, Sara, then moved to Bahir Dar, Ethiopia, where they lived for more than a half-dozen years and where he helped the University of Bahir Dar to establish a program in Chemical Engineering. This work earned him an Alumnus of the Year award from the University of Strathclyde in 2001. Recently, Ralph has been living in Addis, studying Gə_əz, and teaching at Holy Trinity Theological College. Ever the student, Ralph was in the final stages of another PhD program in the Department for the Study of Religions, at the School of Oriental and African Studies, University of London. He has since completed his thesis on the topic of 'Symbolic Interpretations in Ethiopic and Ephremic Literature,' supervised by Dr E C D Hunter. Ephremic literature has formed a rich resource for Ethiopic writings, including Ethiopic musical literature. Almost ten of the manuscripts in the collection at Mekane Yesus seminary come with musical notation. I asked Ralph if he would contribute a small introduction to ―Yaredawi," the musical tradition which flows from Ethiopia's musical genius, Saint Yared.

Dr. Bliese and Mekane Yesus Seminary librarian, *Ato* Meheret-Ab, were in a perfect position to gather information about Meseret's life and they set about working on a draft of his biography.

I had met Dr. Marilyn Heldman in May of 2008 when I gave a talk at the Library of Congress. She had been doing work there in the collection of materials recently acquired from the estate of Thomas Leiper Kane. With enthusiasm she showed us some of the more interesting pieces. She is probably the leading authority in North America on Ethiopian illuminations and editor of the magnificent book called *Africa Zion: the Sacred Art of Ethiopia* (Yale: University Press, 1993). Having completed the digitization of the collection, I knew that there were several nice illuminations in the collection. Dr. Heldman agreed to write an article on these.

All through this time I had ongoing relations with the Pankhursts and Richard was kind enough to agree to write a foreword.

In November of 2009, the International Conference of Ethiopian Studies was held at the Akaki campus of Addis Ababa University a few miles outside of Addis proper. Those who were in Addis for the conference–Ralph Lee, Loren Bliese, Meheret-Ab, Demeke Berhane and I–met at Mekane Yesus Seminary and finalized plans for the production of a catalog.

In late December I was back to Addis to set up the implementation phase of a project to digitize the manuscripts and archives department at the Institute of Ethiopian Studies. The British Library's Endangered Archives Programme provided a grant to complete this project (EAP 286) and it called for six months of digitization on four stations in Addis Ababa. Jeremy Brown, a former student and, more recently, colleague in the Ethiopian Manuscript Imaging Project (EMIP) went to Ethiopia to be the on-site director of digitization for the project. He was there, in Addis, for five of the six months of the project. Jeremy has developed an interest in scribal intervention in Ethiopian manuscripts, and has studied the ways in which scribes add material in margins and between the lines to correct and clarify the text and also how they delete material in an Ethiopian book. In addition to studying this phenomenon in manuscripts in the EMIP and IES collections, he travelled to Collegeville for a week in August of 2009 to study scribal intervention in all of the Ethiopian manuscripts from the seventeenth century and earlier which they have in their collections. Based on this expertise, Jeremy agreed to write an article on the scribal interventions in the Mekane Yesus collection.

While in the final stages of the IES digitization project in Addis, in May and June of 2010, a manuscript of Jubilees and the Minor Prophets came to my attention elsewhere in Addis. The manuscript was in the hands of a dealer. We purchased the manuscript for a reasonable price and, since I am determined not to remove any of Ethiopia's manuscripts from the country, I needed to decide to which institution we would make the donation. In the past few years I have donated five manuscripts to the IES, one to *Mahibere Kiddusan* (a youth organization in the Ethiopian Orthodox Tewahido Church whose offices are adjacent to the Patriarch's compound), and one to the Patriarch's library. In this case, I decided to donate the manuscript to Mekane Yesus Seminary and did so in June of 2010. It became MYS 54 / EMIP 654.

It was just a month or two later that I met Ted Erho in Collegeville. Ted, a former student at Trinity Western University in Langley, British Columbia, Canada, is well into a PhD program at the University of Durham. He was in Collegeville to study old Ethiopian manuscripts, particularly of Enoch and Jubilees. We looked at MYS 54 together and he showed great interest in its age and text. I asked him to write up a brief analysis of the textual affiliations of the manuscript in relation to the families of texts identified by James VanderKam.[1]

Finally, another of my students, Sara Vulgan, has spent some time working with EMIP. While Jeremy and I were in Addis digitizing the IES collection, she reviewed the images of the Mekane Yesus Collection and identified those that were blurry or needed, for various other reasons, to be re-shot. Armed with her list, we took a couple of stations over to Mekane Yesus in June of 2010 and digitized those folios that needed it. Sara has developed an interest in codicology, generally, and Ethiopian codicology, in

---

[1] James C. VanderKam, *The Book of Jubilees*, 2 vols. CSCO 510/511; SA 87/88; (Louvain: Peeters, 1989).

particular. I asked her to work with me on an article which can serve as an introduction to some of the characteristics of Ethiopian codicology.

We experienced one delay during this timeframe. The library staff at the seminary had been unable to locate one of the manuscripts, MYS 44. It had not been digitized as part of the initial work on the collection in July of 2009. We believed that this was an important work and a rare copy (maybe one of only a handful of copies) of a work written in Amharic, in the early twentieth century, by *Aläqa* Tayye Gäbrä Maryam. The work is called *A Theological Critique of Certain Practices of the Orthodox Church*. *Aläqa* Tayye was born in 1858 and lived until August, 1924. We were quite anxious to recover the book and were therefore delighted when we received word that the book had been found. Because of its odd format, it had been stored in a different location from the rest of the collection. But, now that it had been located, we digitized it in June of 2010, at the same time we were re-shooting blurry images from the other manuscripts.

At this point, the scope of the catalogue was growing by stages. We made the decision to separate the catalogue into two part volumes. In the former, we have included the foreword by Pankhurst, the biography by Bliese and Meheret-Ab, the articles by Lee and Erho and the catalogue entries for the fifty-four manuscripts. In the companion volume we placed those articles that are accompanied by color plates: Jeremy's article on scribal intervention, Sara's and my article on Ethiopian codicology and, especially, Marilyn's article on the illuminations in the collection. By segregating these into a separate volume, the cost of the volumes can be kept down.

Our thanks extend to *Ato* Demeke for his help in so many ways when we are in Ethiopia and for the delightful times we have spent together with his family. We are grateful to Ralph Lee for reviewing the Gə‿əz and Amharic text in the volume and for catching some errors. Finally, I mention again Dr. Bliese, with whom this odyssey began. His generosity and hospitality have inspired and guided the project.

Introduction to the Collection

Steve Delamarter

Some might be tempted to ignore the Mekane Yesus Seminary collection of manuscripts. After all, the manuscripts are neither plentiful nor old. But, this would be an error, because many of them are both important and interesting.

MYS 1 contains the largest single collection of Miracles of Mary that is known to us. Further, it contains a previously unknown cycle of eighteen miracles (numbers 97-115) which we call the Zion Cycle. Ostensibly narrated by Ezra, the eighteen miracles tell the story of the tablet given to Moses and which accompanied Israel throughout its history. The tablet is called Zion and symbolizes Mary. Thus, the story of the tablet's sojourn with the people Israel is the story of Mary's sojourn with Israel. According to Professor Getatchew, this cycle is unknown in any other manuscript.

MYS 8 contains a fairly uncommon form of the Ziq chants known as the Yä-Aba Jale Ziq Chants. And in this manuscript, the scribe often identifies the source of the tradition for that particular chant. For instance, Gojjam, Gondar, Tigray and Shewa are mentioned as specific loci from which these forms of the Ziq chants came. Two other manuscripts in the collection (MYS 9 and 10) contain the more common forms of the Ziq chants.

MYS 16 contains a remarkable collection of twenty-five works including an interesting combination of known theological and liturgical works alongside a set of Asmat *prayers.* The latter include *Asmat* Prayers for the seven Archangels and *Asmat* Prayers of Solomon.

MYS 20 contains a set of Lectionary Readings from the Four Gospels. These have been arranged for the festivals of the church and have instructions for readings from the Psalter interspersed.

MYS 21, Antiphonary for the Whole Year, or Dəgg^{w}a, is the manuscript which was microfilmed by the Ethiopian Manuscript Microfilm Library and given the project number 1256. According to Professor Getatchew's catalogue, it was copied by a reliable hand which made a substantial claim in the colophon (folio 201v) that it had used as its exemplar a manuscript known as Mäzgäbä Berhanä Aläm of Betä Leḥem, which was owned by *Qäñ* Masfen Ḥayla Maryam with baptismal name Gäbrä Maryam of Efrata in Mänzih (today Mänz). But, in Getatchew's opinion, it is most probably copied from EMML 1262.

MYS 25 contains the text of the five books of the Pentateuch with marginal mnemonics for the Andemta traditional commentary. The first section of the Ethiopic Old Testament is not a Pentateuch but an Octateuch, including the books of Joshua, Judges and Ruth. There are schools where students went to memorize the huge body of traditional commentary known as the Andemta. The primary mode of transmission of this body of interpretation was memorization and oral recitation. The marginal notes in this codex represent mnemonics to prompt the memory of the one reciting the interpretation.

MYS 28 is the first of four manuscripts in the collection that were produced in or around the government scriptorium. The others are MYS 34, 39, and 51. These provide us, we believe, with more materials to identify the characteristics of the scriptorium.[1]

MYS 29 contains the liturgy for the dedication of a Church. Manuscripts of this work are not very common.

MYS 33 is a fine copy of Acts and Paul (including Hebrews) from the late-eighteenth or early-nineteenth century. It also contains a full introduction to each of the books.

MYS 34 is a lengthy codex containing the full text of the Missal in Gəʿəz and extensive commentary in Amharic. It is a fascinating example of how the history of publishing in Ethiopia influenced the ongoing manuscript tradition. The colophon says, "This commentary of the book of missal was written in 1974 E.C by *Märige(ta)* Gäbrä Maryam, Wäldä Maryam of Saynt [in Wollo] and Lə_ul Wäldä Rufaʿel." Its contents, however, appear to have been copied from the published edition of ትርጓሜ፡ ጸሎተ፡ ኪዳን፡, which was produced in 1918.

MYS 36 is the first of two marvelous manuscripts of the Ethiopian computus, the literary product of elaborate calculations of the movements of the astronomical bodies, useful primarily for the determination of Easter. MYS 36 was copied in the twentieth century and contains, along with the literary texts associated with this genre, a map of the earth (f. 58r) and three diagrams of the path of the Zodiac through the heavens (f. 61r).

---

[1] For a description of ten other manuscripts (EMIP 44, 94, 28, 30, 58, 87, 141, 145, 161, and 176) that may have been produced in the government scriptorium, see our "Introduction to the Collection and Its Codicology," in *Catalogue of the Ethiopic Manuscript Imaging Project, Volume 2: Codices 106–200 and Magic Scrolls 135–284*, EMTS 3 (Eugene OR: Pickwick, 2011) xxvii.

The other copy of the Ethiopian computus is MYS 53. Copied in the eighteenth-century, it includes charts of the orbit and windows of the stars (f. 1r), the cycle of a quarter of the year (f. 1v), and other tables and computations.

MYS 39, like MYS 16, contains a full set of Asmat Prayers of the Seven Archangels. In addition, this manuscript contains 25 fine illuminations by a very competent artist.

MYS 44 is a very rare work by Aläqa Tayye Gäbrä Maryam providing a ―Theological Critique of Certain Practices of the Orthodox Church," in Amharic. The manuscript, held in a modern two-ring binder, is fully 451 folios long.

MYS 49 contains a complete set of Andemta Commentaries on the Epistles of Paul. This manuscript serves as a complement both to MYS 33, with its text of Acts and Paul, and to MYS 25 with its Andemta on Genesis through Deuteronomy.

The collection contains fully six Gädla manuscripts, or lives and miracles of the saints. These include Gäbrä Krestos (MYS 17), Gäbrä Mänfäs Qəddus (MYS 24), Gälawədewos or Claudius (MYS 43), Saint Marqorəwos or Mercurius (MYS 45), Saint George (MYS 47), Krəstos Sämra (MYS 50)

MYS 51 provides a copy of Sword of the Trinity; MYS 52 provides a copy of the same work, but in a variant form. Folios 49v-68r of the latter include this variant form which contains, in part, *Asmat* prayers of the prophet Moses.

Finally, MYS 54 comprises fifty-five folios of a late-fifteenth century or early sixteenth century manuscript with more than half of the book of Jubilees. This copy of the book witnesses to a very interesting set of textual affiliations with other copies of the book of Jubilees.[2] In addition, the manuscript also contains most of the biblical book of Hosea and about half each of the books of Amos and Micah.

It should be clear, then, that Aläqa Meseret had a very discriminating eye in his acquisition of manuscripts and has left to us a collection remarkable for its quality of interesting manuscripts, if not for their quantity and age.

---

[2] See the study by Ted M. Erho below on ―The Textual Character of Jubilees in Mekane Yesus Seminary 54."

Aläqa Mäsärät Səbḥat Lä'ab:[1] A Biography[2]

Dr. Loren Bliese, *Ato* Mehretab Bereke, and *Ato* Walda Estifanos[3]

The scholar who arranged for the purchase of the fifty-three manuscripts in the Mekane Yesus Seminary Library is *Aläqa*[4] Meseret Sebhat Leab. All his life he studied Ethiopian Orthodox Church literature and practice. For twenty-four years he taught these subjects as well as Gə_əz, the ancient language of the manuscripts, to students at Mekane Yesus Seminary. Already in 1965 he showed his concern that Gə_əz manuscript material be made more accessible by getting the equipment from the seminary and doing microfilming. He was concerned that many Gə_əz manuscripts were being taken out of Ethiopia, and proposed to the seminary that manuscripts be collected for the library so they would be available for research in Ethiopia. A grant was obtained from the German Evangelical Church for this purpose, and from 1977 to 1980 Meseret selected and purchased the manuscripts.

---

[1] During his lifetime, when his name was spelled in an anglicized form, the spelling would have been Meseret Sebhat Leab. The form given in the title is the scholarly notation of Ge'ez and Amharic words, but in the body of this article, we will use the common form of his name.

[2] We are especially indebted to Dawit Chibsa, who in 1990, did primary research and wrote his Mekane Yesus Seminary Bachelor of Theology senior paper on Meseret. Tibebu Tedla prepared an obituary read at Meseret's funeral in January 1998. Volume 14 of *Chorra*, a spiritual magazine founded by Meseret, provides many insights in a lengthy interview with him before his death. This was published as a memorial volume after his death. Alemayehu Haile Mariam wrote a student paper on Meseret in 2004 for the Evangelical Theological College. Dr. Dirshaye Menberu wrote an article on him in *Dictionary of African Christian Biography* in 2006. Rev. Dr. Eshetu Abate, who was entrusted to Meseret by his father when Eshetu entered Mekane Yesus Seminary, wrote a short Amharic biography published in Meseret's last published book *Trinity in Unity* (*Sellassie Betewahido*) in 1996. Eshetu helped with the publication of this book. Besides being his student, Eshetu worked with Meseret as a colleague while Eshetu was a professor and principal of the seminary.

[3] Amharic and Gə_əz passages were translated by the writers for this article.

[4] A title given for a church scholar or leader.

Meseret's Early Education

Meseret was born July 7, 1926 in Axum, Ethiopia. His mother was Kassaye Gebray. His father, Sebhat Leab Gebre Mesqel, was a priest and teacher in the historic St. Mary of Zion Church in Axum. Meseret was the first of eight children, five of whom died early. He began school when he was three years old. *Yäneta* (teacher) Wahid, a very good teacher and friend of Meseret's father, had promised him that if he bore a son he would teach him. He began Meseret's training in scripture memorization and liturgical music. Over the years Meseret memorized the prescribed books including Psalms, Song of Songs, the Book of Prayer and the New Testament in Gə_əz. He later took further liturgical training from *Yäneta* Gebre Kristos and *Yäneta* Gesu. He was an exceptional student and eventually memorized the entire Bible except the Pentateuch.

For two years during the Italian occupation after his father was arrested for opposing their rule, Meseret was required to attend their school. However, he continued his traditional church education secretly at night and his service as a deacon in St. Mary's Church in Axum. After the Italian education ended, he returned to full-time study at the church while serving as a deacon with his father.

His father took him to *Yäneta* Aweqe, a recognized teacher in Gə_əz poetry at the Debra Menkol monastery in Axum. In order to avoid a customary early marriage, at 17 he secretly left to Wegera in Gondar province. At Wegera he studied Gə_əz poetry under the great teacher *Yäneta* Kihnet. However, his father found him and brought him back to Axum, where he continued his studies of chanting of hymns or *aqwaqwam* under *Märigeta* Səbuh and *Märigeta* Gäsu.

Two years later, in 1945, he was again pressured to marry, so he left and studied for three years in various monasteries in Tigray and Amhara regions. He studied *qəne* in Lasta from *Yäneta* Aklilu, in Wadla Dälanta (in the place called Bethar) from *Yäneta* Mäṣəhet, in Yänja from *Yäneta* Qäññə Azmač Täkaləñ, in Däqəše from *Aläqa* Wəbe, in Gädäba from *Aläqa* Kasse, and in Däbrä Ṣəge from *Aläqa* Yətbaräk, respectively[5]. After this he studied *Andemta* (traditional biblical commentary) from *Mämhər* Abebe and from *Aläqa* Ḥəruy. In Ashenge again he did advanced study of Gə_əz Poetry from

---

[5] His knowledge of Gə_əz literature and poetry is evident throughout his writings. His love for the poetry was specially evident. At the time of his death, he was preparing a book on ~~one~~ hundred thirty two patterns of Gə_əz Poetry in connection with biblical and patristic books" (see his book *Traditional Computus and its History*).

well-known teacher, *Yäneta* Fetha Selassie Since he had no parental support he wore animal skins for cloths, and had to beg for his food, and build his own huts for shelter, as did the other students.

Meseret's Contact with David Stokes and *Särawitä Kərstos*

In February 1947 Meseret went to Addis Ababa to continue studies in Biblical interpretation. He studied with teachers *Yäneta* Abebe and *Mämhər* Gebre-Amlak, and taught *Qəne* (Gəəz poetry). While he was studying *Andəmta* (traditional biblical commentary) he met David Stokes, a missionary who worked closely with the Orthodox Church and who had a good relationship with well-known Ethiopian scholars. *Särawitä Kərstos*, the Ethiopic name of the missionary organization of Mr. Stokes and his friends, practiced an ecumenical approach and evidenced a deep commitment to the Ethiopian Orthodox church. As a result, Mr. Stokes and his friends had access to interact with the clergy and, in some cases, the laity of the church.

Stokes' manner of preaching attracted Meseret, especially in the way he explain the grace of God. Meseret liked the message, but was confused about seeing a well-to-do man preaching. He considered luxury to be ungodly.

Stokes talked to Meseret and his companion, and they agreed to join his *Amha Desta* Preachers Training School. Part of the program was to go out as field preachers, so after being trained, Meseret and his school mates went to Aleta Wando in Sidamo, and later to Arsi and Bale proclaiming the gospel. At that time the main preachers of the church were the hermits, the *bahətawəyan*. Their approach to preaching was mainly through warning and rebuke. Their sermons were usually based on the stories of the saints or the apocalyptic writings of the Middle Ages. The manner of preaching by Meseret and his friends was considered heretical for those who were familiar with the preaching of the *bahətawəyan*. On the next trip to Ankober, Meseret and his companion were imprisoned for three weeks. Even there they preached to the other prisoners until they were ordered to leave the area. Meseret then stayed with Stokes for about six months. He turned down an invitation to stay longer, and chose, instead, to continue his study of the doctrinal foundations of the

Ethiopian Orthodox Church. In Meseret's later ministry and scholarly labor we can see the influence of David Stokes and his writings.[6]

Meseret's Restorationist Position

Meseret's research eventually led him to what might be called a restorationist or primitivist position. He concluded that the Christian teaching brought to Ethiopia in the fourth century by the first Bishop *Abuna* Selama (Frumentius) was based soundly on scripture. However, during the fifteenth century Emperor Zär'a Ya‗əqob introduced new writings and practices which Meseret did not view as based soundly on scripture. These innovations were even opposed by some scholars of the time, who were beaten and exiled. They were named ―Enemies of Mary." Their leader *Abba* Estifanos died in exile from injuries inflicted as punishment. Meseret advocated going back to ―the faith of the fathers," and for this he was generally opposed.

In 1949 Meseret went to monasteries in Gojjam with Tibebu Tedla. He enrolled as a student since he was not a monk. This also allowed him to beg for food, a traditional privilege of students studying theology. He studied in Aläfa Ṭaqusa with Gebre Kristos and in Gondar Märaba with another Gebre Kristos. His skill in liturgical singing was appreciated, but his theological position as a reformer was usually rejected. He was accused of being an ―Enemy of Mary." Because of plots against him, he went to monasteries near the border of Gondar. He served for four months as a *Merigeta* in the role of the ‗liturgical leader' at Wegera in Gondar. During the two and a half years in Gojjam and Gondar he continued to study the history of development of doctrine in the Ethiopian Orthodox Church. He went to the scholars to learn from them and read the books they recommended. He gave special recognition to *Mämhər* Tsige, *Abba* Wube and *Abba* Azane as being outstanding teachers. At this time Meseret had no plans to write, so he did not take notes. Later, when he became an author, he regretted not having easy access to the materials he had studied formerly.

Even though he was suspect in some quarters, Meseret's command of scripture and theology were also recognized as great strengths. Near the end of his time in Wegera he was invited by a government official to correct

---

[6] Beyond their life-time friendship, Meseret had a deep appreciation for Stokes' Amharic commentaries. Because of their ecumenical approach and very clear application, these commentaries are very popular among the clergy, especially those who preached in the churches.

the theology of the Falasha Jewish priests. He and Tibebu Tedla visited these priests and explained the Old Testament witness to Jesus as the promised Messiah. Further, on the basis of Numbers 20:10–13, they argued that even Moses sinned. By implication, he was arguing that the system of religion based on the sinless Messiah was better than a form of religion based on Moses alone.

Meseret at Saint Paul's Seminary

Likewise, Meseret's skills and knowledge led Stokes and the *Särawitä Kərstos* Association to recommend him to Emperor Haile Sellassie for membership on the theological faculty at the newly-formed Saint Paul's Seminary. Mr. Stokes had been a member of a consultation established by Emperor Haile Sellassie to recommend reform for the Ethiopian Orthodox Church. This resulted in the establishment of St. Paul's Seminary, and a theological faculty at the University in Addis Ababa. Stokes recommended Meseret as a person working for reform. *Ras* Desta, a high government official, was delegated to find Meseret and offer him a position. But, due to the fact that Meseret was continually moving from one place to another for further study, it was a full two years later, in October 1953, that Desta found him. He reluctantly came back to Addis Ababa, having spent twenty-four years in traditional church education. However, because of the lapse of time since the recommendations of the consultation committee, the energy to pursue the reform agenda had waned among the leaders in Addis. *Ras* Desta asked him to stay with him, but Meseret did not want to remain in Addis Ababa, so he set out to return to Gondar. At Fitche he became sick, and was unable to travel further, so he came back to Addis Ababa. He stayed with *Ras* Desta for three months while getting medical treatment at Zewditu Hospital. It had become clear that Meseret was too weak to return to Gondar any time soon, so it was arranged for him to be a student at St. Paul's *Säwasəw Bərhan* Theological Seminary until a position would open for him as a teacher.

At the seminary he shared his restorationist convictions about the renewal of the church and biblical and patristic teaching on salvation. Some students accepted the teaching and others opposed him and this created a controversy at the school. Reports of Meseret's activities reached the patriarch and Queen Menen. Some wanted to send him to Harar as punishment; others wanted to execute him. Emperor Haile Sellassie, however, did not support their plans. He told them that a school was where things were to be studied critically. Because of the Emperor's intervention Meseret was saved from this danger.

Meseret's Writings and the Influence of Gə‗əz Manuscripts

In an interview published in *Čorra*,[7] Meseret told of a special opportunity he had had to do research with manuscripts. At the silver jubilee of Emperor Haile Sellassie, in 1956, an exhibition of manuscripts from various monasteries was set up in Gondar. Stokes arranged with the governor, Prince Asrate Kasa, that Meseret be given access to read and study the books. Meseret went there quickly and was able to take notes of material he wanted. He also made lists of manuscripts he did not have time to study. He noted their content and in which monastery or church they were located. Later, while teaching, he used his vacation times to go to these places and study the manuscripts. He also photographed pages of these manuscripts with pertinent information. He lived frugally and saved his salary during the nine months of teaching in order to have money for these trips. Besides transportation costs, he brought gifts such as books and umbrellas. The locations were sometimes remote and this required that he rent mules or walk through the steep mountains and low valleys in whatever conditions the weather provided at the moment.

Meseret also developed a friendship with a man by the name of *Abba* Habte Sellassie. This clergyman supplemented his work in the ministry with buying and selling books. When he found a book or manuscript that he thought Meseret would want, he brought it to him to examine and purchase if he desired. He charged Meseret only a small commission. This friendship and service lasted until Habte died, which was only a few years before Meseret's death. However, in later years, it was rare to find old manuscripts, since many had been taken out of Ethiopia.

Meseret's labor in studying manuscripts showed itself in his writings. Anyone who studies his published and unpublished books can tell how much he valued the Orthodox fathers and their teachings. His commitment to Orthodox scholarship of the past continues to give his writings high place among modern Ethiopian Orthodox scholars. In what follows, we will examine three of his most important books and see how he incorporated the study of Gə‗əz manuscripts and the teaching and culture of the Ethiopian Orthodox church into his thinking and writing.

---

[7] Volume 14 (1998) 12.

Meseret's First Book: *Indigenous Witness for the Truth: According to the Ancient Orthodox Church Fathers*[8]

Meseret published his first book, *Indigenous Witness for the Truth* (*Səm'a ṣədq Bəherawi*) in 1958. It was a time when reforming the church was the main topic among the Imperial Government and church officials. The main reason for this spirit of renewal was due to the fact that the Ethiopian Orthodox church had recently become autocephalous after 1600 years under Coptic administration. In his lengthy introduction, *Aläqa* Meseret explained how this change inspired him to write the book. "My desire and aim in this book is that our church, which has gained its independence, can reform not the basic faith but those customs which have entered [into the life of our church] without examination, so that the church can be renewed by teaching [our people] the foundation of ancient faith in a clear way."[9]

Meseret believed that the way to accomplish this objective was by providing articles of faith which would explain the teaching of the church according to the ancient Orthodox Church fathers. Meseret saw the importance of the article of faith as a springboard for ecumenical dialogue with other churches and a manual for the renewal of the Ethiopian Orthodox church. He argued that the church needed an article of faith in order to be understood by other churches and to be involved in a constructive dialogue. He said,

> Today, out of the wisdom and knowledge of human beings, one country has come into contact with another country, one government with another government, trying to create friendship and unity. For their part, the churches, which have been separated for so many years, have taken measures to get to know each other.[10] At this time, then, it is important to study the similarity of this church with another or the difference [between it and another], its uniqueness, or how wide is the gap between the churches. In this context, one

---

[8] ስምዓ ፡ ጽድቅ ፡ ብሔራዊ ፡ በጥንታውያን ፡ የኦርቶዶክስ ፡ ቤተ ፡ ክርስቲያን ፡ መምህራን ፡ ፍሊጋ፣ was published in 1951 EC. Meseret often referred to *Bəherawi Betä Kərəstiyan* or the National Church. In this context, the term *Bəherawi* refers to the contrast between the indigenous witness within Ethiopia as compared to the witness to Christianity from other cultures.

[9] *Ibid.*, 9.

[10] This probably refers to recent negotiations for reconciliation which had been held between the Monophysite and Diophysite Orthodox Communions.

> church can learn the doctrine (foundation of faith) of the other church when it is provided in an article (ምዕላድ). As the other church provides their article of faith, this church must provide its own article of faith. . . .[11]

In relation to the renewal of the church, Meseret saw the production of articles of faith as an opportunity to separate those later innovations from the foundation of faith. He described how the article facilitated the process of the renewal of the church in this way:

> . . . every Christian, whose zeal for faith has not grown cold, needs to be able to understand which part [of our Christian tradition] has to be preserved according to the ancient church faith and from which part [of the tradition] he must separate himself; and also it is unavoidable that he must be able to answer any sudden question which arises about his striving (for renewal), about the goal of his faith, or about the history of his church and about the teachings of the ancient fathers: it is important to have a book which has an article which is grounded in the Old and New Testaments and which is supported by the writings of the ancient Church Fathers."[12]

Meseret pointed out that this kind of writing was not new for the Ethiopian Orthodox church. He mentioned two books which had the same goal, each with a slightly different approach: Faith of the Fathers (*Haymanotä Abäw*) and Five Pillars of Mystery (*Aməstu A_əmadä Məstir*). Throughout his life he collected several copies of these two works. For example, in our collection we find a copy of the Five Pillars in MYS 46 / EMIP 646. And, Faith of the Fathers is found in MYS 35 / EMIP 635.

In his book, the *Indigenous Witness*, Meseret's quotation of the patristic writers was abundant:[13] St. John Chrysostom[14], the Homily by Severianus of Gabala[15], St. Yared[16], the Apostolic Creed[17], the Three

---

[11] *Indigeneous Witness* 8.

[12] *Ibid.*, 8–9.

[13] There are difficulties in attempting to provide the full list of patristic works cited by Meseret. Following the Orthodox fathers, he does not provide references for the work cited or quoted. In some cases we have no clue about the source of the quotation other than our own familiarity with the patristic literature.

[14] *Indigeneous Witness* 8, 48, 53, 80, 88, 101–3, 131, 133–4, 138–9, 142–3, 145, 157–8, 160, 176–8, and 181–2.

[15] *Ibid.*, 23. See MYS 41.22.

[16] *Ibid.*, 27, 69, 136, and 167–8.

[17] *Ibid.*, 33.

Hundred Nicene Fathers[18], Mystagogia, *Elmästo 'ägeya*[19], Athanasius' Creed[20], Ignatius of Antioch[21], Severus of Smunay[22], Cyril of Alexandria[23], Biniyamin (Benjamin)[24], Abulidis (Hyppolytus)[25], John, Bishop of Jerusalem[26], Canon of Amonius and Eusebius[27], Bädran son of Sima'on, Bishop of Armenia[28], Anaphora of Epiphanius[29], Philgos' commentary on Galatians[30], The Interpreter[31], Heraclitus[32], Mar Ephrem (of Syria)[33], Anaphora of Our Lord[34], Prayer of the Covenant[35], Book of Hours[36], Book of *Mə'alad*[37], Filəgos' Commentary on Hebrews[38], Filəgos' Commentary on 1 Corinthians[39], Epiphanius, Bishop of Cyprus[40], Severus of Antioch[41], Homily by Proclus of Cyzicus[42], Athanasius, bishop of Alexandria[43], John

---

[18] *Ibid.*, 33 and 126.
[19] This is a variant version of the common Mystagogia, usually found at the beginning of *Haymanotä Abaw*. *Ibid.*, 36, 46, 84–5, 89–90, 109–110, 161, 164, and 166. See MYS 35.2.
[20] *Ibid.*, 38.
[21] *Ibid.*, 43.
[22] *Ibid.*, 48.
[23] *Ibid.*, 48, 67, 84, 94, 96–7, 116–7, 147, 152, and 156–7.
[24] *Ibid.*, 55–56 and 70.
[25] *Ibid.*, 57–58, 81, and 149–150.
[26] *Ibid.*, 58–59 and 172.
[27] *Ibid.*, 61, 90–1, and 151.
[28] *Ibid.*, 62–63 and 107.
[29] *Ibid.*, 63.
[30] *Ibid.*, 66–7.
[31] *Ibid.*, 70. The name of this interpreter or the source of this quotation is unknown. Probably it is from some Gə_əz commentaries which were translated from an Arabic source.
[32] *Ibid.*, 73.
[33] *Ibid.*, 79.
[34] *Ibid.*, 84.
[35] *Ibid.*, 97–8, 154, and 183–4.
[36] *Ibid.*, 105.
[37] *Ibid.*, 112.
[38] *Ibid.*, 113–4, 116, and 170.
[39] *Ibid.*, 121–122.
[40] *Ibid.*, 124.
[41] *Ibid.*, 126, 128–130, and 152.
[42] *Ibid.*, 150 and 153. See MYS 41.22.
[43] *Ibid.*, 152.

Chrysostom's Commentary on Paul's Epistles[44], God of the Luminaries[45], Anaphora of the Three Hundred Fathers[46], and Didascalia[47].

Out of this research, Meseret put forward forty-six articles which contained the phrase "we believe" in each article. He organized his book into three sections, following the Trinitarian formula based on St. Severus' famous quote "The Faith started with the Father, proceeded through the Son and will be completed by the Holy Spirit".[48] In the first section he described the work of God, including discussions about scripture, man, sin, and free will. In the second section he described the incarnation and work of Jesus Christ including repentance, righteousness, faith, good works, and Holy Communion. In the third section, he described the work of the Holy Spirit, which included a description of the unity and greatness of the church, its worship, honoring departed saints, the role of priests, the sacraments of the church, and the resurrection of the dead.

In many quarters his book was a success. Though there were a few objections, the main outcome was that the scholars in the church were able to see Meseret's deep knowledge and appreciation of the Ethiopian Orthodox church fathers.[49] The book was also received well in the Palace. Meseret sent his book to the Emperor via a Minister and the Emperor himself read the book. He liked it and he summoned Meseret to his Palace. Meseret, himself, provided an account of this meeting in *Čorra* 14 (1998), on page 15. Meseret went to the palace chapel on a Sunday morning and greeted the Emperor as he was leaving church. They met for an hour and a half in which time the Emperor expressed his appreciation for Meseret's work. The Emperor was acquainted with Meseret's father. The Emperor first asked about the difficulties which Meseret had been having at St. Paul's Seminary, and expressed regret over the situation. He then asked how and why he had written the book. Meseret answered that he wrote it to help church teachers explain and students understand the "Five Mysteries" that the church has been teaching from ancient times, and to facilitate making references

---

[44] *Ibid.*, 153–4.
[45] *Ibid.*, 154–5.
[46] *Ibid.*, 174.
[47] *Ibid.*, 179–180.
[48] *Ibid.*, 23. Some modern theologians follow the same Trinitarian structure in their presentations of systematic theology. The goal is to employ the categories of patristic theology as the basis for a consensus theological expression of the church. See, for instance, Thomas Oden's systematic theology.
[49] After more than 50 years, the book still has a deep influence among Ethiopian Orthodox scholars and preachers.

supporting these truths. In the book's 46 sections Meseret had added Biblical references that supported the teachings of the church, and explained how the ancient church fathers had understood each of the teachings. The Emperor asked many questions, including where Meseret got the books he quoted. Meseret told him that it was at the exposition in Gondar at the Jubilee of the Emperor, to which Prince Asrate Kasa had invited him and given him permission to read and take notes from the manuscripts. The Emperor then asked what Meseret's future plans were. Meseret told him that he planned to continue studying, writing, and publishing books. The Emperor asked Meseret to ask a favor from him, but Meseret said he didn't want anything. As he was leaving, an official came to him and said it was an offense not to ask for something. He was ordered to stand daily before the palace entrance and greet the Emperor when he left for his office, and stand waiting to greet him when he returned. This punishment was to humble him and break his pride. Several days later, while standing at court with others, Meseret sent word to the Minister through whom he had sent his book to the Emperor. Meseret was taken to the Minister's office where he apologized, saying he meant no offense. The minister later told him that he had been commanded to take a job, either in the palace office or in the Ministry of Education and Fine Arts. He chose the Ministry reluctantly, and served there until 1961.

Meseret's Involvement with Other Christian Groups

Meseret understood that true renewal of the church was not going to be accomplished through a sectarian and denominational mentality. With his passion for the renewal of the Ethiopian Orthodox Church, he combined an ecumenical approach which made it possible, even meaningful, for him to work with other groups and individuals outside the Ethiopian Orthodox Church.

With the Bethel Presbyterian Group
In 1954, while Meseret was teaching at St. Paul's School, he met Rev. Gidada Solon. Rev. Gidada was a leader of the Bethel Evangelical Church, a Presbyterian group.[50] He was also physically impaired with blindness.

---

[50] Before Meseret had came to Bethel, Dr. D. C. Henry, a Presbyterian missionary, had started a worshiping group there. The number of people increased, and an administrative committee was formed. Mamo Charqa was ordained to serve as their pastor. However, the administrative committee collapsed. When Meseret came to

Gidada was explaining the gospel to a young man. Meseret listened for a while, and then joined in the discussion. Afterwards Gidada asked Meseret who he was. A few weeks later he called Meseret and invited him to teach Amharic to some pastors in a short course. This was at a time when Meseret was confused as to what he should do in the face of opposition from his own church. So he accepted the invitation and came to the Bethel Presbyterian compound in Gulale, Addis Ababa. Soon after, he was asked to teach at their *Hiywot Birhan* Girls' School. Meseret saw this as an opportunity for ministry, and did not intend to leave the Orthodox Church. All during his time at the school, he continued to share his vision of working for reform within the Orthodox Church.

    Meseret continued working in the Addis Ababa Gulale Bethel church as coordinator, administrator, teacher and preacher. Some missionaries did not agree with the direction the committee was going, so Meseret decided to stop working in the Presbyterian school. *Ato* Gutema Rufo, who was a Bethel administrator, later expressed admiration for Meseret's patience when challenged. Meseret resigned from Hiywot Birhan School in 1960 in spite of the director's request that he continue. He had served there for about seven years. Although he was no longer on the school staff, Meseret continued his ministry in the congregation until the construction of the church began in 1968. He served the Bethel group for a total of fourteen years.

With the Mekane Yesus Seminary Lutheran Group
The Rev. Badima Yalew, a pioneer of the Ethiopian Evangelical Church Mekane Yesus and member of the organizing committee of Mekane Yesus Seminary, proposed that the history and doctrine of the Ethiopian Orthodox Church be included in the curriculum. This was accepted, and the committee, including Rev. Badima, Dr. Amanuel Gebre-Selassie and Rev. Manfred Lundgren, agreed to ask Meseret to be the teacher. Meseret had been praying that God would prepare a way for him to get out of the Ministry of Education appointment since he wanted to be full-time in religious work. He immediately accepted the offer and applied for a release from the Ministry of

---

Bethel there was no functioning group. He began to share the Word of God in groups as well as privately, and at his request he was provided with the prayer room that the former group had used. Attendance increased, and a committee was formed with Meseret as chairman. The compound with the meeting place was turned over to the committee. A delegation came from the Presbyterian Church USA, approved the committee's work, and gave 125,000 birr toward construction of a church building. A large church was later built. This group later became the Gulale Bethel Mekane Yesus Congregation.

Education. Since it was the Emperor who had arranged the position, it took five months for Meseret to get the release. He began at Mekane Yesus Seminary in 1961.

Meseret taught Gə_əz and Amharic languages as well as the history, doctrine, and practice of the Ethiopian Orthodox Church. His goal was to acquaint the seminary students with knowledge of Ethiopian Christianity to better equip them for ministry. He modeled respect for the Ethiopian Orthodox Church for its foundation in the gospel and faith in Jesus Christ as Savior. He taught students to hold the ancient teachers of the faith in high regard. His criticism of the church was guided by the hope that it would return to its original biblical and theological basis. With his broad knowledge of these subjects and his desire to share ideas, he contributed much to student and staff discussions. His many teaching handouts on the Ethiopian Orthodox Church and Gə_əz and Amharic are kept in the archives of Mekane Yesus Seminary to this day. In 1970–71 he wrote a textbook on Ethiopian Orthodox Church history for the Theological Education by Extension program of the seminary, which continues as part of the certificate/diploma curriculum. He also gave classes in the seminary's program of education for student wives, and served as warden for the students from 1961–74. He was respected and appreciated very much for the fatherly care he gave to students. Dr. Amanuel Gebre-Selassie, the first president of the Ethiopian Evangelical Church Mekane Yesus, noted that Meseret contributed more to the seminary than was expected of him. After four years of working together, Dr. Gustav Aren, the principal, encouraged him to apply for further studies. Meseret studied for some months at Makumira Seminary in Tanzania, and then returned to his teaching.

In those early years at Mekane Yesus Seminary he prepared another book for publication. He was motivated by two sets of experiences. The first was an experience of healing. In 1966, Meseret had a growth removed from his right hand. But the hand got worse after the surgery. When it was almost paralyzed, Meseret had a profound experience of healing in which his hand was restored to health without the intervention of the doctors. During the same timeframe, Meseret had another set of experiences that had left him with a deep concern for Ethiopians who went abroad for theological studies, but had their personal faith destroyed in the process. In this second book, Meseret wrote a novel that combined elements of personal testimony about the experience of physical healing alongside an enumeration of the many bases for faith in God. He called the book *Many Roots* (Sire Bizu) and it was published in 1969. It made the point that well-grounded faith has too many roots to be overthrown by other teachings.

In the late 1960's the seminary was going through a struggle concerning its place in the church. The number of students had decreased, and Meseret left in May 1971. He decided to support himself by farming and preaching and hoped to do more writing. He obtained land near Mizan Teferi in southwest Ethiopia, and set up his farm there. However, the situation at the seminary improved in the following year and the leaders of the church and seminary wanted him back. He returned to his teaching position[51] and in 1974 he married Sehin Seifu who later bore a son, Fekade Sellassie.

With the World Council of Churches in Jerusalem

After the fall of the monarchy in 1974, Meseret was unable to continue going to the monasteries in northern Ethiopia to work with manuscripts. For one thing personal security was a significant problem during this time. For another, his advancing age was beginning to limit his ability to withstand the enormous rigors of these demanding trips. But other opportunities for travel were to present themselves.

The communist leaders executed Emperor Haile Sellassie and replaced his administration with a communist government. Patriarch Theophilos was also arrested and replaced. This action was not accepted by any of the world's churches except for the Russian Orthodox Church. A delegation from the World Council of Churches came to Ethiopia to check on the status of the Ethiopian Orthodox Church. While there, they had contact with the Evangelical Church *Mekane Yesus* which was also one of its members. Meseret was there, and because of his knowledge of the traditions and practice of the Ethiopian Orthodox Church, he was able to interpret the change in patriarch to this delegation. A month later, the secretary general and other officials of the WCC came and met Meseret. A month later, they wrote a letter to the Ethiopian Evangelical Church Mekane Yesus asking for Meseret and Dr. Yaqob Tesfai, both of whom were on the Mekane Yesus Seminary staff, to be members of a committee for dialogue on the issue. They were sent to Jerusalem for meetings in June 1976.

---

[51] Meseret left his property, including 505 books and manuscripts, in the hands of several friends. He expected to bring his property to Addis Ababa later, or to keep it there for when he retired. However, after the fall of Emperor Haile Sellassie, the property was taken by the farmers' association. Only the books in one friend's hands, amounting to less than ten per cent of his collection, were saved, and later brought to Meseret in Addis Ababa.

In London

Due to his own personal interests, Meseret arranged his return trip to go through London. However, he did not know that his air ticket was valid for only forty days. After a short stay in London he went to the airline office to arrange his return, but found his ticket had expired. Now he was stranded and without funds to buy another ticket. A friend helped him get a job in a garage and he used the time to study English. He was also able to meet with some of his friends, including David Stokes. Best of all, he was able to spend time in the Oxford University Library and the British Museum working with their Ethiopic manuscripts. He became a source person about Ethiopia for professors and students. Among them, Oxford lecturer Madame Spenser and Rev. Michael Blair became friends. They encouraged Meseret to continue his studies in London, and he applied to Mekane Yesus Seminary for a scholarship. Instead, they asked to return to his teaching position. The principal, Rev. Dr. Johnny Bakke, went to London and personally talked to him, after which he agreed to return. Madam Spencer and others then consulted with the Anglican Archbishop, and they arranged for Meseret to stay in Oxford as a special student and resource person. Since, since he had promised Dr. Bakke that he would return, Meseret turned down this offer. Finally, in mid-1979, Meseret's stay in London ended and he returned to Ethiopia.

Meseret's Second Major Work: *Traditional Computus and its history: According to the Ethiopian Church*[52]

Aläqa Meseret wrote this book while he was in London. In his introduction, he described how he was inspired to write a book on the Ethiopian computus:
> When he was in London, *Abba* Arägawi, a priest for the newly established Ethiopian Orthodox Tewahido Church, asked me to provide a brief introduction on feast days and seasons which are part of the Ethiopian calendar and different from European culture. I wrote down a few pages and translated them into English. But, instead of satisfying the request, the introduction which I had prepared raised several new questions. Every Sunday, when I met with the people (at the church), our discussions about the Ethiopian

---

[52] ትውፊታዊ ፡ ጎሳብ ፡ ዘመንና ፡ ታሪኩ ። በኢትዮጵያ ፡ ቤተ ክርስቲያን ፡ አቋም፡, (Hong Kong: New Life Literature, 1988 [1976 EC]).

church calendar raised further questions. Out of this process was born *Traditional Computus and Its History*. In short, [the Ethiopian Computus] needs a detailed explanation."[53]

If we analyze the introduction to the book in the context of his life, we receive even further insight about what was happening for Meseret at this time. First, after a nearly-twenty-year hiatus from regular worship in an Ethiopian Orthodox setting, Meseret was reconnecting with his mother church as he was participating in the Sunday liturgy. Second, it was also at this time that he was coming back into contact with the hierarchy of the church. In the appreciation page he wrote: ―I want to express my thanks to the following scholars who encouraged me after reviewing the manuscript: His Grace Abuna Timotiwos, archbishop of Keffa Diocese,[54] and His Excellency *Liqä Ṣəlmanat* Habtä Marəyam,[55] and *Nəburä _ed* Dəmeṭəros Gäbrä Marəyam."[56] As we mentioned above, it was also during this time that Meseret was accessing the British Library's collection of manuscripts from Maqdala. He gave himself to the study of these unique and rare works. In *Traditional Computus and Its History*, the following manuscripts from the British Library are cited:[57] Orient 481[58], Orient 491[59], Orient 492[60] (Book of Wisdom), Orient 501[61], Orient 584[62], Orient 585[63], Orient 699[64], Orient 717[65], Orient 729[66], Orient 735[67], Orient 751[68], Orient 778[69], Orient 782[70], Orient 787[71], Orient 799[72], Orient 809[73], Orient 816[74], Orient 809[75], Orient

---

[53] Ibid., 3.
[54] Current dean of Holy Trinity Theological College in Addis Ababa.
[55] Now Archbishop Abuna Mälkä Ṣedeq.
[56] The late managing director of Ethiopian Orthodox Tewahedo church. His collection of manuscripts were acquired by the Capuchin Friary in Asko, outside of Addis Ababa. There were digitized by EMIP and a catalog is in preparation.
[57] This is only a partial list of the manuscripts that are cited in Meseret's book.
[58] Traditional Computus 72.
[59] *Ibid.*, 143.
[60] *Ibid.*, 20.
[61] *Ibid.*, 150.
[62] *Ibid.*, 30 and 34.
[63] *Ibid.*, 200.
[64] *Ibid.*, 71.
[65] *Ibid.*, 200.
[66] *Ibid.*, 161.
[67] *Ibid.*, 66, 67, and 167.
[68] *Ibid.*, 87 and 150.
[69] *Ibid.*, 231.
[70] *Ibid.*, 38 and 44.
[71] *Ibid.*, 162.

812[76], Orient 814[77], Orient 815[78], Orient 818[79], Orient 824[80], Orient 829[81], Orient 833[82], Orient 890[83], and Orient 13269[84].

He divided *Traditional Computus* into three Parts.[85] In the first part of the book Meseret discussed the contribution of Ethiopian scholars to the formation of the text of the computus. He acknowledged the influence of the Persian, Jewish, Coptic, and Arabic computus on the Ethiopic computus, but he rejected the idea that the whole of the Ethiopian computus was borrowed from foreign sources. He showed that the seasonal division of the Ethiopic computus corresponds with the weather and geography of Ethiopia and argued that this is evidence of the contribution of Ethiopian scholars. He said:

> The division (of the seasons) points to the weather of the land of Ethiopia and its natural seasonal pattern. If we take this division to Persia, Palestine, Europe, and China, does it work? If we follow this logic, then we ask further, from whom did Ethiopia receive this kind of guidance? What foreign person could have arranged these correspondences of the country's geography and seasonal patterns? In my opinion, it would be difficult for anyone who was raised in the country's seasonal pattern and who has studied the indigenous books and culture which synchronize with their natural surroundings, to conclude that Ethiopia received its computus from abroad.[86]

In part two of the book he showed first that the Ethiopian computus is based on biblical genealogy. He went on to demonstrate how the Ethiopian scholars of the computus scholars interpreted these biblical accounts and incorporated them into the life of the church. He showed how the indigenous understanding of the computus was fleshed out in the life of

---

[72] *Ibid.*, 24, 28, and 196.
[73] *Ibid.*, 196.
[74] *Ibid.*, 165.
[75] *Ibid.*, 16, 17, 25, 30, and 33.
[76] *Ibid.*, 16, 19, 21, 22, and 34.
[77] *Ibid.*, 127.
[78] *Ibid.*, 17, 18, 22, 66, and 161.
[79] *Ibid.*, 22 and 41.
[80] *Ibid.*, 132.
[81] *Ibid.*, 52.
[82] *Ibid.*, 130.
[83] *Ibid.*, 12 and 189.
[84] *Ibid.*, 67.
[85] A brief summery of the book is given in English (p. ii) and Amharic (pp. 6–7).
[86] *Ibid.*, 30.

the church, as expressed in its hymns, images, commentaries and Gə͟əz poetry.

In the third and final part of the book, Meseret discussed the calculation of the Ethiopic computus in relation to the church year and the seasons of nature. He showed how the church lectionary follows this seasonal calendar. Meseret collated the Sunday lectionary readings for the entire year with their biblical readings and with their corresponding hymns from Dəggwa.[87] He provided a lection table which was divided into eight columns for each Sunday. The first column showed from which type (*bet*) the Yared song came. The second column designated the melody of the hallelujah. The third gave the title of the hymn. The fourth listed the passage from the Pauline epistles. The fifth listed the passage from the general epistles. The sixth listed the passage from the Acts of the Apostles. The seventh column listed the Psalm which was to be sung just before the Gospel reading (this is the so-called *məsbak*). And finally, in the eighth column, he listed the passage from the Gospel. In his lection table he was able to integrate the nine major feast days of our Lord, the seven fasting seasons of the Ethiopian Orthodox church, as well as the feast days of the Apostles and Evangelists.

Meseret's Third Major Work: *Trinity in Unity*[88]

Following *Traditional Ethiopian Computus*, the Mekane Yesus Literature Program published three more of his books. In 1993, *The Arians* (*Arəyosawəyan*) was published. It applied the ancient Arian discussions to the modern teachings of the group known as Jehovah's Witness. In 1995, *The Word was God* (*Qal Ǝgzi'bəher Näbbärä*) was published by Artistic Printing Press. This book discussed the objections raised by the Arians to the teaching of the Mystery of Incarnation.

Finally, in 1996, Meseret published his *magnum opus*, *Trinity in Unity*, just before his death. *Trinity in Unity* is one of the greatest books published in the modern era of the Ethiopian Orthodox Church. The book is a living testament to Meseret's lifetime of study in the Ethiopian Orthodox Church. It shows not only the depth of his knowledge but also his love and respect for the teaching and tradition of the church.

In the introduction to *Trinity in Unity* he summarized the argument of the book, organized into seven main sections. The first section explored

---

[87] *Ibid.*, 211–28.

[88] ሥላሴ ፡ በተዋሕዶ፡ (Addis Ababa: Bərəhanəna Sälam Printing Press, 1996).

the question of revelation. Meseret argued that God was neither completely hidden, nor was he the god of the philosophers who is easily found in human reasoning. He set forth the thought of the Cappadocian fathers on the transcendent nature of God. As Basil said,

እመሰ ፡ ይርህቀ ፡ ለሕሊናነ ፡ አአምሮተ ፡ ምግባራት ፡ ዘይኔጽሮሙ ፡ ወኢንክል ፡ ተናግር ፡ ዘከመ ፡ ድልወቶሙ፤ እፎኑመ ፡ ንትሀበል ፡ ለተናግር ፡ ዘኢያአምርነ፤

> If the visible works of creation are difficult for our mind to understand how they work, then how can we be so bold as to speak about the things we do not know?[89]

Although God is transcendent in his nature, He is also immanent. His immanence is based on his grace. For Meseret, whether it is human reason or biblical revelation, the foundation of the revelation of God is the Grace of God.[90]

The second section discussed the nature of God. Meseret explored the meaning of the terms nature (ጠባይ), existence (ሁሉና), person (አካል), divinity (መለኮት), and others.

In the third part, he discussed the meaning of personhood in the corporal and spiritual world. Through the analogy of personhood, Meseret tried to explain the existence of the persons of the Trinity in one, triune God.

In part four, Meseret explained the idea of the unity of the Trinity, especially in relation to how the three persons in-dwelled each other and interacted with one another. In this part he discussed the concept of unity in diversity and diversity in unity (ተጋብአ ፡ በተክፍሎ ፡ ወተክፍሎ ፡ በተጋብአ ፡). He presented the idea of Perichoresis which was so important to the patristic theologians.

In the fifth section, Meseret explored the notion of the generation of the Son and the Holy Spirit, explaining how the Father is both Origin and Source.

In the sixth section, he discussed what he called the ―functional names" (አስማተ፡ ግብር፡ in Gə_əz and የግብር፡ ሥሞች፡ in Amharic) and the ―personal names" (አስማተ፡ አቃኒም፡) of the Trinity. The functional names of the trinity are ―Begetter" (ወላዲ), ―Begotten" (ተወላዲ)—describing the eternal generation of the Son from the Father—and the One Who Caused to Proceed (አሥራጊ) and the One Who Proceeded (ሠራጊ)—describing the relationship between Father and Holy Spirit. Meseret explained these terms

---

[89] From section four of Basil's homily in *Haymanotä Abäw*, cited in *Trinity in Unity*, 20.
[90] *Ibid.,* 34.

with many Ethiopian theological expressions and examples. He cited the discussion of Gregory the Wonder Worker and other patristic writers regarding the various understandings of the personal and functional names of the Trinity.

The conclusion of the book (section seven) is a short summary of the fall of humanity and how the Father sent his Son for the salvation of humanity. This seventh section was actually added in the final stages of the preparation of the book as an appendix in order to explain how a proper understanding of salvation flows from correct Trinitarian doctrine.[91]

Like his other books, *Trinity in Unity*, is filled with references to Ethiopian patristic literature. Some of these works cited are: Haymanotä Abäw[92], Homily of John Chrysostom[93], Book of Qerəlos[94], Anaphora of Our Lady Mary[95], Anaphora of Gregory of Armenia[96], Mäṣəhafä Gəṣəw Wätägsaṣ[97], Rətu_a Haymanot[98], Mäṣəhafä Dəggʷa,[99] Homily of Severus of Smunay[100], Ṣomä Dəggʷa[101], Əlmäsṭoʻagəya[102], Fənotä Əgziʻabeḥer of Aläqa Ḥəruy[103], Mäṣəhafä Baḥry[104], Aksimaros[105], Anaphora of Epiphanius[106], Haymanotä Abäw Zä-Qädämt Wäzädäḫart[107], Arägawi Mänfäsawi[108], Image of the Trinity[109], Məʻəlad zä-Aqabe Säʻat Käbte[110], and Mar Yəsḥaq[111].

---

[91] Meseret hoped to publish a further work in the series in which he intended to explore the Mystery of Christology from a Trinitarian perspective. Unfortunately, he died before this hope was realized.
[92] *Trinity in Unity* 19, 20, 34–5, 46, 48–9, 74, 79, 84, 85, 87, 88, 89–90, 100–1, and 103.
[93] Ibid., 20.
[94] Ibid., 28, 45, and 72.
[95] Ibid., 29 and 86.
[96] Ibid., 30 and 91–2.
[97] Ibid., 30.
[98] Ibid., 37–9.
[99] Ibid., 47.
[100] Ibid., 51–3.
[101] Ibid., 55.
[102] Ibid., 74.
[103] Ibid., 76, 82, and 89.
[104] Ibid., 85.
[105] Ibid., 93.
[106] Ibid., 93 and 102.
[107] Ibid., 93.
[108] Ibid., 97.
[109] Ibid., 98.
[110] Ibid., 99.
[111] Ibid., 99.

A reviewer of the book commented[112] that Meseret's writings showed his discernment both for the strengths and the weaknesses of the Church, with the aim always to bring renewal. Indeed, his works contain valuable information on the history, worship and traditions of the Church, and are written with superb Amharic literary skill.

At the time of his death Meseret left several unpublished manuscripts.

Meseret was a founding member of an association called *Maḥəbärä Bäk^wur* (Association of the First-Born). The name comes from Romans 8:29. The aim of the organization was to seek the renewal of the Ethiopian Orthodox Church and a rediscovery of its roots, so that it might become a *beacon of light* (Čorra) to the whole of Ethiopia and beyond. An informational tract about the association referred to Philip, the Evangelist, who taught the way of salvation to the first Ethiopian convert in Acts 8. The organization did not aim to draw members away from the Church. It strove to produce biblically-based materials grounded in patristic thinking and to arrange meetings for fellowship in Bible study and prayer, with the goal that those within the Church would stand firm in the Gospel. The organization sought to join with and encourage the Church in revival and renewal in its teaching, worship and administration. Tibebe Eshete noted[113] that the organization challenged the innovations in the Church that were promoted by literature created during the reign of Emperor Zär_a Ya_ᶐob and forced upon the people by him. Tibebe added the following in describing the organization:

> The group believes that the rich tradition of the Church—such as fasting, liturgical worship, songs, the wearing of traditional vestments during church services, and the fellowship bonds, *Maḥəbärä*, patterned along *maheber,* the secret clubs that the followers of Estifanos formed in the medieval period—is a heritage to be honored and nurtured.

Maḥəbärä Bäk^wur had an ongoing magazine called *Čorra* (beacon of light), which contained many articles written by Meseret before he died, up through volume 13. It played an important part in promoting thoughtful study of the Church's teaching and traditions in the light of Scripture.

Before the Bible Society of Ethiopia published a contemporary translation of the Amharic Bible in 1988, Meseret was asked by the Ethiopian Evangelical Church Mekane Yesus to be on a voluntary review committee for the Old Testament. He read doctrinally significant chapters,

---

[112] *Čorra* 14 (1998) 7.
[113] Evangelical Movement (2009) 47–8.

and worked with the consultant, Rev. Dr. Loren Bliese, to include final recommendations. These meetings were held in Meseret's home since his activities were limited for medical reasons.

Meseret continued teaching at Mekane Yesus Seminary until his retirement, which was unanimously extended by the seminary board for two years beyond 1986 when he became eligible. He served the seminary full time for twenty-three years. During his last years, Meseret suffered from high blood pressure and had to limit his activities. Provision was made for him to be paid for work he would be doing for the seminary after his formal retirement. He continued to live at the seminary with his wife and son. He died on January 14, 1998. A funeral service was held at the Addis Ababa Fifth Kilo Mekane Yesus Church, and he was buried in Saint Joseph's Cemetery.

Meseret's concern for church reform on the basis of biblical teaching and patristic theology lives on. His love for the scholarly tradition of the Ethiopian Orthodox Church is shown in his writings and in his lifetime of study of manuscripts, from the remotest monasteries in Ethiopia to the treasured holdings of the British Library. We feel certain that this catalog of the manuscripts he collected and studied will be a fitting tribute to his life and work.

Postscript: Eulogies for Mäsärät Səbḥat Lä'ab

Various persons have provided formal eulogies in tribute to Meseret. Shortly after his death, volume 14 of *Čorra* was devoted to Meseret's memory.

Derese Birru, a colleague and friend of Meseret, wrote the following note of appreciation in Amharic to be included in this publication. The translation reads,

> God said to the young Jeremiah, ―Before I formed you in the womb I knew you." God knows everyone who comes to the earth. He called Jeremiah to be a prophet, and we know that in every time there are those God calls for a special purpose. Now, and in the future he works through those whom he calls.
>
> The beloved teacher and author Meseret Sebhat Leab is one of those whom God called for his purpose. In his strong faith in Christ and his deep knowledge of Holy Scripture, the life he lived has left a clearly visible fingerprint of his work. This respected servant conducted himself humbly among the students who drank

from the deep knowledge and wisdom he received from the Holy Spirit. He used the time when he was not teaching, in preparing books in which high and deep mysteries are made clear. Of the books Meseret wrote, I personally have been blessed by *Sire Bizu* (*Many Roots*), which has the aim to make clear in the reader's heart that "faith, hope and love remain." The book draws the reader forward with the sweet flavor of its appropriate explanations and chosen examples.

The main characters of the book are church leader Mekbib and Mr. Bedlu. Their questions and answers lead the reader to cross from the known to the unknown. Spiritual mysteries are chosen and explained with the ability to make one hold on to them. Leaving other details of the book to the reader, the message on page 166 paragraph three is as follows: "The good news proclaimed in the Gospel is that although human beings have fallen into the shadow of death and the swamp of darkness, to the extent that they are sinking deeper and cannot get out, God's grace and holy Spirit grasp the hair on their heads and lift them out. The Good Shepherd, who gave his life as a ransom and rose from the dead, lifts them to his shoulders, taking them to live with him, where they will enter the presence of the Father, from whose hand no one can snatch them away."

The spirit of our father and brother Meseret Sebhat-Leab, who by the Holy Spirit's help left us *Many Roots* and other books, is now with Jesus, his beloved Lord. His spirit is waiting for the day of resurrection when it will be united in a new way with the body it left. Now, until we go where he is, we who are alive remember and honor him when we read his works. –Derese Birru, January 22, 2010.

Dr. Johnny Bakke contributed the following words of appreciation for Meseret.

Ato Meseret Sebhat-Leab, or *Abba* Meseret as we also called him, was a very good friend whom I over the years learnt to know, love and respect. Although due to my very limited knowledge of Amharic, we had some communication problems, I learnt to appreciate him quickly after my arrival at the Seminary. He expressed in his humble, patient and careful way his concern regarding the development of the Seminary. These were concerns we shared and tried to express.

We left the Seminary at the same time in 1971. I went to Norway on furlough and he decided to go for contemplation and studies at a plot of land that he had in Illubabor. I was very happy to hear that he, after a year, agreed to return to the Seminary, it was great to meet him there as we returned in 1973.

There were many incidents through the years that could be told describing the fine character of Ato Meseret. He did not ask much for himself, he was happy as long as he was allowed to do his work, helping the students to see the great value of the Ethiopian Orthodox tradition and its importance for the development of the country. I am always thankful to him for having taught me to love and respect that great tradition.

We all rejoiced when he married W/ Sihen Seifu, and it was just appropriate that Seminary could provide them with a proper house. But here too he proved his modesty. He did not want a villa in the same pattern as the other staff residences. The size and the number of rooms were all planned and ordered by him. He did not want anything that separated him from his friends and from his simple way of living.

His teaching and his life were throughout Christocentric. Whenever our discussions, in his opinion, were moving away from that centre, he would object. I remember so well in one staff meeting African theology was on the agenda. When the other staff members had voiced their opinion on the topic, it came carefully and silently from Ato Meseret, "I believe we should concentrate on our Palestinian theology."

Ato Meseret was loved and respected by all. The students, the workers of the Seminary and staff members, we all looked up to him and we are thankful that God gave us the gift of learning to know Ato Meseret Sebhat Leab.

In love and appreciation,
Johnny Bakke a friend and colleague of Ato Meseret, 1969–98

Sources

—Association of the First Born:" Introductory Brochure of the Mahbere Bekur Organization in Amharic, explaining its background, name, vision and goals. Nd and np.

"Meseret Sebhat Le-ab Memorial Volume." *Chorra: Spiritual Magazine* 14 (1998) 4–21.

Dawit Chibsa. "Meseret Sebhat Leab: An Orthodox with Evangelical Conviction," Bachelor of Theology Thesis Mekane Yesus Seminary, Addis Ababa, May, 1990.

Dirshaye Menberu. "Meseret Sebhat Leab (Aleqa), 1926–1996, Mekane Yesus Church Ethiopia." *Dictionary of African Christian Biography*. Available at: www.dacb.org/stories/ethiopia/meseret_.html.

Eshetu Abate. "A Short *Biography* of Meseret Sebhat Le-Ab." In Meseret Sebhat Le-Ab, *Sellassie Betewahido* (Trinity in Unity). Addis Ababa: Berhanena Selam, 1996. Three pages, in Amharic.

Tibebe Eshete. *The Evangelical Movement in Ethiopia*. Waco TX: Baylor, 2009. See especially the section "Reform Initiatives from Within" (44–48), which deals with the Estifanites and with *Aläqa* Meseret as a modern advocate of their fifteenth-century theological position.

Tibebu Tedla. "Memhir Meseret Sebhat Leab Achir Yehiwet Tarik" (Short Biography of Scholar Meseret Sebhat Leab read at Meseret's funeral January 1998 in Amharic). Mekane Yesus Seminary Library. Mimeographed three pages.

The *Dəggʷa* of St Yared and the Musical Manuscripts in the Collection

Ralph Lee

Introduction

The *dəggwa*, attributed to the sixth century CE saint, Yared, is one of the most important books in the tradition of the Ethiopian Orthodox *Tewahido* Church.

In a common introductory inscription for *dəggwa* MYS022 in this collection, a complete *dəggwa*, tells us that the *dəggwa* lists the various types of songs which are written and states their purpose, which is, *'for the feasts and Sabbaths, and the season of flowers[1] and the harvest season[2], of the rainy season[3] and the dry season[4]*'. The *dəggwa* contains all the prescribed songs for all seasons, for all festivals, and all common days of worship, and its purpose is to bring glory to the triune God at all times of day, in all seasons of the year, and on all occasions either feasts or Sabbaths.

The performance of Yared's works is a sacred spectacle for the faithful, performed by *däbtära* or cantors. The songs are set in the *Qəne Mahəlet* which is the outermost of the three sections of an Ethiopian church, except at the festival of *Ṭimqät*, or Epiphany, when the hymns are performed in an open field near water, recalling Christ's baptism in the Jordan. According to one Ethiopian scholar *'its sound is soothing, its movement a gentle swaying of the body sideways and to and fro, its dance a softly rhythmic and undulating march backwards, forwards, and sideways, its percussion minimalistic, and, some say, subtly imitative of the human heart beat'* (Giyorgis 1997: xx). Musical accompaniment with sistrum and drum is important, as is the prayer staff which is used to make elaborate gestures during the performance. The *däbtära* dress in white robes, covered by colored shawls with white turbans on their heads, and they stand in two

---

[1] The season after the end of the rainy season from September until December.
[2] The short rainy season and harvest time from April till July.
[3] The rainy season from July till September.
[4] The dry season from January till March.

groups facing each other, with drummers in the space between. Although obscure even to many of the Ethiopian faithful, the words of the *dəggwa* are rich in subtle biblical allusions. They proclaim clearly the Christian message, using symbolic connections between the Old Testament and the New, with Christian mystical interpretations of prophetic visions. The digitization of a wide range of manuscripts through the EMML project improves the availability of the text to scholars significantly, but still use of the Gəʿəz language makes them relatively inaccessible.

Sacred music is designated as *zema*, meaning harmony or liturgical chant, and incorporates texts, along with melody, rhythms, vocal style, instruments and dance movements associated with them. There are four antiphonaries credited to Yared that come under this broad title: *dəggwa, zəmare, mäwaśəʼt* and *məʿəraf*. Later *dəggwa* manuscripts are marked with cantillation signs indicating the mode of singing, as are found in the manuscripts in this collection. It has been suggested that the musical reciting of the psalms in Ethiopia has Hebraic origin, reflecting the manner of chanting in the Days of David and Solomon. It is notable that some of the few instruments used for liturgical music such as the sistrum (*şänaşəl)*, and beganna (box lyre), are associated with the ancient Middle East. This supports the contention that elements of music including the mode of recitation and notation were preserved from antiquity, possibly coming to Ethiopia with South Arabian migrants in the first millennium BCE (Ullendorff 2006: 95). The *dəggwa* could be described as a style of plainsong, although quite different from other traditions. There is an additional *şomä dəggwa* for fasting periods, which is similar in style. *Zəmare* is the Psalms set to music. The *mäwaśəʼt* are antiphonal chant, the word being derived from the verb meaning ‗answer'. *Məʿəraf* is a complimentary mode of singing to the other forms, and is used in all types of church music (Mondon-Vidailhet 1922; Lepisa 1970).

Studies on the *dəggwa* have focused on the musical style (see for instance Mondon-Vidailhet 1922; Shelemay 1982; Shelemay 1992) and celebrate the uniqueness of the Ethiopian musical expression. Yared's musical compositions show general similarities to Syrian, Egyptian and particularly Armenian ecclesiastical music (Mondon-Vidailhet 1922). Little has been written, however, about the text itself, which also contains a unexplored treasure trove of information about the Ethiopian Church, its theological expression and connections, as well as being poetry of exceptional beauty.

Although obscure their textual content is rich and has the potential to build a picture of indigenous Ethiopian Christian thought and to reveal important elements of the formation and development of Christianity in Ethiopia through indigenous inspiration and external influences which can be identified through a careful study of the *dəggwa*.

St Yared

In the Ethiopian Orthodox *Tewahido* Church it is impossible to talk about the *dəggwa* without mentioning the seminal figure of St Yared. Yared was first a priest and later a monk and hermit, one of the most important saints in Ethiopia, with many churches dedicated to him (Mekarios 1996: 47–8) and frequent representations in paintings. Little is known about the life of St Yared except for that recorded in his hagiography, in documents such as the Acts of Yared (Conti Rossini 1904), in the Ethiopian Synaxarium (Budge 1928: 875–7). The Acts of Yared connect him with another enigmatic figure, King Gebra Meskel, who was the son of King Caleb. The close association with King Caleb's son would, however, place him in the first half of the sixth century CE (Crummey 2006: 461), a date consistent with the theological style of his writing.

The complete *dəggwa* or hymnody is attributed to him, which is a powerful indigenous medium for spreading the Christian message and helped to lay the basis for Gə'əz civilization. It is thought that the basic text has not changed a great deal, apart from additions made by Giyorgis of Gascha in the fifteenth century CE. The musical notational system was developed in the sixteenth century CE (Giyorgis 1997: xvii). Yared was also considered a great biblical exegete and teacher of morals and ethics, and his works communicate the essence of the Oriental Orthodox Christian faith. Ethiopian scholars describe him as extolling theological, moral and social virtues in the light of the Holy Bible. His hymns are written to enhance understanding of sacred texts through the use of melody.

The hagiography of St Yared, recorded in the Acts of Yared (Conti Rossini 1904) stresses the divine inspiration of his music given to him through a mystical ascent into heaven. Yared was said to speak with ‗sweet words' or with a sounds ‗sweet like honey' and he called upon all believers to glorify God with a ‗great sound like the Seraphim'. Whilst for many it is the sound of the music and the visual spectacle which is most appreciated, the words of the hymns represent an ancient indigenous form of theological poetry which should be appreciated in its own right as theological poetry of the highest order. In his hagiography Yared makes an ascent into Paradise with three birds, in the likeness of the Trinity, where he witnesses heavenly worship. This ascent story is resonant of Jewish mysticism of the early centuries CE, which also featured in Semitic Christianity of the same period, and places Yared alongside the biblical characters of Enoch, Moses, Ezekiel, Zechariah and Ezra whose visions Yared interprets in the same mystical pattern in the dəggwa. In Paradise Yared is said to have learned the songs of the twenty four elders who worship before the throne of God (see for instance Revelation 4:10, 5:8, 11:16, 19:4). It should be stressed here that whilst the normal focus in the Ethiopian Church is on his musical style, it is also the words of the heavenly worship that he said to have heard. In whatever way this mode of revelation is to be understood, the hagiography places the character of Yared in the same sphere as the prophets whose visions he interprets in the style of Jewish and Semitic Christian mysticism. The belief in this heavenly ascent also explains the rigidity of the Ethiopian Church in relation to the music, which if heavenly could not be improved on!

St. Yared's initial lack of natural aptitude and his transportation to the heavenly realm are emphasized in the Acts of Yared, thus underlining the idea the music and words were revealed to him, rather than coming just from his own ideas. Before Yared wrote his music the liturgy was not sung distinctly, but was ‗murmured in a low voice'. Yared was trained in the psalms of David by one *Abba* Gideon, initially a poor pupil; he was beaten for his lack of aptitude. Inspired by the perseverance of a caterpillar repeatedly attempting to climb a plant to gain food, he repented and learned the books of the Old and New Testaments in a day. After his ascent with the three birds to Paradise he returned to the cathedral in Axum, at the third hour he sang Hallelujah to the Trinity, attracting the attention of the king, queen, bishop and notables for the rest of the day. It is related that he developed the three modes of chant, in such a way that they did ‗not lack … any of the sounds that are made by men, and birds, and beasts.' Also it is told that while singing before King *Gäbrä Mäskäl* (the son of Kaleb) Yared's beautiful singing so absorbed the king that he unwittingly drove his spear into Yared's foot,[5] who was so taken up in the ecstasy of the song that he did not realize until later. In recompense the King agreed to grant whatever Yared wished, and he chose to retire from the world (Conti Rossini 1904; Budge 1928: 875–7). The Ethiopian Synaxarium celebrates St Yared on the 11th of the Ethiopian month of *Gənbot*, (approximately corresponding to May in the

---

[5] See the cover art.

European calendar) which according to the *Gädlä* Yared is the date of his death.

Theology in Poetry

In the Ethiopian and other Oriental traditions hymns are not only for worship, but they are the primary mode of expressing theology. Yared is described in his hagiography as a ‚spiritual harp' a title connecting with his earlier Syrian counterpart as a theologian-poet, The Harp of the Spirit, St Ephrem. Yared's style and content resembles that of St Ephrem, as well as Ephrem's (Julian 1907: 8) fifth and sixth century CE devotee Jacob of Serugh. In fact in many details the *Yaredawi* use of symbolic theology concurs both in detailed associations and in wider themes.

St Ephrem saw poetry as the best way to express theology, eschewing the theological definitions of the Greek world. St Yared should be classified in the same way, as a theologian-poet who wrote hymns for the Church expressing the deepest mysteries of the faith. The western reader may not fully appreciate the significance of this mode of expression, and should refer to the works of Sebastian Brock, in particular *The Luminous Eye* to appreciate it more deeply.

The text of the *dəggwa* has the potential to reveal the meaning of many of the mysteries of the Ethiopian Church. For instance the following is from the *dəggwa* for the twenty first of the Ethiopian month *Ḥədar* entitled the Teaching of Zechariah:

> *The King of Israel danced before her,*
> *behold her, Zion, our mother, our Lady,*
> *behold her Zion, our mother, our Lady.*
> *This is Mary whom the holy prophets compared with the Ark of Noah*
> *who had Manna concealed inside her,*
>
> *...*
>
> *All of the prophets prophesied about Holy Mary the Ark of Noah,*
> *who had concealed inside her Manna,*
> *wondrous white fleece of David,*
> *the lampstand of Zechariah the priest,*
> *pure bridal chamber,*
> *perfect Tabernacle,*
> *dwelling place of divinity,*
> *adorned with holiness and sealed in virginity,*
> *wrapped in golden clothes in a single piece.*

Contained in these few words is the connection between the Ark, before which David danced (2Sam 6:14); the heavenly city, Jerusalem or Zion, of which the Tabernacle is seen as a representation; Saint Mary is also termed the ‚*dwelling place of divinity*' which conjures up memories of the temple, or the Word becoming flesh and *dwelling* amongst us, and of the Jewish mystical concept of the *shekinah*, a symbol of divine imminence; the Ark of Noah which is perceived symbolically in the same way as the Ark of the Covenant; and of Christ as Manna, which in the Syriac and Ethiopic traditions is taken as a symbol of the heavenly Eucharist celebrated in Paradise on which the faithful feast for eternity. The connection here is also made between the fleece of Gideon, which the Ethiopian *andəmtā* bible commentaries also connect with the LXX version of Psalm 72:6, ‚*He shall come down as rain upon a fleece; and as drops falling upon the earth*'. This verse is seen as interpreting the sign of the fleece given to Gideon in Judges 6, the fleece symbolizing Saint Mary, and the dew Christ, so the two together symbolize the incarnation. Finally the lampstand of Zechariah 4 is also interpreted as Mary, with the light as Christ, by implication. Zechariah's vision is also seen as a vision of Paradise, connected with visions of Moses on Sinai, Ezekiel's chariot vision, and Ezra's vision of a weeping woman in 4Esdras 9.

The following quotation is from the *dəggwa* for the seventeenth of the Ethiopian month *Mäskäräm*, which celebrates Helena's finding of the true Cross, and reveals at least part of the understanding of the Cross:

The cross is the Tree of Life,
the Tree of Salvation,
the light of the Gentiles,
the salvation of kings.

Give thanks to the God of Gods,
Give thanks to the Lord, the liberator
because He is the God of mercy,
by His Cross he unlocked Paradise.
By His Cross he unlocked Paradise,
by the work of salvation,
this is the Cross,
our redemption,
our strength,
and our refuge,
He is always with us.

Here the Cross is the key to Paradise, the means of access for believers. Also it is identified with the Tree of Life, which is symbolically Saint Mary, with Christ as the fruit on which the faithful feast forever. This has connections with the 1Enoch 25, another Jewish mystical source, which also has the Tree of Life symbolized in this way.

In both cases very similar connections can be found in the writing of St Ephrem, in particular in his *Hymns on Paradise* which can be found in translation by Sebastian Brock (Brock 1990), and also in the *Hymns on the Nativity* which form part of Kathleen McVey's translation of a wider set of Ephrem's hymns (McVey 1989). The full significance of the relationship with St Ephrem is only beginning to be understood, and there remains a great wealth of material to study in this literature.

These two short quotations it is hoped indicate some of the richness of the *dəggwa* with its wealth of biblical allusions and symbolic connections. The poetry of the *dəggwa* is formed from a consistent theological framework which does not immediately present itself to those familiar with the systematic approach of theology in the West. Not only does it provide such a rich mine of knowledge for researchers, it is hoped that future translations will also provide spiritual inspiration for many.

Sources

Brock, Sebastian. *St. Ephrem the Syrian: Hymns on Paradise*. New York: Saint Vladimir's Seminary, 1990.

Budge, E. A. Wallis. *The Book of the Saints of the Ethiopian Church*. Volume 3. Cambridge: Cambridge University Press, 1928.

Conti Rossini, Carlo. *Acta Yared et Pantalewon*. CSCO 26/27 SA 9/10. Leipzig: Harrassowitz, 1904.

Crummey, Donald. "The Ethiopian Orthodox *Täwahedo* Church." In *The Cambridge History of Christianity, Volume 5: Eastern Christianity*, edited by M. Angold. Cambridge: Cambridge University Press, 2006.

Giyorgis, L. W. G. *Tentawi ser'ata mahlet za-Abuna Yared (A study of the ancient musical system of Yared - In Amharic)*. Addis Ababa: Maison des Etudes Ethiopiennes & Institut Tigreen des Langues, 1997.

Julian, John. *A Dictionary of Hymnology: Setting forth the Origin and History of Christian Hymns of all Ages and Nations*. New York: Scribner, 1892.

Lepisa, Tito. "The Three Modes and the Signs of the Songs in the Ethiopian Liturgy." In, *Proceedings of The Third International Conference of Ethiopian Studies 1966*, edited by Richard Pankhurst, et. al., 162–87. Addis Ababa: Addis Ababa University Press, 1969–70.

McVey, Kathleen. *Ephrem the Syrian: Hymns*. New York: Paulist, 1989.

Mekarios, A. *The Ethiopian Orthodox Tewahedo Church: Faith, Order of Worship and Ecumenical Relations*. Addis Ababa: Tensae, 1996.

Mondon-Vidailhet, Casimir. "La Musique Ethiopienne." In *Encyclopedie de la Musique et Dictionnaire du Conservatoire, Premiere Partie: Histoire de la Musique*, edited by A. Lavignac and L. de la Laurence, 3178–3196. Paris: Libraire Delagrave, 1922.

Shelemay, Kay Kaufman. "Zemā: A Concept of Sacred Music in Ethiopia." *The World of Music* 24 (1982): 52–64.

———. "The Musician and Transmission of Religious Tradition: The Multiple Roles of the Ethiopian Däbtära." *Journal of Religion in Africa* 22 (1992) 242–60.

Ullendorff, Edward. *Ethiopia and the Bible*. The Schweich Lectures, 1967. London: Oxford University Press, 1968.

The Textual Character of Jubilees in Mekane Yesus Seminary 54

Ted M. Erho

Ever since its appearance in 1989, James C. VanderKam's edition of the Ethiopic *Book of Jubilees* has functioned as a standard reference for scholars working on the text.[1] In a contribution to a 2008 seminar on *Jubilees*, VanderKam provided an update on the manuscript tradition of this book, in which he refers to twenty-seven known copies in Ge'ez.[2] Recent findings, however, have brought forth more than a dozen new manuscripts containing this book or substantial portions thereof, providing further data and insight on the textual history of this important document.[3]

Among the more significant of these is Mekane Yesus Seminary number 54 (hereafter denoted by the siglum _54'), a late-fifteenth or early-sixteenth century manuscript rebound in abject disorder, which preserves approximately half of *Jubilees*, primarily from the latter portion of the book,

---

[1] James C. VanderKam, *The Book of Jubilees* (2 vols.; CSCO 510/511; SA 87/88; Louvain: Peeters, 1989).

[2] James C. VanderKam, ―The Manuscript Tradition of Jubilees," in *Enoch and the Mosaic Torah* (ed. Gabriele Boccaccini and Giovanni Ibba; Grand Rapids: Eerdmans, 2009), 3–21 (on Ethiopic text at 18–21).

[3] While most of these manuscripts have only been digitized in the past few years (e.g. Gundä Gunde nos. 146 and 162), this figure also includes four previously unmentioned copies of *Jubilees* known since the early 1970s, when they were microfilmed and catalogued (see *Catalogue of Manuscripts Microfilmed by the UNESCO Mobile Microfilm Unit in Addis Ababa and Gojjam Province* [Addis Ababa: Ministry of Education and Fine Arts, Department of Fine Arts and Culture, 1970], nos. 2.13, 2.26, 10.48, 10.77 and [in Amharic] *Catalogue of the Ethiopian Manuscripts in the National Library of Ethiopia* [Imperial Ethiopian Government and Antiquities Administration: Addis Ababa, 1962 EC], nos. 15, 26). However, these microfilms, of which a master set was stored at the Institute of Ethiopian Studies in Addis Ababa, have been relatively inaccessible to Western scholars. The Ethiopian Manuscript Imaging Project has recently digitized the reels and the resultant images will be deposited in the Hill Museum & Manuscript Library in Collegeville, MN and at the Institute of Ethiopian Studies in Addis Ababa.

along with piecemeal sections of Hosea, Micah, and Amos.⁴ In the following, the textual character of this new exemplar shall be examined, first through a listing of the variants found in five leaves of 54 (ff. 12r–13v [*Jub.* 26:27–27:21]; ff. 39r–41v [*Jub.* 31:28–32:9, 44:12–45:13]) as collated against the critical text of VanderKam, and second through a brief analysis of the accumulated data with regard to the probable affiliation of this copy of *Jubilees*.⁵

Variants

f. 12r–*Jub.* 26:27–33
26:27 በኩርክ]om. 54 | ወልድክ]+በኩርክ 54; +ዘበኩርክ 44
26:28 ድማመ]ድማሜ 54; om. 21 | እንበለ]እምቅድመ 54; pr. ዘ 12 21 | ባረክዎ]+ውእቱ 54 35 | ይኩን]ይከውን 54 35; +እስከ ፡ ለዓለም 44
26:29 ወ(መራር)]om. 54 | ለአቡሁ]om. 54 20 25 35
26:30 በረክታቲክ]በረክታት 54; በረክታተክ 12; በረከተክ 63; +ኩሎ 35 | ያዕቆብ]+ወ 54 21; +እስመ 58
26:31 ወ(ኩሎሙ·)]+ለ 54 21 35 44 63; om. 38 | አንዊሁ]አኃዊክ 54; አንዊ 44; አበዊሁ 58 | ወሁብክዎ]pr. ወ 54 21 35 38 44
26:32 ይቤ]ይቢሎ 54 44 63 | በረክትክ]በረክተክ 54; በረከት 12 35; በረከት 20 25; +ኢተርፈት ፡ እም- 63 | ኪያየኒ]ኪያየ 54 9 38 39ᵗ
26:33 ይኩን ፡ ንብረትክ]tr. 54 | እምጠለ]እምቆለ 54

f. 12v–*Jub.* 26:34–27:6
26:34 ተሐዩ]ሕያው 54 35 38; +ሕያው 48ᶜ(?); om. 21; +ወሕያው 63 | ትትቀነይ]ተቀነይ 54 12 21 35 | ወይኩን]om. 54 35 | ዐበይክ]አበይክ 54 12 20 21 44 47; ዕበይክ 38 | አሜሃ]አሚሃ 54; om. 47 | ዘርእክ]pr. ኩሉ 54 44 48 58 63; pr. ኩሎ 9 38 42 47; +ኩሎ 17

---

⁴ For the precise listing of contents, see the catalogue entry below.
⁵ It must be stressed that the list provided in the following is made solely on the basis of a collation of 54 against the critical text of VanderKam, and, as such, does not incorporate all variants that are present amongst the various copies of *Jubilees*. Moreover, orthographic variants of either consonantal (e.g. ሐ/ኀ or ኣ/ዐ) or vowel (e.g. interchangeability between the first and fourth or fifth and sixth orders in certain instances) types are not included. The sigla used in the following are taken from VanderKam, *The Book of Jubilees*, I:xv.

26:35 ያዕቆብሃ]+እኍሁ 54 35; ለያዕቆብ 21; om. 25 | ይእዜኒ]ማእዜኑ 54; ማዕዜ 35 | እቀትሎ]እቅትሎ 54 25 38 42 44 47
27:3 ከራንሃ]ከራን 54 9 12 17 38 44 63; ራን 21; pr. ኅበ 44; ከራንሂ | ኅዳጠ]ሕዳጠ 54
27:4 ይቤ]ይቤላ 54 35 | እመ]pr. ወ 54 35 58
27:5 ትቤሎ]+እሙ 54 35; +ርብቃ ፡ ለያዕቆብ 12; +ሐር 58
27:6 ናሁ]om. 54

f. 13r–*Jub.* 27:6–13
27:6 ኢየሐውር]ወኢይሐውር 54; ወኢየሐውር 38 | ወእመ]ወለእመ 54; ወእመኒ 12 17; እመ 20 25; ለወእመ 35; ወእመሰ 38 | ባሕቱ]om. 54
27:7 ለያዕቆብ]om. 54
27:8 ርብቃ]+ኅበ ፡ ይስሐቅ 54 17 35 58 63 | ለይስሐቅ]om. 54 17 35 63 | ኬጥ]ኬጢ 54 | እመ]ለእመ 54; እመኒ 17 | ሎቱ]om. 54 12 | እምውስት (om. 21; እምነ 20) ፡ አዋልደ]እምአዋለደ 54 | እለ]እሱ 54 12; እላ 35 39 42ᶜ 44 48; om. 38 42ᵗ 47 58 63 | ሲተ (om. 12 21) ፡ እንከ]tr. 54 | አሐዩ]ሐዩው 54
27:9 ገሥጸ]ገሥጾ 54 35 47
27:10 ሐር]pr. ወ 54 12 17 21 35 38 39 42 44 47 48 58 63 | አቡሃ]pr. ለ 54 9 20 39 48
27:11 ሰዳይ]ሰዳዲ 54; ሰማይ 20 21 25 35 39 42 47 48 58; ሰዱይ 63(?) | ያልህቀ]om. 54; ያልህቅ 9; ያልህቃ 21 | ኩላ]ኩሎ 54 21 44; ኩሉ 12 38 | ወሀቦ]ወሀበ 54 9 17 38 44; ወሀበከ 12

f. 13v–*Jub.* 27:13–21
27:13 ሐዘነ]እንዛ 54
27:14 ትብኪዩ]ትብክዩ 54; ትብኪይ 9 | ወልድየ ፡ እስመ]ወእስመ 54
27:15 የኃንድኅ]ይሐድን 54; የኃንድን 9 17; ያኃንድን 12
27:16 እስመ]om. 54 39; +ከሙ 12 | ኅቤነ]ኅቤየ 54
27:17 ወፍጹም ፡ ውእቱ]om. 54 44 | ምእመን]መእመን 54 17; ማእመን 9; pr. ወ 21 38 | ምእመን ፡ ውእቱ]+ወፍጹም 54 | ትብክዩ]ትፍርሂ 54; ትብከይ 9 12
27:19 ካራንሃ]ከራን 54; ካራን 9 12 17 21 38 44 63 | ኢዮቤሌዉ]ኢዮቤሌም 54 | ወስተ ፡ ሉዛ ፡ እንተ ፡ ውስተ ፡ ደብር ፡ እንተ ፡ ይእቲ ፡ ቤቴል ፡ በሥርቀ ፡ ወርኅ ፡ ዘቀዳሚ ፡ ዘዘ ፡ ሱባዔ ፡ ወበጽሐ]ኅበ ፡ የሐውር 54 | መሲዮ]ወመሰየ 54; መሰዮ 9; ምሴተ 12; ወመሲዮ 17 35; om. 21; መሳዮ 58 | ተግሕሠ]ተግሡ

54 | እምፍጦተ]እፍጦት 54; እምፍጦት ፡ እንተ 12; እምፍጦት 17;
እምፍጦቱ 25 | ዛቲ]ይቲ 54; ይእቲ 12 35
27:20 አእባነ]አእባን 54 9; om. 44 | ውእቱ]pr. እም 54; ይእቲ 44 |
አንበር]አንበሮሙ· 54; አንበረ 12 63; አንበራ 44
27:21 ትለክፍ]ይበጽሕ 54 | ውስተ]እስከ 54 21 35 58 63

f. 41r–*Jub.* 31:28–32:2
31:29 ወ(ተሰራሕ)]om. 54 | ታጎንዲ]ትጎንዲ 54 21 44; ተጎንዲ 17
| ጸሎተክ]ጸሎትክ 54 9 17 44; ዘጸለይክ 21 | ጸሎተ]ጸሎትክ 54
35; ጸሎት 25 39 42 44 47 48 | ትግበራ]ትግበር 54 9 12 21
38 63; ተግባረ 17 58; ግበራ 20 | ይሠመር]ይሠምር 54 9;
ይሠመር 44 48 58; ሠምረ 21; +ቦቱ 63 | ዘገብረ]ዘገበርክ 54;
ዝግብረ 17; om. 21
31:31 እንተ]pr. ወ 54 58
31:32 ተስፋ]ተስፋየ 54ᶜ | ያዐርጉ]ያዐርጉ· 54 20 39 42 47 |
ስምዕ]ስም 54
32:1 እምንዋሙ·]om. 54
32:2 መጽአ]አምጽአ 54 35 | እስከ]pr. ወ 54 21 44 | እስከ²]pr. ወ 54
21

f. 41v–*Jub.* 32:2–9
32:3 ይእቲ]om. 54 21 35 58; ይእቲኒ 20 25 39 42 44 47 48 |
ኖለቄ]ኖለቆ 54; ኖለቁ 9 12; ጕለቄ 20 35 38 58; ጕለቆ 39
42 47 48 | ያዕቆብ]ያዕቆብሃ 54 21 39 42 47 48 63 |
አልባሰ]ልብሰ 54 12; አልባስ 47
32:4 እም(አልህምት)]ወ 54 48; om. 58 63; +ወስተ 25 |
አልህምት]አልህምተ 54 48 63 | ስላ]ጽ 54; om. 17, 58; ሶሲራ 21
| ዕሥራ]om. 54 (blank space) | ተስዐተ]om. 54 (blank space);
ተስዐቱ 25; ትስዐት 9 | ጽንሐሕ]pr. ወ 54 21 | ሥሙረ]ሥሙር
54 9 38 42 47; ሥሙር ፡ ለግሙራ 21
32:6 ስኒነ ፡ ዲቤሁ]tr. 54 | ለ]ወይወዲ ፡ ውስት 54 35 |
ወ(ለመሥዋዕት)]om. 54 35 | አርባዕት]om. 54 (blank space) 12
17 63 | ከመዝ]pr. ወ 54
32:7 ሰቡዐ]ሰቡዑ 54; ሱቡዓ 63 | ይባርክ]ይባርክዎ 54 21 44; ይባርኩ
9 12 17 38 63 | ያእኩቶ]ያእኩትዎ 54 9 12 17 21 38 44 63;
የአኩቶ 39 58 ያእኩቶ 42 47(?) | ባልሓ]ባልሐ 54 9 25 38;
ይባልሐ 58 | ጸሎቶ]ጸሎቱ 54
32:8 ንጹሕ]+ወዘኢኮነ ፡ ንጹሕ 54 35 58 | ወ(ገብር)]om. 54 |
ገብር]ገብረ 54 9 12 38 39 42 47 48 | ኩሎ]ኩሉ· 54

f. 39r–*Jub.* 44:12–22

44:12 ኤስሮም]አስሮም 54 21; ኤሴሮም 9 47; -ሙ 38 | ኀምስቱ] om 54 (erasure, but only of one or two letters)

44:13 አምት]አምታ 54 21; አውት 9 38; አወት 44 58 | ፍኒሰወት]ፍንሳዋት 54; -ዊት 9; ፍኔሰዋት 12; -ተ 17; ሲፍነዋት 20 25 35 44; ፍንሰዋት 21; ፌኒሳዋት 38; ፍንሰዋት 39 48 (-ሰ-) 58; ስፍንስዋት 42 47 | ሰብንቱ] om 54

44:14 ሌዊ]ለዊ 54 | ቃንድ]ቃንት 54 21 35 38 42 47 48 58 | ሚራሪ]ሜራሪ 54 17 35 38 48 63; ምራሪ 9; ሚራሪ 12; ሜራሪ 58

44:15 ሴሎም]ሴሎሙ 54 21; ሰሎሞን 12; ሰሎም 25

44:16 ፉአ]ፉላ 54 21; ፉአ 9; ፉእ 12; ፎአ 20; ፌአ 38; ለአፉአ 39; ለፉአ 42 47 48; ለፉዕ 58 | ሳምሮም]ሰምሮሙ 54 17 21; ሰመሮሚኒ 9 38; ሰመሮሙ 12; ስምሮሙ 63

44:17 ኢያሊኤል]ኢያልኤል 54 25 39; ኢያሉኤል 9; ኢያሲኤን 20; ኢያአል 21; ኢያሎኤል 38; ኢያሲኢል 42; እያልኤል 44; ኤልያ 58; om 63

44:18 እለ]ዘ 54 21

44:19 ውሉደ]ውሉያ 54 | ለአክታ]ላእካታ 54; ልእክታ 12 20 21 35 | ብሲተ]ብእሲቱ ፡ ለ 54 9 12 21 38 39 42 47 48 58 63

44:20 ምስሉሁ]ምስሌሆሙ 54 9 21 38ᵗ 39 42 47 48 58; om 38ᶜ | ሴፍዮን]ሰፍዮን 54; ሴፋዮን 17; ስፍዮን 21 42 47ᶜ(?) 58; ሶፍዮን 39 48; ሲፋንዮስ 63; ስፍንዮን 47ᵗ | ኢጋቲ]ጋቲ 54 17 20 21; ኢጋቲ 9; pr. ሐዲ፡ወ 58 | ሱኒ]ሰኒ 54 (ሳኒ) 21; አሱኒ 20; ሶኒ 38; ኡኒ 58 | አሲቦን]ሳቦኒ 54 21; አሰብን 9 38; አሲባን 12; ሲቦን 20; አሶን 39 42 47 48 58 | አሪሊ]አረሊ 54 21 42 47 48; አሪሊ 9; አሪሊ 12 39; አሪቢ 17; አሊረ 25; አሮሊ 38 63; እረሊ 58 | አሩዲ]አረዲ 54 21 39 42 47 48 58; አሩዲ 9 38; ሩዲ 12; +ወአሊአሪ 44; +ወኢራሱ 58

44:21 ኢዮምን]ኢያምን 54; አይምን 12; ኢያምኒ 21 47 48 58; እዮምን 42 | ይሱአ]ይስእ 54 21; ይሱዕ 58; ይሶአ 38; ይሴዋሕ፡ወይሰቡአ 44 | ቤርያ]በራያ 54; ቤሪየ 12; ቦራያ 21; ባሪያ 39 48; ባርያ 42 47 58 ቡየ 44

44:22 ነፍስ]+ዘዘለፋ 54 21 35; ዘዘ[ ] 58; om. 48 | ኩሉ]ዘኩሉ 54 | አርባዕቱ]om. 54 (blank space); ፫ 58

f. 39v–*Jub*. 44:23–34

44:24 ተጢፋሪ]ጢፋሪ 54; ተጢፋራ 12 39(?) 42 47 48 58 ተጢፋሬ 17; ተጢፍራ 25; ጊጥፋራ 38ᶜ; ፈጢፋሬ 63

44:25 ባላ]ለወባኤል 54; ባላኤል 17ᶜ; ለባውኤል 21; ለውባኤል 39 42 47 48; ለውሰብኤል 58 | ወባኮር (ባከር 12 17; ቦኮር 20 35)] om. 54 21 39 42 47 48 58 | አስቢ.ል]አሳቤል 54 12 21 39; ኢሶቤል 9 38 63; አባሲል 17; አስቢ.ር 20; አክቤል 48; አስቤል 42 47; አሰባኤል 58; +ወ 20 58 | ጉአድ]ጉአው· 54 21 (ጉ·-) 39 42ᵗ 47 48 58; ጉኢ.ድ 9 12 17 63; ጉድ 20ᵗ (ጉ·አድ 20ᶜ); ጉኤል 38 | አብዮድ]ብሮድዮ 54 21; አብብድዮ 9 17 63 (አበ-); አብድዮ 12 38 (-ድይ); አብሮድዮ 39 42 47 48; ብዮድ 44; አብራድዮ 58 | ራኤ]ራኤፍስ 54 21 39 (-ኢ.-) 42 47 48 58 | ሰናኒም]ያኒግ 54 42 47 48 58; ዓኒግ 21; ያሚና 39 | አፈም]አፌን 54 21; አፈል 20ᶜ (አፍል 20ᵗ [?]) 25 35 44; ኩፈም 38; አፈሞ 48; አፈም 58; +ወዮአዮ 39 58; +ወየአም 42 47 48 | ጋአም]ያኢ.ሞ 54 21; ጋአስ 39; ጋዕም 58

44:27 ለአክታ]ላእክታ 54 39 58; ላእክታ 12; ልእክታ 20 21 25 35 | ዘወለደት]om. 54 20 | ለያዕቆብ]om. 54 21 | ዳንሃ]ዳን 54 9 20 21 38 42 47 48

44:28 ግብጽ]+ወ 54 9 12 17 21 39 42 47 48 63 | አሱዴ]አሱድ 54 21 39 42 47 48 58; አሲ.ዲ 20 | ስድስቱ]፮ 54

44:29 ወተረፎ]ወተረፈ 54 21 38 | ለዳን]om 54 21

44:30 ጋሄኒ]ጋሐን 54 21 39 42 47 48 58 | አሰአር]አሳዓር 54; ኢ.ሶአር 9; ኢ.ሰአር 17; እስአር 25; አስአር 35 42 44 47 48 58; ኢ.ሲ.አር 38; አይስአር 63 | ሰሉ·ም]ያኩ·ም 54 39 42 47 48 58; ያኩም 21; ስሉም 12; ስሉ·ም 35; ሱሉ·ም 38; ሰሉም 44 | ኤው]አው 54 21 42 47 48 58; ኢ.ው 12; ኤዊ. 25; ኢ.ም 38; +፪ 42 47

44:31 ኤው]አው 54 21 42 47 48 58; ኢ.ው 12; ኤዊ. 25; ኢ.ም 38

44:32 ኮኑ]ኮነ 54 21 39 42 47 58 | ኩሎሙ·]ኩሉ· 54; ኩሉ.ሙ· 21 38 39 42 47 58; +ነፍስ 38 | ዘ]+ወሉ.ደ 54 21; እም 48; +እም 39 42 47 58 | ስድስቱ]፮ 54; ፱ 47ᶜ

44:33 ·ንምስቱ]+ወ 54 21; +ነፍስ ፡ ወ 35; +ነፍስ 58 | ዘእንበለ]እንበለ 54 21; እለ 38; እለኢ. 38ᶜ; om. 39ᵗ

44:34 ደቁ]ዮቁ 54; ደቂቁ 9 38 48; ደቅ 35; ውሉ.ዱ· 20

f. 40r–*Jub*. 44:34–45:6

45:1 ውስተ]om. 54 21 35

45:2 አባሁ·]አቡ·ሁ· 54 9 12 38 39 48; እጐሁ· 58

45:3 ይእዜሰ]pr. እም 54 21 35 38 44 | እስራኤል ፡ ወ (om. 9 12 20 38 39 42 47 48 58) አምላከ (om. 58)]om. 54 21 35
45:4 ቤቴል]+ወ 54 21
45:5 እስመ ፡ ርእዮ ፡ ለዮሴፍ ፡ እንዘ ፡ ይበልዕ ፡ ምስለ ፡ አኀዊሁ ፡ ወይሰቲ ፡ በቅድሜሁ·]om. 54 21
45:6 ወሀቦ]ወሀቦሙ· 54 21; ወሀበ 12 20 38 | ራሜሲና]ራሜሴና 54 20 21; ራሜሴና 12; ራሚሲኑ 38; ራሚሲቲና 39 42 47 48; ራምሲቲና 58; ራሚሲና 63 | ኵሎ]ኵሉ· 54 21 35 39 47 58 | ይኤንት]ኵነኑ 54 21; ይኤንን 12 38; ይኤነኑ 44 | በቅድሜሁ·]ዘቅድሜሁ 54 | ወ(ነደረ)]om. 54 21 | ነደረ]ነደሩ· 54 9 12 | ምሥናዪሃ]ምሥናይሃ 54 12 20 21 35 38 39 42 47 58 63; ምሥናዪሃ 44

f. 40v–*Jub.* 45:6–13
45:6 ሠላሳ]+ወእርባዕቱ 54 35
45:7 ወጥሪቶሙ·ሂ]ወለጥሪቶሙ·ሂ 54 21 38 42ᶜ(?)
45:8 ኵለንታሃ]ኵልንታሃ 54; ኵለንተሃ 12
45:9 ዘ(ውስተ)]om. 54 21 58 | ምድር]ምድረ ፡ ግብጽ 54 21 35 38 58 | ኵላ]ኵሉ· 54 9 12 17 21 38 39 42 44 47 58 63
45:10 ውኁዳት]ውሑዳት 54 12 21; ወሑዳት 17; ውኁዳን 35; ውሐዳት 44; ውኅዳት 58
45:11 ኢዮቤሌው·]ኢዮቤሌፆ 54
45:12 እደ]እድ 54 9 12 20 21 35 38; om. 39ᵗ 42 47 58; እዴሁ· 44 | ረሰዮ]ረሰየ 54 9 17 21 58 | ዕለት]ሰኑት 54 21
45:13 ሰብዓት]ፀ 54 21; om. 12; ሰብዓቱ 25 35 | ኢዮቤሌውስ]ኢዮቤሌፆስ 54; ኢዮቤሌዋት 44 63; +ወ፫ኢዮቤሌው· 42 47 48 58 | ሰብዓቱ]ቷ 54 21 35 | ዓመት]ዓመተ 54 9 17 38 | ወሞተ ፡ በዓመት ፡ ራብዕ ፡ ዘሱባዔ ፡ ኃምስ ፡ ዘአርብዓ ፡ ወኅምስቱ ፡ ኢዮቤሌውስ]om. 21

Analysis

The initial section of text (*Jub.* 26:27–27:21) maintains a close affinity with 35, which VanderKam gathers together with 20 and 25 into group one.[6] Primary exemplars of this singular relationship include unique readings such

---

[6] These manuscript groupings, the data supporting them, and the rationale behind their various weightings are given in VanderKam, *The Book of Jubilees*, II:xxiv-xxxi.

as the addition of ውእቱ after ባረክዎ in 26:28, እኑሁ after ያዕቆብሃ in 26:25, and እሙ after ትቤሎ in 27:5, as well as the omission of ወይኩን in 26:34. Indeed, on the fourteen occasions when 35 preserves a previously unattested variant, 54 agrees with the former almost as many times as not, a fairly high degree of congruence in such circumstances. Nevertheless, this similarity generally does not extend to the other constituents of group one when the three jointly preserve a variant reading, though one exception to this pattern is found in the common omission of ለአቡሁ (26:29). At the same time, 54 also remains affiliated with 21, though this occurs most often in instances wherein the latter is in agreement with 35.[7] In addition, a considerable amount of unique readings are present in this portion of the text, none more remarkable than ኀበ ፡ የሐውር rather than ውስተ ፡ ሉዛ ፡ እንተ ፡ ውስተ ፡ ደብር ፡ እንተ ፡ ይእቲ ፡ ቤቴል ፡ በሡርቀ ፡ ወርኅ ፡ ዘቀዳሚ ፡ ዘዝ ፡ ሱባዔ ፡ ወበጽሐ in 27:19. Nevertheless, this section can be broadly characterized as most akin to 35, albeit with substantial autonomy.

The second selection of text (*Jub.* 31:28–32:9) does not consistently display a close relationship with any particular manuscript or group thereof. Like the preceding section, there are several points of affinity with 35, such as the inclusion of ወይወዲ ፡ ውስተ in 32:6 and ወዘአ.ኮነ ፡ ንጹሕ two verses later, but this association is mitigated by other significant instances in which the two offer dissimilar readings.[8] Nevertheless, these two manuscripts remain the most compatible counterparts. At the same time, 54 occasionally agrees with various minor textual variants found in each of the earliest witnesses except for 17, reading, for instance, ይሠምር rather than ይሥመር (31:29) with 9 and ልብሰ rather than አልባሰ (32:3) with 12. There is also some slight similarity with 21, especially in the insertion of the conjunction ወ in supplementary positions (32:2, 4). However, this miscellany offers little foundation for the plausible dependence of 54 by or upon other manuscripts or groups, save for perhaps 35 to some degree; indeed, as 54 includes a large number of unique readings here,[9] it can be considered even more independent in this section than in the previous one.

---

[7] E.g. 26:31 ወሁብክዎ ed.]pr. ወ 54 21 35 38 44 | 26:34 ትትቀነይ ed.]ተቀነይ 54 12 21 35 | 27:21 ውስተ ed.]አስከ 54 21 35 58 63

[8] Note esp. 31:31 አቡሁ ፡ ወ ed. 54]አቡሁ ፡ ይስሐቅ ፡ ምስለ 35 58 | 32:1 እምንዋሙ ed.]om. 54 | 32:6 ስኒነ ፡ ዲቤሁ ed.]tr. 54

[9] 31:29 ወ(ተሰራሕ)]om. 54 | 31:32 ስምዕ]ስም 54 | 32:1 እምንዋሙ]om. 54 | 32:6 ስኒነ ፡ ዲቤሁ]tr. 54 | 32:6 ከመዝ]pr. ወ 54 | 32:7 ጸሎቶ]ጸሎቱ 54 | 32:8 ወ(ገብር)]om. 54 | 32:8 ኩሎ]ኩሉ 54

Unlike those dealt with in the preceding, the final selection of text (*Jub.* 44:12–45:13), displays a very close correlation to 21, which is the second earliest member of group five.[10] Quantitatively, the degree of agreement extends to approximately two-thirds of all variants: 54 provides the same reading as 21 in twenty-three of forty-one instances of otherwise non-attested variants (56%), while in cases where other manuscripts corroborate variant readings in 21, the level of congruency rises to 75%. Qualitatively, these readings vary from minor letter differences to large phrasal divergences, for which the joint omission of እስመ ፡ ርእዩ ፡ ለዮሴፍ ፡ እንዘ ፡ ይበልዕ ፡ ምስለ ፡ አንዊሁ ፡ ወይሰቲ ፡ በቅድሜሁ (45:5) provides the most noteworthy example. However, despite these wide-ranging similarities, it is improbable that either 54 or 21 are slavishly dependent upon the other: apart from the differences noted in the preceding sections, *Jub.* 45:11 is omitted entirely in 21,[11] but is fully included in 54. In addition, at the very end of this section 21 again does not include a sizable passage (ወሞተ ፡ በኃሙት ፡ ራብዕ ፡ ዘሱባዔ ፡ ኃምስ ፡ ዘአርብዓ ፡ ወኢምስቱ ፡ ኢዮቤልውስ), in contradistinction to its counterpart.

One subfeature of the close relationship between these two manuscripts at this juncture deserves additional treatment, namely the virtually complete agreement among variants that are also attested by 35, which was noted to be perhaps the closest textual exemplar to 54 in the previous sections. In fact, notwithstanding a potential exception in a primarily orthographic distinction within a variant in 44:27,[12] this trio offers total congruity in the eleven remaining joint attestations. As such, and particularly in light of the somewhat divergent character of 35 from the other members of group one,[13] this data suggests a need for the reassessment of these categorizations and their restructuring if necessary, along with, accordingly, a re-evaluation of the evidential weight placed upon the various families and manuscripts.

Conclusion

Although incomplete, MYS 54 remains an important early witness to the Ethiopic text of the *Book of Jubilees*. However, its textual affiliation, which

---

[10] 12, which can be dated to the early fifteenth century, is the oldest manuscript belonging to group five.

[11] About half the verse is restored by a corrector.

[12] ለአክታ]ለአክታ 54 39 58; ላአክታ 12; ልአክታ 20 21 25 35

[13] As even noted by VanderKam, *The Book of Jubilees*, II:xxxi.

vacillates between independence and affinity with both 21 and 35 in different sections, and hence between VanderKam's groups one and five, is multifaceted. This raises questions about the consistency of these categorizations. As a result, and especially in view of the considerable number of new, early, and important manuscripts of *Jubilees* that have recently come to light, this indicates a need for a reappraisal of the textual groupings that have been proposed.

Catalogue of the Manuscripts

Melaku Terefe, Steve Delamarter, and Jeremy Brown

MYS 1 – EMIP 601
Three Hundred Seventy-One Miracles of Mary, ተአምረ፡ ማርያም፡

Parchment, 415 x 342 x 102 mm, six Coptic chain stitches are visible between the quires, neither their attachment nor the boards themselves are visible, leather bound with tooled red leather, headband and tailband, protection quire + 24 full quires, v + 199 folios, top margin 35–45 mm, bottom margin 65 mm, fore edge margin 45 mm, gutter margin 17 mm, ff. 1r–197v three columns, 33–35 lines, Gə_əz, twentieth century.

Quire descriptions: protection quire and quires 1–7 and 9–24 balanced; quire 8 adjusted balanced.

Major Works:

Ff. 1r–197v: Three Hundred Seventy One Miracles of Mary, ተአምረ፡ ማርያም፡, each with a rhyming summary at the end. There are similarities with Princeton Ethiopic MS 41 which leaves four blank lines at the end of each miracle to be filled in later with the concluding summarizing hymn. The standard works on the miracles of Mary are Cerulli, *Maria*, and Budge, *Mary*.

1. Ff. 1r–3v: Introductory Rite from *Mu_älläqa*.
2. Ff. 5r–6r: How the Virgin Mary accepted the Book of Miracles compiled by Saint Däqsəyos and how she punished a bishop who usurped the garment and chair of Däqsəyos (Budge, I; Princeton Ethiopic MS 41, ff. 30r–32r).
3. Ff. 6rv: How Däqsəyos healed the sick and the demon possessed by means of the covering of the icon.
4. Ff. 6v–7r: How an aged Jew of Akhmim, who had spent his whole life in ministering in a church of the Virgin Mary, fell down one day during the service and broke his back, and how the Virgin Mary touched his backbone and made it whole, and made him to stand by her on the right-hand side of the altar (Budge, III).

5. Ff. 7rv: How the scribe Damianus used to write the name of the Virgin Mary in gold and colored paints, and how the Virgin appeared to him when dying, and took his soul to Paradise and showed him his name inscribed upon a pillar of gold (Budge, IV; Princeton Ethiopic MS 41, ff. 55v–56r).
6. Ff. 7v–8r: How Abbas, Bishop of Rome, cut off his hand which had been kissed by a woman when he was celebrating the Eucharist, and how the Virgin Mary rejoined it to his arm (Budge, V; Princeton Ethiopic MS 41, ff. 55rv).
7. Ff. 8rv: How Isaac, monk and verger, heaped ascetic labors upon himself, and for seven years devoted his nights to prayers to the Virgin whilst the brethren were asleep, and how the Virgin Mary appeared to him and promised to take him to herself after three days (Budge, VI; Princeton Ethiopic MS 41, ff. 56r–57r).
8. Ff. 8v–9r: How a certain God-fearing man took his two elder daughters and went to church, leaving in his house Mary, his youngest daughter, in spite of her protests and wish to go in order to receive the Sacrament; and how the Virgin Mary appeared from out of her picture to the child, and told her that she would take her to herself in Paradise after three days; and how a godly man saw the child three days later, clad in purple and following the Virgin up into heaven (Budge, VII; Princeton Ethiopic MS 41, ff. 57rv).
9. Ff. 9r–10r: How a certain painter was decorating a church with pictures of the blessed in and his friends in hell; how the Devil overturned the scaffolding, and how the painter was caught by the arm by the Virgin Mary as he fell, and how she lowered him little by little uninjured to the ground (Budge, VIII; Princeton Ethiopic MS 41, ff. 57v–58v).
10. F. 10r: How the Virgin Mary carried a sick monk from the Monastery of the Pilgrims[1] to Palestine, and showed him Jerusalem and Bethlehem, and bathed him in the waters of Jordan (Budge, IX; Princeton Ethiopic MS 41, ff. 58v–59r).
11. Ff. 10r–11r: How a certain youth called Zacharias, a native of Constantinople, crowned the head of a picture of the Virgin daily with fifty roses, and how when the season of roses was past he recited fifty Aves before it, and how the Virgin Mary appeared to him in the desert, and how the thieves who were waiting to attack him repented and become monks when they saw the roses that

---

[1] Budge has ―Monastery of Beggars."

dropped from his mouth when he addressed her (Budge, X; Princeton Ethiopic MS 41, ff. 59r–60v).

12. Ff. 11rv: How two women called Juliana and Barbara, went on a pilgrimage to Jerusalem, were attached by robbers who stole their provisions; and how, when the thieves tried to eat them, the Virgin Mary turned the bread into stones upon which the thieves broke their teeth; and how the thieves repented and restored twofold what they had stolen from the women, when the Virgin Mary had healed their wounded mouths and mended their broken teeth (Budge, XI; Princeton Ethiopic MS 41, ff. 60v–61r).

13. Ff. 11v–12r: How three Arabs set sail for Rif, and were overtaken by a storm which sank their boat and hurled them into the water; how two of them appealed to the Virgin Mary for help, and were saved by her, whilst the third, who jeered at their prayers and called upon Muhammad the Prophet, was swallowed up by a crocodile; and how the men who were saved paid their vow and sent a camel-load of dates to the Monastery of Kalman, where there was a church dedicated to the Virgin Mary (Budge, XII; Princeton Ethiopic MS 41, ff. 61r–62r).

14. Ff. 12rv: How the Virgin Mary removed the Monastery of Si_əqona[2] from the site on which it had been built in the desert to the side of a running stream; and how the removal was effected by night whilst the monks were sleeping (Budge, XIII; Princeton Ethiopic MS 41, ff. 62rv).

15. Ff. 12v–13r: How the Virgin Mary anointed the eyes of John Bakansi, a blind priest of the Church of Saint Mercurius in Cairo, with milk from her breasts and restored his sight when he was one hundred years old (Budge, XIV; Princeton Ethiopic MS 41, ff. 62v–63v).

16. Ff. 13rv: How a merchant from the Island of Colossae[3] was shot in the eye by the arrow of a pirate in the Mediterranean; how his friends made an image in wax of the wounded man with an arrow fixed in one eye and took it to a church of the Virgin Mary; and how she withdrew the arrow from the eye of the figure, whereupon the eye of the Greek was healed (Budge, XV; Princeton Ethiopic MS 41, ff. 63v–64r).

---

[2] Budge has ―Monastery of _Akona."
[3] Budge has ―Greek Merchant" in his table of contents.

17. Ff. 13v–14v: How the Virgin Mary restored the sight of Elizabeth, a blind girl of Badraman, by breathing upon her eyes and sprinkling them with milk from her breasts (Budge, XVI; Princeton Ethiopic MS 41, ff. 64v–65v).

18. Ff. 14v–15r: How the Virgin Mary arranged marriages for three poor girls,[4] called Mary, Martha and Yawahita, with the sons of Tewog, the blacksmith of Makmas (Budge, XVII; Princeton Ethiopic MS 41, ff. 65v–66v).

19. F. 15r: How the Virgin delivered from devils the soul of a scribe who was engaged in writing a copy of the Book of her Miracles. This scribe had a brother who had sinned, but not knowing him they seized the innocent man and tried to carry him off to hell (Budge, XVIII; Princeton Ethiopic MS 41, ff. 66v–67v).

20. Ff.15rv: How the Virgin Mary delivered from prison a certain man called ―George the New"[5] who had been condemned to suffer by the judges, and how she healed the wound in his head which had been inflicted by those who beat him (Budge, XIX; Princeton Ethiopic MS 41, ff. 67v–68r).

21. Ff. 15v–16r: How a cruel sacristan evilly entreated an aged priest called Qāṭir, and thrust him out of the church, and how the Virgin Mary restored the strength of her servant, and caused two men to bastinado the sacristan, whom she smote with paralysis (Budge, XX; Princeton Ethiopic MS 41, ff. 68rv).

22. F. 16rv: How a certain Qadi caused a Christian dyer called Nazib to be beaten and shut up in prison in order to compel him to embrace Islam, and how, at the intercession of Tag,[6] the Virgin Mary sent to the Kadi St. George of Lydda, who threatened to kill him if he did not release Nazib (Budge, XXI; Princeton Ethiopic MS 41, ff. 68v–69v).

23. Ff. 16v–17r: How the Virgin Mary cured a man in his lameness (Budge, XXII; Princeton Ethiopic MS 41, ff. 70rv).

24. Ff. 17rv: How the Virgin Mary cleansed Bishop Mercurius of his leprosy by touching her body with her hand (Budge, XXIII; Princeton Ethiopic MS 41, ff. 70v–71r).

---

[4] Budge's table of contents lists only ―two girls" but the account in the body of his work lists ―three poor sisters."

[5] Budge has simply ―George."

[6] Budge does not mention Tag.

25. Ff. 17v–18r: How the Virgin Mary used to appear in person in the church at Ḫärtälomä, and how she healed the broken foot of a woman therein (Budge, XXIV; Princeton Ethiopic MS 41, ff. 73v–74v).
26. Ff. 18r–19r: How Sophia, Abbes of Mount Carmel, became with child; how the Virgin Mary caused an angel to deliver her of her child before the arrival of the bishop who came to enquire into the matter; and how the child was reared by the monks and Bishop Severus, whom he succeeded in the episcopate (Budge, XXV; Princeton Ethiopic MS 41, ff. 89r–91r).
27. Ff. 19rv: How the Virgin Mary received the soul of Barok, a dissolute man who worshipped her, and took it to Paradise (Budge, XXVI; Princeton Ethiopic MS 41, ff. 85v–86v).
28. Ff. 19v–20r: How the Virgin Mary received the soul of Anastasius, a deacon of Rome[7], who addressed the "Five Gaudes" to her at all times, and took it to Paradise (Budge, XXVII; Princeton Ethiopic MS 41, ff. 84r–85r).
29. Ff. 20r–21r: How the Virgin Mary helped a pious monk of the Monastery of *Abba* Samuel of Qälmon to escape from the persecution of the brethren by making a breach in the wall of the church when he smote it with his skull cap (Budge, XXVIII; Princeton Ethiopic MS 41, ff. 104r–106r).
30. Ff. 21rv: How the Virgin Mary delivered from crucifixion the son of a poor widow, who had become a thief and a robber (Budge, XXX; Princeton Ethiopic MS 41, ff. 80rv).
31. Ff. 21v–22r: How the Virgin Mary protected a woman, great with child, who was overtaken by an inrush of the sea, and how the woman brought forth her child and escaped from drowning (Budge, XXXII; Princeton Ethiopic MS 41, ff. 83r–84r).[8]
32. Ff. 22rv: How a certain rich man hurled a loaf at the head of a beggar and wounded him, and how the Virgin Mary delivered his soul from the devils (Budge, LXXXVI; Princeton Ethiopic MS 41, ff. 71v–72v).
33. Ff. 22v–23r: How the Virgin Mary saved a daughter of a wealthy man from labor pain (Princeton Ethiopic MS 41, f. 72v).

---

[7] Budge has Constantinople.
[8] Up to this point, the order and content of the miracles is very close to Budges order and content; after this the relationship breaks down.

34. Ff. 23rv: How the Virgin Mary healed the blind daughter of a woman who, in a dream, threw her daughter into the sea (Princeton Ethiopic MS 41, ff. 73rv).
35. Ff. 23v–24r: How the Virgin Mary raised the dead son of a wealthy man from Cappadocia who refused to bury the son and who took the body to the church and prayed to Mary for his son (Princeton Ethiopic MS 41, ff. 74v–75r).
36. F. 24r: How a certain woman, living with her mother-in-law, was devoted to an icon of Mary in her house; how her mother-in-law criticized her for her devotion to the icon; how Mary appeared in a dream and told her that she could not stay in the home because of the criticisms of the mother-in-law; and how, when she awoke, the icon was gone (Princeton Ethiopic MS 41, ff. 75rv).
37. Ff. 24rv: How the Virgin Mary saved a certain military officer of the King when he became mentally distressed by anointing his lips with her breast milk (cp., Princeton Ethiopic MS 41, ff. 75r–76v).
38. Ff. 24v–25r: How a certain woman was bereft of her nine children; how the Virgin Mary appeared to her and promised three children who would become priests; how she conceived three children who became priests and presided at her funeral (Princeton Ethiopic MS 41, ff. 76v–77r).
39. Ff. 25rv How the Virgin Mary saved Qiras, the bandit who was devoted to Mary, when the people caught him and led him to the gallows; and how he later became a monk (Princeton Ethiopic MS 41, ff. 80rv; cf. Budge, XXXI).
40. Ff. 25v–26r: How a certain man slew an evil-living deacon and buried him where he fell, and how the Virgin Mary had his body dug up and buried in consecrated ground (a version of Budge, CIII; Princeton Ethiopic MS 41, ff. 80v–81v).
41. Ff. 26rv: How the Virgin Mary cut out and sewed a garment for Philotheus, a bishop of Upper Egypt (Budge, XL; Princeton Ethiopic MS 41, ff. 81v–82r).
42. Ff. 26v–27r: How the Virgin Mary revealed herself to Bishop Philotheus when he refused to receive the repentance of a man called Paraqos (Princeton Ethiopic MS 41, ff. 82r–83r).
43. Ff. 27rv: How Nicodemus, an evil-living Persian knight, became a Christian, but was unable to learn the Lord's Prayer, and could only master the Salutation to Mary; and how these words were found

written on every leaf of a tree which grew on his grave (Budge, XXXVIII; Princeton Ethiopic MS 41, ff. 85rv).

44. Ff. 27v–28r: How a certain bishop removed a priest from his office owing to complaints of his ignorance of the Eucharistic service, and how the Virgin Mary rebuked the bishop (Budge, CII; Princeton Ethiopic MS 41, ff. 86v–87r).
45. Ff. 28rv: How a certain Hebrew man called Alexander was swallowed by a large serpent and cried out to the Virgin Mary; how the serpent spat him out; how he further developed leprosy, cried out to the Virgin Mary again, became a Christian and was healed (Princeton Ethiopic MS 41, ff. 87v–88r).
46. Ff. 28v–29r: How a certain righteous governor, Armatyas of Ephesus, was falsely accused, and the authorities attempted to behead him, but the Virgin Mary prevented the beheading and also sustained his life when they attempted to hang him (Princeton Ethiopic MS 41, ff. 88v–89r).
47. F. 29r: How a generous, wealthy woman attended prayers with the monks at a monastery and saw the Virgin Mary descending from heaven with a multitude of angels (Princeton Ethiopic MS 41, ff. 91r–92r; Princeton Ethiopic MS 8, ff. 45v–46v).
48. Ff. 29rv: How a certain Ishmaelite was converted when he saw oil and milk flowing from the breasts of a picture of the Virgin Mary (Budge, LXI; Princeton Ethiopic MS 41, ff. 92r–93r).
49. Ff. 29v–30r: How the Virgin Mary helped a young, impoverished man and how the church keeper gave his daughter to him [when he saw the icon of the Virgin Mary bow down to him] (Princeton Ethiopic MS 41, ff. 93r–94r; and Princeton Ethiopic MS 20, ff. 25r and 72rv).[9]
50. Ff. 30rv: How the Virgin Mary delivered from the devils the soul of an avaricious farmer who had given alms in her name during his life (Budge, CIX; Princeton Ethiopic MX 41, ff. 94r–95r).
51. Ff. 30v–31r: How the Virgin Mary commanded the bishop to bury in the believers' burial the body of a hanged thief who had been devoted to Mary; and how a tree with healing powers grew up from his grave.

---

[9] Not included in the Budge collection, but the theme of the bowing icon appears in other miracle stories.

52. Ff. 31rv: How the Virgin Mary revealed herself as a woman with wings like an eagle's wings to John the Righteous, the priest at Mäqarəs monastery (Princeton Ethiopic 41, f. 97r).
53. F. 31v: How the Virgin Mary appeared to a certain nun and commanded her to continue reciting the Hail Mary (Princeton Ethiopic 41, ff. 96rv).
54. Ff. 31v–32v: How the Virgin Mary saved, by the intercession of *Abba* Samuel of the monastery of Qäləmon, a fallen angel who had failed to execute judgment on a city by saving a beautiful young child (Princeton Ethiopic 41, ff. 97v–98v; and Princeton Ethiopic 43, ff. 53v–55v).
55. Ff. 32v–33r: How the Virgin Mary saved Timothy, a drunken monk, from a lion and a savage dog (Budge, XXXVIII and Princeton Ethiopic 41, ff. 98v–99v).
56. Ff. 33rv-: How the Virgin Mary saved from a sinking ship a certain devoted person who cried out to Mary, who then came and covered him with her garment (cf. Princeton Ethiopic 41, f. 99v).
57. Ff. 33v–34r: How the Virgin Mary appeared to a man from France (Färäsawi) when he denied Christ but kept devotion to the Virgin Mary (cf. Princeton Ethiopic 41, ff. 100v–101v).
58. Ff. 34rv: How the Virgin Mary appeared to the man from France named Nifon and led him to the monastic life (cf. Princeton Ethiopic 41, ff. 106r–107v).
59. Ff. 34v–35r: How the Virgin Mary appeared to a monk from the Island Ṭegəros (Tigris?) when he couldn't walk and his friends carried him to church (Princeton Ethiopic 41, ff. 107v–108r).
60. F. 35rv: How the Virgin Mary took a Shepherd into paradise in seven days (Princeton Ethiopic 41, ff. 108r–109r).
61. Ff. 35v–37r: How the Virgin Mary recovered for a deacon named Mika'el a ring stolen by a Muslim and swallowed by the fish (Princeton Ethiopic 41, ff. 101v–104r).
62. Ff. 37r–41r: How the Virgin Mary at the intercession of John the priest caused the Khalifah of Athribis to spare her church in that city (Budge, XXXIV).
63. Ff. 41r–43r: How the Virgin Mary helped *Abba* Abraham the Syrian, archbishop of Alexandria, move a mountain when he was challenged by the Jewish advisor of a Muslim King (cf. *TM89* 150–4).

64. Ff. 43r–46r: How the Virgin Mary gave to a certain couple a child and how, when he was grown and falsely accused of stealing, the Virgin Mary saved him.
65. Ff. 46r–47r: How the Virgin Mary recovered the scissors of Jacob the Short, a tailor, when Arabs stole it from him (Princeton Ethiopic 41, ff. 122rv, but 122v has been painted over with an added illumination).
66. Ff. 47rv: How a certain monk converted to Judaism and denied Christ and the Virgin Mary and how a Christian governor put to death the monk.[10]
67. Ff. 47v–49r: How the Virgin Mary helped a certain man named Aboli to borrow money from a rich Jew and how the icon of the Virgin Mary testified when the Jew denied receiving the borrowed money (*TM89* 261–3).
68. Ff. 49rv: How the Virgin Mary commanded the demon to serve the monks in the monastery in Egypt (Princeton Ethiopic 46, ff. 93v–94v; *TM89* 165–8).
69. F. 49v: How the Virgin Mary recovered a silver dish from the river (Princeton Ethiopic 46, ff. 94v–95r).
70. Ff. 49v–50r: How the Virgin Mary saved the abbot of Däbrä Q^{w}usq^{w}am from flogging when the Muslim governor tried to plunder the monastery.
71. Ff. 50r–51r, How the Virgin Mary saved a young widow from the wiles of a certain knight, who forthwith became a monk and retired to the desert (Budge, LV).
72. Ff. 51rv: How the icon of the Virgin Mary healed a woman who suffered from hemorrhage (Princeton Ethiopic 41, ff. 132r–133v).
73. Ff. 51v–52r: How the Virgin Mary punished a Muslim man when he tried to take the clothes of two monks (*TM89* 124–6).
74. Ff. 52rv: How the Virgin Mary made the tears of a sinful maiden, when weighed in the scales of Justice, to outweigh her sins; and how Mary commanded Saint Mika'el to baptize the woman and add her to the virgins of the monastery (cf. miracle 201 below and Budge, LXXI and *TM89* 227–31).

---

[10] This miracle has been considered relevant for the discussion of the origin of the Falasha group in Ethiopia. See, Stephen Kaplan's *The Monastic Holy Man and the Christianization of Early Solomonic Ethiopia* (Weisbaden: Franz Steiner Verlag, 1984) 40, etc.

75. Ff. 53r–54r: How the Virgin Mary was born to Joakim and Anna (Princeton Ethiopic 41, ff. 13r–14v; *TM89* 16–9).
76. Ff. 54rv: How Saint Gabriel took the body of the Virgin Mary and put it under the tree of life in Paradise, and how 600 Jews who tried to burn the body of the Virgin Mary were baptized when they saw the earth swallow one of their number who had insulted Christ and the Virgin Mary (*TM89* 19–21).
77. Ff. 54v–55v: How the Virgin Mary punished the camel caravan leader of Däbrä Mətmaq monastery when he stole property from the monastery (Princeton Ethiopic 41, ff. 150r–2r).
78. Ff. 55v–56v: How the Virgin Mary punished the King of Egypt named al-Sharif when he plundered the monastery of Däbrä Mətmaq and how Christians in Egypt sent a message to Emperor Zärə_a Ya_əqob, king of Ethiopia, about the destruction of Däbrä Mətmaq and how he built a church and named it Däbrä Mətmaq (*TM89* 59–64).
79. Ff. 56v–59r: How the Virgin Mary appeared to Muslim traders at Däbrä Mətmaq after its destruction and how the Virgin Mary commanded them to tell her miracle and how she led them to Christianity (*TM89* 64–9).
80. Ff. 59rv: How the angel of God cut the hand of Tawəfanya when he tried to burn the body of Mary (*TM89* 21–3).
81. Ff. 59v–60r: How Saint John greeted the Virgin Mary when he embalmed her body (*TM89* 23–5).
82. Ff. 60r–61r: How the apostles did not leave the body of Mary for fear of the Jews and how the angel of God encouraged them to claim the body (*TM89* 25–30).
83. Ff. 61rv: On the Assumption of Mary; How Jesus Christ took the body of the Virgin Mary to heaven (*TM89* 30–2).
84. Ff. 61v–63r: How the icon of the Virgin Mary came from Jerusalem to the city of Ṣedenya (*TM89* 32–7).[11]
85. Ff. 63rv: How the Virgin Mary gave birth to Jesus Christ and how the wise men came to present their gifts (*TM89* 39–41).
86. Ff. 63v–64r: How the Virgin Mary gave birth while she was with Joseph in Bethlehem for the census (*TM89* 41–3).
87. Ff. 64r–66r: How the Virgin Mary received the covenant of mercy from her son; and how the Virgin Mary saved the soul of the cannibal of Kemer, who had killed and eaten his wife and two

---

[11] This miracle is mentioned in the introductory rite of Mu_alqqa, see Budge xlvii.

children and a large number of men and women (Budge, XXIX; *TM89* 43–52).[12]

88. Ff. 66rv: How, when the Virgin Mary was weaving silk and gold in the temple, God sent Gabriel to announce the birth of Jesus Christ (*TM89* 52–4).
89. Ff. 66v–67r: How the Virgin Mary conceived Jesus Christ on Maggabit 29 (*TM89* 54–5).
90. Ff. 67r–69v: How Jesus predicted to his mother the Virgin Mary that a church (Däbrä Mətmaq) would be constructed in Egypt where they had stayed and how the Virgin Mary appeared to the people of Egypt (Princeton Ethiopic 46, ff. 80r–84r; *TM89* 69–80).
91. F. 69v: How the Virgin Mary appeared to the apostles with Jesus Christ (*TM89* 84–5).
92. Ff. 69v–70v: How, when the people of Damot worked on the day of Mary's festival, the Virgin Mary uprooted a tree that they worshipped, and how when the people tried to cut up the tree, the Virgin Mary raised the tree upright again and how Zärə_a Ya_əqob, king of Ethiopia built a church at that place (See ff. 89r–90v in this manuscript; *TM89* 88–94).
93. F. 71r: How Joachim and Hanna presented the Virgin Mary to the temple (cf. Princeton Ethiopic 41, ff. 14v–15v; Princeton Ethiopic 47, ff. 13r–15r; and cf. *TM89* 18–9).
94. Ff. 71r–72r: How Saint Gabriel announced the birth of Jesus Christ to Mary as she was spinning silk for the temple; how Joseph received the Virgin Mary in order to protect her; and how she gave water in her shoe to a thirsty dog (regarding the annunciation, cf. Princeton Ethiopic 37, ff. 67r–68v; Princeton Ethiopic 41, ff. 15v–17r; regarding water for a thirsty dog, cf., Princeton Ethiopic 20, ff. 83r–84r; Princeton Ethiopic 47, ff. 92v–93r; Princeton Ethiopic 55, ff. 150r–152r; Budge, XXXIII; and *TM89* 217–18).
95. F. 72r. How *Abba* Samu'el levitated from the ground and spewed fire from his mouth and was not touched by the rain when he read the praises of the Virgin Mary (Princeton Ethiopic 43, ff. 52v–53v).
96. Ff. 72rv: How Zechariah, the prophet, saw a vision of Zion and seven lamp stands which symbolized Mary.

---

[12] In this manuscript and in *TM* the miracles are combined in one account; in Budge the miracle of the cannibal of Kemer is a separate miracle.

97. Ff. 72v–73r: [The beginning of the Zion Cycle:] How Moses received Zion, the tablet—which is a symbol of the Virgin Mary—with the ten commandments on Mount Sinai.[13]
98. F. 73r: How, after the death of Moses, Joshua received Zion, the tablet—which is a symbol of the Virgin Mary—; and how he parted the Jordan River, circled Jericho and stopped the movement of the sun with it, and how he built a home for Zion, the tablet, in Jericho; and how it was there throughout the period of the Judges.
99. Ff. 73rv: How David received with praise Zion, the tablet—which is a symbol of the Virgin Mary—and how he put it in the temple until Solomon became King, and how Menelik the son of Solomon and the Queen of the South took it to Aksum; and how, when he was pursued by the army of Solomon, escaped when the Red Sea opened before him.
100. F. 73v. How the army of Solomon became sad when they realized that Zion, the tablet—which is a symbol of the Virgin Mary— was beyond their power to regain, how Menelik, also called Əbnä Ḥakim, came to Aksum with his army, how they built a temple and put Zion, the tablet, there, and how they celebrate her festival every year on Ḥədar 21.
101. F. 73v–74r: How Zion, the tablet—which is a symbol of the Virgin Mary—parted the Jordan River.
102. Ff. 74rv: About the glory of Zion, the tablet—which is a symbol of the Virgin Mary—and how it protected the people of Israel and later saints?
103. F. 74v: How the Philistines took Zion, the tablet—which is a symbol of the Virgin Mary—and killed Eli's sons Afənin and Finəḥäs.
104. Ff. 74v–75r: How Eli died when he heard the news of the death of his sons and the capture of Zion, the tablet—which is a symbol of the Virgin Mary; and how Zion, the tablet, punished the Philistines and their idols.
105. F. 75r: How the Philistines discussed in what manner they had to return Zion, the tablet—which is a symbol of the Virgin Mary.

---

[13] The following cycle of miracles, which we call "The Zion Cycle," continues in nineteen sections through f. 78r. In the upper corners of ff. 72rv and 73r is written the word "Ẓon." The cycle is narrated, ostensibly, by Ezra (see, miracles 114 and 115 on ff. 78r). This cycle is known in no other copy of the Miracles of Mary with which we are familiar.

106. Ff. 75rv: How the Philistines sent toward the territory of Israel, with gold, Zion, the tablet—which is a symbol of the Virgin Mary.
107. Ff. 75v: How Zion, the tablet—which is a symbol of the Virgin Mary—punished the house of Samis, and how Zion dwelt in the house of Aminidab.
108. Ff. 75v–76r: How King David brought Zion, the tablet—which is a symbol of the Virgin Mary—from the house of Aminidab and how Zion punished Ḥoza, and how David put Zion in the house of Abidara, and how, after three months, he brought Zion to his city and placed it in the tabernacle, and how Meləkol, daughter of Saul, despised David for his dancing.
109. Ff. 76rv: How David tried to build a temple for Zion, the tablet—which is a symbol of the Virgin Mary—and how God told him that his son, Solomon, would build the temple, and how David brought material for the temple from Tyre, and how Solomon built the temple.
110. Ff. 76v–77r: How the various parts and accoutrements of the temple built by Solomon symbolized Zion, the tablet—which is a symbol of the Virgin Mary—, the prophets and the apostles.
111. F. 77r: How Kiram, king of Tyre, helped Solomon to build the temple, and how Solomon put Zion, the tablet—which is a symbol of the Virgin Mary—in the holy of holies, and how he blessed the temple, and how God made a covenant with Solomon.
112. Ff. 77rv: How, in Babylon, Ezra saw a vision about Zion, the tablet—which is a symbol of the Virgin Mary—
113. F. 77v: How Ezra saw that Zion, the tablet—which is a symbol of the Virgin Mary—was glorified by angels and archangels praising Zion.
114. F. 78r: How the spirit of the Virgin Mary's Son prepared the author (Ezra) to praise her.
115. F. 78r: [Conclusion to the Zion Cycle:] How the spirit of the Virgin Mary's Son commanded the author (Ezra) to read out to others the praise of the Virgin.
116. Ff. 78r–79r: How the Virgin Mary revived the child Saint Fiqəṭor when the wife of Emperor Diocletian killed him.
117. Ff. 79rv: How a Muslim girl converted to Christianity and became a martyr after she recovered a lost belonging by the power of the Virgin Mary (Princeton Ethiopic 46, ff. 88v–89r).

118. F. 79v: How the Virgin Mary gave a cup full of the water of life and joy to an Ethiopian pilgrim who was going to Jerusalem.
119. Ff. 79v–80r: How Jesus Christ cast out a demon from wild animals when the holy family was in Egypt; and how He healed sick people when the holy family was at the place called Qwusqwam.
120. Ff. 80r: How the Virgin Mary asked her Son to bless the place called Qwusqwam.
121. Ff. 80rv: How the Virgin Mary asked her son to bless the people who visit the place called Q^{w}usq^{w}am.
122. Ff. 80v–81r: How the Virgin Mary appeared to Säräbamon, the Martyr.
123. F. 81r: How the Virgin Mary gave a garment to Saint Nicolaus who had given his possessions to the poor (see similar themes in Budge, XL, and Princeton Ethiopic 8, ff. 13v–15v).
124. Ff. 81rv: How the Virgin Mary punished a certain woman with leprosy when the woman killed her sister in order to take her husband; and how the earth swallowed her; and how Basil told this story.
125. F. 81v: How Jesus commanded John, the disciple, to take, by fiery chariots, the body of Saint Mary to paradise under the tree of life.
126. Ff. 81v–82r: How Matthew, the priest, fled to the monastery to avoid becoming archbishop; how the abbot of the monastery of Saint Anthony sent him back to become archbishop; and how he cut out his own tongue; and how the Virgin Mary appeared to him with instructions for the healing of his tongue by reading her homilies (Princeton Ethiopic 46, ff. 138v–139v).
127. Ff. 82rv: How the Virgin Mary cut off the hands and feet of a certain man when he insulted her and refused to listen to her pleas.
128. Ff. 82v: How the Virgin Mary was revealed to a certain lady from a noble family of Rome when that lady tried to enter the Church of the Holy Sepulcher in Jerusalem; and how the Virgin Mary led her to repentance.
129. F. 82v: How the Virgin Mary turned the water into sweet, white bread to feed the priests who burned incense to her icon.
130. Ff. 82v–83r: How the Virgin Mary appeared to reassure an ascetic woman about the purity of her friends, other ascetic women in the monastery (Princeton Ethiopic 8, ff. 19v–21r; Princeton Ethiopic 20, ff. 5v–6r, 31r, and 75rv).

131. F. 83r: How the Virgin Mary raised the saints who died at the monastery of Scete (Asqeṭəs) (cp. Budge, XCI; Princeton Ethiopic 20, ff. 1rv and 66rv; Princeton Ethiopic 41, ff. 155v–156r).
132. F. 83rv: How the Virgin Mary appeared to the abbot of Scete (Asqeṭəs) when he was afraid of demons.
133. F. 83v: How the Virgin Mary anointed the woman of Q‍ʷusq‍ʷam and how she described to Anthony of Q‍ʷusq‍ʷam the future glory of that place (Princeton Ethiopic 20, ff. 85v–86v; Princeton Ethiopic 46, ff. 49v–50v).
134. Ff. 83v–84r: How the Virgin Mary blessed the Monastery of Q‍ʷusq‍ʷam with its people and animals and how she anointed them again (see 133 above and the cross references there).
135. F. 84r: How the Virgin Mary appeared to Timothy, archbishop of Alexandria, and how she commanded him to build the church (Princeton Ethiopic 46, ff. 51v–53v).
136. Ff. 84rv: How the Virgin Mary appeared to a certain Muslim man, how she rebuked him when he insulted Christians, how he converted to Christianity, how she commanded him to be a witness and how he was martyred for his faith (Princeton Ethiopic 41, ff. 143r–144r).
137. Ff. 84v–85r: How the archangel Gabriel appeared to the Virgin Mary at Bethlehem and told her about her assumption to heaven.
138. F. 85r: How, because of his devotion, the Virgin Mary saved a bandit leader when the other bandits tried to kill him.
139. Ff. 85rv: How the Virgin Mary appeared to a priest named Yoḥannəs as a woman with wings like a bird (Princeton Ethiopic 41, f. 97r; Princeton Ethiopic 43, ff. 13rv).
140. F. 85v: How the Virgin Mary healed the sick deacon who recited her sälam song by anointing him with her breast milk (Princeton Ethiopic 8, ff. 2r–4r; Princeton Ethiopic 41, ff. 75r–76v).
141. Ff. 85v–86r: How the Virgin Mary saved a certain bandit from hanging because he always recited her sälam song and how he became a pious monk (Princeton Ethiopic 8, ff. 4r–6r; Princeton Ethiopic 20, ff. 65r–66r; Princeton Ethiopic 41, ff. 95r–96r; cp. Budge, XXX).
142. Ff. 86rv: How a certain man slew an evil-living deacon and buried him where he fell and how the Virgin Mary had his body dug up and buried in consecrated ground (Budge, CIII; Princeton Ethiopic 8, ff. 9r–10v; Princeton Ethiopic 41, ff. 80v–81v; Princeton Ethiopic 43, ff. 25r–26r; Princeton Ethiopic 46, ff. 128rv).

143. F. 86v: How [Nicodemus,] an evil-living [Persian] knight, became a Christian, but was unable to learn the Lord's Prayer, and could only master the Salutation to Mary; and how these words were found written on every leaf of a tree which grew on his grave (Budge, XXXVIII, Princeton Ethiopic 8, ff. 10v–12v).

144. Ff. 86v–87r: How the Virgin Mary gave a garment to a certain bishop and how she commanded him to receive a person who wanted to repent before him (Budge, XL and CII; Princeton Ethiopic 8, ff. 13v–15v; Princeton Ethiopic 41, ff. 81v–82r; Princeton Ethiopic 43, ff. 49v–50v).

145. Ff. 87rv: How the Virgin Mary appeared a certain deacon who was sick and how she took him into paradise (Princeton Ethiopic 8, ff. 14v–17v).

146. F. 87v: How the scribe [Damianus] used to write the name of the Virgin Mary in gold and colored paints, and how the Virgin appeared to him when dying, and took his soul to Paradise and showed him his name inscribed upon a pillar of gold (Budge, IV; Princeton Ethiopic 20, ff. 43r–44r; Princeton Ethiopic 41, ff. 55v–56r; Princeton Ethiopic 46, ff. 11v–12v; Princeton Ethiopic 47, ff. 22r–23v).

147. Ff. 87v–88r: How a certain Ishmaelite was converted when he saw oil and milk flowing from the breasts of a picture of the Virgin Mary (Budge, LXI, Princeton Ethiopic 20, ff. 73rv; Princeton Ethiopic 41, ff. 92r–93r; Princeton Ethiopic 43, ff. 17r–18v).

148. Ff. 88rv: How the Virgin Mary, in Bethlehem, blessed a certain government official and how she healed his son.

149. Ff. 88v–89r: How the Virgin Mary raised up a dead knight who had been buried in the cemetery of a convent, to fight an enemy of the church called Goləyad (Goliath), and how the knight fought against him and slew him (Budge, LX; Princeton Ethiopic 20, ff. 73v–74r).

150. Ff. 89r–90v: How, when the people of Damot worked on the day of Mary's festival, the Virgin Mary uprooted a tree that they worshipped, and how when the people tried to cut up the tree, the Virgin Mary raised the tree upright again and how Zärə_a Ya_əqob, king of Ethiopia built a church at that place (See ff. 69v–70v in this manuscript, and *TM89* 88–94).

151. Ff. 90v–91v: How the light descended into the Emperor's city when the Emperor killed a certain group of monks who refused to bow down for Mary and the cross (*TM89* 94–8).

152. Ff. 91v–92v: How the light remained in the Emperor's city until a monk appointed by the Emperor arrived. (*TM89* 98–101).[14]
153. Ff. 92v–93r: How a light descended upon the Ethiopian traveler during the Easter celebration in Jerusalem when the other communities rejected him and cast him out of the Church of the Holy Sepulcher because he was black (*TM89* 101–4).
154. Ff. 93rv: How the Virgin Mary punished a wealthy man when he insulted a priest who only knew how to recite the Anaphora of Our Lady (*TM89* 104–6; cp. Budge, CII).
155. Ff. 93v–94v: How the Virgin Mary warned the people of a certain city when they put their wealth inside the church, and how she burned down the church with lightning, while protecting the priests as they celebrated the Mass (*TM89* 106–9).
156. Ff. 94v–95r: How Our Lord descended from Heaven and how He honored the Virgin Mary before the Apostles (*TM89* 109–110).
157. Ff. 95rv: How the Virgin Mary punished those who denied the doctrine of the millennial feast of Mount Zion during the reign of Zärə̣a Ya ᵊqob (*TM89* 110–4).
158. Ff. 95v–97r: How the Virgin Mary helped the priest of a certain church when a Muslim warrior tried to burn down the church (*TM89* 114–9).
159. F. 97r: How the Virgin Mary performed a miracle through the icon of the city of Ṣedenəya when a certain merchants tried to cut a piece from the icon and blood flowed out (*TM 89*, 119–20).
160. Ff. 97rv: How the Virgin Mary saved a harlot from stoning by the people of a certain city (*TM 89* 121).
161. F. 97v: How the Virgin Mary provided food for a monastery when a young helper of the monks he prayed to her (*TM 89* 122).
162. Ff. 97v–98r: How the Virgin Mary protected a monk from the temptations of the devil (*TM89* 122–3).
163. Ff. 98rv: How the Virgin Mary punished a certain man when he attacked a priest and a deacon from the monastery of Fiqəṭor (*TM89* 124–6; cp. Princeton 41, ff. 136v–138r).

---

[14] These two miracles are understood to be in reference to the Estifanosite movement. See Getatchew, *Däqiqa Ǝsṭifanos Bäḥəg Amlak*, Collegeville, MN, 1996; *The Gəʿəz Acts of Abba Ǝsṭifanos of Gʷəndagʷəndе*, CSCO 619/620; SA 110/111 (2006); "Religious Controversies and the growth of Ethiopic Literature in the Fourteenth and Fifteenth centuries," *Orient Christianus* 65 (1981) 102–136; "The Cause of the Ǝsṭifanosites: A Fundamentalist Sect in the Church of Ethiopia" *Paideuma* 29 (1983) 93–119.

164. Ff. 98v–99r: How our Lord Jesus Christ appeared with His Mother and Saints Michael and Gabriel to a certain man named Pifamon during his martyrdom (*TM89* 126–8; Princeton 43, ff. 55v–57r).
165. Ff. 99r–100r: How the Virgin Mary appeared to a certain woman named Tekəla, sister of *Abba* Asi (*TM 89*, 128–32).
166. Ff. 100rv: How the Virgin Mary appeared in Däbrä Q"usq"am when Bishop Gabriel stayed there and died during the celebration of the passion week (*TM89* 132–4).
167. Ff. 100v–101r: How the Virgin Mary punished a certain Muslim when he attacked the abbot of Däbrä Q"usq"am and when Qozəmos Yoḥannəs prayed (*TM89* 134–6).
168. Ff. 101rv: How the Virgin Mary appeared to a certain deacon Yoḥannəs as a pillar of light (*TM89* 136–9; Princeton 20, ff. 68r–69v; Princeton 41, ff. 153r–154r; Princeton 46, ff. 86v–87v).
169. Ff. 101v–102r: How the Virgin Mary brought water to the well of the monastery of Däbrä Mətmaq (*TM89* 139–141; Princeton 20, ff. 66r–68r; Princeton 41, ff. 154r–155v).
170. Ff. 102rv: How the Virgin Mary saved a prince's son named Bätergela Maryam (*TM89* 141–3).
171. Ff. 102v–103r: How the Virgin Mary prayed to God that He would reveal his Trinity to a certain man named Ṗeṭros (*TM89* 143–5; Princeton 46, ff. 104v–105v).
172. Ff. 103r–104r: How the Virgin Mary appeared to a certain man called Silan to warn him about the money he had lent to Filipos and how she led him to righteous life (*TM89* 145–9).
173. Ff. 104r–105v: How the Virgin Mary appeared to Abraham, Archbishop of Alexandria when he was challenged by a Jew and Muslims to move a mountain, how she led them to Simon, the shoemaker, and how he moved the mountain. (*TM89* 150–4).
174. Ff. 105v–106v: How a certain woman named Sophia received a candle in her dream when her husband forbade her to go to the church, and how she found the candle in her hand when she awoke (*TM89* 154–9).
175. Ff. 106v–107r: How when bishop Nestorius commanded the people to spit on the menstrual blood of a woman in the church, John Chrysostom kissed her instead and the icon in the church called him ‒golden mouth" (*TM89* 159–161).
176. F. 107r: How Jesus asked Mary about her five lamentations (*TM89* 161–2; Princeton 46, f. 102v; Princeton 47, ff. 102v–103v).

177. Ff. 107r–108r: How the Virgin Mary punished a certain Jew when he challenged a monk who converted from Judaism (*TM89* 162–5; cp. Princeton 46, ff. 152v–153v).
178. Ff. 108rv: How the Virgin Mary commanded the devil to be a servant for the monastery; and how the pagans converted to Christianity when they saw the devil acting as servant for the monastery (*TM89* 165–8).
179. Ff. 108v–109v: How the Virgin Mary appeared to a certain deacon when he went to a certain woman to give her holy communion and when the priest who loved money refused to go (*TM89* 168–71).
180. Ff. 109v–110v: How the Virgin Mary healed a certain monk when he was bitten by a snake and how he and his friends served the Virgin Mary until they died in martyrdom (*TM89* 171–5).
181. Ff. 110v–111r: How the Virgin Mary took a certain abbot with her into heaven when the people accused him and how she punished them like Dothan and Abiram (i.e., the earth swallowed them) (*TM89* 176–7).
182. Ff. 111rv: How a certain harlot swore falsely about her pregnancy by the name of saint Mary at which moment the harlot delivered two cows horns and two sheep horns from her womb and how she lost her mind and died (*TM89* 176–9).
183. Ff. 111v–113r: How the Virgin Mary appeared to a certain monk named Giyorgis and how she gave to him the cup of knowledge when he was rejected by his teacher due to a lack of money (*TM89* 179–83).
184. Ff. 113rv: How the Ark of the Virgin Mary performed a set of miracles in the palace of a certain king: the ark came out of the box without aid, it turned the tents of the king from white to black and it punished wicked priests (*TM89* 183–6).
185. Ff. 113v–114v: How a certain priest was carried away by the angel of God out of the gate of the Virgin Mary church when he was sleeping and had a nocturnal emission (*TM89* 186–8).
186. Ff. 114v–115r: How the angel of God punished a certain man with hemorrhage when he entered into the Virgin Mary Church after he had committed adultery (*TM89* 189–90).
187. F. 115r: How the ark of the Virgin Mary fell into the hands of an army of unbelievers and how the Virgin Mary punished a certain man when he sat down on the ark by cutting him into two pieces (*TM89* 190–1).

188. Ff. 115r–116r: How the Virgin Mary appeared to those who were trying to steal the holy articles from the church; how she punished the thieves when they did not listen; how she appeared to the governor of that land and how she led him to the thieves; and how the thieves were thrown into prison (*TM89* 191–4).

189. Ff. 116rv: How the Virgin Mary saved a certain man named Alexander the Jew after he was swallowed by a serpent for three days and three nights and how she led him to the Jordan River to wash him and heal him (*TM89* 194–6; Princeton 41, ff. 87v–88r; Princeton 43, ff. 23v–25r).

190. Ff. 116v–117v: How the Virgin Mary enabled a man to slay a serpent nearly one hundred feet in length and thirty-three feet in diameter, how the man took from the brain of the serpent a pearl of great price, which he placed in a martyrium of Mary that he built at Sidon (Budge, LIII; *TM89* 196–9).

191. Ff. 117v–118r: How the Virgin Mary appeared to a certain monk after had become depressed concerning a nocturnal emission and how she comforted him and gave him a sign of assurance in his hand (*TM89* 199–202).

192. Ff. 118r–119r: How the Virgin Mary gave a child to a certain couple and how they turned aside from their promise to raise him for the service of God; how he became very sick on his wedding day and the Virgin Mary appeared to him, comforted him and sent him to a monastery (*TM89* 202–5).

193. Ff. 119r–120r: How the Virgin Mary appeared to a certain priest; how she commanded him to go to Gäbrä Krestos [known as Alexis in the West], son of Theodotius, king of Constantinople; when Gäbrä Krestos lived among the beggars for fifteen years (*TM89* 205–9).

194. Ff. 120rv: How the Virgin Mary saved a certain Jew when his father threw him into the fire because of his conversion to Christianity (Budge, LIX; *TM89* 209–11; Princeton 20, ff. 37r–39r).

195. Ff. 120v–121r: How the Virgin Mary appeared to a certain priest to go to Abədäl Mäsih [Arabic form of Gäbrä Krestos], son of the king of Constantinople; and how she commanded the priest to bring him back to the church to live there (*TM89* 211–3; see miracle 193 above and the references there).

196. F. 121r: How the icon of the Virgin Mary appeared in a beehive when a certain beekeeper, commanded by a sorcerer to multiply his

beehive, brought the elements from holy communion to put in his beehive (Budge, CVII; *TM89* 215–7).

197. Ff. 121r–122v: How the Virgin Mary punished a certain young man when he revealed the whereabouts of the hiding place of the Holy Family in Egypt; and how she heard the prayer of the governor of that land who interceded for the young man (*TM89* 218–22).

198. Ff. 122v–123r: How the Virgin Mary gave water to a thirsty dog with her shoe (Budge, XXXIII; *TM89* 217–8; Strelcyn 32.16. 32; Princeton 20, ff. 83r–84v; Princeton 47, 92v–93r; Princeton 56, ff. 150r–152v).

199. Ff. 123rv: How, when she was fleeing from Herod, the Virgin Mary visited a certain king when he sent a message to her to bless him and his people (*TM89* 222–5; Princeton 41, ff. 44v–45v).

200. Ff. 123v–124r: How the Virgin Mary gave birth to Jesus while she was in Judea; how the midwife Salome burned her hand when she touched the body of the Virgin; and how her hand healed when she touched the body of the infant Jesus (*TM89* 225–7; cp. the miracle associated with Salome glorifying Jesus at his birth, Princeton 23, ff. 36r–37v; Princeton 41, ff. 179rv; Princeton 46, ff. 57v–58r; Princeton 47, ff. 20r–22r).

201. Ff. 124r–125r: How a certain woman promised herself to live as a virgin for Saint Mary; how she committed adultery with many men, how she repented on her deathbed; how her tears and her sin were put on a scale and the tears outweighed the sin; how the Virgin Mary commanded Saint Michael to baptize her and put her with other virgins (*TM89* 227–31; cf. Budge, LXXI and miracle 74 above).

202. Ff. 125rv: How the Virgin Mary helped two monks when they prayed on behalf of a certain man who had lost his mind when he made a covenant with Satan to protect his cattle (*TM89* 231–3).

203. Ff. 125v–126r: How a certain rich man called Paqlima hurled a loaf at the head of a beggar and wounded him, and how the Virgin Mary delivered his soul from demons (Budge, LXXXVI; *TM89* 233–4; Princeton 20, ff. 54r–55r).

204. Ff. 126rv: How a certain Jew of Constantinople threw into the water [to the ground a picture of the Virgin Mary and when it was restored it exuded oil that healed many (Budge, LXV; cp. Budge, LXI and LXVIII; *TM89* 237–8; Princeton 20, ff. 78rv).

205. F. 126v: How the Virgin Mary protected an adulterous deacon from his attackers until he had confessed his sin to the priest; and

how she directed the bishop to bury his body among the faithful (*TM89* 238–9; cp. Budge, CIII, "How the Virgin Mary commanded a deacon to dig up and rebury in consecrated ground the body of an adulterous deacon from the island of Jericho in the city of Gärisat who was killed by the people;" cp. also Princeton 8, ff. 9r–10v; Princeton 40, ff. 80v–81v; Princeton 43, ff. 25r–26r; Princeton 46, ff. 128rv, which all follow Budge, CIII).

206. Ff. 126v–127r: How the Virgin Mary carried a sick monk from the Monastery of the Pilgrims [Budge, has "Beggars"] to Palestine, and showed him Jerusalem and Bethlehem, and bathed him in the waters of the Jordan (Budge, IX; *TM89* 239–40; Princeton 20, ff. 47r–48r; Princeton 23, ff. 29v–30r; Princeton 41, ff. 58v–59r; Princeton 43, ff. 30rv; Princeton 46, ff. 15v–16r; Princeton 47, ff. 35v–37v).

207. Ff. 127rv: How Sybil the prophetess saw a vision of the Virgin Mary holding her child within a circle around the sun and revealed this vision to a king who refused to be worshipped (*TM89* 241–2; Princeton 8, ff. 6r–8v; Princeton 20, ff. 39r–40r; Princeton 41, ff. 37v–39r).

208. Ff. 127v–128v: How the Virgin Mary saved the servant of a certain king when a co-worker accused him falsely; and how she caused the co-worker to be executed instead of the innocent man (*TM89* 243–7).

209. Ff. 128v–129r: How the Virgin Mary healed a certain man named Ṭiras who had became a deaf mute (*TM89* 247–8)

210. F. 129r: How a monk [named in this manuscript Gärdan] who had defiled himself mutilated himself and died under the influence of Satan; how Satan tried to carry off his soul to Sheol; and how the Virgin Mary obtained forgiveness for him, and restored life to his body (Budge, CI; *TM89* 248–9).

211. Ff. 129r–130r: How the Virgin Mary saved a certain woman from a knight who wanted to marry her and how she became a nun; how the knight repented from his sins and how, when he died, a tree sprang from him tomb; and how the icon of the Virgin was on every leaf of the tree (*TM89* 250–3; compare Budge, XXXVIII and Princeton 8, ff. 10v–12v; Princeton 41, ff. 85rv; Princeton 43, ff. 22v–23v).

212. F. 130v: How the Virgin Mary saved a young Jew of Tyre from the fiery furnace into which his father had cast him (Budge, XLIV; *TM89* 209–11; compare with Budge, LIX; Princeton 20, ff. 37r–39r).

213. Ff. 130v–131r: How the Virgin Mary protected a woman, great with child, who was overtaken by an inrush of the sea, and how the woman brought forth her child and escaped from drowning (Budge, XXXII; *TM89* 255–6; Princeton 20, ff. 82v–83r; Princeton 41, ff. 83r–84r; Princeton 46, ff. 31v–32v).
214. Ff. 131rv: How a certain woman whose husband had left her for another woman begged the Virgin Mary to kill the other woman; and how the Virgin Mary brought the other woman, who was devoted in worship of the Virgin, to repentance (*TM89* 256–8).
215. Ff. 131v–132r: How the Virgin Mary delivered a thief, the son of a poor widow) (Budge, XXX; *TM89* 259–260; Princeton 47, ff. 88v–89v).
216. Ff. 132r–133r: How the Virgin Mary became a guarantor on a loan from a certain Jew to a certain knight; how she delivered the money when the knight prayed to the Virgin Mary; and how the icon of the Virgin Mary testified when the Jew denied having received his money (Budge, XLVII; *TM89* 261–3).
217. Ff. 133rv: How the Virgin Mary appeared to the son of a king and asked him to remain celibate; how his father, the king, wanted him to marry a woman; and how the son died on his wedding day; and how the Virgin Mary received his soul and took it to heaven (*TM89* 264–7).
218. Ff. 133v–134v: How the Virgin Mary appeared to a certain king when he repented of his sin and how she told him that God received his repentance (*TM89* 267–71).
219. Ff. 134v–135r: How the Virgin Mary appeared to a certain priest named Askänafər who was sad over his lack of church education and how she told him that she found him more blessed than educated ones (*TM89* 271–3).
220. Ff. 135rv: How the Virgin Mary appeared to a certain pilgrim when he was travelling to Jerusalem; how she showed him a river of milk when he was exhausted from the heat of the sun; and how he arrived in Jerusalem in peace (*TM89* 273–4).
221. Ff. 135v–136r: How the Virgin Mary punished a certain treasurer of the church who disobeyed the monks and the bishop and how he died (*TM89* 274–6).
222. Ff. 136rv: How the Virgin Mary saved a certain monk when a demon tried to drown him (*TM89* 276–8; cf. Budge, LXIX and Princeton, 20, ff. 27r–28v).

223. Ff. 136v–137r: How the Virgin Mary saved a certain blind teacher when his students pushed him from a cliff and how she punished those students (*TM89* 278–81).
224. Ff. 137v–138r: How the Virgin Mary with her mother, Anna, and Elsabet, mother of John the Baptist, appeared to Tawkəlaya and how the Virgin Mary told her of her martyrdom along with her husband, Yosəṭos, and her son, Aboli (*TM89* 281–3).
225. Ff. 138r–139r: How King Marqos became the king of Rome and was pressed to marry, how he left his palace and went to church to pray before the Icon of Mary and how he entered the monastery of Tormaq (*TM89* 284–7; Princeton 8, ff. 34r–35v). The scribe has marked with red and black dotted lines a section on f. 138v, columns 1 and 2, which were copied erroneously.
226. Ff. 139r–143v: How the Virgin Mary appeared to Archbishop Tewofəlos of Alexandria and told him about the events surrounding Jesus' birth and the flight of the Holy Family into Egypt (*TM 89* 287–303; Princeton 41, ff. 21r–30r and ff. 113r–115v; cf. Princeton 41, ff. 146r–147v).
227. Ff. 143v–144r: How King Herod ordered the murder of the children [of Bethlehem]; how the angel of God appeared to Joseph to take the holy family to Egypt; and how the Sycamore tree opened itself and hid the holy family when they were threatened by bandits (Princeton 41, ff. 39v–42v).
228. Ff. 144r–145r: How, when fleeing to Egypt, the Virgin Mary asked water of a wealthy woman; how the woman insulted her; how the servant of this woman threw the infant Jesus to the ground; how the wealthy woman descended to Sheol and how her family turned into wild animals (cf. the next miracle).
229. Ff. 145rv: How the Virgin Mary cursed the people of a certain city in Egypt, while the Holy Family was there, when they treated her with disdain and how the city was swallowed by the ground (Princeton 41, ff. 42v–43v).
230. Ff. 145v–146r: How, when the holy family fled to Egypt; how Jesus brought forth water from under the feet of the Virgin Mary; and how the Virgin Mary healed the daughter of bandits (cf. Princeton 41, ff. 45v–48r, How the Holy Family visited Egypt and blessed Asqeṭəs and how Jesus caused water to well up from the ground using Joseph's rod);

231. Ff. 146rv: How the Virgin Mary saved the robber's soul from judgment because he drank from water that sprang from her feet (Princeton 20, ff. 5rv).
232. F. 146v: How the Virgin Mary healed a certain man who had been sick for forty-seven years.
233. Ff. 147rv: How the Virgin Mary healed a certain man with a foot of stone (Budge, XXII (has lame foot); Princeton 20, ff. 63rv; Princeton 41, ff. 70rv; Princeton 46, ff. 24rv; Princeton 47, ff. 67v–69v).
234. Ff. 147v–148r: How the Virgin Mary appeared to a Jeweler to forbid him from making an icon for certain arrogant people; and how she showed an icon of her which had been made by the angels to *Abba* Basiliyos (cf. Princeton 46, ff. 55v–56r).
235. F. 148r: How the Virgin Mary saved the drunken monk from a lion (See Budge, XXXVII and XLVIII which include an incident with a savage dog as well; Princeton 8, ff. 21r–22r; Princeton 20, ff. 9rv; Princeton 20, ff. 87rv; Princeton 41, ff. 98v–99v; Princeton 43, ff. 15v–17r).
236. Ff. 148rv: How the Virgin Mary helped a sick monk, who had left the monastery without the permission of the abbot, to repent and to receive holy communion before he died (cf. Princeton 20, ff. 89r).
237. F. 148v: How the Virgin Mary appeared to a wise monk who had criticized his fellow monks about the fish they were eating and how she chided him.
238. Ff. 148v–149r: How the Virgin Mary received the gift of a certain woman who was forbidden to fast by her husband (cf. Budge, XCIX; Princeton 20, ff. 6rv; Princeton 43, ff. 58r–61r).
239. F. 149r: How the Virgin Mary rescued from the clutches of the Devil the soul of a libertine monk who was crossing a stream one night to visit a paramour (Budge, LXIX; Princeton 20, ff. 27r–28v).
240. Ff. 149rv: How the Virgin Mary appeared to a certain sick man and commanded him to stay at the gate of the church during her fasting season and how she healed him on the feast day of her assumption to heaven.
241. F. 149v: How the Virgin Mary made a stream to reverse its course and water to run uphill in order to assist a poor man (Budge, XXXVI; Princeton 41, f. 54r; Princeton 8, ff. 43rv).
242. Ff. 149v–150r: How the Virgin Mary commanded [Budge says ―taught"] the Syrian potter [Ephrem] to learn by heart and to recite

the weekly service of her Book of Praise (Budge, XXXV; Princeton 8, ff. 30r–33v; Princeton 41, ff. 77r–79r; Princeton 43, ff. 40r–43r; Princeton 46, ff. 47r–48v; Princeton 47, ff. 103v–106v).

243. Ff. 150r–151r: How the Virgin Mary saved the cupbearer of a king who was accused by his fellow and how the accuser received the judgment which was planned for the cupbearer (Princeton 40, ff. 163r–164r; cf. miracle 208 above).

244. Ff. 151rv: How the Afrənəgawi [European man] took the gate lock from the Church of Bethlehem and how the Virgin Mary revealed her power when the Afärəngi was strangled by it (Princeton 41, ff. 141r–143v).

245. Ff. 151v–154r: The Cycle of the Vision of John, Son of Thunder: how the Virgin Mary appeared as a lady with twelve stars in her crown (ff. 151v–152r); how the Virgin Mary was glorified by all creation (f. 152r); how the glory of the Virgin Mary was preordained before the creation of heaven and earth (ff. 152rv); how the Virgin Mary appeared when the whole world was in darkness (f. 152v); how the Virgin Mary was given great wings (ff. 152v–153r); how the Virgin Mary is pure in her mind and in her body (f. 153r); how the Virgin Mary is a perpetual virgin (ff. 153rv); how King Solomon prophesied about her virginity (f. 153v); how the apostles taught their synod about the virginity of Saint Mary (f. 153v); and how the Virgin Mary is praised by all creation (ff. 153v–154r).

246. F. 154r: How the Virgin Mary made a garment for a devoted bishop and how, when the bishop refused to accept the repentance of a sinner, she revealed herself to the sinner and told him to go tell the bishop that he was wearing her garment (cf. Budge, XL; Princeton 8, ff. 13v–15v).

247. Ff. 154rv: How the Virgin Mary appeared to a certain wealthy man as great bird on a pillar of light (Princeton 46, ff. 41rv).

248. Ff. 154v–155r: How Saint Paul saw the glory of the Virgin Mary when he went to the third heaven.

249. Ff. 155rv: How the angels appeared to *Abba* Mardäri and how they praised the Virgin Mary with him.

250. Ff. 155v–156r: How the Virgin Mary appeared to *Abba* Bəḥor, disciple of Amoni (Princeton 46, ff. 42v–43r).

251. F. 156r: How the Virgin Mary appeared to Säwla, wife of Giyorgis, the new martyr after he had endured his martyrdom.

252. Ff. 156rv: How the holy family stayed in a place near to the Jordan River and how Jesus and his mother, the Virgin Mary, blessed that place.
253. F. 156v: How the Virgin Mary revealed a vision of the departed saints of the monastery of Asqeṭəs to the monks who were praying there (Princeton 41, ff. 155v–156r).
254. F. 156v: How the Virgin Mary saved a devoted monk from the deceptions of Satan.
255. Ff. 156v–157r: How the Virgin Mary saved a certain priest from Satan's temptation.
256. F. 157r: How the Virgin Mary saved from a lion a certain laundryman of a king.
257. F. 157r: How the Virgin Mary gave a garment to a devoted monk (Budge, XC; cf. Budge, XL; Princeton 47, ff. 93r–94r; Princeton 20, f. 84r).
258. Ff. 157rv: How the Virgin Mary gave a male child to a certain barren woman and how on his wedding day he refused to sleep with his bride; how the Virgin Mary anointed him with fragrance and he went to his bride.
259. F. 157v: How the Virgin Mary saved a certain governor when the king wrongly accused him and tried to kill him with the sword (cf. Princeton 20, ff. 31–32r; Princeton 41, ff. 88v–89r; Princeton 43, ff. 20v–21v).
260. Ff. 157v–158r: How the Virgin Mary protected a certain virgin when a nobleman took her by force to be his wife.
261. F. 158r: How the Virgin Mary saved a fisherman when a great sea serpent swallowed him (cf. *TM 89* 194).
262. Ff. 158rv: How the Virgin Mary took to safety the Abbott of the monastery when the monks wrongly accused him of adultery.
263. F. 158v: How the Virgin Mary interceded on behalf of a certain sinner when God ordered the angels to put his soul in hell; and how the tears of the Virgin Mary washed the sin away.
264. Ff. 158v–159r: How the Virgin Mary sent priests to a certain man when he prayed to receive holy communion.
265. F. 159r: How the Virgin Mary saved the drunken monk from a lion and a savage dog (see miracle 235 above; Budge, XXXVII and XLVIIII; cf. Princeton 8, ff. 21r–22r; Princeton 20, ff. 9rv; Princeton 20, ff. 87rv; Princeton 41, ff. 98v–99v; Princeton 43, ff. 15v–17r).

266. Ff. 159rv: How the painted figures of the Virgin Mary and Christ on an icon bled when a Jew cast the board into a pit, and how the magistrate had the Jew burnt alive (Budge, LXVIII; Princeton 20, ff. 29v–30v).
267. F. 159v: How a certain woman consigned to the Devil the son whom, against her desire, she conceived on Good Friday, and how the Virgin Mary rescued the young man from the clutches of the Devil (Budge, XLIX which has the day of conception as Easter Eve; Princeton 20, ff. 35v–37r.).
268. Ff. 159v–160r: How the Virgin Mary gave food to a certain poor beggar to be able to share with a guest.
269. F. 160r: How the Virgin Mary healed the son of a certain Roman governor while she was at Bethlehem and how she blessed him and his family and how he returned to Rome in peace.
270. Ff. 160rv: How the Virgin Mary, with other apostles, appeared to John Chrysostom and encouraged him in the exercise of the office of the keys.
271. F. 160v: How the angels protected the house of the Virgin Mary in Bethlehem when the Jews tried to burn it down (Princeton 46, ff. 53v–54r).
272. Ff. 160v–161r: How a certain man wished to build a martyrium to the Virgin Mary but lacked the necessary money and how she showed him in a dream where a pot of gold coins was to be found (Budge, LXXXVIII).
273. F. 161r: How the icon of the Virgin Mary wept for the sins of this world and how the icon spoke to a child to hide this from anyone and how the child followed the Blessed Virgin in a holy life of celibacy (Budge, XCII).
274. F. 161r: How a certain man used to put fifty roses on the icon of the Virgin Mary and how, when roses were out of season he would recite fifty Hail Mary's instead; and how fifty roses sprang from his grave three months after he died with their roots springing from his heart (cf. Budge, X and Princeton 8, ff. 39r–41r; Princeton 23, ff. 31r–34v; Princeton 41, ff. 59r–60v; Princeton 43, ff. 30v–32v; Princeton 46, ff. 16r–17r; Princeton 47, ff. 39r–42r.
275. F. 161r: How the Virgin Mary, because of his devotion, protected a thief who was stealing from the church.
276. Ff. 161rv: How the icon of the Virgin Mary spoke to a certain woman whose mother-in-law was opposed to her devotion to the

icon of the Virgin and how the icon disappeared because of the mother-in-law's objection (Princeton 20, ff. 52v–53r; Princeton 41, ff. 75rv).

277. F. 161v: How the Virgin Mary made a stream to reverse its course and water to run uphill in order to assist a poor man (see miracle 241 above; Budge, XXXVI; Princeton 41, f. 54r; Princeton 8, ff. 43rv).

278. F. 161v: How Jesus Christ appeared with his Mother to the apostles; how he appointed Peter to be the father of the people of Israel (*TM89* 109–10).

279. Ff. 161v–162v: How a certain Ethiopian monk named Qäleməntos went to lower Egypt to a city called Säbət in order to make a pilgrimage to Jerusalem; how he stayed in the house of the mother of Yohannəs, a lady who was known for her love of pilgrims; how her house was filled with light when he was reading from the miracles of Mary and how the lady decided to follow the monk to Jerusalem (Princeton 41, ff. 139r–141r; Princeton 46, ff. 129v–131r).

280. F. 162v: How a certain lady of Roman nobility tried to enter into the tomb of Jesus Christ in Jerusalem; how she was forbidden to enter because of her unbelief and how she came to faith, received holy communion and entered into the tomb to receive a blessing (cf. Budge, XXXIX; Princeton 43, ff. 57r–58r).

281. Ff. 162v–163r: How the Virgin Mary and her son, Jesus Christ, with the Apostles and archangels, blessed a certain church near to the Jordon River (see miracle 252 above).

282. F. 163r How the Holy Spirit taught about the honor of the day Sunday and how Jesus Christ appeared in honor of the Virgin Mary (Princeton 46, ff. 54rv).

283. F. 163r: How the Virgin Mary gave a garment to a devoted monk See miracles 41 and 257 above; Budge, XC; cf. Budge, XL; Princeton 20, f. 84r; Princeton Ethiopic MS 41, ff. 81v–82r; Princeton 47, ff. 93r–94r).

284. Ff. 163rv: How the Virgin Mary saved a certain wealthy lady from Syria from the pain of childbirth (cf. Princeton 23, ff. 34v–35r; Princeton 41, f. 72v which identifies the woman as from Caesarea).

285. F. 163v: How the Church of the Virgin Mary in Jerusalem at the gate of Mount Olives will serve as a ship [like the ark of Noah] at the time of the second coming of Jesus Christ.

286. Ff. 163v–164r: How the Virgin Mary saved a drunken monk named Matewos from a lion and a savage dog. (see miracles 55 and

235 above; and Budge, XXXVII and XLVIII; Princeton 8, ff. 21r–22r; Princeton 20, ff. 9rv; Princeton 20, ff. 87rv; Princeton 41, ff. 98v–99v; Princeton 43, ff. 15v–17r).

287. F. 164r: How the Virgin Mary punished Nəsṭur [Nestorius] who had insulted her.

288. Ff. 164rv: How the Virgin Mary saved the people on a certain ship on the sea when they were caught in a powerful storm (Princeton 20, ff. 57v–58v).

289. F. 164v: How the Virgin Mary appeared to a wealthy woman at a monastery while the monks were in prayer (Princeton 8, ff. 45v–46v; Princeton 20, ff. 25v–26v).

290. Ff. 164v–165r: How a certain Roman prefect was prevented by a Ram from entering the Tomb of our Lord, and how he was not able to go in until he had become a follower of the Virgin Mary (Budge, XXXIX; Princeton 43, ff. 57r–58r).

291. F. 165r: How the Virgin Mary appeared to *Abba* Bärsuma as a white dove.

292. Ff. 165rv: How Jesus Christ carried the body of the Virgin Mary to heaven on the day of her assumption and how he gave her a covenant (cf. Synaxarium entry for the sixteen day of Yäkatit).

293. Ff. 165v–166r: How Emperor Tiberius sent a letter to our Lord Jesus Christ with the body of his son and how his son was raised from the dead when they put him in the tomb of Jesus and how the Emperor and Empress tried to bring our Lady Mary to the palace in Rome (cf. a similar account in Gäbrä Haymamat).

294. Ff. 166r–167r: How Jesus Christ commanded John to go to Emperor Tiberius; how Tiberius asked John to make an icon like the one he had seen on the day of the crucifixion of Jesus; how John made the icon and when he finished how John kissed the icon for several hours and how the icon called John "my beloved." (cf. a similar account in Gäbrä Haymamat).

295. F. 167r: How Jesus Christ commanded John the Apostle to carry the body of the Virgin Mary in a heavenly chariot and how the angels received the body of Mary with incense and praise (Princeton 46, ff. 65rv).

296. Ff. 167rv: How the Virgin Mary was exalted more than the angels and how the One born from the Virgin Mary saved the world (cf. Princeton 46, ff. 64v–65r).

297. Ff. 167v–168v: How the Virgin Mary took the position from a certain abbot who had forbidden the praise of Mary among the monks; and how the Ethiopians and Copts received the light at Jerusalem and they were singing and dancing during the Easter celebration with the line "for us who believe in your resurrection, send us your light" (cf. *TM89* 101–4).

298. F. 168v: How the Virgin Mary returned a child to a certain woman when the child was taken by a hyena and the mother went to the local church, took an icon of Jesus and said, "I will return your son, when you return my son."

299. F. 168v: How the Virgin Mary gave a garment and food to a poor, devoted monk (see miracles 41 and 257 above; Budge, XC; cf. Budge, XL; Princeton 20, f. 84r; Princeton Ethiopic MS 41, ff. 81v–82r; Princeton 47, ff. 93r–94r).

300. Ff. 168v–169v: How the Virgin Mary healed the hand of Atenatewos, a converted Muslim, who had became a priest, after he cut off his hand because a woman had kissed it during the celebration of the Eucharist (*TM89* 319–21; cf., Budge, V; Princeton 41, ff. 55rv).

301. F. 169v: How the Virgin Mary healed a certain sinful woman when she swallowed a scorpion because she was depressed about her sin and how a voice from the icon led her to a certain priest for repentance and healing; and how she gave birth to forty scorpions when she had completed her repentance (*TM89* 330–2; Princeton 20, ff. 57rv).

302. F. 170r: How the Virgin Mary healed a sick deacon by anointing him with her breast milk (Princeton 41, ff. 75r–76v).

303. Ff. 170rv: How the Virgin Mary appeared at the time of prayer for a certain wealthy woman who was a patron for a certain monastery (Princeton 8, ff. 45v–46v; Princeton 20, ff. 25v–26v).

304. F. 170v: How, because of his devotion to her, the Virgin Mary saved the soul of a wicked monastic leader from hell when he died; and how he appeared to his disciple in a dream and told him how the Virgin Mary saved him from damnation (Princeton 20, f. 62v).

305. Ff. 170v–171r: How a certain Muslim was converted when he saw oil and Myron exuded from the breast of icon of the Virgin Mary (see miracle 48 above; Budge, 61; Princeton 41, ff. 92r–93r; Princeton , ff. 17r–18v; cf. Budge, LXV and LXVIII).

306. Ff. 171rv: How the Virgin Mary healed an elderly priest of Alexandria when he fell and broke his back during the church service because of his old age (Budge, III, which identifies the man as an elderly Jew of Akəmim; Princeton 20, ff. 42r–43r; Princeton 43, ff. 8v–9v; Princeton 46, ff. 11rv).

307. F. 171v: How the Virgin Mary spoke from her picture to a devout worshipper and said to him, "Blessed art thou among men" (Budge, II; Princeton 20, ff. 41v–42r; Princeton 23, ff. 28v–29v; Princeton 41, ff. 54v; Princeton 43, ff. 8rv; Princeton 46, ff. 10v–11r).

308. Ff. 171v–172r: How the Virgin Mary received the soul of a sick and devout monk who was unable to go to church and how she took his soul to Paradise (cf. Budge, XXVII; Princeton 20, ff. 81rv; Princeton 41, ff. 84r–85r; Princeton 43, ff. 6v–8r; Princeton 43, ff. 50v–51v; Princeton 46, ff. 27v–28r; Princeton 47, ff. 80v–81r).

309. Ff. 172rv: How the icon of the Virgin Mary helped a young impoverished man and how the church keeper saw this miracle and how he gave his daughter to the young man in marriage (Princeton 20, f. 25r; Princeton 20, ff. 72rv; Princeton 41, ff. 93r–94r).

310. F. 172v: How the Virgin Mary appeared to reassure an ascetic woman about the purity of her friends, other ascetic women held with her in prison (cf. Princeton 8, ff. 19v–21r; Princeton 20, ff. 5v–6r, f. 31r and ff. 75rv).

311. Ff. 172v–173r: How the Virgin Mary received the gift of gold from a certain woman when the woman was forbidden by her husband to fast (see miracle 238 above and cf. Budge, XCIX; Princeton 20, ff. 6rv; Princeton 43, ff. 58r–61r).

312. F. 173r: How the Virgin Mary delivered from devils the soul of a scribe who was engaged in writing a copy of the Book of her Miracles. This scribe had a brother who had sinned, but not knowing him they seized the innocent man and tried to carry him off to hell (Budge, XVIII; Princeton 20, ff. 51v–52v; Princeton 41, ff. 66v–67v; Princeton 46, ff. 21v–22r; Princeton 47, ff. 58r–59r).

313. Ff. 173rv: How the Virgin Mary revealed a vision of the departed saints of the monastery of Asqeṭəs, among them *Abba* Mäqars, *Abba* Yoḥannəs, *Abba* Bəsoy, *Abba* Muse, *Abba* Yoḥannəs Käma, to the monks who were praying there (see miracle 253 above and Princeton 41, ff. 155v–156r).

314. F. 173v: How; during the reign of Gabriel the eighty-eighth Archbishop of Alexandria, the Virgin Mary punished a certain man

who insulted the icon of the Virgin; and how the icon spoke to the abbot when he interceded for the man.
315. F. 174r: How the Virgin Mary received the soul of the king of Constantinople who was a devout follower of the Virgin Mary.
316. F. 174r: How the Virgin Mary saved a certain nun who died before she finished her penitence and how she appeared to the Abbess and told her how the Virgin Mary saved her (Princeton 20, ff. 28r–29v).
317. Ff. 174rv: How the Virgin Mary saved the people on a certain ship on the sea when they were caught in a powerful storm and they cried out to her (Princeton 20, ff. 57v–58v).
318. Ff. 174v–175r: How the Virgin Mary saved a certain man from drowning when the ship was sinking (Princeton 41, ff. 99v–100v).
319. F. 175r: How the monk Ḥərdaw had defiled himself, mutilated himself and died under the influence of Satan; how Satan tried to carry off his soul to Sheol; and how the Virgin Mary obtained forgiveness for him and restored life to his body (Budge, CI; Princeton 20, ff. 40r–41v).
320. Ff. 175rv: How the Virgin Mary saved a certain Jew from the fiery furnace into which his father had cast him (Budge, XLIV; cf. Budge, LIX; and Princeton 20, ff. 37r–39r).
321. F. 175v: How the Virgin Mary saved a certain painter when he fell from his scaffolding (Princeton 20, ff. 3v–4r; cf. Budge, VIII; Princeton 20, ff. 46r–47r; Princeton 41, ff. 57v–58v; Princeton 46, ff. 14v–15v and ff. 145v–146r; Princeton 47, ff. 32v–35v).
322. Ff. 175v–176r: How the Virgin Mary gave a garment to a certain bishop and how she appeared to a certain man and commanded him to go again to make repentance with the bishop who had previously refused to grant forgiveness (cf. Budge, XL; Princeton 8, ff. 13v–15v; Princeton 41, ff. 81v–82v; Princeton 43, ff. 49v–50v).
323. F. 176r: How the icon of the Virgin Mary in Jerusalem spoke to the people of Ethiopia when they entered into the place with their shoes still on their feet (*TM89* 342–3).
324. Ff. 176rv: How Jesus Christ took the body of the Virgin Mary to heaven and how the angels praised her and cast upon her the leaves of the tree of life; and how John commanded his secretary Abərokos [Prochorus] to write down the account of the assumption of the Virgin on the sixteenth of Näḥase (cf. Princeton 46, ff. 65rv).
325. Ff. 176v–177r: How the apostles assembled to witness the assumption of the Virgin Mary and how the archangels Gabriel,

Michael and Rufael commanded the earth to give up the body of the Virgin Mary.
326. Ff. 177rv: How a certain man named Afəlaṭon [Plato?] came to see the assumption of the Virgin Mary.
327. Ff. 177v–178r: How the Holy Spirit commanded Thomas, the apostle, who was in India, to go back to Jerusalem and receive blessing from Saint Mary during her assumption to heaven.
328. Ff. 178rv: How the Virgin Mary prayed to Jesus Christ to send an angel to take her from this world.
329. Ff. 178v–179r: How the apostles buried the body of the Virgin Mary when she died, part one (*TM89* 25–7).
330. Ff. 179rv: How the apostles buried the body of the Virgin Mary when she died, part two (*TM89* 27–30).
331. Ff. 179v–180r: How Saint John greeted the Virgin Mary holding the shroud of the Virgin Mary (*TM89* 23–5).
332. F. 180r: How the Virgin Mary appeared to a certain man named Yoləyo in a dream; how she commanded him to bury the martyrs; how she put the sign of the cross on his hand and how he found it when he awoke.
333. Ff. 180rv: How the Virgin Mary kept the container of oil suspended in the air after its attachments had broken (Princeton 41, ff. 135r–136v).
334. F. 180v: How the angel of God transported a certain man eighty cubits outside the church when he had a nocturnal emission. (see miracle 185 above, for which this is a longer version, and *TM89* 186–8).
335. Ff. 180v–181v: How the Virgin Mary appeared to Timothy, the archbishop, and how she told him about the holy family and the flight to Egypt (*TM89* 321–6; Princeton 46, ff. 51v–53v and ff. 146r–147v; cf. the appearance to Tewoflos with a similar vision, Princeton 41, ff. 21r–30r, ff. 113r–115v).
336. Ff. 181v–182r: How Hanna, the mother of the Virgin Mary, went to the funeral of Samər, son of Ṭolit, in Jericho and how, when she was weeping and holding his body, he awoke and praised her saying, ―Greetings to you, O Mother of the sun of righteousness" (*TM89* 149–50).
337. Ff. 182rv: How Gregory, the Seer of Mystery (Rä'aye Ḥəbu'at), saw the glory of the Virgin Mary in heaven (*TM89* 332–5; Princeton 46, ff. 43r–44r).

338. Ff. 182v–183v: How a certain woman, Abrəsqəla, and her husband, Särges, consigned to the Devil the son whom, against the woman's desire, she conceived on Easter Eve, and how the Virgin Mary rescued the young man from the clutches of the Devil (see miracle 267 above; Budge, XLIX; Princeton 20, ff. 35v–37r).

339. Ff. 183v–184v: How a certain man named Ṭəbrəyanos became poor and Satan came to him and tempted him to deny Jesus Christ, the Virgin Mary, and the angels and he denied all except the Virgin Mary; and how he repented and appealed to the Virgin Mary and how she obtained forgiveness for him from Jesus Christ (*TM89* 339–42; cf. Princeton 20, ff. 26r–27v, and ff. 77rv; Princeton 41, ff. 100v–101v).

340. Ff. 184v–185r: How a stone from the mountain of Ṭir served as a ship when the holy family returned from Egypt and the captain of another ship refused to transport them (*TM89* 37–9).

341. Ff. 185r–186r: How the Virgin Mary raised from the dead a young man who had fallen into a deep pit when he tried to bring water to Däbrä Q^{w}usq^{w}am; how, when he was still lost, his mother prayed to the Virgin Mary during the feast of Däbrä Q^{w}usq^{w}am and how the young man awoke from the dead and came to his mother (cf. Princeton 41, ff. 158v–161r).

342. Ff. 186r–187r: How the Virgin Mary appeared to Ṭimotewos, the Archbishop and son of Deyosəqoros, and how she told him about the meeting with the witch Ṭäludar during the flight of the Holy Family into Egypt (cf. Princeton 46, ff. 146r–147v).

343. Ff. 187r–188r: How the Virgin Mary appeared to Tewoflos the Archbishop of Alexandria and told him about the flight of the Holy Family into Egypt (cf. Princeton 41, ff. 21r–30r).

344. Ff. 188r–189r: How the Virgin Mary saved the wife of King Constantine when the brother of the king accused her falsely of adultery when she refused to sleep with him; and how the Virgin Mary gave her the power of healing, and how she led a life of chastity.

345. F. 189r: How a certain Christian who was the treasurer for a Muslim prince gave all of the food in the treasury to the poor and needy; and how the servants of the prince found nothing in the treasury during a time of drought; and how the Virgin Mary saved the treasurer when he was thrown into prison.

346. Ff. 189rv: How the Virgin Mary, through her icon, told Dänasəyos, the Archbishop of Rome, that King Marqos had entered a monastery (Princeton 8, ff. 33v–34r).
347. F. 189v: How the Virgin Mary gave a child to the king of Rome, Mäsfəyanos, and his wife, Səfnəgəya.
348. Ff. 189v–190r: How Nicodemus, an evil-living Persian knight, became a Christian, but was unable to learn the Lord's Prayer, and could only master the Salutation to Mary; and how these words were found written on every leaf of a tree which grew on his grave (Budge, XXXVIII; Princeton 8, ff. 10v–12v; Princeton 40, ff. 85rv; Princeton 43, ff. 22v–23r).
349. Ff. 190rv: How the Virgin Mary gave a child to a certain woman named Martha from a royal family in the East; how the Virgin Mary raised the child from the dead when the wife of the Emperor Diocletian threw the child to the floor out of jealousy.
350. Ff. 190v–191v: How the Virgin Mary appeared to Tewoflos the Archbishop of Alexandria and told him about the events surrounding Jesus' birth and the flight of the Holy Family into Egypt (cf., Princeton 41, ff. 21r–30r; Princeton 41, ff. 110v–113r and ff. 113r–115v).
351. Ff. 191v–192r: How the Virgin Mary appeared to a certain deacon who loved to sing her praises and how she received his soul into paradise (Princeton 8, ff. 14v–17v).
352. F. 192r: How the Virgin Mary saved a certain man from drowning when the ship was sinking (see miracle 318 above; Princeton 41, ff. 99v–100v).
353. Ff. 192r–193r: How a certain woman whose husband had left her for another woman begged the Virgin Mary to kill the other woman; and how the Virgin Mary brought the other woman, who was devoted in worship of the Virgin, to repentance (see miracle 214 above; *TM89* 256–8).
354. F. 193r: How Sybil the prophetess saw a vision of the Virgin Mary holding her child within a circle around the sun and revealed this vision to a king who refused to be worshipped (Princeton 8, ff. 6r–8v; Princeton 20, ff. 39r–40r; Princeton 41, ff, 37v–39r).
355. Ff. 193rv: How [Abbas,] Bishop of Rome, cut off his hand which had been kissed by a woman when he was celebrating the Eucharist, and how the Virgin Mary rejoined it to his arm (incomplete at the end; cf. Budge, V and Va; Princeton 41, ff. 55rv; Princeton 46, ff.

11v–12v; Princeton 47, ff. 23v–25v; and fused with the story of); How the Virgin Mary appeared to reassure an ascetic woman about the purity of her friends, other ascetic women held with her in prison (incomplete at the beginning, see miracle 310 above; cf. Princeton 8, ff. 19v–21r; Princeton 20, ff. 5v–6r, f. 31r and ff. 75rv).

356. Ff. 193v–194r: How the Virgin Mary saved the soul of a certain woman who died without repentance and how this woman appeared at the church of her friend and told her how the Virgin Mary had saved her because of the blessing of the feast day in that church (see miracle 316 above and Princeton 20, ff. 28r–29v).

357. Ff. 194rv: How the Virgin Mary helped two brothers when they prayed on behalf of a certain man who had lost his mind when he made a covenant with Satan to protect his cattle (see miracle 202 above; *TM89* 231–3).

358. Ff. 194v–195r: How the Virgin Mary raised up a dead knight, who had been buried in the cemetery of a convent, to fight against an enemy of the church called Gǝlǝyanos (Budge, LX; Princeton 20, ff. 73v–74v).

359. F. 195r: How the Virgin Mary sent priests to a certain man when he prayed to receive holy communion (see miracle 264 above).

360. Ff. 195rv: How one of Herod's soldiers saved the Christ child and the Virgin Mary from the slaughter of the innocents.

361. F. 195v: How the Virgin Mary saved the soul of a man who had committed great sin but who had also built a martyrium; and how the Virgin Mary asked her Son to show mercy on this man.

362. F. 195v: Ff. 110v–111r: How the Virgin Mary took a certain abbot with her into heaven when the people accused him and how she punished them (a variation of miracle 181 above; *TM89* 176–7).

363. Ff. 195v–196r: How the Virgin Mary healed a man who had spent all of his money on medicine but who, at the end, prayed to the Virgin Mary for healing.

364. F. 196r: How the Virgin Mary provided for a poor family the meal for the feast of Saint Mary.

365. Ff. 196rv: How the Virgin Mary helped a hunter to catch a wild animal with the face of a dog and how she commanded him to eat the flesh of that animal.

366. F. 196v: How the icon of the Virgin Mary wept for the sins of this world and how the icon spoke to a child to hide this from anyone and

how the child followed the Blessed Virgin in a holy life of celibacy (see miracle 273 above; Budge, XCII).

367. F. 196v: How a certain man wished to build a martyrium to the Virgin Mary but lacked the necessary money and how she showed him in a dream where a pot of gold coins was to be found (see miracle 272 above; Budge, LXXXVIII).

368. Ff. 196v–197r: How the Virgin Mary saved a certain governor when the king wrongly accused him and tried to kill him with the sword; and how the Virgin Mary appeared to the king and said, ‒Don't harm my servant" (see miracle 259 above; cf. Princeton 20, ff. 31–32r; Princeton 41, ff. 88v–89r; Princeton 43, ff. 20v–21v).

369. F. 197r: How the Virgin Mary appeared to a certain sick man and commanded him to go into the church on the sixteenth of Näḥase (the feast day of her assumption); and how he was healed on that day (see miracle 240 above).

370. Ff. 197rv: How the Virgin Mary gave a male child to a certain barren woman and how on his wedding day he refused to sleep with his bride; how the Virgin Mary anointed him with fragrance and he went to his bride (see miracle 258 above).

371. Ff. 197v: How the Virgin Mary saved the soul of the monk who had no other good works beside observing the fast of Mary which is known as the Assumption.

Miniatures:
1. F. iii v(erso): Saint George and the Dragon.
2. F. iv r(ecto): Madonna and Child.
3. F. vi v(erso): How the Virgin Mary was crowned by the Trinity.
4. F. 4v: How the Virgin Mary gave garment and chair to Saint Hildefonsus (Däqsəyos), Bishop of Toledo.
5. F. 58v: The Assumption of the Virgin Mary and how she gave Saint Thomas her handkerchief (cf. the four miracles beginning on f. 59r which recount the death and assumption of the Virgin Mary).

Notes:
1. Ff. ii r(ecto)-iii r(ecto), iii v(erso)-vi r(ecto), 4r, 58r and 198rv: blank.
2. Ff. i and 199 are pasted beneath the tooled leather.
3. Decorative designs: ff. 1r, 5r (ornate and colorful ḥaräg); ff. 2r, 138v, 154r (a line of alternating red and black dots); multiple full stops are used as section dividers throughout (e.g., ff. 2r, 5r, 7r); f. 43r (a line of black dots).
4. The word Mary is rubricated.

5. F. 197v: Scribal prayer: ―Oh our lady, may your prayer and blessing be with your servant—and the scribe *Abunä* Gäbrä Qiros—forever and ever, amen."
6. Scribal intervention: words of text are written interlinearly (ff. 1v, 6r, 26r, 30r, 41r, etc.); and lines of text are written interlinearly (f. 176v); and in the upper margin with a symbol (+) marking the location where the text is to be inserted (f. 31v, col. 3, line 9); text has been removed (e.g., ff. 44v, 51v, 79v).
7. F. 144r, col. 3, lines 16–17: two lines of text have been crossed out to correct homeoteleuton (see lines 11–12).
8. F. 43r, col. 2, contains the beginning of the miracle know as ―How the Virgin Mary call John, the priest, ‗Golden Mouth' after he kissed the woman with an issue of menstrual blood who had been challenged by Nestorius." Cf. *TM89* 159–61. But, the scribe stopped, put removal dots above and below the account, and someone has made ink lines through the text.

Quire Map

Protection Quire:

F. i is three inches wide and pasted beneath the tooled leather.

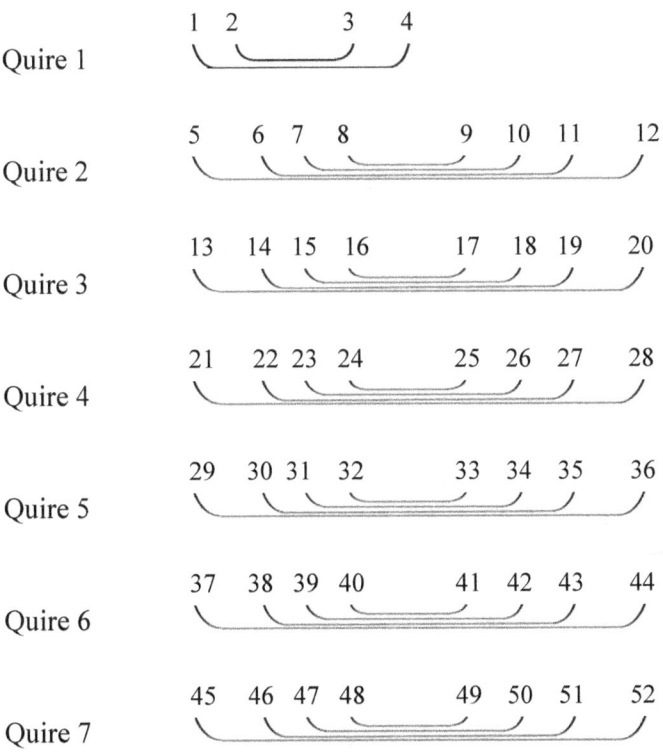

Quire 8: 53 54 55 56 57 58 59 60 61
Folio stub is visible between ff. 55 and 56.

Quire 9: 62 63 64 65 66 67 68 69

Quire 10: 70 71 72 73 74 75 76 77

Quire 11: 78 79 80 81 82 83 84 85

Quire 12: 86 87 88 89 90 91 92 93 94 95

Quire 13: 96 97 98 99 100 101 102 103

Quire 14: 104 105 106 107 108 109 110 111 112 113

Quire 15: 114 115 116 117 118 119 120 121 122 123

Quire 16: 124 125 126 127 128 129 130 131 132 133

Quire 17: 134 135 136 137 138 139 140 141

Quire 18: 142 143 144 145 146 147 148 149 150 151

Quire 19: 152 153 154 155 156 157 158 159

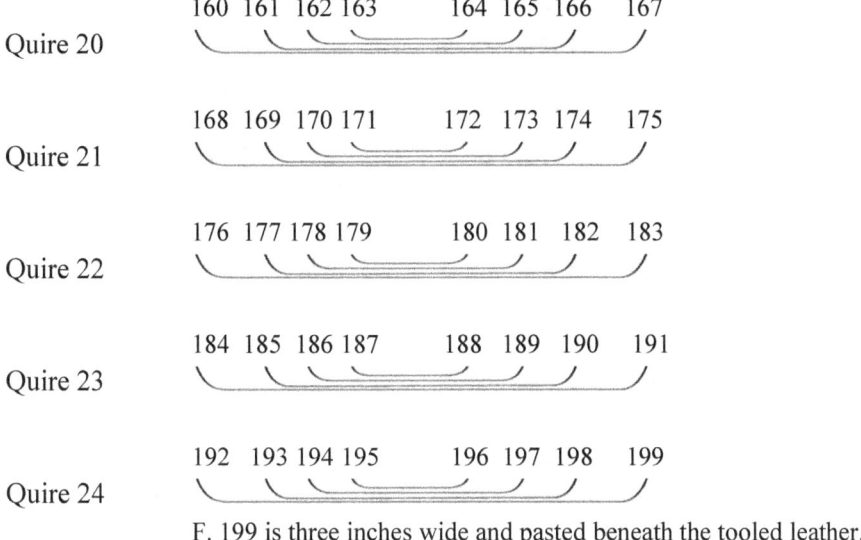

F. 199 is three inches wide and pasted beneath the tooled leather.

MYS 2 – EMIP 602
Printed Reproduction of the Ḥaylä Śəllase Bible, in Amharic and Gə͡əz, volume 1, Genesis through Esther, መጽሐፍ፣ ቅዱስ፣ (በግዕዝና፣ በአማርኛ፣ የተጻፈ።) ጀኛ፣ ክፍል፣

Paper, 420 x 290 x 40 mm, printed reproduction, iv +233 folios, ff. 1r–231v four columns, 66 lines, Gə͡əz and Amharic, twentieth century.

Major Works:

Holy Bible, written in Gə͡əz and Amharic, Part 1, መጽሐፍ ፣ ቅዱስ ፣ (በግዕዝና ፣ በአማርኛ ፣ የተጻፈ ፣) ጀኛ ፣ ክፍል ፣,

1. Ff. 1r–23r: Genesis, ኦሪት፣ ዘልደት፣. See, Augustus Dillmann, *BVTA* (Leipzig, 1853) 3–95; *AIP* 12–57. J. Oscar Boyd, *The Octateuch in Ethiopic According to the Text of the Paris Codex, with the variants of five other manuscripts, Part I, Genesis* (Leiden: Brill, 1909).
2. Ff. 24r–42v: Exodus, ኦሪት፣ ዘጸአት፣. See, Augustus Dillmann, *BVTA* (Leipzig, 1853) 96–169; *AIP* 58–98.
3. Ff. 43r–56v: Leviticus, ኦሪት፣ ዘሌዋውያን፣. See, Augustus Dillmann, *BVTA* (Leipzig, 1853) 170–228; *AIP* 99–118.
4. Ff. 57r–76r: Numbers, ኦሪት፣ ዘኍልቍ፣. See, Augustus Dillmann, *BVTA* (Leipzig, 1853) 229–309; *AIP* 119–139.
5. Ff. 77r–93r: Deuteronomy. Augustus Dillmann, *BVTA* (Leipzig, 1853) 310–380; *AIP* 139–164.

6. Ff. 93v–104v: Joshua, ኦሪት ዘኢያሱ. Augustus Dillmann, *BVTA* (Leipzig, 1853) 381–428; *ALJJR*, 167–191.
7. Ff. 105r–116v: Judges, ኦሪት ዘመሳፍንት. See, Augustus Dillmann, *BVTA* (Leipzig, 1853) 431–478; *ALJJR*, 192–215.
8. Ff. 117r–118r: Ruth, ኦሪት ዘሩት. See, Augustus Dillmann, *BVTA* (Leipzig, 1853) 479–485; *ALJJR*, 215–219.
9. Ff. 118v–134r: 1 Kings (Gə_əz) / 1 Samuel (Amharic), መጽሐፈ፡ ነገሥት፡ ቀዳማዊ፡. Dillmann *BVTA, Tomus Secundus 1* (Leipzig, 1861) 1–53.
10. Ff. 134r–146v: 2 Kings (Gə_əz) / 2 Samuel (Amharic), መጽሐፈ፡ ነገሥት፡ ካልዕ፡. Dillmann *BVTA, Tomus Secundus 1* (Leipzig, 1861) 54–96.
11. Ff. 147r–162v: 3 Kings (Gə_əz) / 1 Kings (Amharic), መጽሐፈ፡ ነገሥት፡ ሣልስ፡. Dillmann *BVTA, Tomus Secundus 2* (Leipzig, 1871) 1–51.
12. Ff. 162v–177v: 4 Kings (Gə_əz) / 2 Kings (Amharic), መጽሐፈ፡ ነገሥት፡ ራብዕ፡. Dillmann *BVTA, Tomus Secundus 2* (Leipzig, 1871) 52–98.
13. Ff. 177v–193v: 1 Parileipomenon (Gə_əz) / 1 Chronicles (Amharic), መጽሐፈ፡ ሕውያን፡ ቀዳማዊ፡ አው፡ መጽሐፈ፡ ዜና፡ መዋዕል፡ ቀዳማዊ፡. Sylvain Grébaut, *Les Paralipomènes, Livres I et II, Version Ethiopienne*, PO 23 (Paris: Firmin-Didot, 1932).
14. Ff. 193v–212v: 2 Parileipomenon (Gə_əz) / 2 Chronicles (Amharic), መጽሐፈ፡ ሕውያን፡ ካልዕ፡ አው፡ መጽሐፈ፡ ዜና፡ መዋዕል፡ ካልዕ፡. Sylvain Grébaut, *Les Paralipomènes, Livres I et II, Version Ethiopienne*, PO 23 (Paris, 1932).
15. Ff. 213r–226r: Ezra Nehemiah, መጽሐፈ፡ እዝራ፡ ነህምያ፡. Francisco Maria Esteves Pereira, *Le troisième livre de _Ezrâ (Esdras et Néhémie canoniques): version éthiopienne*, PO 13.5 (Paris: Firmin-Didot, 1919).
16. Ff. 227r–231v: Esther, መጽሐፈ፡ አስቴር፡. Francisco Maria Esteves Pereira, *Le Livre d'Esther*, PO 9 (1913) 1–56.

Notes:
1. Blank: ff. i rv, 23v, 76v, 226v, 232r–233v.
2. F. ii r(ecto): Title Page: ―Holy Bible, written in Gə_əz and Amharic, First Part"
3. F. ii v(erso): ―Translated from Gə_əz into Amharic by Ethiopian Church scholars."

4. F. iii r(ecto): The Canon. Part One Genesis to Esther. Part Two: Job to Malachi. Part Three: Jubilees to Additions to Daniel.
5. F. iv r(ecto): The Canon, continued: Part Four: Matthew to Revelation.
6. F. 93r, 226r: seal.
7. Decorative designs: ff. ii r(ecto), 1r, 24r, 43r, 77r, 93v, 105r, 117r, 118v; 147r, 213r, 227r (ḥaräg); ff. 57r, 152v, 177v, 193v (space for ḥaräg).

MYS 3 – EMIP 603
Printed Reproduction of the Ḥaylä Śəllase Bible, in Amharic and Gə,əz, መጽሐፍ፡ ቅዱስ፡ (በግዕዝና፡ በአማርኛ፡ የተጻፈ፡), Volume 2, Psalms and New Testament

Parchment, 410 x 285 x 33 mm, printed reproduction, 153 folios, ff. 1r–152r four columns, 66 lines, Gə_əz and Amharic, twentieth century.

Major works:

F. ii r(ecto): Title Page: "New Testament and Psalms in Gə_əz and Amharic. Translated from Gə_əz into Amharic by Ethiopian Church scholars." See Thomas Pell Platt, ed., *Evangelia Sancta Aethiopice* (London, 1826).

1. Ff. 1r–33r. Psalms of David. Hiob Ludolf, *Psalterium Davidis Aethiopice et Latine*, 1701.
2. Ff. 34r–47v: Gospel of Matthew. Rochus Zuurmond, *Novum Testamentum Aethiopice: the Synoptic Gospels, volume 1, General Introduction*, AF 27 (Wiesbaden: Steiner Verlag, 1989). Rochus Zuurmond, *Novum Testamentum Aethiopice, part III - The Gospel of Matthew*, AF 55 (Wiesbaden: Harrassowitz Verlag, 2001).
3. Ff. 48r–56r: Gospel of Mark. Rochus Zuurmond, *Novum Testamentum Aethiopice, the Synoptic Gospels, volume 2, The Gospel of Mark*, AF 27 (Wiesbaden: Steiner Verlag, 1989).
4. Ff. 56v–71r: Gospel of Luke.
5. Ff. 71v–82v: Gospel of John. Michael G. Wechsler, *Evangelium Iohannis Aethiopicum*, CSCO, SA 109 (Louvain, Peeters, 2005).
6. Ff. 83r–97v: Acts of the Apostles. See Curt Niccum, "The Book of Acts in Ethiopic (with critical text and apparatus) and its relation to the Greek textual tradition," unpublished dissertation, Universtiy of Notre Dame, 2000.

7. Ff. 99r–135v: Paul's Epistles. See Petrus Aethiops, ed. *Testamentum Novum cum epistula Pauli ad Hebraeos* (Rome, 1548), and *Epistulae XIII divi Pauli* (Rome, 1549).
   a. Ff. 99r–105v: Romans
   b. Ff. 105v–112r: 1 Corinthians
   c. Ff. 112r–116r: 2 Corinthians
   d. Ff. 116v–118v: Galatians
   e. Ff. 118v–120v: Ephesians. See Siegbert Uhlig and Helge Maehlum, *Novum Testamentum aethiopice: die Gefangenschaftsbriefe*, AF 33 (Stuttgart: Franz Steiner Verlag, 1993).
   f. Ff. 120v–122v: Philippians. See Siegbert Uhlig and Helge Maehlum, *Novum Testamentum aethiopice: die Gefangenschaftsbriefe*, AF 33 (Stuttgart: Franz Steiner Verlag, 1993).
   g. Ff. 122v–123v: Colossians. See Siegbert Uhlig and Helge Maehlum, *Novum Testamentum aethiopice: die Gefangenschaftsbriefe*, AF 33 (Stuttgart: Franz Steiner Verlag, 1993).
   h. Ff. 123v–125r: 1 Thessalonians
   i. Ff. 125r–126r: 2 Thessalonians
   j. Ff. 126r–127v: 1 Timothy
   k. Ff. 127v–129r: 2 Timothy
   l. Ff. 129r–130r: Titus
   m. F. 130r: Philemon. See Siegbert Uhlig and Helge Maehlum, *Novum Testamentum aethiopice: die Gefangenschaftsbriefe*, AF 33 (Stuttgart: Franz Steiner Verlag, 1993).
   n. Ff. 130r–135v: Hebrews
8. Ff. 137r–152r: Catholic Epistles and Revelation
   a. Ff. 137r–138v: 1 Peter. See Josef Hofmann and Siegbert Uhlig, *Novum Testamentum Aethiopice: die katholischen Briefe*, AF 29 (Stuttgart: Franz Steiner Verlag, 1993).
   b. Ff. 138v–140r: 2 Peter. See Josef Hofmann and Siegbert Uhlig, *Novum Testamentum Aethiopice: die katholischen Briefe*, AF 29 (Stuttgart: Franz Steiner Verlag, 1993).
   c. Ff. 140r–141v: 1 John. See Josef Hofmann and Siegbert Uhlig, *Novum Testamentum Aethiopice: die katholischen Briefe*, AF 29 (Stuttgart: Franz Steiner Verlag, 1993).

d. Ff. 141v–142r: 2 John. See Josef Hofmann and Siegbert Uhlig, *Novum Testamentum Aethiopice: die katholischen Briefe*, AF 29 (Stuttgart: Franz Steiner Verlag, 1993).
e. Ff. 142r: 3 John. See Josef Hofmann and Siegbert Uhlig, *Novum Testamentum Aethiopice: die katholischen Briefe*, AF 29 (Stuttgart: Franz Steiner Verlag, 1993).
f. Ff. 142r–143v: James. See Josef Hofmann and Siegbert Uhlig, *Novum Testamentum Aethiopice: die katholischen Briefe*, AF 29 (Stuttgart: Franz Steiner Verlag, 1993).
g. Ff. 143v–144r: Jude. See Josef Hofmann and Siegbert Uhlig, *Novum Testamentum Aethiopice: die katholischen Briefe*, AF 29 (Stuttgart: Franz Steiner Verlag, 1993).
h. Ff. 144v–152r: Revelation. See Josef Hoffmann. *Die äthiopische Übersetzung der Johannes-Apokalypse*, CSCO 281 (Louvain, 1967).

Notes:
1. Ff. i rv, ii v(erso), 33v, 98rv, 136rv and 152v–153v: blank.
2. F. 152r, column 1: Colophon book was copied by the order of Ḫaylä Śəllase I, King of Kings of Ethiopia, son of the blessed, his highness Ras Makonnen, his baptismal name is Wäldä Amlak. May God write his name in the Book of Life. May the blessing of David dwell upon him and upon our Empress Mänän. Her baptismal name is Wälätä Giyorgis, his wife, servant of God, with his chosen children and his family. This book was written in 1927 E. C. when our Archbishop was *Abba* Qerəlos, with the blessed bishops of Ethiopia, *Abba* Abraham, *Abba* Peṭros, *Abba* Mikaʻel, *Abba* Isaac, with our teacher *Əčäge* Gäbrä Giyorgis who sits on the throne Täklä Haymanotä. The one who commissioned is the Minister of Pen, Ḫayle. The Old Testament was translated from the Gəʻəz tongue into the Amharic tongue by Mälə'akä Gänät Kəfle, Mälə'akä Bərhan Ṣəge, Mäməhər Täkle of Mänagäša Maryam, *Aläqa* Bəluy Täkle [i.e., *Aläqa* Täkle of the Old Testament] of Gondar, *Aläqa* Tamänä of Amhara Sayənt of Gondar, *Aläqa*; Beluy Takle. And for the New Testament books, it was translated by *Nəburä əd* Täkle [i.e., Hadis Täkle], *Aläqa* Ḫəruy of Gondar, *Aläqa* Lamma of Mäkanä Śəlasse, and *Aläqa* Qäṣäla of Əntoto Maryam. The name of the scribes are: Yäšäwawärq of Aratä Maryam, Wändəmagäñähu of Sälale, Śahəle of Bulga, Habtä Maryam of Däbrä Libanos, Täsäma of Bulga, Täkle Ṣadəq of Däbrä Libanos, Habtä Mikʻael of Sälale, Ləsanä Wärq of Däbrä Libanos,

Wäldä Maryam of Däbrä Libanos, Abäbä of G^woha Ṣəyon. Glory to God who led us up to this time and to his Mother, virgin and holy Mary. Let his mercy and forgiveness be upon us.

3. F. 152r, column 2: Notice of Royal Commission to publish and distribute this work and give the profits to Betä Säyda hospital. The original manuscript is given to the memorial house [probably, church or traditional school] of my father [i.e., Ras Makonnen].
4. F. 152r: two examples of the large seal of Ḥaylä Śəllase:
"Conquering Lion of the Tribe of Judah, Ḥaylä Śəllase I, King of Kings of Ethiopia."
5. F. 152r: two examples of the smaller seal of the Minister of Pen: Ḥayle Wäldä Rufe.
6. F. ii r(ecto): title page.
7. Decorative designs: ff. 1r, 2v, 6v, 11v, 13r, 15v, 18r, 20v, 28v, 29v, 31v, 34r, 48r, 56v, 71v, 83r, 99v, 105v, 112r, 116v, 120v, 122v, 123v, 125r, 126r, 127v, 129r, 130r, 137r (ḥaräg); ff. 2v, 34r, 37r, 45r, 68r, 105v, 118v, 135v, 151v, 152r (line of full stops).

MYS 4 – EMIP 604
Printed Reproduction of the Ḥaylä Śəllase Bible, in Amharic and Gə,əz, volume 3, Apocrypha, መጽሐፍ፡ ቅዱስ፡ (በግዕዝና፡ በአማርኛ፡ የተጻፈ፡) ፫ኛ፡ ክፍል፡, a gift from Emperor Ḥaylä Śəllase

Paper, 410 x 285 x 33 mm, printed reproduction, covered with double pouch linen cloth in white with small pink and blue flowers, iii + 147 folios, ff. 1r–145r four columns, 66 lines, Gə_əz and Amharic, twentieth century.

Major Works:
Holy Bible, written in Gə_əz and Amharic, Part 2, መጽሐፍ፡ ቅዱስ፡ (በግዕዝና፡ በአማርኛ፡ የተጻፈ፡) ፫ኛ፡ ክፍል፡,

1. Ff.1r–28v: Book of Jubilees, August Dillmann, መጽሐፈ ፡ ኩፋሌ ፡ *sive Liber Jubilaeorum, qui idem a Graecis Η ΛΕΡΤΗ ΓΕΝΕΣΙΣ inscribitur versione Graeca deperdita nunc nonnisi in Geez lingua conservatus nuper ex Abyssinia in Europam allatus* (Kiel and London, 1859); James C. VanderKam, *The Book of Jubilees, Text and Translation*, CSCO 87 and 88 (Louvain, 1989).
2. Ff. 29r–44v: Book of I Maccabees, መጽሐፈ፡ መቃብያን፡ ቀዳማዊ፡.
3. Ff. 44v–53r: Book of II Maccabees, መጽሐፈ፡ መቃብያን፡ ካልዕ፡.
4. Ff. 53r–57r: Book of III Maccabees, መጽሐፈ፡ መቃብያን፡ ሣልሱ፡.
5. Ff. 57v–80v: Book of Enoch, መጽሐፈ፡ ሄኖክ፡. August Dillmann, *Liber Henoch, Aethiopice* (Leipzig, 1851); R. H. Charles, *The Ethiopic*

Version of the Book of Enoch (Oxford: Clarendon, 1906); Johannes Paul Gotthilf Flemming, *Das Buch Henoch: Äthiopischer Text* (Leipzig, 1901); Michael Knibb, *The Ethiopic Book of Enoch: A New Edition in the Light of the Aramaic Ded Sea Fragment, 1: Text and Apparatus*; *2: Introduction, Translation and Commentary.* (Oxford, Clarendon, 1978 and 1979).

6. Ff. 81r–91v: Book of Ezra (Sutuʻel), መጽሐፈ፡ እዝራ፡ ሱቱኤል፡. August Dillmann, *BVTA, Tomus Quintus, quo continentur Libri Apocryphi, Baruch, Epistola Jeremiae, Tobith, Judith, Ecclesiasticus, Sapientia, Esdrae Apocalypsis, Esdrae Graecus* (Berlin, 1894).

7. Ff. 92r–99v: Book of Second Ezra, መጽሐፈ፡ እዝራ፡ ካልዕ፡. August Dillmann, *BVTA, Tomus Quintus, quo continentur Libri Apocryphi, Baruch, Epistola Jeremiae, Tobith, Judith, Ecclesiasticus, Sapientia, Esdrae Apocalypsis, Esdrae Graecus* (Berlin, 1894).

8. Ff. 100r–103v: Book of Tobit, መጽሐፈ፡ ጦቢት፡. August Dillmann, *BVTA, Tomus Quintus, quo continentur Libri Apocryphi, Baruch, Epistola Jeremiae, Tobith, Judith, Ecclesiasticus, Sapientia, Esdrae Apocalypsis, Esdrae Graecus* (Berlin, 1894).

9. Ff. 103v–110r: Book of Judith, መጽሐፈ፡ ዮዲት፡. August Dillmann, *BVTA, Tomus Quintus, quo continentur Libri Apocryphi, Baruch, Epistola Jeremiae, Tobith, Judith, Ecclesiasticus, Sapientia, Esdrae Apocalypsis, Esdrae Graecus* (Berlin, 1894).

10. Ff. 110v–118v: Book of Wisdom of Solomon, መጽሐፈ፡ ጥበበ፡ ሰሎሞን፡. August Dillmann, *BVTA, Tomus Quintus, quo continentur Libri Apocryphi, Baruch, Epistola Jeremiae, Tobith, Judith, Ecclesiasticus, Sapientia, Esdrae Apocalypsis, Esdrae Graecus* (Berlin, 1894).

11. Ff. 119r–137r: Book of Ecclesiaticus, መጽሐፈ፡ ሲራክ፡. August Dillmann, *BVTA, Tomus Quintus, quo continentur Libri Apocryphi, Baruch, Epistola Jeremiae, Tobith, Judith, Ecclesiasticus, Sapientia, Esdrae Apocalypsis, Esdrae Graecus* (Berlin, 1894).

12. Ff. 137v–138v: Book of (4) Baruch, መጽሐፈ፡ ባሮክ፡. August Dillmann, "Liber Baruch," *CA* 1–15 (cf. Enno Littmann's corrigenda in the 1967 reprint of Dillmann's book).

13. Ff. 139rv: Letter of Jeremiah to the Captives in Babylon, ተረፈ፡ ኤርምያስ፡. (also, አርአያ መጽሐፍ ዘኤርምያስ.)

14. Ff. 139v–143r: Prolegomenon of Baruch, ተረፈ፡ ባሮክ፡ (ትንቢተ፡ ኤርምያስ፡).

15. Ff. 143v–144r: Book of Susanna, መጽሐፈ፡ ሶስና፡.

16. Ff. 144v–145r: Book of Paraleipomenon of Daniel (Bel and the Dragon), ተረፈ፡ ዳንኤል፡.

Notes:
1. Ff. i rv and 146r–147r: blank.
2. F. ii r(ecto): title page. Holy Scripture, written in Geʻez and Amharic, Third part
3. F. ii v(erso): Translated by Ethiopian church scholars from Geʻez into Amharic.
4. F. iii r(ecto): Table of Contents for Three Volumes; the Table of Contents for volume four, the New Testament, is on f. iii v(erso).
5. F. iii v(erso): in blue ink, top of page: ―This book belongs to Agafari Täkläyäs Wolde Mikaʻel, given to him from Emperor Ḫaylä Śəllase to be a memorial for the era of exile, in 1929 (EC =1936/7) when we are in a foreign land."
ዝንቱ ፡ መጽሐፍ፡ ዘአጋፋሪ ፡ ተክለየስ ፡ ወልደ ፡ ሚካኤል ፡ ዘተውሕበ ፡ ሎቱ ፡ እምቀዳማዊ ፡ ኃይለ ፡ ሥላሴ ፡ ንጉሡ ፡ ነገሥት ፡ ከመ ፡ ይኩን ፡ ለዝክረ ፡ ነገር ፡ በመዋዕለ ፡ ስደት ፡ አመ ፡ ፩ሺ፱፻፳፱ ፡ ዓመት ፡ እንዘ ፡ ሀሎነ ፡ ውስተ ፡ ብሔረ ፡ ባዕድ ፡
In blue ink at bottom of page: ―*Ato* Ḫəruy Ṭəbäbu bought this book with his money on 19 Mäskäräm 1969 (EC)."
6. F. 145v: in blue ink, ―[This is the] ninth [copy of the published book]; Agafari Täkläyäs was given this book." ―This book belongs to *Ato* Ḫəruy Ṭəbäbu who bought it with his money from a woman named *Wayzero* Azänäč Aba Šawəl, wife of Agafari Täkläyäs in 1969 (EC)."
7. Decorative designs: ff. ii r(ecto), 1r, 29r, 57v, 81r, 92r, 100r, 103v, 110v, 119r, 137v, 139r, 143v, 144v (*ḥarägs* in black ink); multiple full stops are often used as section dividers.

MYS 5 – EMIP 605
Fifty-Eight Miracles of Jesus, ተአምረ፡ ኢየሱስ፡

Parchment, 295 x 220 x 65 mm, four Coptic chain stitches attached with bridle attachments to rough-hewn boards of the traditional wood, covered with tooled leather, headband and tailband, protection sheet + 13 full quires, ii + 96 folios, top margin 30 mm, bottom margin 57 mm, fore edge margin 30 mm, gutter margin 15 mm, ff. 1r–95v two columns, 24 lines, Gə_əz, twentieth century.

Quire descriptions: protection sheet and quires 1–8 and 10–12 balanced; quires 9 and 13 adjusted balanced.

Major Works:
1. Ff. 1r–95v: Fifty-Eight Miracles of Jesus, *Tä'ammərä Iyyäsus*, ተአምረ፡ ኢየሱስ፡ . S. Grébaut, *Les Miracles de Jésus, texte éthiopien publié et traduit par S. Grébaut*, PO 60 (Paris: Firmin-Didot, 1919). See also Strelcyn, *BL* entry 16 [OR. 8824]. Prefatory matter: በስመ ፡ አብ ፡ ወወልድ ፡ . . . ዝንቱ ፡ ምሥጢር ፡ አምላካዊ ፡ ዘነገር ፡ እግዚእን ፡ ወአምላክን ፡ ወመድኃኒን ፡ ኢየሱስ ፡ ክርስቶስ ፡ ለረድኡ ፡ ዮሐንስ ፡ ወልደ ፡ ዘብዴዎስ ፡ እምቅድመ ፡ ዕርገቱ ፡ ለእግዚእን ፡ ኢየሱስ ፡ ክርስቶስ ፡ ውስተ ፡ ሰማይ ፡ . . .

Miniatures:
1. F. ii v(erso): The Crucifixion.

Notes:
1. Ff. i r(ecto)-ii r(ecto) and 96rv: blank.
2. Decorative designs: f. 95v (multiple full stops).
3. The words Mary and Jesus are rubricated.
4. Numbered quires: quires 2–12.
5. Scribal intervention: words of text are written interlinearly (f. 68v); text has been removed (e.g., ff. 10r, 26v, 37v).
6. F. 9r, col. 1, line 18: lines have been drawn above and below to indicate its erasure in order to correct repeated text.

Quire Map

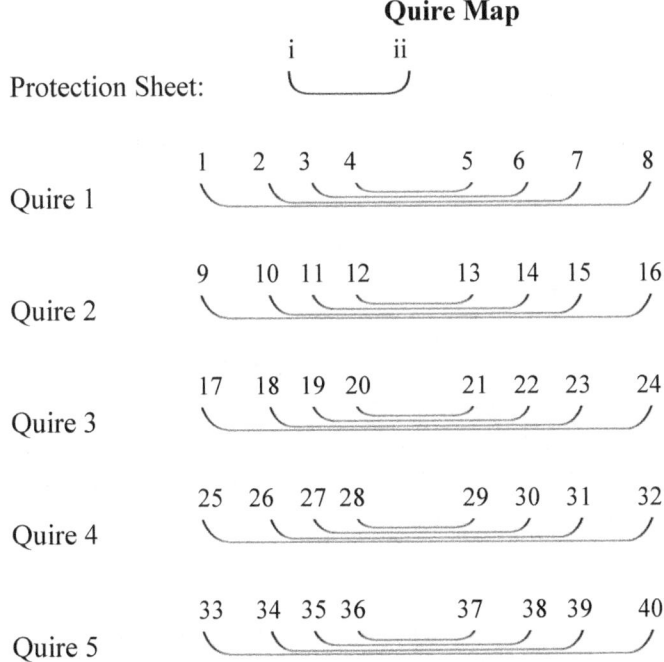

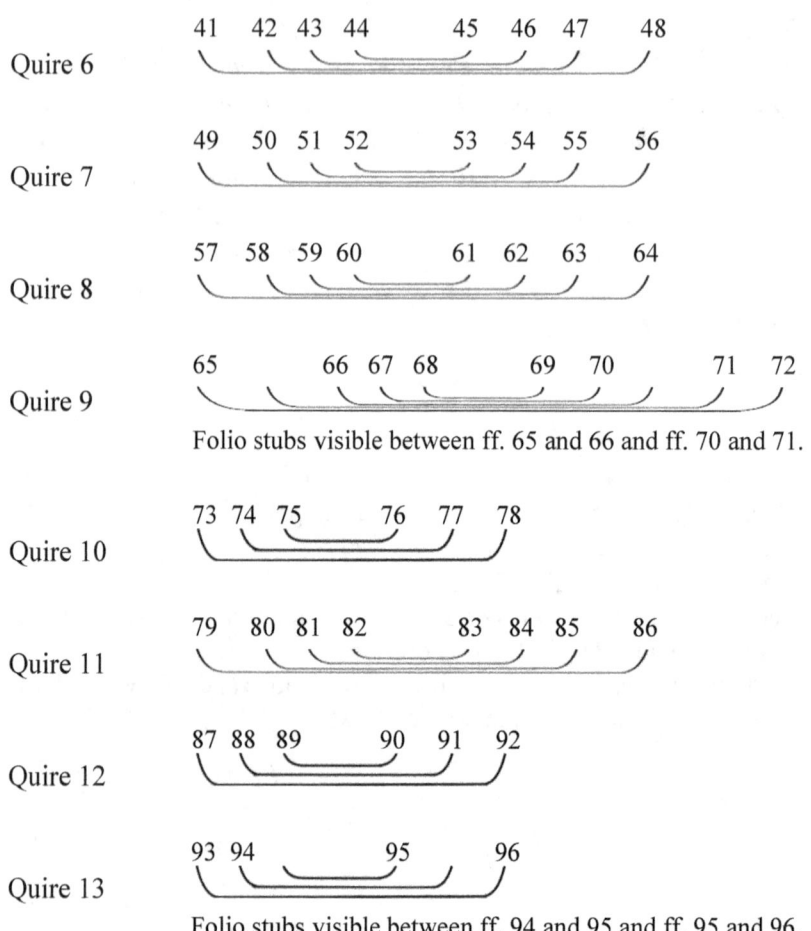

Folio stubs visible between ff. 65 and 66 and ff. 70 and 71.

Folio stubs visible between ff. 94 and 95 and ff. 95 and 96.

MYS 6 – EMIP 606

Images of Mary, መልክአ፡ ማርያም፡, Michael, መልክአ፡ ሚካኤል፡, Gabriel, መልክአ፡ ገብርኤል፡, and Saint George, መልክአ፡ ጊዮርጊስ፡, Hymn to Saint George, "O, who is quick for help," አ፡ ፍጡነ፡ ረድኤት፡

Parchment, 117 x 82 x 47 mm, four Coptic chain stitches attached with bridle attachments to rough-hewn boards of the traditional wood, covered with tooled leather, headband and tailband, protection quire + 10 full quires, iv + 121 folios, top margin 13 mm, bottom margin 31 mm, fore edge margin 11 mm, gutter margin 7 mm, ff. 1r–120v one column, 10 lines, Gəʿəz, twentieth century.

Quire descriptions: protection quire and quires 1–2, 4–6 and 8–10 balanced; quires 3 and 7 adjusted balanced.

Major Works:
1. Ff. 1r–38v: Image of Mary, መልክአ፡ ማርያም፡. Chaîne, *Répertoire* 220; *MG59* 735ff.
   ሰላም ፡ ሰላም ፡ ለዝክረ ፡ ስምኪ ፡ ሐዋዝ ፡
   እምነ ፡ ከልበኔ ፡ ወቁስጥ ፡ ወእምነ ፡ ስንበልት ፡ ምዑዝ ፡
   ማርያም ፡ ድንግል ፡ ለባሲተ ፡ ዐቢይ ፡ ትእዛዝ ፡
   ይስቀየኒ ፡ ለእለ ፡ ጸባሑ ፡ ወይነ ፡ ፍቅርኪ ፡ አዚዝ ፡
   ከመ ፡ ይስቅዮ ፡ ውኒዝ ፡ ለሡናይ ፡ አርዝ ፡
2. Ff. 39r–66v: Image of Michael, *Mälk_a Mika'el*, መልክአ፡ ሚካኤል፡. Chaîne, *Répertoire* 119; *MG59* 290ff. EMIP 16, f. 92v; EMIP 56, f. 1r, beginning:
   በሰመ ፡ እግዚአብሔር ፡ አብ ፡ እምቅድመ ፡ ዓለማት ፡ ሰፋኔ ፡
   በሰመ ፡ እግዚአብሔር ፡ ወልድ ፡ ሥጋ ፡ ማርያም ፡ ተከዳኔ ፡
   በሰመ ፡ እግዚአብሔር ፡ መንፈስ ፡ ቅዳስ ፡ ዘይሥእር ፡ ግብረ ፡ ግማኔ ፡
   አሰመ ፡ ወጠንኩ ፡ ውዳሴከ ፡ ማእከለ ፡ ሐዳስ ፡ ኩርንኔ ፡
   ቤዘወኒ ፡ ሚካኤል ፡ እምሲኦል ፡ ወኮንኔ ፡
   ሰላም ፡ ለዝክረ ፡ ስምከ ፡ ምስለ ፡ ስመ ፡ ልዑል ፡ ዘተሳተፈ ፡ ...
3. Ff. 67r–85v: Image of Gabriel, መልክአ ገብርኤል፡. Chaîne, *Répertoire* 246; *MG59* 312ff.; EMIP 56, f. 63r.
   በሰላመ ፡ ገብርኤል ፡ መልዓክ ፡ በሳስ ፡ ማርያም ፡ ዘአዝለፈ ፡
   ከመ ፡ እዜኑ ፡ ሕዳጠ ፡ ወአኮ ፡ ትሩፈ ፡
   እግዚአብሔር ፡ ጎበኒ ፡ ሲሳየ ፡ ልቡና ፡ መጽሐፈ ፡
   ወአፉየ ፡ ሙሴ ፡ ለእመ ፡ ኮነ ፡ ጸያፈ ፡
   ጸራቅሊጦስ ፡ አርን ፡ ይኩንኒ ፡ ክንፈ ፡
   ሰላም ፡ ለተፈጥሮትከ ፡ በሌሊተ ፡ እሁድ ፡ ዘቀዳሚ ፡ ...
4. Ff. 86r–117v: Image of Saint George, *Mälk_a Giyorgis* [zä-Säleda Mogäs], መልክአ፡ ጊዮርጊስ፡. Chaîne, *Répertoire* 147.
   ሰላም ፡ ለዝክረ ፡ ስምከ ፡ በሰሌዳ ፡ ሞገስ ፡ መጽሐፉ ፡
   ዘያሜኒ ፡ ኩሎ ፡ ወዘያስተሴፉ ፡
   ጥዑመ ፡ ዜና ፡ ጊዮርጊስ ፡ ለሐሊበ ፡ እጕልት ፡ ሱታፉ ፡
   ሰላምከ ፡ ወረድኤትከ ፡ በሳዕሌየ ፡ ያእርፉ ፡
   አኮ ፡ ለምእር ፡ ዳእሙ ፡ ለዝላፉ ፡
5. Ff. 117v–120v: Hymn to Saint George, –Ө, who is quick for help," ኦ፡ ፍጡን፡ ረድኤት፡, EMML 1214, f. 38a. Cf. Chaîne, *Répertoire* 380.
   ኦ ፡ ፍጡን ፡ ረድኤት ፡ ለጽኑእ ፡ ወለድኩም ፡
   ወለነፍስ ፡ ኩሉ ፡ ቃውም ፡
   ጊዮርጊስ ፡ የዋሕ ፡ እንበለ ፡ መስፈርት ፡ ወአቅም ፡
   ከመ ፡ እግዝእትክ ፡ ቡርክት ፡ ማርያም ፡
   ርኁን ፡ ልብ ፡ አንተ ፡ እምበቀል ፡ ወቂም ፡

Notes:
1. F. i r(ecto): pen trial.
2. Ff. i v(erso)-iv v(erso): blank.
3. F. 121r: pen trial.
4. F. 121v: pen trial. Wäldä Ṣadəq. Upside down at the bottom of the folio is written "–$120,–"
5. Decorative designs: ff. 1r, 39r, 67r, 86r (colorful ḥaräg).
6. The words Mary, Michael, Gabriel and George are rubricated.
7. Scribal intervention: text has been removed (e.g., ff. 3v, 64v).
8. Ff. 36r, lines 3–5; 57r, line 4: text has been crossed out to correct repeated text.

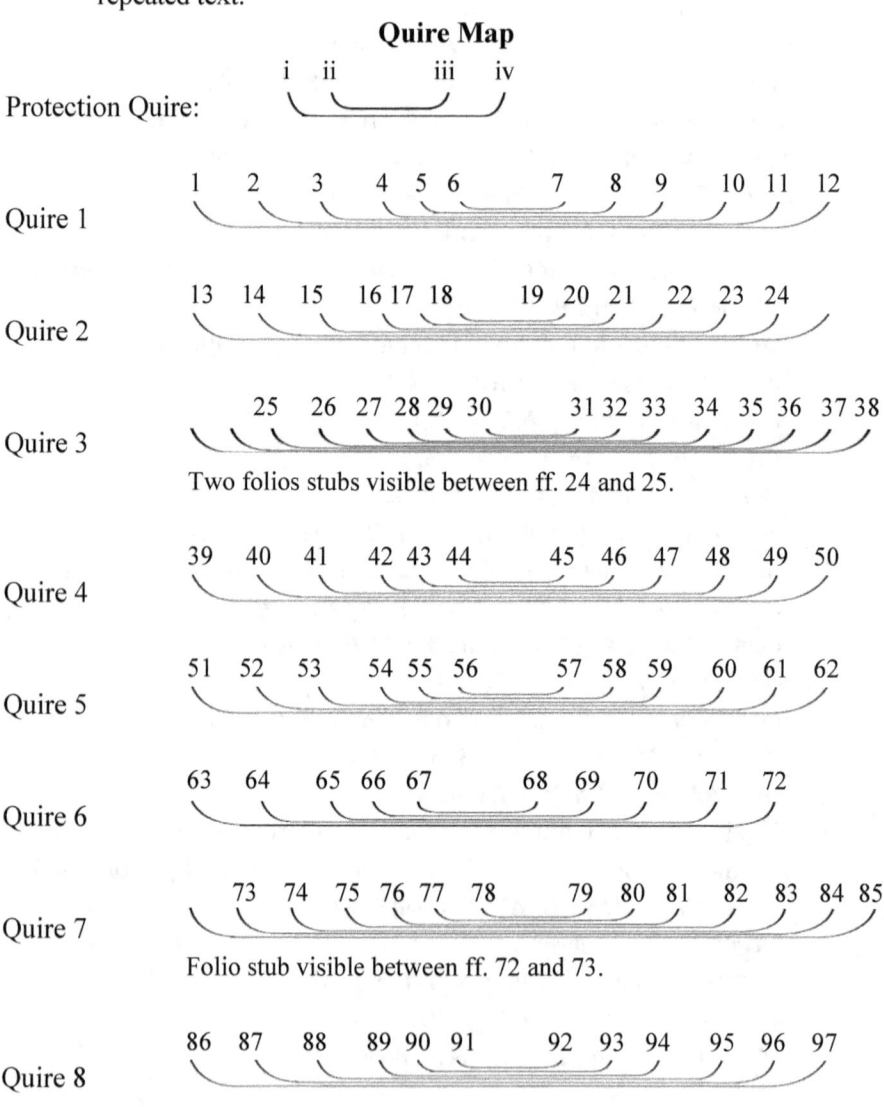

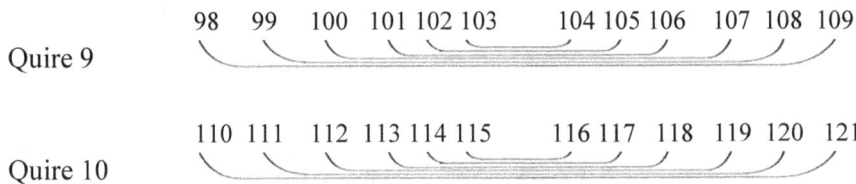

MYS 7 – EMIP 607
Canticle of the Flower, ማሕሌተ፡ ጽጌ፡

Parchment, 112 x 82 x 32 mm, four Coptic chain stitches attached with bridle attachments to rough-hewn boards of the traditional wood, covered with a double-pouch, plain linen cover, protection sheet + 9 full quires, i + 85 folios, top margin 13 mm, bottom margin 22 mm, fore edge margin 9 mm, gutter margin 4 mm, ff. 1r–83v one column, 10 lines, Gə_əz, twentieth century. Double-slip *maḥdär*.

Quire descriptions: quires 2, 4–6 and 8–9 balanced; protection sheet and quires 3 and 7 adjusted balanced; quire 1 unbalanced. Navigation system: pink yarn is sewn into the fore edge of ff. 12, 25 and 37 to mark content; purple yarn is sewn into the fore edge of ff. 63 and 73 to mark content.

Major Works:
1. Ff. 2r–83v: Canticle of the Flower, *Maḥletä Ṣəge*, ማሕሌተ፡ ጽጌ፡, Grohmann, *Marienhymnen* (ff. 4r–5v are written in a different hand on an inserted leaf), arranged for the days of the week, Monday (2r), Tuesday (12v), Wednesday (25r), Thursday (37r), Friday (50v), Saturday (63r), Sunday (73r). In each case a piece of thread has been sewn into the upper fore edge.

   ጽጌ ፡ አስተርአየ ፡ ሡሪፃ ፡ እም ፡ አዕሙ ፡
   ለዘአምታኪ ፡ ጽጌ ፡ ለገብርኤል ፡ ምስለ ፡ ሰላሙ ፡
   ወበእንተዝ ፡ ማርያም ፡ ሰበ ፡ ጋወዘኒ ፡ መዓዛ ፡ ጣዕሙ ፡
   ለተአምርኪ. ፡ ጽጌ ፡ አሃሊ. ፡ እሙ ፡
   ማኅሌተ ፡ ጽጌ ፡ ዘይሰመይ ፡ ሰሙ ፡

Miniatures:
1. F. 85v: crude drawing of a figure, in pencil.

Varia:
1. Ff. irv: Calendar of the Weevily and Unweevily Months.
2. Ff. 1rv: Excerpt from Canticle of the Flower.

Notes:
1. Ff. irv: ―Theon Mäskäräm 15 it will be weevily"

2. F. 1v: remnant of a seal is visible.
3. F. 83v: later owner's name (in blue ink) Wäldä Sändät Däsəta.
4. F. 84r: blank
5. F. 84v: pen trial
6. F. 85r: Trinitarian formula
7. Decorative designs: f. 2r (ornate *ḥaräg* in black ink); ff. 12v, 25r, 37r and 50v (line of red dots); ff. 1v and 83v (multiple full stops).
8. The word Mary is rubricated.
9. Scribal intervention: words of text are written interlinearly (ff. 4r, 5v, 8r, 18v, 20v, etc.); and lines of text are written interlinearly (ff. 54v, 83v).

Quire Map

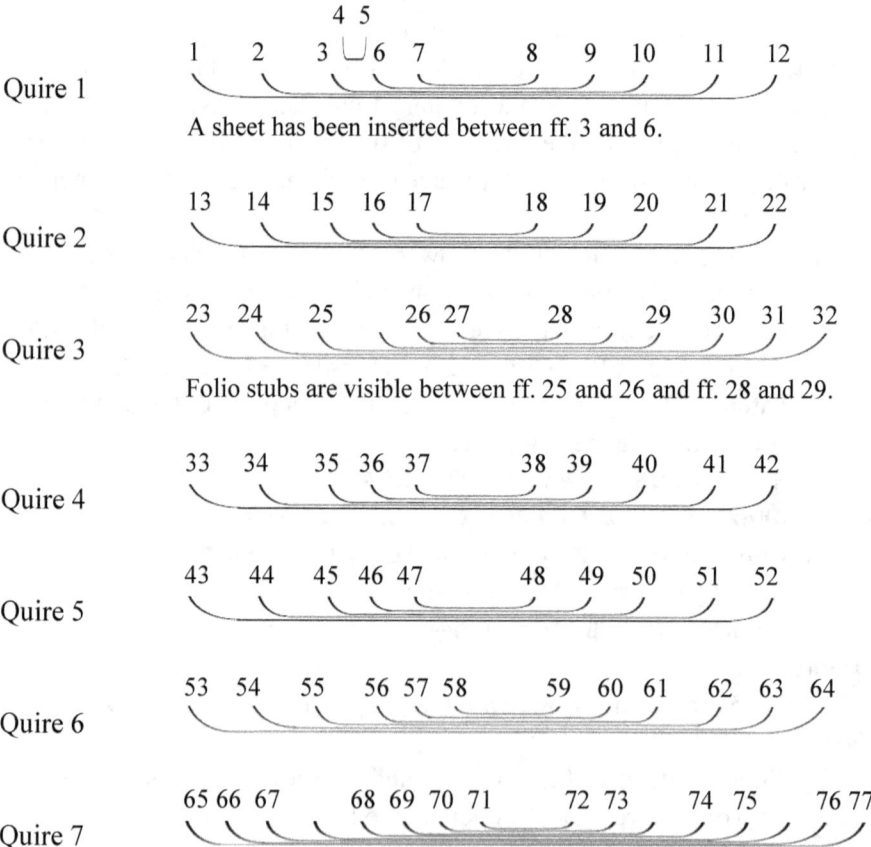

Folio stubs are visible between ff. 67 and 68, ff. 73 and 74 and ff. 75 and 76

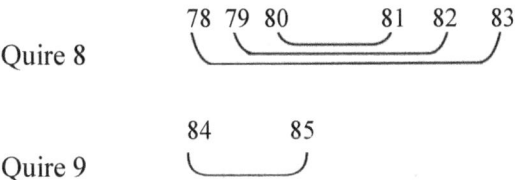

Quire 8

Quire 9

MYS 8 – EMIP 608
Yä-Aba Jale Ziq Chants, የአባ፡ ጃሌ፡ ዚቅ፡

Parchment, 168 x 120 x 65 mm, four Coptic chain stitches attached with bridle attachments to rough-hewn boards of the traditional wood, protection quire + 15 full quires, iv + 125 folios, top margin 17–20 mm, bottom margin 30 mm, fore edge margin 10–14 mm, gutter margin 8 mm, ff. 1r–122r two columns, 22–23 lines, Gəʿəz, twentieth century. Double-slip *maḥdär*.

Quire descriptions: protection quire and quires 1–4 and 7–14 balanced; quires 5–6 and 15 adjusted balanced. Navigation system: marginal notation throughout, some of which may be overlooked text.

Major Works:
1. Ff. 1r–122r: Yä-Aba Jale Ziq Chants, የአባ፡ ጃሌ፡ ዚቅ፡, see, *AṢZ* 249–373.
    በስመ ፡ አብ ፡ ወወልድ ፡ . . . እዌጥን ፡ በረድኤተ ፡ እግዚአብሔር ፡ ጸሐፊ ፡ ዚቅ ፡ እምዮሐንስ ፡ አስከ ፡ ዮሐንስ ፡ ዋዜማ ፡ ዚቅ ፡ አሰመ ፡ ለዓለም ፡ አቡን ፡ ዓራራይ ፡ ምስለ ፡ ሰላም ፡ ወኩሉ ፡ ድሙር ፡ ዘአስተጋብእም ፡ ሊቃውንተ ፡ ጎንደር ፡ ጐራያን ፡ ዘምስለ ፡ መምህራን ፡ ጥዑማን ፡ ልሳን ፡ ወአፍ ፡ ዘሸዋ ፡ ወዘጎንደር ፡ ዘትግሬ ፡ ወዘጎጃም ፡ ሥኩራን ፡ በመንፈስ ፡ ቅዱስ ፡ መኃትዊ ፡ ለቤተ ፡ ክርስቲያን ፡ ሥርጉት ፡ . . . በጴ ፡ ብዑዕ ፡ አንተ ፡ ዮሐንስ ፡ ዘሀለወክ ፡ ታእምር ፡ ወተሐውር ፡ ቅድመ ፡ እግዚአብሔር ፡ ጸሊ ፡ በእንቲአነ ፡ ውስተ ፡ ርእስ ፡ አውደ ፡ ዓመት ፡ ተጸሕፈ ፡ ተዘካርከ ፡ ባርከኒ ፡ እንሣዕ ፡ በረከተከ ፡ . . .

Notes:
1. F. iii r(ecto): a piece of paper that indicates that this work is Yä-Aba Jale Ziq Chants.
2. Ff. i r(ecto)-iv v(erso) and 122v–125v: blank.
3. At various points in the manuscript, the writer indicates instructions for the ziq and often identifies the source of the tradition for that particular chant. Gojjam, Gondar, Tigray and Shewa are mentioned.

E.g., f. 1r identifies the order of the following Ziq as from Gojjam. Then, in folio 40r the writer identifies the source of the following festival ziq order as from Gondar.

4. Decorative designs: lines of alternating red and black dots are used as section dividers, often with geometric patterns connected to the lines (e.g., ff. 1v, 2rv).
5. The word Mary is rubricated.
6. Scribal intervention: words of text are written interlinearly (ff. 3v, 7v, 17r, 22r, 48r, etc.); and lines of text are written interlinearly (ff. 17v, 24r, 25r, 65v, 71v, etc.); and in the upper margin with a symbol (⊥) marking the location where the text is to be inserted (ff. 5v, col. 1, line 8; 8v, col. 1, line 13; 29r, col. 1, line 11; 68r, col. 1, line 2; 74v, col. 1, line 4; 75v, col. 1, line 10), or in the bottom margin (f. 11v, col. 2, line 20); erasure markings are visible (ff. 69r, 70v, 90v, 101v, 112r); text has been removed (e.g., ff. 15v, 19v).

Quire Map

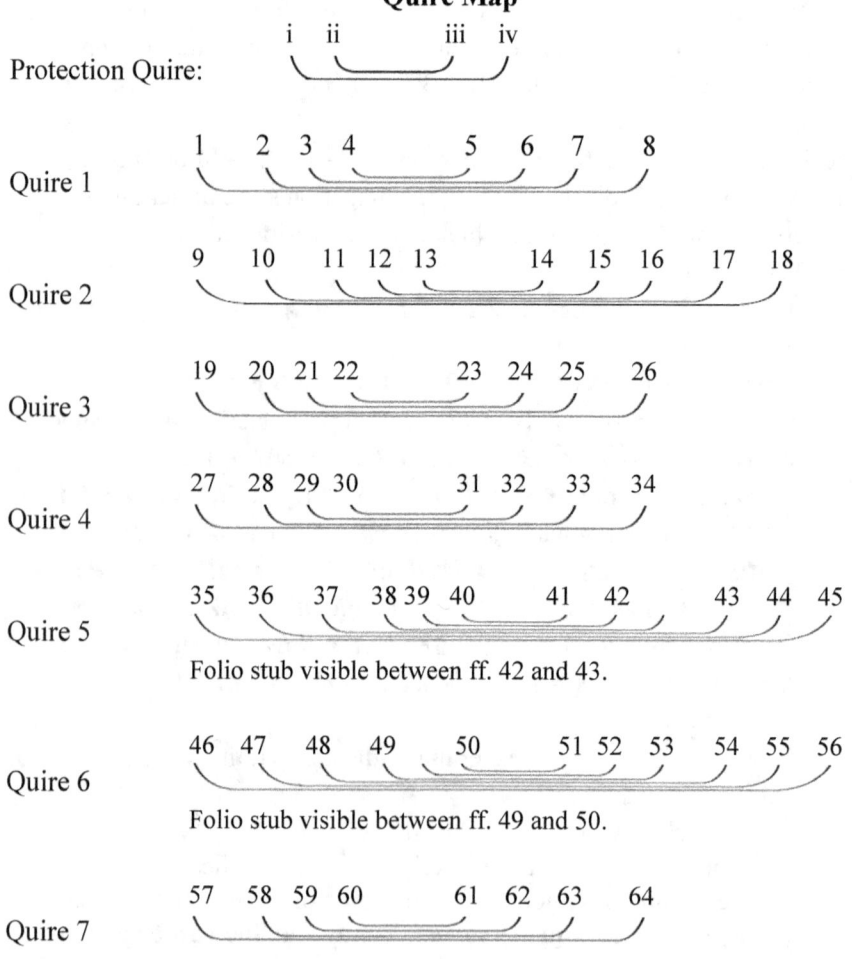

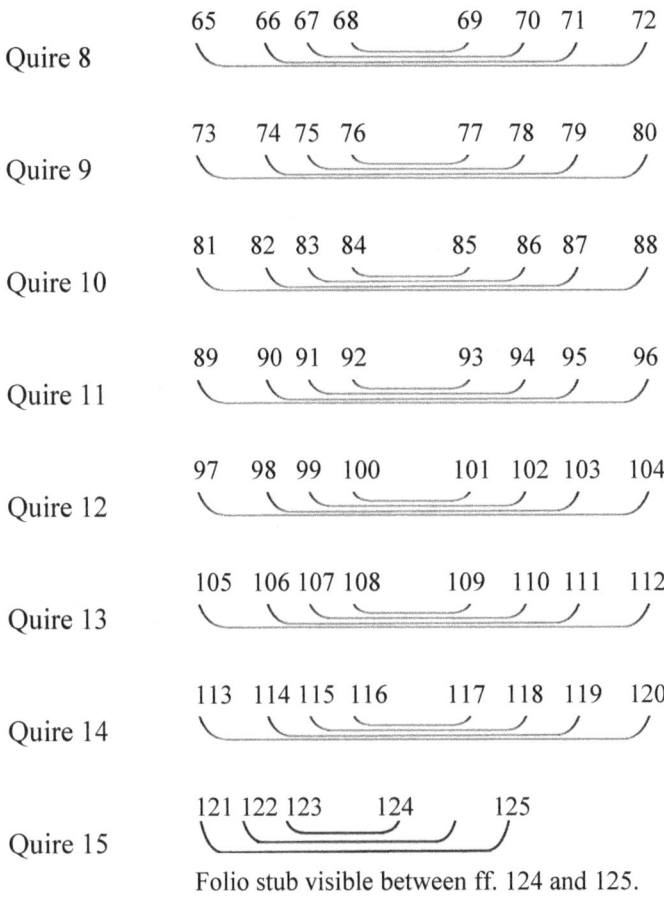

Folio stub visible between ff. 124 and 125.

MYS 9 – EMIP 609
Ziq Chants, መጽሐፈ፡ ዚቅ፡

Parchment, 170 x 133 x 52 mm, two Coptic chain stitches attached with bridle attachments to rough-hewn boards of the traditional wood, protection sheet + 12 full quires, ii + 112 folios, top margin 18–20 mm, bottom margin 35 mm, fore edge margin 15 mm, gutter margin 10 mm, ff. 1r–110v two columns, 22 lines, Gə‗əz, twentieth century.

Quire descriptions: protection sheet and quires 1, 4–9 and 12 balanced; quires 2–3 and 10–11 adjusted balanced. Navigation system: marginal notation throughout, some of which may be overlooked text.

Major Works:
1. Ff. 1r–110v. Ziq Chants, መጽሐፈ፡ ዚቅ፡. See *AṢZ* 249–373. It begins:

በስመ ፡ አብ ፡ . . . ንቒጥን ፡ በረድኤተ ፡ እግዚአብሔር ፡ ጸሐፊ ፡ ዚቅ ፡
ዘአስተጋብዖ ፡ ሊቃውንተ ፡ ገንደር ፡ አምዮሐንስ ፡ አስከ ፡ ዮሐንስ ፡
ለዓለ ፡ ዓለም ፡ አሜን ። በጀ ፡ ብዐዕ ፡ አንተ ፡ ዮሐንስ ፡ ዘሀለወከ ፡
ታዕምር ፡ ወተሀውር ፡ ቅድመ ፡ እግዚአብሔር ፡ . . .

Notes:
1. F. i r(ecto): $115.
2. Ff. i v(erso)-ii v(erso) and 111r–112v: blank.
3. Decorative designs: lines of alternating red and black dots are used as section dividers (e.g., ff. 2v, 3v, 4r).
4. The word Mary is rubricated.
5. Numbered quires: quires 2–10.
6. Scribal intervention: words of text are written interlinearly (ff. 5r, 11r, 15r, 38v, 99r, etc.); and lines of text are written interlinearly (f. 40v); and in the upper margin with a symbol (⊥) marking the location where the text is to be inserted (ff. 6r, col. 1, line 8; 55r, col. 1, line 19; 86v, col. 2, line 11; 88v, col. 2, line 16), and in another case where the symbol (⊤) is used (ff. 77v, col. 1, line 1; 80v, col. 2, line 5), and in another case where the symbol (+) is used (f. 90v, col. 1, line 18); erasure markings are visible (ff. 69r, 74v); text has been removed (e.g., ff. 37v, 49r, 65r).

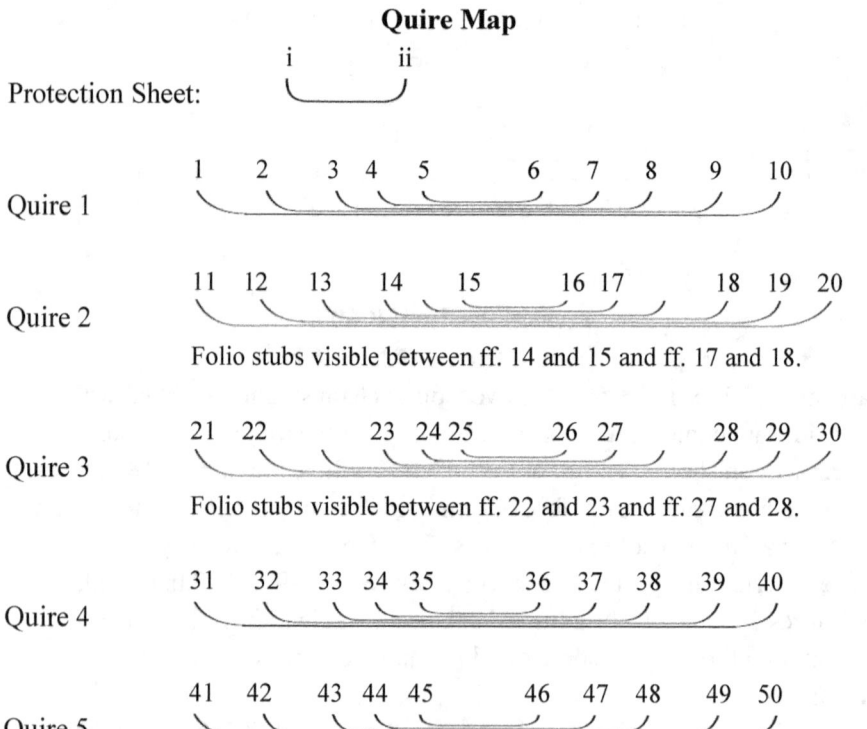

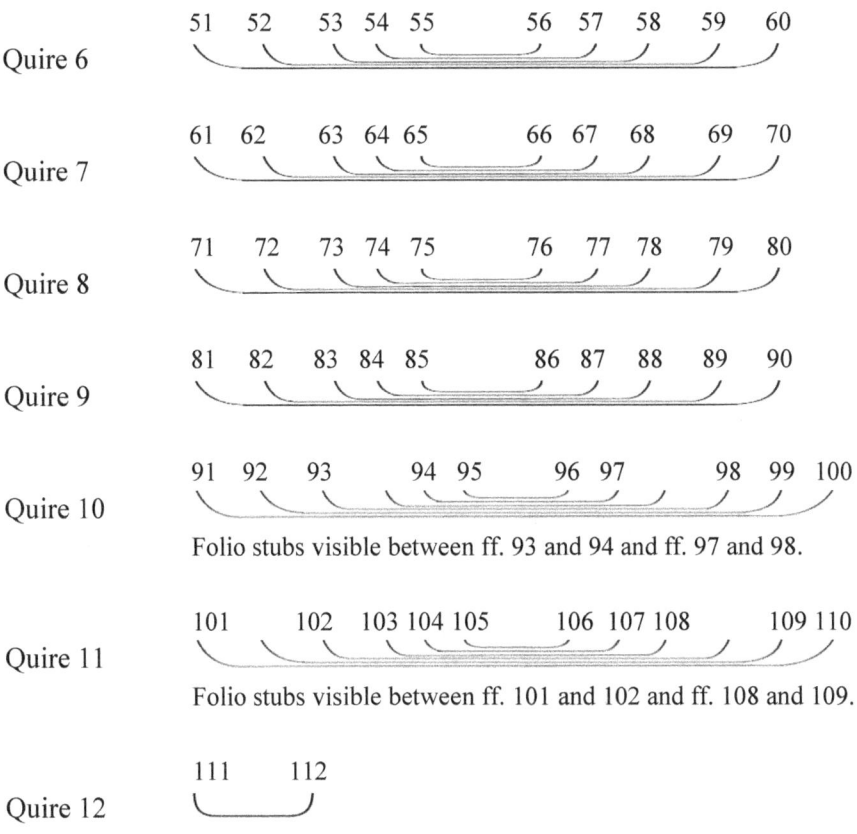

Folio stubs visible between ff. 93 and 94 and ff. 97 and 98.

Folio stubs visible between ff. 101 and 102 and ff. 108 and 109.

MYS 10 – EMIP 610
Ziq Chants, መጽሐፈ፣ ዚቅ፣

Parchment, 150 x 112 x 60 mm, four Coptic chain stitches attached with bridle attachments to rough-hewn boards of the traditional wood, protection sheet + 13 full quires, ii + 118 folios, top margin 15 mm, bottom margin 25 mm, fore edge margin 16 mm, gutter margin 6 mm, ff. 1r–116v two columns, 19 lines, Gə_əz, twentieth century.

Quire descriptions: protection sheet and quires 1–13 balanced. Navigation system: marginal notation throughout, some of which may be overlooked text.

Major Works:
1. Ff. 1r–116v: Ziq Chants, መጽሐፈ፣ ዚቅ. See *AṢZ* 249–373. It begins: በስመ ፣ አብ ፣ . . .ንዌጥን ፣ በረድኤተ ፣ እግዚአብሔር ፣ ጽሐፈ ፣ ዚቅ ፣ ዘአስተጋብዕዎ ፣ ሊቃውንተ ፣ ጐንደር ፣ አምዮሐንስ ፣ አስክ ፣ ዮሐንስ ፣

ወአንተኒ ፡ ሕጻን ፡ ነቢየ ፡ ልዑል ፡ ትሰመይ ፡ እስመ ፡ ተሐውር ፡ ቅድመ ፡ እግዚአብሔር ፡ከመ ፡ ትጼሕ ፡ ፍኖቶ ፡ . . .

Notes:
1. F. i r(ecto): "This book belongs to Mälakä Gänät Ṭərunäh." Cp. f. iii v(erso) and ff. 117r.
2. Ff. i v(erso)-ii v(erso) and 117r–118v: blank except for a few isolated words.
3. F. 1r mentions the scholars of Gondar.
4. Decorative designs: lines of black dots or of alternating red and black dots are used as section dividers (e.g., ff. 2r, 3r, 4rv).
5. The word Mary is rubricated.
6. Numbered quires: quires 2–3.
7. Scribal intervention: words of text are written interlinearly (ff. 4v, 16v, 19r, 28r, 29v, etc.); and lines of text are written interlinearly (ff. 18r, 40r, 78r, 85rv, etc.); and in the upper margin with a symbol (⊥) marking the location where the text is to be inserted (f. 27r, col. 1, line 11), and in another case where the symbol (⊤) is used (f. 89r, col. 1, line 6).

Quire Map

Protection Sheet: i ii

Quire 1: 1 2 3 4 5 6 7 8 9 10

Quire 2: 11 12 13 14 15 16 17 18 19 20

Quire 3: 21 22 23 24 25 26 27 28 29 30

Quire 4: 31 32 33 34 35 36 37 38 39 40

Quire 5: 41 42 43 44 45 46 47 48 49 50

Quire 6: 51 52 53 54 55 56 57 58 59 60

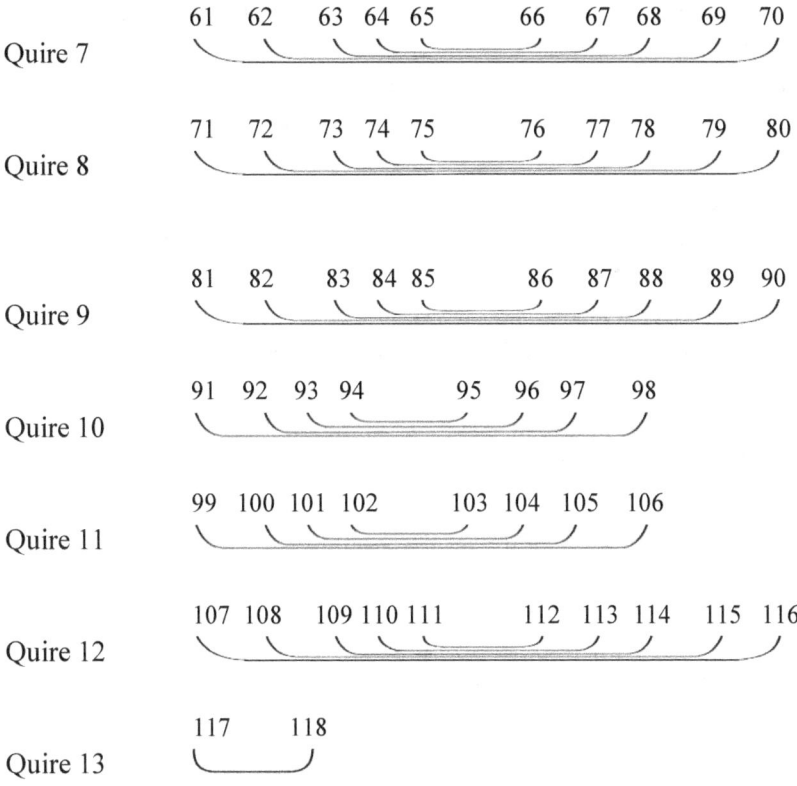

MYS 11 – EMIP 611
Homiliary in Honor of the Monthly Feast of the Archangel Michael, ድርሳነ፡ ሚካኤል፡, Asmat Prayer for the Archangel Michael, Images of Michael, መልክአ፡ ሚካኤል፡, and Gabriel, መልክአ ገብርኤል፡

Parchment, 220 x 151 x 54 mm, four Coptic chain stitches attached with bridle attachments to rough-hewn boards of the traditional wood, covered with tooled leather, headband and tailband, protection sheet + 14 full quires, ii + 133 folios, top margin 18 mm, bottom margin 37 mm, fore edge margin 21 mm, gutter margin 5 mm, ff. 1r–133r two columns, 20 lines, Gə_əz, early-twentieth century.

Quire descriptions: protection sheet and quires 1–3, 5–10 and 12–14 balanced; quires 4 and 11 adjusted balanced.

Major Works:
1. Ff. 1r–111r: Homiliary in Honor of the Archangel Michael, *Dərsanä Mika'el*, ድርሳነ፡ ሚካኤል፡. Published several times in Ethiopia; see

for example, *DM* 11–205. See also BL Or. 4849, Strelcyn *BL* 94–7; EMML 1133.

a. Ff. 1r–4r: Introductory homily. It begins:

በስመ ፡ አብ ፡ . . .ሰምዑ ፡ ሕዝበ ፡ ክርስቲያን ፡ ወነጽሩ ፡ አጋውየ ፡ ወፍቁራንየ ፡ ዕበዮ ፡ ወክብሮ ፡ ለሊቀ ፡ መላእክት ፡ ሚካኤል ፡ ለአለ ፡ ይስእልዎ ፡ በጻሕቅ ፡ ኅቤሁ ፡ በትውክልት ፡ ልብ ፡ ወበንጹሕ ፡ ሥጋ ፡ መፍትው ፡ ለነ ፡ ንግበር ፡ ተዝካር ፡ በኵሉ ፡ ጊዜ ፡ ከመ ፡ ይስአል ፡ ለነ ፡ ወይጼሊ ፡ በእንቲአነ ፡ . . .

b. Ff. 4v–16r: Ḫədar.
   (1) Ff. 4v–12v Homily by Dämatewos, bishop of Alexandria.
   (2) Ff. 12v–14r: Miracle.
   (3) Ff. 14r–16r: Synaxary Entry: Mission to Joshua, son of Nun.
   (4) F. 16r: Greeting to the Archangel, *Sälam*.

c. Ff. 16v–23r: Taḫśaś.
   (1) Ff. 16v–21v: Homily, author not given.
   (2) Ff. 21v–22v: Miracle.
   (3) Ff. 22v–23r: Synaxary Entry: Mission of the Archangel to rescue the three holy children.
   (4) F. 23r: Greeting to the Archangel, *Sälam*.

d. Ff. 23v–30v: Ṭərr
   (1) Ff. 23v–29v: Homily, author not given.
   (2) Ff. 29v–30v: Miracle.
   (3) F. 30v: Synaxary Entry: Mission of the Archanel to save Jacob from the wrath of Esau.
   (4) F. 30v: Greeting to the Archangel, *Sälam*.

e. Ff. 31r–35v: Yäkkatit.
   (1) Ff. 31r–34r: Homily, author not given.
   (2) Ff. 34r–35r: Miracle.
   (3) Ff. 35rv: Synaxary Entry: Mission of the Archangel to Samson, the giant.
   (4) F. 35v: Greeting to the Archangel, *Sälam*.

f. Ff. 36r–56v: Mäggabit.
   (1) Ff. 37r–53r: Homily by the archbishop of Antioch
   (2) Ff. 53r–56r: Miracle.
   (3) Ff. 56rv: Synaxary Entry: Mission of the Archangel to Balaam.
   (4) F. 56v: Greeting to the Archangel, *Sälam*.

g. Ff. 56v–65r: Miyazya.
   (1) Ff. 56v–63r: Homily, author not given.

(2) Ff. 63r–65r: Miracle.
(3) F. 65r: Synaxary entries: Mission of the Archangel to the Prophet Isaiah [sic].
(4) F. 65r: Greeting to the Archangel, *Sälam*.

h. Ff. 65v–64v: Gənbot.
(1) Ff. 65v–67r: Homily by Yoḥannəs, Bishop of Ethiopia, who came after Bishop Yəsḥaq, on the conflict between the consort of King Arqadewos and John Chysostom.
(2) Ff. 67r–69r: Miracle.
(3) Ff. 69rv: Synaxary entry: Mission of the Archangel to Habakkuk.
(4) F. 69v: Greeting to the Archangel, *Sälam*.

i. Ff. 69v–85v: Säne
(1) Ff. 69v–77r: Homily by Yoḥannəs, Bishop of Aksum on the family of Astäraniqos and Euphemia.
(2) Ff. 77r–78v: Miracle.
(3) Ff. 78v–85v: Synaxary entry: The building of the church of the Archangel in place of a pagan temple in Alexandria.
(4) F. 85v: Greeting to the Archangel, *Sälam*.

j. Ff. 86r–92v: Ḥamle
(1) Ff. 86r–91r: Homily [by Bishop Yoḥannəs] on the wicked wealthy man whose property was inherited by the son of his poor neighbor.
(2) Ff. 91r–92r: Miracle.
(3) Ff. 92rv: Synaxary entry: Mission to the camp of Sennacherib.
(4) F. 92v: Greeting to the Archangel, *Sälam*.

k. Ff. 92v–97v: Näḥase
(1) Ff. 92v–96r: Homily (anonymous) on the book of the angels that came from Jerusalem.
(2) Ff. 96r–97r: Miracle.
(3) F. 97r: Synaxary entry: Mission of the Archangel to the Emperor Constantine.
(4) Ff. 97rv: Greeting to the Archangel, *Sälam*.

l. Ff. 97v–103v: Mäskäräm.
(1) Ff. 97v–100v: Homily (anonymous) on not worshipping other gods.
(2) Ff. 100v–103r: Miracle.
(3) Ff. 103rv: Synaxary entry: Mission to Prophet Isaiah.

(4) F. 103v: Greeting to the Archangel, *Sälam*.
m Ff. 103v–111r: Ṭəqəmt.
- (1) Ff. 103v–107v: Homily (anonymous) on the need to make the angels sureties by honoring them.
- (2) Ff. 107v–110r: Miracle.
- (3) Ff. 110rv: Synaxary entry: Mission to Prophet Samuel.
- (4) Ff. 110v–111r: Greeting to the Archangel, *Sälam*.

2. Ff. 114r–115v: Asmat Prayer of the Archangel Mikaʻel which is written on his left and right wings. It begins:
በስመ ፡ አብ ፡ . . . ድርሳን ፡ ዘቅዱስ ፡ ሚካኤል ፡ ሊቀ ፡ መላእክት ፡ አስማቲሁ ፡ ለእግዚአብሔር ፡ እለ ፡ ተጽሕፈ ፡ በየማናዊ ፡ ክንፉ ፡ ለቅዱስ ፡ ሚካኤል ፡ ሊቀ ፡ መላእክት ፡ ኤኮስ ፡ አሰሌ ፡ ኤፓስ ፡ ኤንክምካም ፡ ለካፍ ፡ ፌ ፡ ኤ ፡ ሎኬ ፡ ወአውርናኬ ፡ ን ፡ አበስኩ ፡ . . .

3. Ff. 115v–119v: Second of Image of Michael, "Ⲑ, One Who Saved Them," ኦ፡ ዘአድኃንሙ፡. Not listed in Chaîne, *Répertoire*.
ኦ ፡ ዘአድኃንኮሙ ፡ እምተሠጥሞ ፡ ባሕር ፡ ለሕዝብ ፡ ትስእል ፡ ምሕረት ፡ ጎበ ፡ ንጉሥክ ፡ አብ ፡ ሚካኤል ፡ ሊቆሙ ፡ ለአሳታውያን ፡ አርባብ ፡ ለጸድቃን ፡ በቤተ ፡ መርዓ ፡ አመ ፡ ይትገበር ፡ ክብካብ ፡ አድኅነነ ፡ እምቀዊም ፡ በአንቀጽ ፡ ጸባብ ፡ . . .

4. Ff. 119v–120r: Concluding Prayer for Synaxarium, ዘአቅረብኩ፡ ማኅሌተ፡.
ዘአቅረብኩ ፡ ማኅሌተ ፡ አዘኪርየ ፡ አዕላፈ ፡ እምእለ ፡ ተጸምዱክ ፡ ዘልፈ ፡ ለለአነብብ ፡ ተወክፍ ፡ ዘንዴትየ ፡ መጽሐፈ ፡ እንተ ፡ ረሰይክ ፡ እግዚኦ ፡ ጽሪቀ ፡ መበለት ፡ ውኩፈ ፡ እምእለ ፡ አብኡ ፡ ብዑላን ፡ ዘተርፈ ፡

5. Ff. 120r–128v: Image of Michael, *Mälk_a Mikaʻel*, መልክአ፡ ሚካኤል፡. Chaîne, *Répertoire* 119; *MG59* 290ff. EMIP 16, f. 92v; EMIP 56, f. 1r; MYS 6, ff. 39r–66v.
ሰላም ፡ ለዝክረ ፡ ስምክ ፡ ምስለ ፡ ስመ ፡ ልዑል ፡ ዘተሳተፈ ፡ ወልደ ፡ ያሬድ ፡ ሄኖክ ፡ በከመ ፡ ጸሐፈ ፡ ሰብ ፡ እጼውዕ ፡ ስመከ ፡ ከሚትየ ፡ አፈ ፡ ረዳኤ ፡ ምንዱባን ፡ ሚካኤል ፡ በከመ ፡ ታስምድድ ፡ ዘልፈ ፡ ለረዲኦትየ ፡ ነዓ ፡ ሰፊሐክ ፡ ክንፈ ፡ . . .

6. Ff. 128v–133r: Image of Gabriel, መልክአ ገብርኤል፡. Chaîne, *Répertoire* 246; *MG59* 312ff.; EMIP 56, f. 63r; MYS 6, ff. 67r–85v.
በሰላም ፡ ገብርኤል ፡ መልአክ ፡ በሳዕለ ፡ ማርያም ፡ ዘአዕረፈ ፡ ከመ ፡ እዜኑ ፡ ኃዳጠ ፡ ወአኮ ፡ ትሩፈ ፡

እግዚአብሔር ፡ ንብኒ ፡ ሲሳየ ፡ ልቡና ፡ መጽሐፈ ፡
ወአፉየ ፡ ሙሴ ፡ ለአመ ፡ ኮነ ፡ ጸያፈ ፡
ጸራቅሊጦስ ፡ አርአን ፡ ይኩነኒ ፡ አፈ ፡ . . .

Notes:
1. F. i r(ecto): Trinitarian formula.
2. Ff. i v(erso)-ii v(erso), 111v–112r and 113r: blank and pen trials.
3. First owner, Gäbrä Mika'el, ff.13r and *passim*; secondary owner, Kidanä Maryam, ff. 4v and *passim*, and as the primary owner from ff. 114r and following.
4. F. 110v: name of scribe, Täklä Śəllase.
5. F. 112v: a few lines from Säwasəw.
6. F. 113v: In a later hand, in blue ink: ~~Gənbot~~ 12, 1964 (EC). This *Dersana Mika'el* awarded to *Märigeta* Ḫayla Mäsqäl Kəbrät. Awarded by Bərəhane Asäfa, his baptismal name Wäldä Tənsa'e."
7. F. 133v, top: name of the scribe for folios 114r–133r, Gäbrä Iyasus. Bottom (in blue ink), note of ownership, erased.
8. Decorative designs: ff. 1r, 4v (colorful, ornate *ḥaräg*); ff. 4r, 14r, 16r, 23r, 34r, 35rv, 53r, 57r, 65r, 67r, 69rv, 77r, 85v, 91r, 92v, 97r, 107v, 110rv, 115rv, 120r, 133r (multiple full stops); ff. 16v, 31r, 57r, 120r (ornate *ḥaräg* in pencil or black ink); ff. 119v, 128v (line of alternating red and black dots).
9. The words Mary and Michael are rubricated.
10. Numbered quires: quires 2–11.
11. Scribal intervention: words of text are written interlinearly (ff. 13v, 14r, 15r, 16r, 21v, etc.); and lines of text are written interlinearly (ff. 14r, 79r); erasure markings are visible (ff. 2r, 3v, 15r, 28r, etc.); text has been removed (e.g., f. 58v).

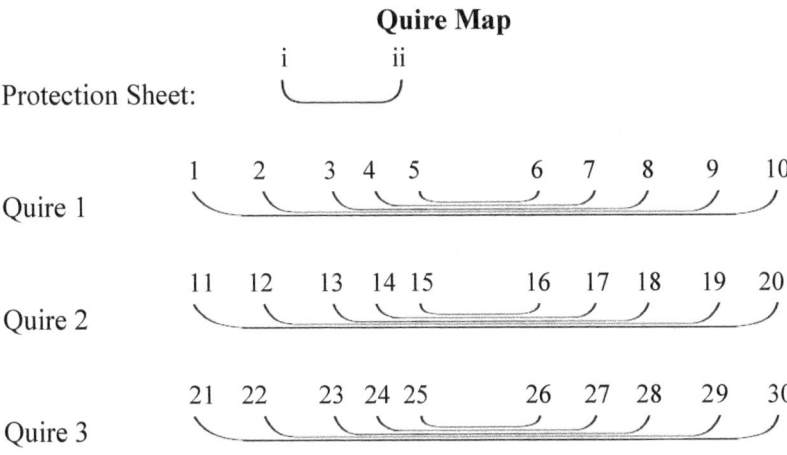

Quire Map

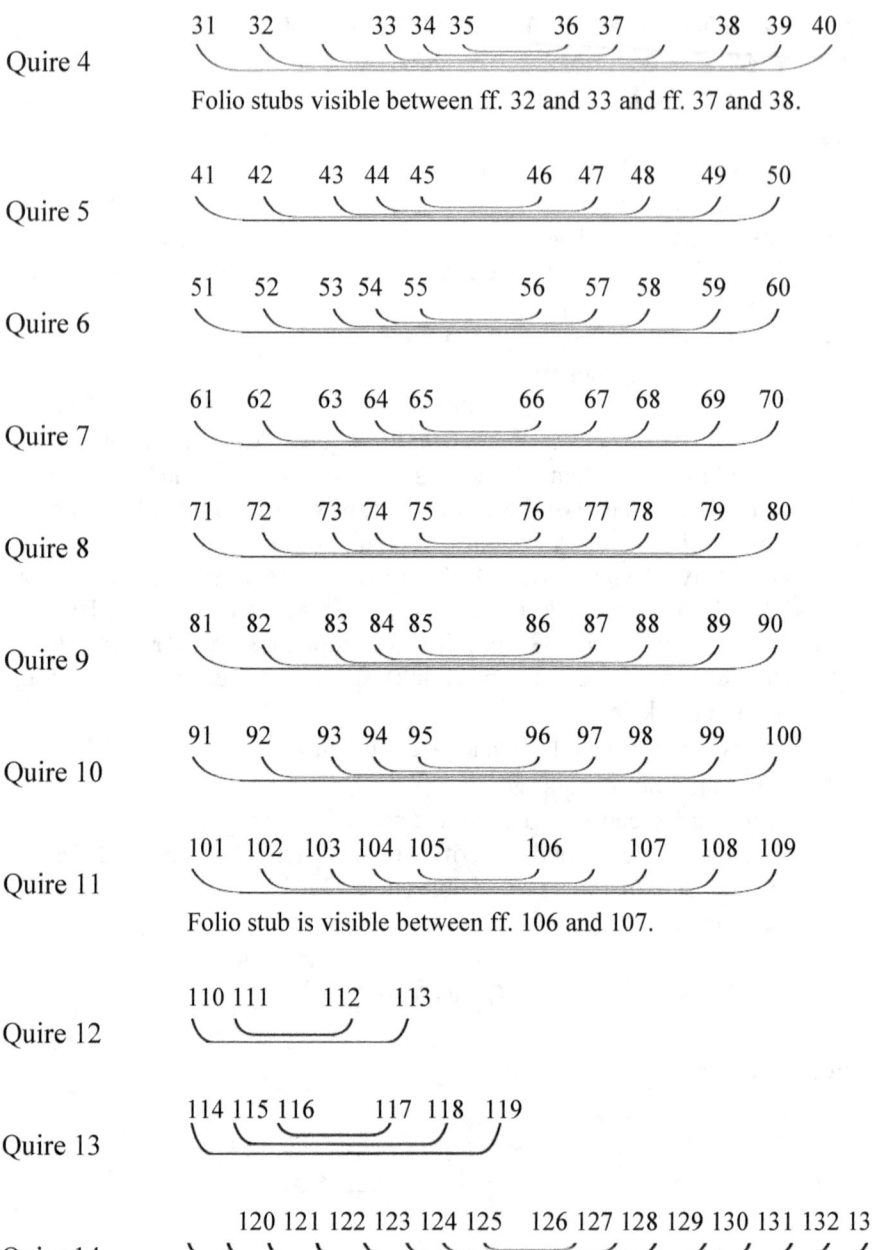

MYS 12 – EMIP 612
Homiliary in Honor of the Monthly Feast of the Archangel Michael, ድርሳነ፡ ሚካኤል፡

Parchment, 255 x 215 x 68 mm, four Coptic chain stitches attached with bridle attachments to rough-hewn boards of the traditional wood, covered with tooled leather, protection quire + 9 full quires, iv + 70 folios, top margin 30 mm, bottom margin 57 mm, fore edge margin 37 mm, gutter margin 13 mm, ff. 1r–68v two columns, 23 lines, Gə_əz, twentieth century.

Quire descriptions: quires 1–3 and 5–9 balanced; protection quire and quire 4 adjusted balanced.

Major Works:
1. Ff. 1r–68v: Homiliary in Honor of the Archangel Michael, Dərsanä Mika'el, ድርሳነ፡ ሚካኤል፡. Published several times in Ethiopia; see for example, *DM* 11–205. See also BL Or. 4849, Strelcyn *BL* 94–7; EMML 1133.
   a. Ff. 1r–3r: Introductory homily, with a beginning identical to 11a.
   b. Ff. 3v–10v: Ḫədar.
      (1) Ff. 3v–9r Homily by Dämatewos, bishop of Alexandria.
      (2) Ff. 9r–10r: Miracle.
      (3) Ff. 10rv: Synaxary Entry: Mission to Joshua, son of Nun.
      (4) F. 10v: Greeting to the Archangel, *Sälam*.
   c. Ff. 11r–15r: Taḫśaś.
      (1) Ff. 11r–14r: Homily by Bishop John, the Orthodox.
      (2) Ff. 14rv: Miracle.
      (3) Ff. 14v–15r: Synaxary Entry: Mission of the Archangel to rescue the three holy children.
      (4) F. 15r: Greeting to the Archangel, *Sälam*.
   d. Ff. 17r–22r: Ṭərr
      (1) Ff. 17r–21r: Homily, author not given.
      (2) Ff. 21rv: Miracle.
      (3) F. 21v–22r: Synaxary Entry: Mission of the Archangel to save Jacob from the wrath of Esau.
      (4) F. 22r: Greeting to the Archangel, *Sälam*.
   e. Ff. 22v–25v: Yäkkatit.
      (1) Ff. 22v–24v: Homily, author not given.
      (2) Ff. 24v–25r: Miracle.
      (3) Ff. 25rv: Synaxary Entry: Mission of the Archangel to Samson, the giant.

(4) F. 25v: Greeting to the Archangel, *Sälam*.
- f. Ff. 26r–38r: Mäggabit.
    - (1) Ff. 26r–37r: Homily by the archbishop John, of Antioch
    - (2) Ff. 37rv: Miracle.
    - (3) Ff. 37v–38r: Synaxary Entry: Mission of the Archangel to Balaam.
    - (4) F. 38r: Greeting to the Archangel, *Sälam*.
- g. Ff. 38r–43v: Miyazya.
    - (1) Ff. 38r–42r: Homily, author not given.
    - (2) Ff. 42r–43r: Miracle.
    - (3) Ff. 43rv: Synaxary entries: Mission of the Archangel to the Prophet Jeremiah.
    - (4) F. 43v: Greeting to the Archangel, *Sälam*.
- h. Ff. 44r–46v: Gənbot.
    - (1) Ff. 44r–45r: Homily by Yoḥannəs, Bishop of Ethiopia, who came after Bishop Yəsḥaq, on the conflict between the consort of King Arqadewos and John Chrysostom.
    - (2) Ff. 45r–46r: Miracle.
    - (3) Ff. 46rv: Synaxary entry: Mission of the Archangel to Habakkuk.
    - (4) F. 46v: Greeting to the Archangel, *Sälam*.
- i. Ff. 47r–53r: Säne
    - (1) Ff. 47r–51v: Homily by Yoḥannəs, Bishop of Aksum on the family of Astäraniqos and Euphemia.
    - (2) Ff. 51v–52r: Miracle.
    - (3) Ff. 52rv: Synaxary entry: The building of the church of the Archangel in place of a pagan temple in Alexandria, abbreviated version.
    - (4) F. 53r: Greeting to the Archangel, *Sälam*.
- j. Ff. 53r–57v: Ḥamle
    - (1) Ff. 53r–56v: Homily [by Bishop Yoḥannəs] on the wicked wealthy man whose property was inherited by the son of his poor neighbor.
    - (2) Ff. 56v–57r: Miracle.
    - (3) Ff. 57rv: Synaxary entry: Mission to the camp of Sennacherib.
    - (4) F. 57v: Greeting to the Archangel, *Sälam*.
- k. Ff. 57v–60v: Näḥase

(1) Ff. 57v–59v: Homily (anonymous) on the book of the angels that came from Jerusalem.
(2) Ff. 59v–60r: Miracle.
(3) F. 60v: Synaxary entry: Mission of the Archangel to the Emperor Constantine.
(4) Ff. 60v: Greeting to the Archangel, *Sälam*.

l. Ff. 60v–63r: Mäskäräm.
(1) Ff. 60v–62v: Homily (anonymous) on not worshipping other gods.
(2) Ff. 62v–63r: Miracle.
(3) F. 63r: Synaxary entry: Mission to Prophet Isaiah.
(4) F. 63r: Greeting to the Archangel, *Sälam*.

m Ff. 63v–68v: Ṭəqəmt.
(1) Ff. 63v–67v: Homily (anonymous) on the need to make the angels sureties by honoring them.
(2) Ff. 67v–68r: Miracle.
(3) Ff. 68rv: Synaxary entry: Mission to Prophet Samuel.
(4) F. 68v: Greeting to the Archangel, *Sälam*.

Notes:
1. Ff. i r(ecto)–iv v(erso), 15v–16v, 66rv, 69r–70v: blank.
2. Decorative designs: ff. 3r, 8r, 10v, 14r, 15r, 21rv, 22r, 25rv, 37rv, 38r, 43rv, 45r, 46v, 53r, 56v, 57v, 60v, 62v, 68v (multiple full stops, often without red ink); ff. 24v, 37v (line of alternating red and black dots).
3. The words Michael and Mary are rubricated.
4. Scribal intervention: erasure markings are visible (f. 67r).

Quire Map

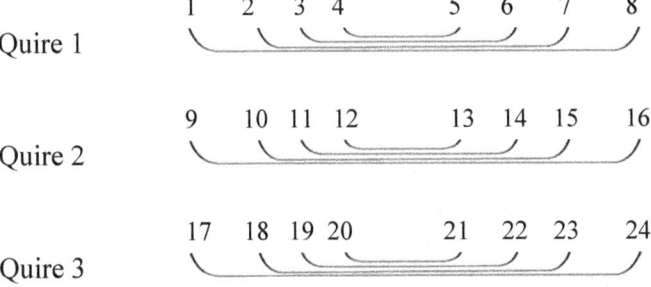

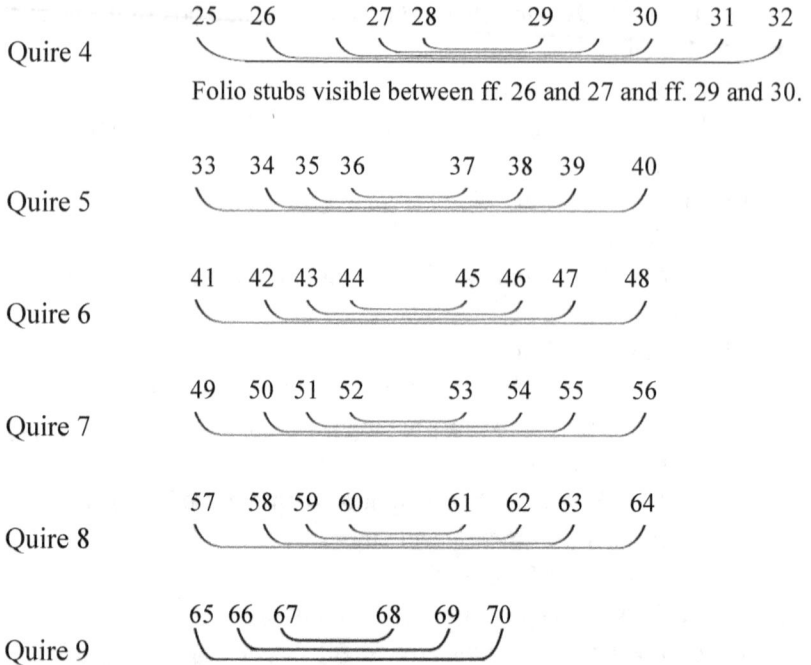

Folio stubs visible between ff. 26 and 27 and ff. 29 and 30.

MYS 13 – EMIP 613
Image of John the Baptist, መልክአ፡ ዮሐንስ፡ መጥምቅ፡, God Reigns, ነግሠ፡, Images of Gäbrä Mänfas Qəddus, መልክአ፡ ገብረ፡ መንፈስ፡ ቅዱስ፡, Saint George, መልክአ፡ ጊዮርጊስ፡, Michael, መልክአ፡ ሚካኤል፡, and Gabriel, መልክአ፡ ገብርኤል፡

Parchment, 135 x 88 x 30 mm, four Coptic chain stitches attached with bridle attachments to rough-hewn boards of the traditional wood, protection sheet + 7 full quires, ii + 55 folios, top margin 8–10 mm, bottom margin 33 mm, fore edge margin 13 mm, gutter margin 7 mm, ff. 1r–55r one column, 13–14 lines, Gə_əz, early-twentieth century.

Quire descriptions: protection sheet and quires 1–4 and 6–7 balanced; quire 5 adjusted balanced.

Major Works:
1. Ff. 1r–10v: Image of John the Baptist, መልክአ፡ ዮሐንስ፡ መጥምቅ፡. Chaîne, *Répertoire* 279; *MG59* 394ff.

    በስመ ፡ እግዚአብሔር ፡ አሳት ፡ በሕቅለ ፡ ሕሊና ፡ ነዳዲ ፡
    ወበስመ ፡ ማርያም ፡ ድንግል ፡ መጥበቢተ ፡ ዓለም ፡ ዓባዲ ፡
    ማኅቶተ ፡ ጽልል ፡ ዮሐንስ ፡ ጽልመተ ፡ አበሳ ፡ ሰዳዲ ፡
    ከመ ፡ እዜኑ ፡ ኒፉተክ ፡ ዐዳ ፡ ኃማውዕየ ፡ ፍዳ ፡

በአየረ ፡ ሰማይ ፡ ዘይጻርን ፡ ቃልክ ፡ ዓዋዲ ፡ . . .

2. Ff. 13r–14v: First part of God Reigns, እግዚአብሐር፡ ነግሠ፡ (ነግሥ፡), ascribed to Zär'a Ya_əqob. See Getatchew Haile, *The Different Collection of Nägś Hymns of the Ethiopic Literature*, Oikonomia 19 (Erlangen, Germany: Lehrstuhl für Geschichte und Theologie des christlichen Ostens, 1983) 29–52; EMML 3128, ff. 2a-10b, and 92r–94a.

በስመ ፡ አብ ፡ ወወልድ ፡ . . . ሃሌ ፡ ሉያ ፡ ዘውእቱ ፡ ብሂል ፡
ንወድሶ ፡ ለዘሁሎ ፡ እግዚአብሐር ፡ ልዑል ፡
ስቡሕ ፡ ወውዱስ ፡ ዘሣረረ ፡ ኵሎ ፡ ዓለመ ፡ በአሐቲ ፡ ቃል፡

3. Ff. 14v–21v: Image of Gäbrä Mänfas Qəddus, *Mälk_a Gäbrä Mänfas Qəddus*, መልክአ፡ ገብረ፡ መንፈስ፡ ቅዱስ፡. Chaîne, *Répertoire* 196; *MG59* 553ff.

ሰላም ፡ ለዕንስትክ ፡ መሠረተ ፡ ነገር ፡ ወውጣኔ ፡
ወለልደትክ ፡ ሰላም ፡ በብሥራተ ፡ መልአክ ፡ ሥናየ ፡ ቅኔ ፡
ገብረ ፡ መንፈስ ፡ ቅዱስ ፡ ጸውሎስ ፡ ሰባኪ ፡ ሃይማኖት ፡ ውስተ ፡ ኵርንኔ ፡
ተማኅፀንኩ ፡ በኪዳንክ ፡ከመ ፡ ኢይርአይ ፡ ኩነኔ ፡
በእንተዝ ፡ ኃሥሥኩ ፡ ኪያክ ፡ መድኃኔ ፡

4. Ff. 22r–28v: Image of Saint George, *Mälk_a Giyorgis*, መልክአ፡ ጊዮርጊስ፡. Chaîne, *Répertoire* 208.

ሰላም ፡ ለጽንስትክ ፡ ወለልደትክ ፡ ቡሩክ ፡
በበዓለ ፡ ቅድስት ፡ ድንግል ፡ ወመስቀለ ፡ ክርስቶስ ፡ አምላክ ፡
ገባሬ ፡ መንክራት ፡ ጊዮርጊስ ፡ በኃውደ ፡ ዳድያኖስ ፡ ምዑክ ፡
አጸራርየ ፡ እለ ፡ ተንሥኡ ፡ በነገረ ፡ ክንቱ ፡ ወበክ ፡
ሐመደ ፡ ለይኩን ፡ በጸባሕ ፡ ወሠርክ ፡

5. Ff. 29r–44v: Image of Michael, *Mälk_a Mika'el*, መልክአ፡ ሚካኤል፡. Chaîne, *Répertoire* 119; *MG59* 290ff. EMIP 16, f. 92v; EMIP 56, f. 1r; MYS 6, ff. 39r–66v.

6. Ff. 45r–53r: Image of Gabriel, *Mälk_a Gäbra'el*, መልክአ ገብርኤል፡. Chaîne, *Répertoire* 246; *MG59* 312ff.; EMIP 56, f. 63r; MYS 6, ff. 67r–85v.

Miniatures:

1. F. ii r(ecto): Madonna and Child. Captions: ―Saint Gabriel" and ―Saint Michael" and ―with her beloved son."
2. F. 21v: Gäbrä Mänfäs Qəddus. Caption: ―Abuna Gäbrä Mänfäs Qəddus."
3. F. 28v: Angel with sword and scabbard standing with his foot on a demon.

Varia:
1. Ff. 11r–12v: Psalm 26, in a different hand.
2. F. 53v: Asmat prayer of the Trinity, listing the Hebrew alphabet as names of God.
3. F. 55r: Prescription for diarrhea.

Notes:
1. F. i r(ecto): $90. Note, illegible, written upside down.
2. F. i v(erso): Deposition, in pencil: *Fitawərari* Taddäsä when he took the hand of Dañe, he said, "Yes, I have a bank debt of 300 birr." The guarantors are *Gərazəmač* Šəfäraw and *Ləj* Alämayähu Ṭäna. Written on 1 Ṭəqemt 1915.
3. Ff. ii v(erso), 54r and 55v: blank.
4. F. 10v: Colophon: Oh, God of Yoḥannəs, protect me and save me from the suffering of flesh and soul, me, your beloved Wäldä Yoḥannəs (owner) and his scribe, Gäbrä Mädḫən.
5. F. 34r, top: faded text: prescription for stubborn bull (abäya bäre).
6. F. 44v: complete name of owner, Wäldä Yoḥannəs Dəl Naśahu.
7. F. 53r: list of names, in blue ink.
8. F. 54v: faded text: excerpt from the book of Psalms.
9. Decorative designs: ff. 1r, 13r, 29r, 45r (interlocking, colorful *ḥarägs*); ff. 10v, 21r, 27r, 28v, 44v, 53r (multiple full stops); f. 10v (line of alternating red and black dots).
10. The words John, Mary, Gäbrä Mänfäs Qəddus, George, God and Michael are rubricated.
11. Scribal intervention: words of text are written interlinearly (ff. 3r, 6r, 8r, 44r, 50r, etc.); erasure markings are visible (f. 19v); text has been removed (e.g., ff. 14r, 20v).

Quire Map

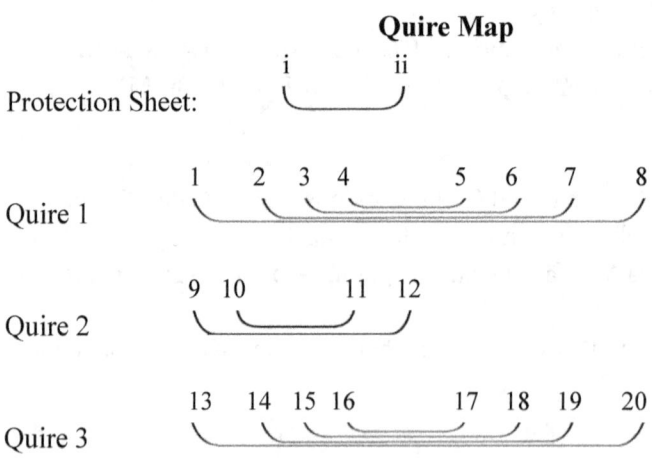

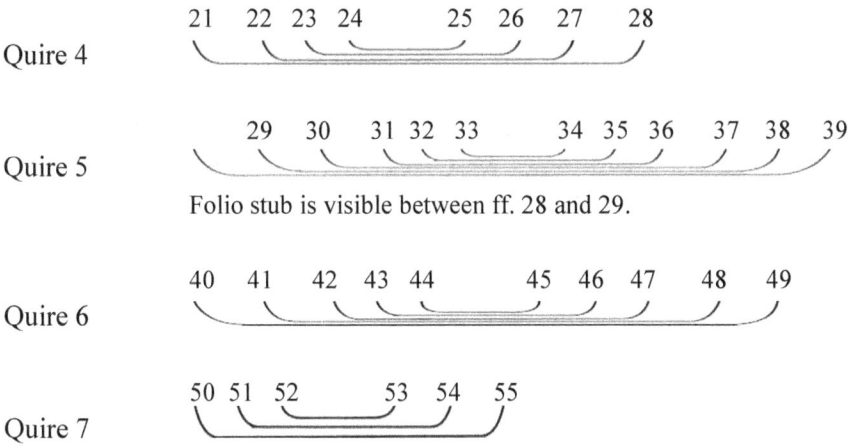

Folio stub is visible between ff. 28 and 29.

MYS 14 – EMIP 614
Sword of Trinity, ሠይፈ፡ ሥላሴ፡, and Book of Disciples, መጽሐፈ፡ አርድእት፡

Parchment, 164 x 102 x 34 mm, remnants of four Coptic chain stitches attached with bridle attachments to rough-hewn boards of the traditional wood, rebound, 6 full quires, i + 58 folios, top margin 10 mm, bottom margin 40 mm, fore edge margin 14 mm, gutter margin 7 mm, ff. i r(ecto)-58v one column, 22 lines, Gə_əz, early-twentieth century.

Quire descriptions: quires 2–5 balanced; quire 6 adjusted balanced; quire 1 unbalanced.

Major Works:
1. Ff. 1r–30v: Sword of the Trinity, *Säyfä Śəllase*, ሠይፈ፡ ሥላሴ፡. Arranged for days of the week. *AbbCat* 244, f. 13r; Conti Rossini, *Notice* 106; Strelcyn, *Lincei*, no. 53 and 62; EMML 1170 and EMIP 7. See ሰይፈኝ ሥላሴኝኛ ወመልክአ ሥላሴኝ ዘደረስኝ አባኝ ስብሐትኝ ለአብኝኛ Addis Ababa: Täsfa Press, 1947 EC.
    a. Ff. 1r–5v: Monday.
    b. Ff. 5v–10v: Tuesday.
    c. Ff. 10v–13v: Wednesday.
    d. Ff. 13v–17v: Thursday.
    e. Ff. 18r–23v: Friday.
    f. Ff. 23v–27v: Saturday.
    g. Ff. 27v–30v: Sunday.

2. Ff. 31r–58v: Book of Disciples, *Ardə't*, መጽሐፈ፡ አርድእት፡. Arranged for the days of the week.
በስመ ፡ አብ ፡ ወወልድ ፡ . . . ነገር ፡ ዘ ፡ Ĭ ፡ ወ ፡ ፪ ፡ አርድዕት ፡ መገረፌ ፡ ፀር ። መድኃኒተ ፡ ነፍስ ፡ ወመድኃኒተ ። ሥጋ ፡ ወመጽሐፈ ፡ ሕይወት ፡ ዘነገረሙ ፡ እግዚእ ፡ ኢየሱስ ፡ ለአርዳኢሁ ፡ በዘተድግኑ ፡ እምኃጢአት ፡ ወለክሙሂ ፡ አነ ፡ በዝትድግኑ ፡ እምኃጢአት ፡ . . .

   a. Ff. 31r–34v: Monday.
   b. Ff. 34v–37r: Tuesday.
   c. Ff. 37r–42v: Wednesday.
   d. Ff. 42v–46v: Thursday.
   e. Ff. 46v–52v: Friday.
   f. Ff. 52v–58v: Saturday.

Varia:
1. F. i rv: Excerpt from Sword of the Trinity.

Notes:
1. F. 1r and *passim*: owners name, Bərəhanä Mäsqäl.
2. F. 23v: name of the scribe, Gäbrä Ṣəyon.
3. Decorative designs: ff. 1r, 13v, 18r, 23v (*ḥaräg*); ff. 26v, 27v, 34v, 58v (multiple full stops).
4. The word Mary is rubricated.
5. Scribal intervention: words of text are written interlinearly (ff. 9v, 11r, 36v, 52v, 54r); and in the upper margin with a symbol (⊥) marking the location where the text is to be inserted (f. 39v, line 18), and in another case where the symbol (+) is used (f. 45v, line 22); erasure markings are visible (f. 30r); text has been removed (e.g., ff. 38v, 44v).

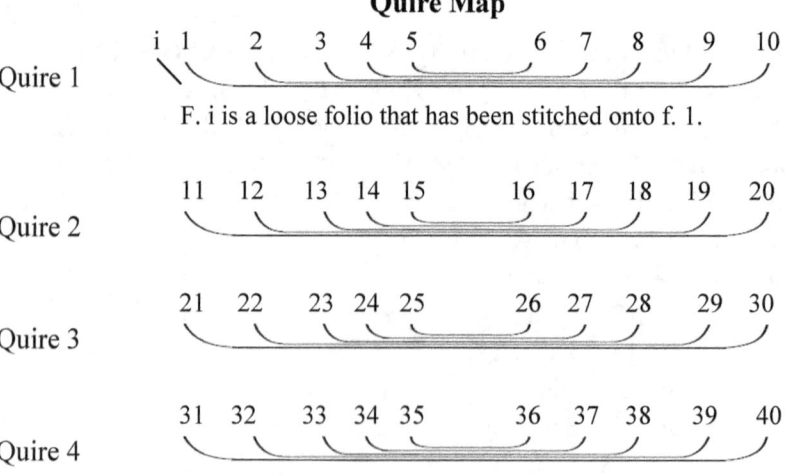

Quire Map

Quire 1: i 1 2 3 4 5 6 7 8 9 10
F. i is a loose folio that has been stitched onto f. 1.

Quire 2: 11 12 13 14 15 16 17 18 19 20

Quire 3: 21 22 23 24 25 26 27 28 29 30

Quire 4: 31 32 33 34 35 36 37 38 39 40

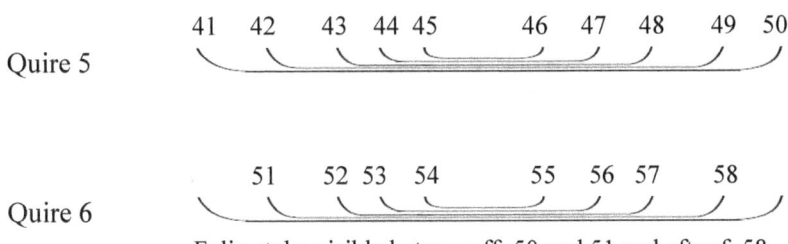

Folio stubs visible between ff. 50 and 51 and after f. 58.

MYS 15 – EMIP 615
Book of Penance, መጽሐፈ፡ (አንቀጸ፡) ንስሐ፡, Book of Confession, መጽሐፈ፡ ኑዛዜ፡

Parchment, 164 x 121 x 29 mm, two Coptic chain stitches attached with bridle attachments to sawed boards, covered with linen, protection quire + 5 full quires, iv + 41 folios, top margin 20 mm, bottom margin 34 mm, fore edge margin 16 mm, gutter margin 9 mm, ff. 1r–38v one column, 13 lines, Gə_əz and Amharic, twentieth century.

Quire descriptions: protection quire and quires 1–4 balanced; quire 5 adjusted balanced.

Major Works:
1. Ff. 1r–25v: Book of Penance, *Mäṣəḥäfä Nəsḥa*, መጽሐፈ፡ ንስሐ፡ in this manuscript called *Anqäṣä Nəsḥa*, አንቀጸ፡ ንስሐ፡ or Article of Penance, (list of sins and their corresponding penance).
   በስመ ፡ አብ ፡ ወወልድ ፡ . . . አንቀጸ ፡ ንስሐ ፡ ዘይመይጥ ፡ ኀበ ፡ ንስሐ ፡ ዘወጽአ ፡ አምኟወዬ ፡ መጻሕፍት ፡ ከመ ፡ ኃጢአቱ ፡ ዘወሀበ ፡ ቀሲስ ፡ ሉብአሲ ፡ ወሉብእሲት ፡ ጾመ ፡ ወጸሎተ ፡ ወሰጊደ ፡ ዘኢተምሕረ ፡ ቀሲስ ፡ ዘንተ ፡ መጽሐፈ ፡ ወኢወ ፡ (ሀ)በ ፡ ከመ ፡ ኃጢአቱ ፡ ወአበሳሁ ፡ ዘይቤ ፡ ዝኑቱ ፡ መጽሐፍ ፡ አልቦቱ ፡ ሥልጣን ፡ ይስዓር ፡ እግዕርጊሁ ፡ በእደ ፡ መልአክ ፡ ይከውን ፡ ክፍሉ ፡ ከመ ፡ አርዮስ ፡ . . .

2. Ff. 25v–38v: Book of Confession, *Mäṣəḥäfä Nuzaze*, መጽሐፈ፡ ኑዛዜ፡, in Amharic, then switching to Gə_əz at f. 34r. See EMML 1334:8 (IV, 368) = IES 00041, which has this text fully in Gə_əz.
   በስመ ፡ አብ ፡ ወወልድ ፡ . . . መጽሐፈ ፡ ኑዛዜu ፡ በዘዖአምሩ ፡ ኃጢአቶሙ ፡ ዘገብሩ ፡ በድፍረት ፡ የኃጢአት ፡ ሥሩ ፡ እግዚአብሔርን ፡ መካድ ፡ ገንዘብን ፡ መውደድ ፡ ነገው ። ገበርኩ ፡ ማለት ፡ ኃጢትን ፡ ሠራሁ ፡ ማለት ፡ ነው ። የሚናዘዝ ፡ መጽፈን ፡ ይዞ ፡ ያንብብ ፡ ያልተማረ ፡ እንደሆነ ፡ መምህሩ ፡ ያንብብ ፡ እግዚአብሔር ፡ ይፍታህ ፡ ይበል ፩ የሚናዘዝ ፡ ይፍቱኝ ፡ ይበል ፡ . . .

Notes:
1. Ff. i r(ecto)-iv v(erso) and 39r–41v: blank.
2. The word Mary is rubricated.
3. Numbered quires: quires 3–4.
4. Scribal intervention: words of text are written interlinearly (f. 16v).

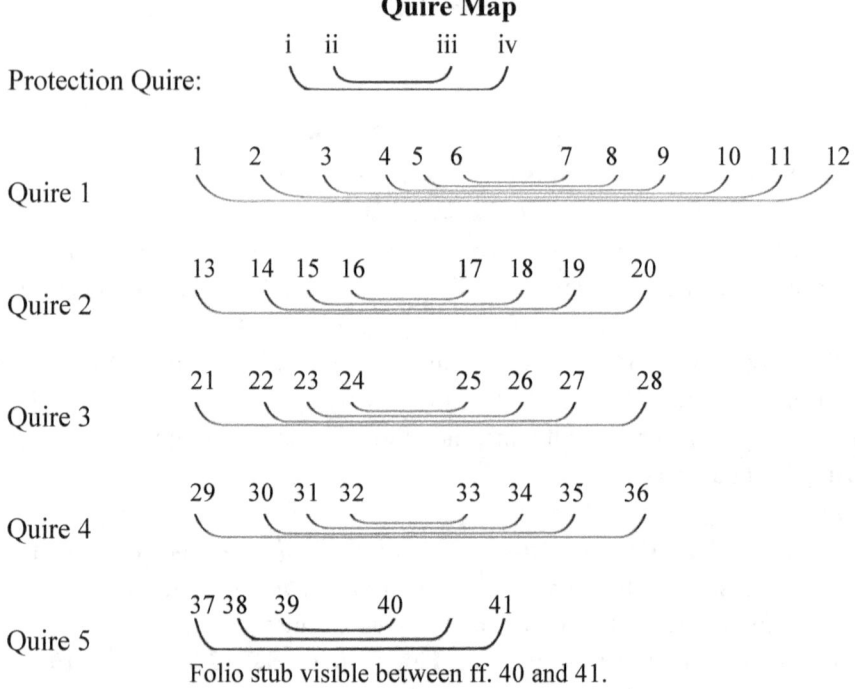

Folio stub visible between ff. 40 and 41.

MYS 16 – EMIP 616
Prayer of the Covenant, ጸሎተ፡ ኪዳን፡, Supplications, መስተብቍዕ፡, God of the Luminaries, እግዚአብሔር፡ ዘብርሃናት፡, Mystagogia, ትምህርተ፡ ኅቡዓት፡, Prayer against the Tongue of People, ልሳነ፡ ሰብእ፡, Asmat Prayers of the Seven Archangels, ድርሳን፡ ዘሰባቱ፡ ሊቃነ፡ መላእክት፡, Asmat Prayers, Prayers, Net of Solomon, መርበብተ፡ ሰሎሞን፡, Prayer of Mary at Golgotha, ጸሎተ፡ እግዝእትነ፡ ማርያም፡ ዘሰኔ፡ ጎልጋታ፡, Image of Fanuel, መልክአ፡ ፋኑኤል፡, Anaphora of Mary, ቅዳሴ፡ ማርያም፡, Sword of Divinity, ሠይፈ፡ መለኮት፡, and Litanies, ሊጦን፡

Parchment, 139 x 106 x 50 mm, four Coptic chain stitches attached with bridle attachments to rough-hewn boards of the traditional wood, protection sheet + 13 full quires, ii + 131 folios, top margin 12 mm, bottom margin 27 mm, fore edge margin 19 mm, gutter margin 9 mm, ff. 1r–129r one column, 19 lines, Gəʽəz, 2. 21 May 1937–29 July 1939 (f. 18r which mentions Bishop Qerəlos III, 2 June 1929–1950, and Bishop Abreham, Bishop of Gondar, to whom Bishop Qerəlos III entrusted interim care of the arch episcopate when he left for Italy on 21 May 1937 and who died on 29 July 1939) . Single-slip *maḥdär*.

Quire descriptions: protection sheet and quires 1, 3–9 and 11–12 balanced; quires 2, 10 and 13 adjusted balanced.

Major Works:

1. Ff. 1r–8r: Prayer of the Covenant, *Ṣälotä Kidan*, ጸሎተ፡ ኪዳን፡. As part of the liturgy, the prayer has been copied and printed many times, e.g. *MQ51* 256–62; *MD59* 602–14; see also *DChr* 46–50; Velat *Me_erāf* I:1–6; and (tr.) Velat, *Me_erāf* II:170–74; Sebastian Euringer, ―Übersetzung der _Preces officii matutini' in Dillmann's _Chrestomathia Aethiopica,'" *Or* NS 11 (1942) 333–66; and Daoud-Mersie, *Liturgy* 314–21.

2. Ff. 8r–13r: Supplications, መስተብቍዕ፡. Cf. *MQ51* 270ff. On the controversial supplications, see ጌታቸው፡ ኃይሌ፡ ደቂቀ፡ እስጢፋኖስ፡ Collegeville (Minnesota) 1996 EC, 36–41.
    ወካዕበ ፡ ናስተበቍዖ ፡ ለኵሉ ፡ ይእገዝ ፡ እግዚአብሔር ፡ አብ ፡ ለእግዚእ ፡ ወመድኃኒነ ፡ ኢየሱስ ፡ ክርስቶስ ፡ በእንተ ፡ ዳያን ፡ አኃዊነ ፡ ከመ ፡ ኵሉ ፡ ወኵሉ ፡ ሕማመ ፡ ያሰስል ፡ እምኔሆሙ ፡ መንፈሰ ፡ ደዌ ፡ ሠዒር ፡ ሕይወተ ፡ የሀቦሙ ፡ ዘኵሉ ፡ ፈውስ ፡ ሥልጣን ፡ ቦቱ ፡ እግዚአብሔር ፡ አምላክነ ፡ . . .

3. Ff. 13r–16r: God of the Luminaries, *Ǝgzi'abḥer zä-bərhanat*, እግዚአብሔር፡ ዘብርሃናት፡. Chaîne, *Répertoire* 363; EMML 4001 (10: 1); and Princeton Ethiopic 13, ff. 44r–46r. See also, *EA* 2: 249; and *Säbattu Kidanat, Qəddase Maryam, Mälkə'a Guba'e*. Addis Ababa: Täsfa, 1959 EC. 38ff.
    እግዚአብሔር ፡ ዘብርሃናት፤ እግዚአብሔር ፡ ዘሥልጣናት ፡ እግዚአብሔር ፡ ዘአርስተ ፡ መላእክት ፡ ዘእምታሕ ፡ እኂዘትከ ፡ ኵሉ ፡ ፍጥረተ ፡ ንጉሠ ፡ ነገሥት ፡ ወእግዚእ ፡ አጋዕዝት ፡ . . .

4. Ff. 16r–18r: Absolution of the Son, *Fəthat zä-Wäld*, ፍትሐት፡ ዘወልድ፡. As part of the liturgy, this prayer has been copied and printed many times, e.g. *MD59* 640–4; *MQ51* 23–5; Daoud-Marsie, *Liturgy* 31–3; see also Carl Bezold, ―The Ordinary Canon of the Mass according to the Use of the Coptic Church," in *The Greek Liturgies Chiefly from Oriental Authorities*, Charles Anthony Swainson, ed., 366–68 (New York, 1871).

እግዚእ ፡ እግዚኦ ፡ ኢየሱስ ፡ ክርስቶስ ፡ ወልደ ፡ እግዚአብሔር ፡ አብ ፡
ዘበተከ ፡ እምኔነ ፡ ኵሎ ፡ ማዕሠረ ፡ ኃጣውኢነ ፡ በሕማቲከ ፡ ማኅየዊት ፡
ወመድኃኒት ፡ ... .

5. Ff. 18r–24r: Mystagogia, *Təmhərtä Ḫəbu_at*, ትምህርተ፡ ኅቡዓት፡.
Hammerschmidt, *Texte* 48–72; Lifchitz, *Textes* 40–52; Velat,
Me_erāf I:215–7; *MG59* 9ff.
በእንተ ፡ ትምኅርተ ፡ ኅቡዓት ፡ ቅድመ ፡ ዘትትነገር ፡ እጽርስ ፡ ፫ራ ፡
ለምዕመናን ፡ ኅቡዓት ፡ ትምኅርተ ፡ ኅቡዓትስ ፡ ከመዝ ፡ ነገር ፡ ዘቅድመ ፡
ሁሎ ፡ ወይሄሉ ፡ ዘመጽ ፡ ዘሐመ ፡ ወሞተ ፡ ወተቀብረ ፡ ወተንሥአ ፡ ዓዐረ ፡
ዘሞተ ፡ ፈትሐ ፡ ወዘእሙታን ፡ ተንሥአ ፡ ...

6. Ff. 24r–32r: Prayer Against the Tongue of People, ልሳነ፡ ሰብእ፡
(በእንተ፡ ልሳነ፡ ዘመድ፡ ወባእድ፡). Chaîne, *Répertoire* 314. S. Grébaut,
⊥'Hymne-invocation Lesâna sab'e," *Aethiopica. Revue
philologique*, 3 (1936) 6–12; *MG59* 271ff.
በስመ ፡ አብ ፡ ወወልድ ፡ . . . ጸሎት ፡ በእንተ ፡ ልሳነ ፡ ሰብእ ፡ ዘመድ ፡
ወባዕድ ፡ . . .
ናሁ ፡ ተማኅፀንኩ ፡ በኖያተ ፡ ሰምከ ፡ ካፍ ፡
ወበቀዳማይ ፡ የውጣ ፡ ዘፖንተ ፡ ፈደሉ ፡ አሌፍ ፡
ከመ ፡ ታድኅነኒ ፡ ክርስቶስ ፡ እምትንሣኤ ፡ ልሳን ፡ ወአፍ ፡
እስመ ፡ ልሳን ፡ ቀተሎሙ ፡ ለማኅበረ ፡ ሰማዕት ፡ አዕላፍ ፡
በነገረ ፡ ውደት ፡ ፀኑዕ ፡ ዘይበልእ ፡ እምሰይፍ ፡

7. Ff. 32r–37v: *Asmat* Prayer of the Seven Archangels, *Dərsanä
Zäsäbatu Liqənä Mäla'kət*, ድርሳን፡ ዘሰባቱ፡ ሊቃነ፡ መላእክት፡.
   a. Ff. 32r–33r: Asmat Prayer of the Archangel Michael which is
   written on his left and right wings.
   በስመ ፡ አብ ፡ ወወልድ ፡ . . . ድርሳን ፡ ዘቅዱስ ፡ ሚካኤል ፡
   ዘይትነበብ ፡ አመ፲ወ፪ ፡ ለኅዳር ፡ ያኮስ ፡ አሜዕ ፡ ለኬ ፡ ኤንካ ፡
   ካዘዕ ፡ ኤርናኬ ፡ ኦሞዕ ፡ ዘዖን ፡ . . .
   b. Ff. 33rv: Asmat Prayer of the Archangel Gabriel.
   በስመ ፡ አብ ፡ ወወልድ ፡ . . . ድርሳን ፡ ዘቅዱስ ፡ ገብርኤል ፡
   ዘይትነበብ ፡ አም ፡ ፲ወ፱ ፡ ለታኅሣሥ ፡ ጤድጎናኤል ፡ ሕዉታኤል ፡
   አውዳኤል ፡ ተርቡታኤል ፡ ቡኤል ፡ ግኤል ፡ ዝኤል ፡ እሎንተ ፡ ቃላተ ፡
   ዘነገር ፡ እግዚአብሔር ፡ ለቅዱስ ፡ ገብርኤል፡
   c. Ff. 33v–34r: Asmat Prayer of the Archangel Rufa'el.
   በስመ ፡ አብ ፡ ወወልድ ፡ . . . ድርሳን ፡ ዘቅዱስ ፡ ሩፋኤል ፡
   ዘይትነበብ ፡ አም ፡ ፲፫ ፡ ለታኅሣሥ ፡ ብርሃናኤል ፡ መብሳኤል ፡
   ክስትኤል ፡ በጎድናኤል ፡ አስሕናኤል ፡ እሎተ ፡ ቃላተ ፡ ዘነገር ፡
   እግዚአብሔር ፡ ለቅዱስ ፡ ሩፋኤል ፡ አም ፡ አብርሃ ፡ ዓይኖ ፡ ለጠቢት ፡
   . . .

d. Ff. 34rv: Asmat Prayer of the Archangel Saquʻel.
በስመ ፡ አብ ፡ ወወልድ ፡ . . . ድርሳን ፡ ዘቅዱስ ፡ ሳቁኤል ፡
ዘይትነበብ ፡ አመ ፡ ፳፯ ፡ ለሕምሌ ፡ ጓድኤል ፡ ሳህልኤል ፡ ዛኤል ፡
እሎንተ ፡ አስማተ ፡ ዘነገር ፡ አምላክኩ ፡ ለቅዱስ ፡ ሳቁኤል ፡ አመ ፡
ተራድኦሙ ፡ ለነገሥተ ፡ ጎንደኬ ፡ ከማሁ ፡ ተራድኣኒ ፡ ሊተ ፡ . . .

e. Ff. 34v–35r: Asmat Prayer of the Archangel Fanuʻel.
በስመ ፡ አብ ፡ ወወልድ ፡ . . . ድርሳን ፡ ዘቅዱስ ፡ ፋኑኤል ፡
ዘይትነበብ ፡ አመ ፡ ፫ ፡ ለታጎሣሥ ፡ ቅርታኤል ፡ ትትያል ፡ ትያል ፡
አውሴፋኤል ፡ እሎንተ ፡ ቃላተ ፡ ዘነገር ፡ እግዚአብሔር ፡ ለቅዱስ ፡
ፋኑኤል ፡ አመ ፡ ሰደዶሙ ፡ ለሰይጣናት ፡ በፈለግ ፡ ዮርዳኖስ ፡ ዮምሰ ፡
ስደዶሙ ፡ ለፀርየ ፡ ወፀላእትየ ፡ . . .

f. Ff. 35rv: Asmat Prayer of the Archangel Raguʻel.
በስመ ፡ አብ ፡ ወወልድ ፡ . . . ድርሳን ፡ ዘቅዱስ ፡ ራጉኤል ፡
ዘይትነበብ ፡ አመ ፡ ፮ ፡ ለመስከረም ፡ አካዕ ፡ ቤቃ ፡ ክስብኤል ፡
አማኑኤል ፡ አጓድኤል ፡ ቡኤል ፡ እሎንተ ፡ ቃላተ ፡ ዘነገር ፡
እግዚአብሔር ፡ አመ ፡ ተጻብኦሙ ፡ ለንጉሥ ፡ ሮም ፡ ከመ ፡ ፅብኦሙ ፡
ለፀርየ ፡ . . .

g. Ff. 35v–36r: Asmat Prayer of the Archangel Afənin.
በስመ ፡ አብ ፡ ወወልድ ፡ . . . ድርሳን ፡ ዘቅዱስ ፡ አፍኒን ፡
ዘይትነበብ ፡ አመ ፡ ፷ ፡ ለወርኃ ፡ ጓዳር ፡ አልፋኤል ፡ ላኤል ፡
ግዔል ፡ ዘነገር ፡ እግዚአብሔር ፡ ለቅዱስ ፡ አፍኒን ፡ አመ ፡ ተራድኦ ፡
ለአስቡ ፡ ከማሁ ፡ ሊተኒ ፡ ተራድኣኒ ፡ እምክራ ፡ ሥጋ ፡ ወነፍስ ፡
ወእምቴዜውአ ፡ በጊዜ ፡ ተፅናን ፡ ወባዕስ ፡ . . .

8. Ff. 36r–37r: Hymn to Sebastian, "Greeting to your hands which were bound behind your back," ሰላም ታ ዘሰብስትያኖስ. Cf. Chaîne, *Répertoire* 217.

9. Ff. 37v–38v: *Asmat* Prayer to Fanuʻel the archangel against disease, miscarriage, bleeding, and the evil eye. Cf. Chaîne, *Répertoire* 49.
በስመ ፡ አብ ፡ ወወልድ ፡ . . . ጸሎት ፡ በእንተ ፡ ሕማመ ፡ ተያሾ ፡
ወቁራኛ ፡ ደም ፡ ወሽተላይ ፡ . . .
ሰላም ፡ ለከ ፡ ለሰዳይ ፡ አጋንንት ፡ ፋኑኤል ፡ እምገጸ ፡ ፈጣሪ ፡ ልዑል ፡
ኢያስተዋድዩኒ ፡ ሰብእ ፡ በነገር ፡ ዘሕጉል ፡
እስመ ፡ አንተ ፡ መልአከ ፡ ኃይል።

10. Ff. 38v–40v: *Asmat* Prayer against evil spirit, evil eye, epilepsy, and Legewon.
በስመ ፡ አብ ፡ ወወልድ ፡ . . . በስሙ ፡ ለእግዚአብሔር ፡ አብ ፡ በስሙ ፡
ለእግዚአብሔር ፡ ወልድ ፡ በስሙ ፡ ለእግዚአብሔር ፡ መንፈስ ፡ ቅዱስ ፡
ታአስ ፡ አዝያስ ፡ ወለሚልካስ ፡ አክሴፍር ፡ አሐፌፌክር ፡ ወወጁን ፡

ዘሐጿን ፡ ዋክ ፡ ፍልፍልማየን ፡ አብሲ.ትር ፡ አፍርርዋቀ ፡ ወገኡ ፡ ዘፍጹም ፡
በጽልመት፡

11. Ff. 41r–44r: Prayer to Mary: "Take Refuge," ተማኅፀንኩ፡. Chaîne, *Répertoire* 297.

በስመ ፡ አብ ፡ ወወልድ ፡ . . . ተማፀንኩ ፡ በኵሉ ፡ ሕማሙ ፡ ዘዐለተ ፡
ዓርብ ፡ ለፍቁር ፡ ወልድኪ። ተማኅፀንኩ ፡ ኦ ፡ እግዝእትየ ፡ ማርያም ፡
በተእንዞቴ ፡ በመጣብሕ ፡ ወእብር። ተማኅፀንኩ ፡ ኦእግዚእትየ ፡ ማርያም ፡
በበዊአቴ ፡ ውስተ ፡ ቤተ ፡ ሊቀ ፡ ካህናት ፡ እንዘ ፡ ሕሙይ ፡ ወእሑር ፡
ለፍቁር ፡ ወልድኪ ፡ . . .

12. Ff. 44r–46v: Hymn to Mary, "In heaven and on earth," በስማይ፡
ወበምድር፡. Abbadie, *AbbCat* 171, f. 99v; Conti Rossini, *Notice* 104; Chaîne, *Répertoire* 248.

በስማይ ፡ ወበምድር ፡ ልብየ ፡ ክህደ ፡ [አልብየ ፡ ባዕደ ፡]
አብ ፡ ወእመ ፡ እኅት ፡ ወውሉደ ፡
ማርያም ፡ እትአመነኪ ፡ ገሀደ ፡
ኪያኪ ፡ ተስፋ ፡ ወኪያኪ ፡ መፍቅደ ፡
ኪያኪ ፡ ዓውቀ ፡ ወኪያኪ ፡ ዘመደ ፡ . . .

13. Ff. 46v–50v: Prayer to Jesus: I Take Refuge, ተማኅፀንኩ፡. Chaîne, *Répertoire* 370.

በስመ ፡ አብ ፡ ወወልድ ፡ . . . ኦ ፡ እግዚእየ ፡ ኢየሱስ ፡ ክርስቶስ ፡ ወልደ ፡
እግዚአብሔር ፡ ሕያው ፡ በእንተ ፡ ማርያም ፡ ወላዲትክ ፡ ርድአኒ ፡ ኦ ፡
እግዚእየ ፡ ኢየሱስ ፡ ክርስቶስ ፡ (በእንተ ፡) ማርያም ፡ ወላዲትክ ፡
ተሣሃለኒ ፡ . . .

14. Ff. 51r–53v: Net of Solomon, *Märbäbtä Solomon*, መርበብተ ሰሎሞን. Cf. Euringer, "Das Netz," *ZS* 6 (1928) 76–100, 300–314, and 7 (1928) 86–85; and Löfgren, "Wandamulette," 109–116.

በስመ ፡ አብ ፡ ወወልድ ፡ . . . በእንተ ፡ ሕማመ ፡ ባርያ ፡ ወሌጌዖን ፡
መርበብተ ፡ ሰሎሞን ፡ ዘከመ ፡ ረበቦሙ ፡ ለአጋንንት ፡ ከመ ፡ መርበብተ ፡
ዓሣ ፡ ባሕር ፡ እንዘ ፡ ይብል ፡ ሰዱቃኤል ፡ አዳታኤል ፡ ክኤስኤል ፡
ኤንኤል ፡ እምእላ ፡ እፍ ፡ ጸልሰኒ ፡ እግዚኦ ፡ ...

15. Ff. 53v–61v: *Asmat* Prayer to protect the shinbone (aq^{w}uyaṣat) and against a witch doctor who killed a person before his time, ጸሎት
በእንተ አቁያጻት ወዓቃብያነ ሥራይ.

በስመ ፡ አብ ፡ ወወልድ ፡ . . . ጸሎት ፡ በእንተ ፡ አቁያጻት ፡ ወዓቃብያን ፡
ሥራይ ፡ እለ ፡ ይቀትሉ ፡ ነፍስ ፡ ዘእንበለ ፡ ጊዜሁ ፡ እለ ፡ ቦሙ ፡ ዕፀ ፡
ወመሠውር ፡ እለ ፡ ይትሜሰሉ ፡ በሕልም ፡ ሌሊት ፡ ወመዓልት ፡ በራዕይ ፤
እለ ፡ ይትሜሰሉ ፡ ዘዕበ ፡ ወቁንጸል ፡ ነምረ ፡ ወአርዓሪ ፡ ቁዓ ፡ ወሆባየ ፡
. . .

16. Ff. 61v–64r: *Asmat* Prayer of Solomon against demons and witch doctors.
በስመ ፡ አብ ፡ ወወልድ ፡ . . . በእንተ ፡ ዘክመ ፡ ጸውያሙ ፡ ሰሎሞን ፡ ለአጋንንት ፡ ርኩሳን ፡ ወዓቃብያነ ፡ ሥራይ ፡ በዘአምሕሎሙ ፡ ወአውገዞሙ ፡ ወይቤሎሙ ፡ ንዑ ፡ መሕሉ ፡ ወተወገዙ ፡ ወበዝንቱ ፡ አስማተ ፡ ክርስቶስ ፡ ወኃሥርሙ ፡ በእሉ ፡ ቃላት ፡ ወይቤልዋ ፡ አምሕለነ ፡ ወአውግዘነ ፡ ከመ ፡ ኢይንብር ፡ ሥራየ ፡ በላዕለ ፡ ይትአመኑ ፡ በእሉ ፡ ቃላት ፡ ወአስማተ ፡ እግዚአብሔር ፡ . . .

17. Ff. 64r–65r: Asmat Prayer against an enemy.
በስመ ፡ አብ ፡ ወወልድ ፡ . . . ሹተክላሽ ፡ ኢላሽ ፡ ሽቱላሹር ፡ ሺ.ር.ታር ፡ አይኤል ፡ ገዴት ፡ አላላሂም ፡ እሩቤል ፡ በርዶም ፡ ኮር ፡ በእልፍውል ፡ ኪ.ኢ.ላዕ ፡ . . . በዝንቱ ፡ አስማቲክ ፡ ቀጦጠሙ ፡ ወዘርያሙ ፡ ከመ ፡ ሐመድ ፡ ወሞቁሎሙ ፡ ወአድክም ፡ ሃይሎሙ ፡ ወደምስስ ፡ ዝክሮሙ ፡ ንስቶሙ ፡ ወኢትሕንጾሙ ፡ ለዐርፍ ፡ ወጸላእየ፥ . . .

18. Ff. 65rv: Asmat Prayer against a demon.
በስመ ፡ አብ ፡ ወወልድ ፡ . . . ኢያሄል ፡ ሱራሄ ፡ ደጣሄ ፡ አቅብያዴር ፡ አብያቴር ፡ አምናቴር ፡ አደናይ ፡ ኬኒያ ፡ ግዮን ፡ ሴቃ ኤቃ ፡ ቀተናዊ ፡ ሰተናዊ ፡ አማኑኤል ፡ አስጠአ ፡ አፍራኤል ፡ ምርዮን ፡ ምናቴር ፡ ኤል ፡ ኤሎሄ ፡ አካ ፡ ሄጣ ፡ ሄድ ፡ . . .

19. Ff. 66r–81v: Prayer of Mary at Golgotha, ጸሎተ፡ እግዝእትነ፡ ማርያም፡ ዘሰኔ፡ ጎልጎታ፡. Copied and printed several times in its Gəʿəz and Amharic versions, e.g., ጸሎተ፡ እግዝእትነ፡ ማርያም፡ ዘሰኔ፡ ጎልጎታ፡ኛ በመቃብረኛ እግዚእነኝ ኢየሱስኝ ክርስቶስኝኛ (Addis Ababa: Täsfa Press, 1949 EC); ጸሎቶኝ እግዝእትነኝ ማርያምኝ (ዘሰኔኝ ጎልጎታኛ) በአማርኛኛ Addis Ababa: Täsfa Press, 1963 EC.; see also Sylvain Grébaut, "La prière de Marie au Golgotha," *JA* 226 (1935) 273–86; and Basset, *Apocryphes,* V:30–47; Strelcyn, *Lincei* 47, f. 73r; EMML 1213, f. 1a.
በስመ ፡ አብ ፡ ወወልድ ፡ . . . ጸሎት ፡ ዘእግዝእትነ ፡ ማርያም ፡ ወላዲተ ፡ አምላክ ፡ ቅድስት ፡ ድንግል ፡ አሙ ፡ ለብርሃን ፡ አብርኮርስ ፡ ረድአ ፡ ዮሐንስ ፡ . . . ጸሎት ፡ ዘጸለየት ፡ ባቲ ፡ አመ ፡ ጀወጀ ፡ ለዐርጋ ፡ ሰኔ ፡ በዲብረ ፡ ጎልጎታ ፡ ዝ ፡ ውእቱ ፡ መቃብር ፡ እግዚእነ ፡ ኢየሱስ ፡ ክርስቶስ። እንዘ ፡ ትብል ፡ ኦ ፡ እግዚአየ ፡ ኢየሱስ ፡ ክርስቶስ ፡ ዘተወለድክ ፡ አምኔየ ፡ በፈቃድክ ፡ ወበጠበውኩክ ፡ ሐሊብ ፡ አምአጥባትየ ፡ . . .

20. Ff. 81v–94r: Prayer to Jesus, "Guard me," ዕቀብኒኝ. Chaîne, *Répertoire* 371.

በስመ ፡ አብ ፡ ወወልድ ፡ . . . ኦ ፡ እግዚእየ ፡ ኢየሱስ ፡ ክርስቶስ ፡
ዕቀበኒ ፡ . . . አንተ ፡ ዘኃደርክ ፡ ውስተ ፡ ከርሠ ፡ እግዝእትን ፡ ማርያም ፡
ኦ ፡ እግዚእየ ፡ ኢየሱስ ፡ ክርስቶስ ፡ ዕቀብኒ ፡ . . .

21. Ff. 94r–96v: *Asmat* prayer against the evil eye with the story of Jesus and the Disciples at the Sea of Tiberias, Ṣälota Nədra, ጸሎተ፡ ንድራ፡. Cf. EMIP Magic Scroll 3:1.
በስመ ፡ አብ ፡ ወወልድ ፡ . . . ጸሎተ ፡ በእንተ ፡ ሕማሙ ፡ ዓይነ ፡ ጽላ ፡
ወዓይነ ፡ ወርቅ ፡ ወዓይነ ፡ አጋንንት ፡ ወዓይነ ፡ ወርቅ ፡ ወዓይነ ፡
አጋንንት ፡ . . . ጸሎተ ፡ ንድራ ፡ ወእንዘ ፡ የሐውር ፡ እግዚእን ፡ ኢየሱስ ፡
ክርስቶስ ፡ ውስተ ፡ ባሕረ ፡ ጥብርያደስ ፡ ምስለ ፡ ፲ወ፪ ፡ አርዳኢሁ ፡
ርእዩ ፡ መልእክ ፡ ብእሲት ፡ አረጊት ፡ ሕስምት ፡ መፍርሕት ፡
ወመደንግፅት ፡ . . .

22. Ff. 96v–100v: Image of Fanuel, *Mälk_a Fanu'el*, መልክአ፡ ፋኑኤል፡. Not in Chaîne, *Répertoire* but, cf. 166. *MG59* 376ff.
በስመ ፡ አብ ፡ ወወልድ ፡ ወመንፈስ ፡ ቅዱስ ፡ ወጠነ ፡
ማኅሌተ ፡ ክቡር ፡ ፋኑኤል ፡ ወዘመልክዑ ፡ ድርሳን ፡
እመስ ፡ ልሳንየ ፡ ላዕላዓ ፡ ኮነ ፡
ነዓ ፡ ፋኑኤል ፡ ትርድአኒ ፡ ወታድኅነኒ ፡ ፍጡነ ፡
እንዘ ፡ ለክ ፡ አጋዝ ፡ ወእዊጦን ፡ አነ ፡
ሰላም ፡ ለተፈጥሮትከ ፡ ምስለ ፡ መላእክት ፡ ኅቡረ ፡
እንዘ ፡ ይትከውን ፡ ቅድም ፡ ወእንዘ ፡ ኢትከውን ፡ ድኃሪ ፡
ሰዳዬ ፡ ሰይጣናት ፡ ፋኑኤል ፡ እምላዕለ ፡ ሰብእ ፡ ወትረ ፡
ስድደሙ ፡ ለሰይጣናት ፡ ወአርእዮሙ ፡ ኃሣረ ፡
ከመ ፡ ኢይግበሩ ፡ ኪያየ ፡ ማደረ ፡ . . .

23. Ff. 101r–120v: Anaphora of Mary attributed to Cyriacus of Bəhənsa, *Qəddase Maryam G^w äs'a*, ቅዳሴ፡ ማርያም፡.
አኮቴት ፡ ቀርባን ፡ ዘእግዝእትን ፡ ማርያም ፡ ድንግል ፡ ወላዲተ ፡ አምላክ ፡
ዘደረሰ ፡ ላቲ ፡ በመንፈስ ፡ ቅዱስ ፡ አባ ፡ ሕርቆስ ፡ ኤጲስ ፡ ቆጶስ ፡
ዘሀገረ ፡ ብህንሳ ፡ . . . ጉሥዓ ፡ ልብየ ፡ ቃለ ፡ ሠናየ ፡ ጉሥዓ ፡ ልብየ ፡
ቃለ ሠናየ ፡ ጉሥዓ ፡ ልብየ ፡ ቃለ ፡ ሠናየ ፡ ወእነ ፡ ዓየድዕ ፡ ቅዳሴሃ ፡
ለማርያም ፡ . . .

24. Ff. 121r–124v: Sword of Divinity, *Säyfä Mäläkot*, ሠይፈ፡ መለኮት፡, Abbadie, *AbbCat* 171, f. 29v; Conti Rossini, *Notice* 104; Abbadie 186, f. 104, Conti Rossini, *Notice* 233; Strelcyn, *Lincei* 47, f.88v; EMML 1169, f. 120b, EMIP 33:10.
በስመ ፡ እግዚአብሔር ፡ ሥሉስ ፡ ቀዳማዊ ፡ ዘእንበለ ፡ ትማልም ፡
ወማዕከላዊ ፡ ዘእን(በ)ለ ፡ ዮም ፡ ወደኃራዊ ፡ ዘእንበለ ፡ ጌሠም ፡ ብሉየ ፡
መዋዕል ፡ ዘእንበለ ፡ ሕማም ፡ ገባሬ ፡ ኩሉ ፡ ዘእንበለ ፡ ድካም ፡ . . .

25. Ff. 124v–129r: Litanies, ሊጠኒ፡. Cf. Velat, Me_erāf I:7–12; MQ51 262ff., for the days of the week: Monday, Enzä Nä'äk*ʷəto, እንዘ፡ ነአኩተ፡ (f. 124v); Tuesday, Səməkä Ḥəyaw, ስምከ፡ ሕያው፡ (f. 125v); Wednesday, Lä-tərus Egziʻo, ለትሩጽ፡ እግዚኡ፡ (f. 126r); Thursday, Kämä Tadäḫnännä, ከመ፡ ታድኅነነ፡ (f. 126v); Friday, Täzäkkär Egziʻo, ተዘከር፡ እግዚኡ፡ (f. 127v); Saturday, Qädame Ṣägga, ቀዳሚ፡ ጸጋ፡ (f. 128r); Sunday, Lä-'amǝlakä Məḫrät, ለአምላከ፡ ምሕረት፡ (f. 128v). The scribe failed to enter the first word of the title for each section, but left a space in each case.

Miniatures:
1. Talismanic charts and symbols: ff. 61v (based on the palindrome lofəḥäm), 64r and 65v, and 66r (based on the palindrome, Sälomon lofəḥämon).

Notes:
1. F. 1r and *passim*: name of owner, Gäbrä Śəllase.
2. F. 18r: Bishop Qerəlos III (2 June 1929–22 October 1950) and Bishop Abreham (Bishop of Gondar, to whom Bishop Qerəlos III entrusted interim care of the arch episcopate when he left for Italy on 21 May 1937 and who died on 29 July 1939).
3. Ff. i rv, 130v–131r: blank.
4. F. 101r: owner's wife, Amätä Śəllase.
5. F. 102r: Bishop Qerəlos III (2 June 1929– 22 October 1950) and Bishop Yohannes XV (1939–1945).
6. F. 129r, lower, in blue ink: pen trial.
7. F. 129v: –for your servant, Wäldä Giyorgis."
8. F. 130r: a name, *Ato* Bäyänägobaw.
9. F. 131v: scrawl.
10. Decorative designs: ff. 51r, 66r (*ḥaräg*); ff. 13r, 32r, 81v, 94r, 96v, 120v, 124v (multiple full stops).
11. The word Mary is rubricated.
12. Numbered quires: quires 2–4, 8–10 and 12.
13. Scribal intervention: words of text are written interlinearly (ff. 44r, 49r, 55r, 87r, 91v, etc.); and in the upper margin with a symbol (⊥) marking the location where the text is to be inserted (ff. 14r, line 6; 102r, line 8), and in another case where the symbol (⊤) is used (f. 26v, line 8); erasure markings are visible (ff. 17r, 118r, 125r, 126r); text has been removed (e.g., f. 15r).

Catalog of the Manuscripts

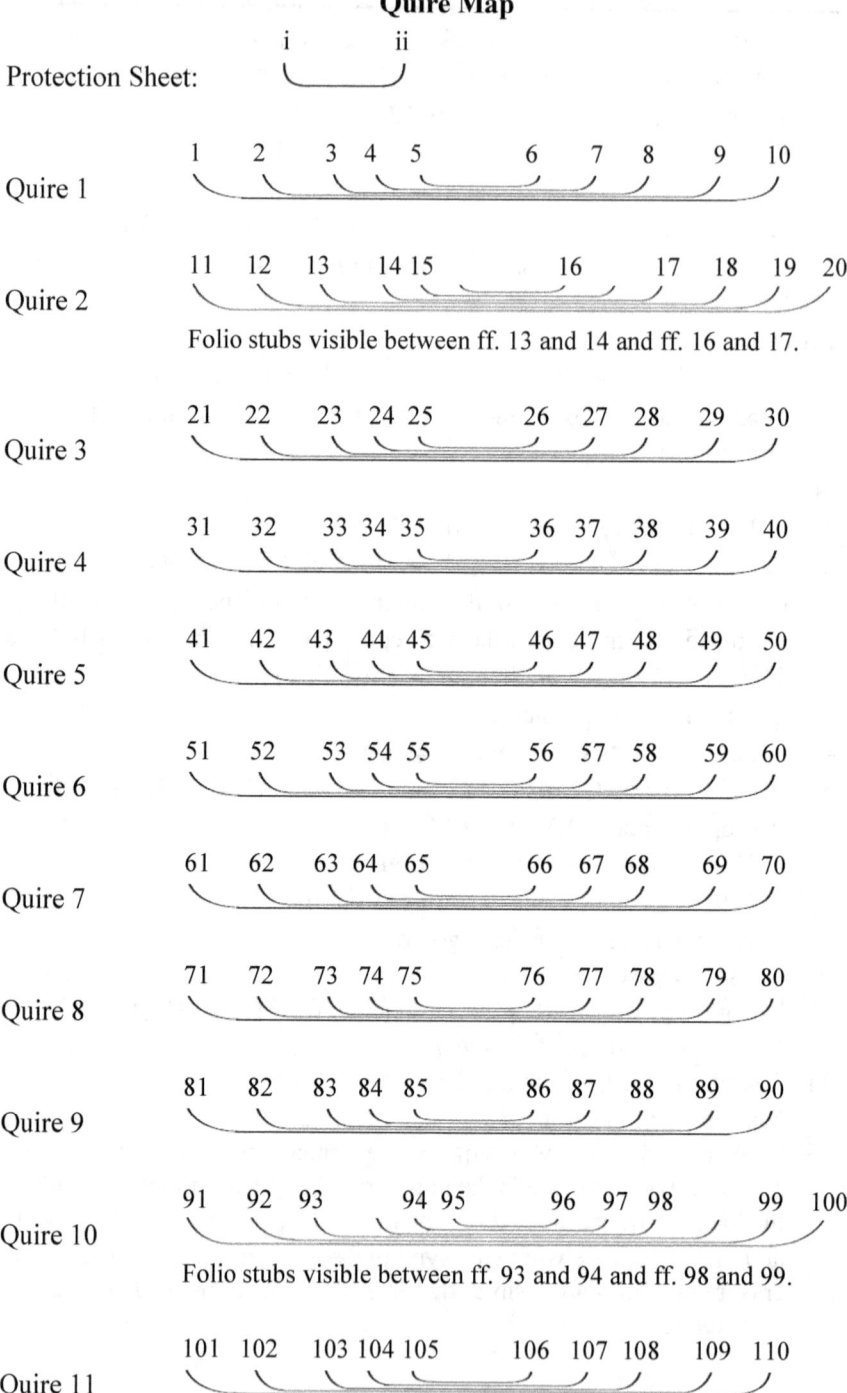

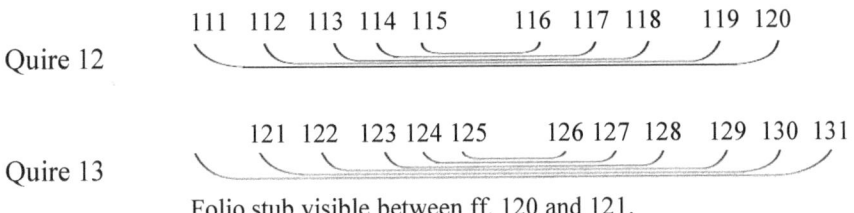

Folio stub visible between ff. 120 and 121.

MYS 17 – EMIP 617
Acts of Gäbrä Krestos, ገድለ፡ ገብረ፡ ክርስቶስ፡

Parchment, 178 x 120 x 50 mm, four Coptic chain stitches attached with bridle attachments to rough-hewn boards of the traditional wood, covered with tooled leather, linen visible between the turn-ins, protection quire + 6 full quires, iv + 54 folios, top margin 19 mm, bottom margin 27 mm, fore edge margin 16 mm, gutter margin 17 mm, ff. 1r–51v one column, 14 lines, Gə_əz, twentieth century.

Quire descriptions: protection quire and quires 1–6 balanced.

Major Works:
1. Ff. 1r–51v: Acts of Gäbrä Krestos, ገድለ፡ ገብረ፡ ክርስቶስ፡, divided into sections: section 1 (f. 1r); section 2 (f. 10r), section 3 (f. 15v), section 4 (f. 22r), section 5 (f. 28v), section 6 (f. 32v), section 7 (f. 35r), synaxarium entry (f. 47r).
   በስመ ፡ አብ ፡ ወወልድ ፡ . . . ንጽሕፍ ፡ በረድኤተ ፡ እግዚአብሔር ፡ ኦ ፡ እግዚእነ ፡ ኢየሱስ ፡ ክርስቶስ ፡ ዜናሁ ፡ ለቅዱስ ፡ ብእሴ ፡ እግዚአብሔር ፡ ገብረ ፡ ክርስቶስ ፡ ወልደ ፡ ቴፓደሎፖስ ፡ ንጉሠ ፡ ቁስጥንጥንያ ፡ ጸሎቱ ፡ . . . ወቴፓደስፖስ ፡ መፍቀሬ ፡ እንግዳ ፡ ወውቱ ፡ ይገብር ፡ ምጽዋተ ፡ ብዙኃ ፡ ለነዳያን ፡ ወለምስኪናን ፡ ለእቤራት ፡ ወለእጽለ ፡ ማውታ ፡ ወሐነጸ ፡ ቤተ ፡ ክርስቲያናት ፡ ወአብዓ ፡ መሥዋዕተ ፡ ወቁርባን ፡ ወአሥመር ፡ ለእግዚአብሔር ፡ . . .

Notes:
1. Ff. i r(ecto)-iv v(erso) and 52r–54v: blank.
2. F. 47r: name of scribe: Ḥaylä Giyorgis.
3. Decorative designs: ff. 22r, 28v, 35r, 47r, 51v (multiple full stops).
4. The words God, Gäbrä Krestos, Mary and George are rubricated.
5. Scribal intervention: words of text are written interlinearly (ff. 8r, 34v); erasure markings are visible (ff. 3v, 5v, 7v, 17r, etc.).

Quire Map

Protection Quire:

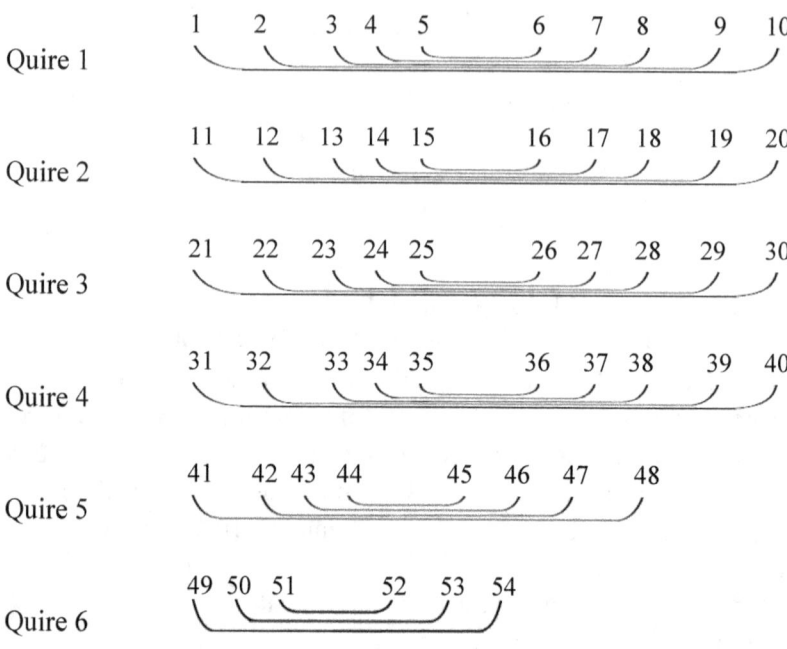

MYS 18 – EMIP 618
Mere„afChants, ምዕራፍ፡

Parchment, 222 x 162 x 48 mm, four Coptic chain stitches attached with bridle attachments to rough-hewn boards of the traditional wood, covered with tooled leather, linen visible between the turn-ins, headband and tailband, protection quire + 10 full quires, iv + 98 folios, top margin 22 mm, bottom margin 35–40 mm, fore edge margin 18 mm, gutter margin 8 mm, ff. 1r–97v two columns, 22 lines, Gəʿəz, twentieth century. Double-slip *maḥdär*.

Quire descriptions: protection quire and quires 1–10 balanced. Navigation system: marginal notation throughout, some of which may be overlooked text.

Major Works:
1. Ff. 1r–97v: *Mə_raf* chants, ምዕራፍ፡, with musical notation. Velat, *Me_erāf* I, and Velat, *Me_erāf* II; *AṢZ* 103–246. Supplications (f. 6v); chants for the season of the flower (*Zämänä Ṣəge*, f. 18v), Gate of Light (f. 39r), chants for Lent (f. 50r), Homily called ―Word of Blessing (Qalä Bäräkät) from our father, Yarəd" (f. 82r), Praises of Mary (90r), Mystagogia (f. 96r).

ምዕራፍ ፡ አምዮሐንስ ፡ እስከ ፡ ዮሐንስ። ቅዱስ ፡ እግዚአብሔር ፡ ቅዱስ ፡
ኃያል ፡ ቅዱስ ፡ ሕያው ፡ ዘኢይመውት ፡ . . . ለእግዚአብሔር ፡ ምድር ፡
በምልዓ ፡ ይቤ ፡ ዮሐንስ ፡ ወውእቱ ፡ ባሕር ፡ ሣረራ ፡ ም ፡ ወበአፍላግኒ ፡
ውእቱ ፡ አጽንዓ ፡ ዘጎብረት ፡ ወመኑ ፡ ይቀውም ፡ ውስተ ፡ መካነ መቅደሱ ፡
ም ፡ ዘንጹሕ ፡ ልቡ ፡ ወንጹሕ ፡ እደዊሁ ፡ ...

Notes:
1. Ff. i r(ecto)-iv v(erso) and 98rv: blank.
2. Decorative designs: ff. 4v–6v, 8v, 18v, 63v–64v, 89v, 90r (line of alternating red and black dots); ff. 6v, 11v, 42r, 49v, 88r, 97v (multiple full stops).
3. The words Mary and Michael are rubricated.
4. Numbered quires: quires 1–10.
5. Scribal intervention: words of text are written interlinearly (ff. 1r, 15v, 17v); erasure markings are visible (ff. 4v, 6r, 14v, 16v, etc.); text has been removed (e.g., f. 31r).

Quire Map

```
                           i    ii          iii   iv
Protection Quire:          _____/____/
```

```
                  1    2    3    4    5        6    7    8    9    10
Quire 1
```

```
                  11   12   13   14   15       16   17   18   19   20
Quire 2
```

```
                  21   22   23   24   25       26   27   28   29   30
Quire 3
```

```
                  31   32   33   34   35       36   37   38   39   40
Quire 4
```

```
                  41   42   43   44   45       46   47   48   49   50
Quire 5
```

```
                  51   52   53   54   55       56   57   58   59   60
Quire 6
```

```
                  61   62   63   64   65       66   67   68   69   70
Quire 7
```

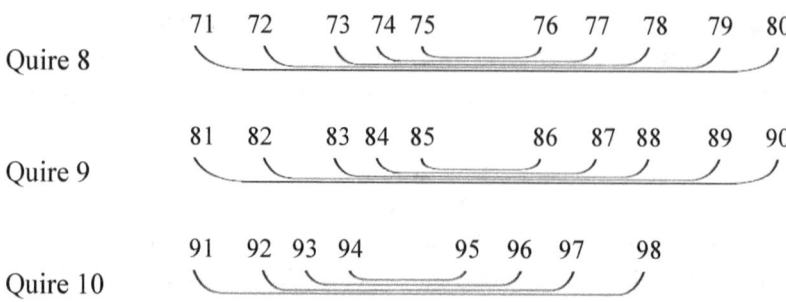

MYS 19 – EMIP 619
Horologium for the Daytime Hours, ሰዓታት፡ ዘመዓልት፡, One Miracle of Mary, ተአምረ፡ ማርያም፡, Readings from Scripture, and One Miracle of Jesus, ተአምረ፡ ኢየሱስ፡

Parchment, 160 x 120 x 45 mm, four Coptic chain stitches attached with bridle attachments to rough-hewn boards of the traditional wood, protection sheet + 7 full quires, ii + 52 folios, top margin 17 mm, bottom margin 23 mm, fore edge margin 14 mm, gutter margin 8 mm, ff. 1r–52r two columns, 19 lines, Gə_əz, twentieth century.

Quire descriptions: protection sheet and quires 1–7 balanced.

Major Works:
1. Ff. 1r–48v: Horologium for Daytime Hours, ሰዓታት፡ ዘመዓልት፡, arranged by the hours.
   መዝሙር ፡ ዘንግህ ፡ ሃሌ ፡ ሃሌ ፡ ሃሌ ፡ ሉያ ፡ ሃሌ ፡ ሃሌ ፡ ሉያ ፡ በጽሐ ፡ አዕንትየ ፡ ለገይሥ ፡ ከአንብብ ፡ ቃለ ፡ ስማዕ ፡ እግዚኦ ፡ ቃልየ ፡ ወለቡ ፡ ጽራኅየ ፡ ተወክፈኒ ፡ ጸሎትየ ፡ ከመ ፡ ዕጣን ፡ በቅድሜክ ፡ ዘይሰማዕ ፡ ግብር ፡ ሊተ ፡ ምሕረትክ ፡ በጽባሕ ፡ . . .
2. F. 48v–50v One Miracle of Mary: ተአምረ፡ ማርያም፡, How the Virgin Mary commanded the Archangel Uriel to show to a certain Roman monk the place where the sinners were held. The standard works on the miracles of Mary are Cerulli, *Maria*, and Budge, *Mary*.
3. F. 50v: Excerpt from the book of Leviticus 23.
4. Ff. 50v–51r: Excerpt from the book of Jeremiah 17: 26–27.
5. F. 51r: Excerpt from the Acts of the Apostles, chapter 17.
6. F. 51v–52r: One Miracle of Jesus, ተአምረ፡ ኢየሱስ፡, How Jesus, when he was seven years old, went to school and mastered the Old and New Testament books in seven days; and how Jesus mixed the red and black ink of the teacher and when the teacher punished him he separated the inks. S. Grébaut, *Les Miracles de Jésus, texte éthiopien*

publié et traduit par S. Grébaut, PO 60 (Paris: Firmin-Didot, 1919). See also Strelcyn *BL* entry 16 [OR. 8824] and the extensive bibliography there.

Notes:
1. Ff. i rv: blank.
2. F. ii r(ecto): "daytime hours."
3. F. ii v(erso): "This daytime hours belongs to (erased)."
4. Ff. 48v and following: name of the owner, Gäbrä Sänbät.
5. Decorative designs: f. 16r (line of alternating red and black dots); f. 48v (multiple full stops).
6. The words Mary and Michael are rubricated.
7. Scribal intervention: words of text are written interlinearly (ff. 2r, 6v, 9v, 10rv, etc.); and lines of text are written interlinearly (ff. 3rv, 47v, 48r); and in the upper margin with a symbol (+) marking the location where the text is to be inserted (ff. 13r, col. 1, line 12; 32r, col. 1, line 13), and in another case where the symbol (⊥) is used (f. 39v, col. 2, line 17); erasure markings are visible (f. 8r).

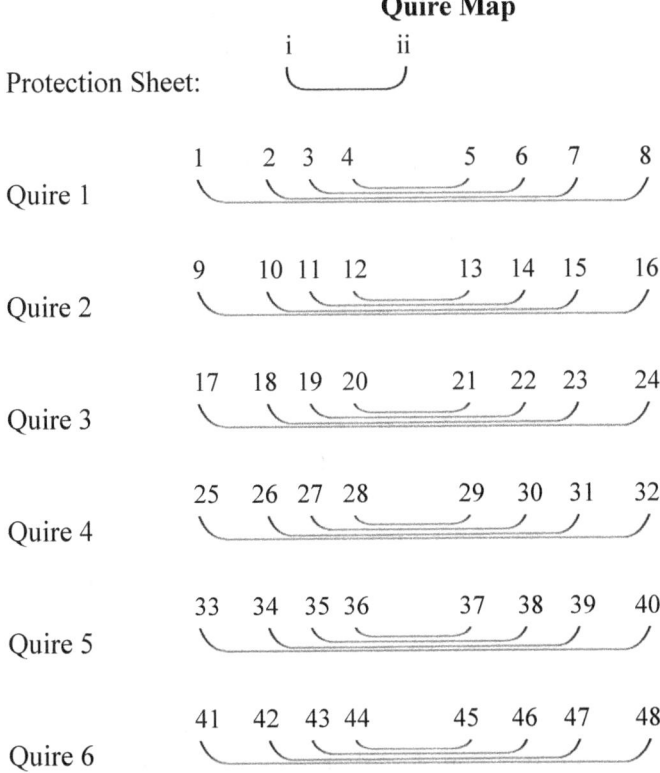

Quire 7   49 50   51 52

MYS 20 – EMIP 620
Lectionary from the Four Gospels, መጽሐፈ፡ ግጻዌ፡

Parchment, 169 x 122 x 55 mm, four Coptic chain stitches attached with bridle attachments to rough-hewn boards of the traditional wood, protection quire + 8 full quires, iii + 62 folios, top margin 12 mm, bottom margin 30 mm, fore edge margin 17 mm, gutter margin 6 mm, ff. 1r–60v two columns, 17 lines, Gəʿəz, twentieth century.

Quire descriptions: quires 1–8 balanced; protection quire adjusted balanced.

Major Works:
1. Ff. 1r–19v: Excerpts from the Gospel of Matthew in order, arranged for the festivals of the church, with instructions for readings from the Psalter interspersed: Nativity (f. 1r), Nativity [Bäʿala Ǝgzi] (3r), Q"usq"am (4v), Nazareth (5v), John (6r), Baptism [of Jesus] (6v), Saints (7r), Flower Season (8v), Apostles (9r), Martyrs (10v), Zion (12r), Night (13r), Good Servant Sunday (14r), Angels and Second Coming (15v), (Breaking) Bread (17r), Resurrection (f. 17v), Good Friday, Ninth Hour (19r).
2. Ff. 20r–31r: Excerpts from the Gospel of Mark in order, arranged for the festivals of the church, with instructions for readings from the Psalter interspersed. John the Baptist (20r), Baptism of Jesus (20v), Seed (21r), Rainy Season (21v), John (f. 23), Mount Tabor (24v), Hosanna (Palm Sunday) (26r), Synagogue (27r), Abraham, Isaac, Jacob and for the Departed (27r), Second Coming and Morning Praise (28r), (Breaking) Bread (28v), Good Friday (29r), Resurrection (30r), Ascension (31r).
3. Ff. 31v–42v: Excerpts from the Gospel of Luke in order, arranged for the festivals of the church, with instructions for readings from the Psalter interspersed. Luke and Zechariah (31v), Mary and Gabriel (32v), Mary (34r), Epiphany (35r), Good Shepherd Sunday and Nativity [Bäʿala Ǝgzi] (35v), Simon and Circumcision of Jesus (36v), Baptism (37r), Evening Prayer (38v), Advent (39v), Mount of Olives and Pagumen (the thirteenth month) (40v), Martyrs (41r), (Breaking) Bread and Resurrection (41v), Ascension (42v).
4. Ff. 43r–60v: Excerpts from the Gospel of John in order, arranged for the festivals of the church, with instructions for readings from the

Psalter interspersed. Trinity and Light Sunday (Advent) and for Cana (43r), Sunday and for Nicodemus (44v), The Paralytic and for Saturday (46v), Good Shepherd Sunday (Advent) and for Saints (48r), Church (50r), Hosanna (Palm Sunday) (51r), Maundy Thursday (52r), Paraclete (54v), ―We have finished" (for the week after Easter) (55r), Good Friday (57v), Virgins (58v), Resurrection (59r).

Notes:
1. Ff. i r(ecto)-iii v(erso) and 61r–62v.
2. Decorative designs: ff. 1r, 43r (multiple full stops between lines of alternating red and black dots); ff. 3r, 13r, 14r, 15v, 17v, 21v, 27r, 28r, etc. (multiple full stops); ff. 19r, 20r, 31v (line of alternating red and black dots).
3. The words Mary and Jesus are rubricated.
4. Numbered quires: quires 2–8.
5. Scribal intervention: words of text are written interlinearly (ff. 3r, 27v, 32r, 33v, 45r, etc.); and lines of text are written interlinearly (f. 35v).

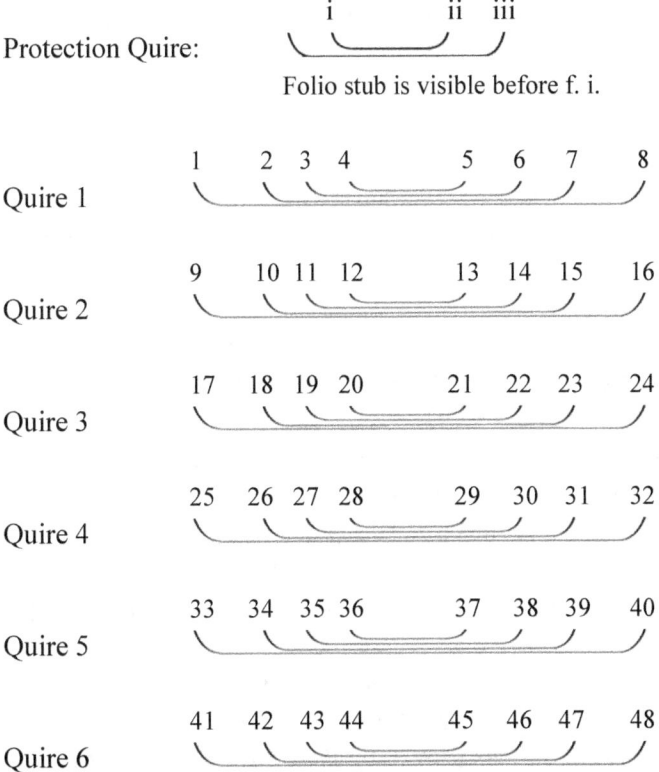

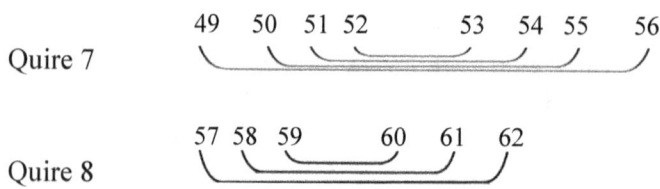

MYS 21 – EMIP 621
Dəggwa for the whole year, ድጓ፡, EMML 1256

The Ethiopian Manuscript Microfilm Library rendered this manuscript into microfilm and gave it the project number 1256. The microfilm was catalogued by Professor Getatchew and appears in volume IV, page 250. The information below includes information from that catalogue.

Parchment, 295 x 255 x 73 mm, four Coptic chain stitches attached with bridle attachments to rough-hewn boards of the traditional wood, covered with tooled leather and the leather is protected by a linen cover, protection sheet + 23 full quires, ii + 204 folios, top margin 18–28 mm, bottom margin 51–55 mm, fore edge margin 25 mm, gutter margin 13–15 mm, ff. 4r–204r in three columns, 38 lines, Gə_əz, dated, Sane 5, 1939 EC (f. 5a), Miyazya 28, 1941 EC (f. 201b), and 1942 EC (f. 128r) (= 12 June 1947–1950 A.D.).

Quire descriptions: protection sheet and quires 1–6, 8–12, 16 and 20–23 balanced; quires 7, 13–15 and 17–19 adjusted balanced. Navigation system: marginal notation throughout, some of which may be overlooked text.

Major Works:
1. Ff. Antiphonary for the Whole Year, Dəgg^wa, ድጓ፡. Published in Ethiopia, መጽሐፈ፡ ድጓ፡ ቅዱስ፡ ያሬድ፡ የደረሰው፡ Addis Ababa: Bərhanənna Sälam Press, 1959 EC, and see now, Kay Kaufman Shelemay and Peter Jeffery, eds., *Ethiopian Christian Religious Chant: An Anthology* (Madison WI: A-R Editions, Inc., 1993–1997); *Introduction*, Volume I (1993); *Performance*, Volume 2 (1994); and *History of Ethiopian Chant*, Volume 3 (1997).

   a. Ff. 4rv: Introduction dealing also with the history of the Dəgg^wa in Gə_əz.

   በስመ ፡ አብ ፡ ወወልድ ፡ . . . ንጽሕፍ ፡ መቅድመ ፡ ድጓ ፡ በረድኤተ ፡ እግዚአብሐር ፡ አሜን። አስመ ፡ ዝንቱ ፡ መጽሐፍ ፡ መንፈቁ ፡ ተረክበ ፡ እመጻሕፍተ ፡ ካህናት ፡ ቀደምት ፡ ወመንፈቁ ፡

ተጽሕፈ ፡ በመዋዕሊሁ ፡ ለንጉሥነ ፡ ዘርዓ ፡ ያዕቆብ ፡ ወልደ ፡ ሥርዐ ፡
ድንግል ፡ ንጉሠ ፡ እስራኤል ፡ ወበመዋ ፡ ንግሥትነ ፡ መልአክ ፡
ሞገሳ ፡ በጋ ፡ እግዚአብሔር ፡ ማርያም ፡ ስና ፡ እንዘ ፡ ሊቀ ፡
ጳጳስነ ፡ ዘኢትዮጵያ ፡ አባ ፡ ጴጥሮስ ፡ ወእንዘ ፡ አባ ፡ አብርሃም ፡
መምህር ፡ ዘደብረ ፡ ሊባኖስ ፡ ወእንዘ ፡ ወልደ ፡ ክርስቶስ ፡ ወልደ ፡
ጌራ ፡ ርእስ ፡ ሠራዊት ፡ ወሊቀ ፡ ሐራ ፡ ወአትናቴዎስ ፡ ወልዱ ፡
ተክለ ፡ ሃይማኖት ፡ ወልደ ፡ ወሰን ፡ ሰገድ ፡ መኰንን ፡ መኳንንት ፡
ወመልአክ ፡ ትእይንት ፡ ወጸሐፋሁኒ ፡ ኃጥእ ፡ ወአባሲ።

b. Ff. 5r–68r: Season of John the Baptist (Yoḥannəs).

በሥምረተ ፡ እግዚአብሔር ፡ አምላክ ፡ ዘአካላቲሁ ፡ ርስቱ ፡ ወአሐዱ ፡
መለኮት ፡ እንዘ ፡ አምኔሁ ፡ ትራዕዕ ፡ ክሂለ ፡ ወንትመራህ ፡ ፍኖተ ፡
ፍጻሜ ፡ ንዌጥን ፡ አስተጋብኦተ ፡ መዝሙር ፡ ዓቢይ ፡ ዘስሙ ፡ እንለ ፡
ፀሐይ ፡ አምብዙሀ ፡ መዛግብት ፡ . . .ምልጣን ፡ ዘሥርክ ፡ ዘዮሐንስ ፡
መጥምቅ ፡ በጀ ፡ ብዑዕ ፡ እንተ ፡ ዮሐንስ ፡ ዘሀለወክ ፡ ታእምር ፡
ወተሐውር ፡ ቅድመ ፡ እግዚአብሔር ፡ ጸሊ ፡ በእንቲአነ ፡ ውስተ ፡
ርእስ ፡ ዓውደ ፡ ዓመት ፡ ተጽሕፈ ፡ ተዝካርክ ፡ ባርከኒ ፡ እንሣእ ፡
በረከተክ ፡ ...

c. Ff. 69r–128v: Season of Astamḫero. The chant for the fifth of Mäggabit is separated from the rest (f. 128v).
d. Ff. 129r–200v: Season of Easter (Tenśa'e).
e. Ff. 200v–201v: Index of types of melodies, *Anqaṣa Halleta*.
f. Ff. 203r–204r: The chants for Yakkatit 16 (f. 203a) and for Taḫśaś 12 (f. 203v).

Miniatures:
1. F. 1r: Yarəd, to whom the authorship of the Dəggʷa is ascribed, with other clergymen chanting in front of King Gäbrä Mäsqäl, who is also standing crowned and surrounded by his army–not so indicated.

Notes:
1. Edges of the folios have been dyed red.
2. This codex is EMML 1256 (IV: 250).
3. Ff. i r(ecto)-ii v(erso), 1v–3v, 68v and 204v: blank.
4. At the end of each section, the number of different chants in each section is indicated by a different hand (ff. 68r, 128rv, 202r) and the number 10,702, which is the total of all the chants, is indicated on f. 202rv.
5. Beautiful multi-colored *ḫarags*: ff. 3r, 69r, and 129r.
6. Copied by a reliable hand, according to the colophon (f. 201v), from a manuscript known as Mäzgäbä Berhanä _Aläm of Betä Leḫem, which is owned by *Qäñ* Masfen Ḫayla Maryam with baptismal name

Gäbrä Maryam of Efrata in Mänzih (today Mänz). But it is most probably copied from EMML 1262.

7. Decorative designs: ff. 5r, 67v, 69r, 129r (*ḥaräg*); ff. 4v, 31r (lines of alternating red and black dots and lines of full stops); lines of red and black dots are used as section dividers throughout (e.g., ff. 5v, 6r, 7r); ff. 49r, 67v, 76v, 107r, 114r, 123v, 126v, 145v, 175v, 177r, 188r, 193v, 200v, 201v (multiple full stops).
8. The word Mary is rubricated.
9. Scribal intervention: words of text are written interlinearly (ff. 8v, 10rv, 13v, 21r, etc.); and lines of text are written interlinearly (ff. 10r, 53v, 133v, 142v, 170r, etc.); and in the upper margin with a symbol (+) marking the location where the text is to be inserted (ff. 11r, col. 3, line 23; 59v, col. 2, line 2; 70v, col. 1, line 16; 81r, col. 3, line 8; 101r, col. 1, line 19, etc.), and in another case where the symbol (+) is used interlinearly (f. 23r, col. 3, line 37), and in another case where the symbol (+) is used in the bottom margin (ff. 28r, col. 2, line 37; 47r, col. 2, line 29; 47r, col. 3, line 15; 49v, col. 2, line 30; 57v, col. 2, line 31, etc.); erasure markings are visible (f. 39v); text has been removed (e.g., ff. 14v, 43v, 82r, 111v).

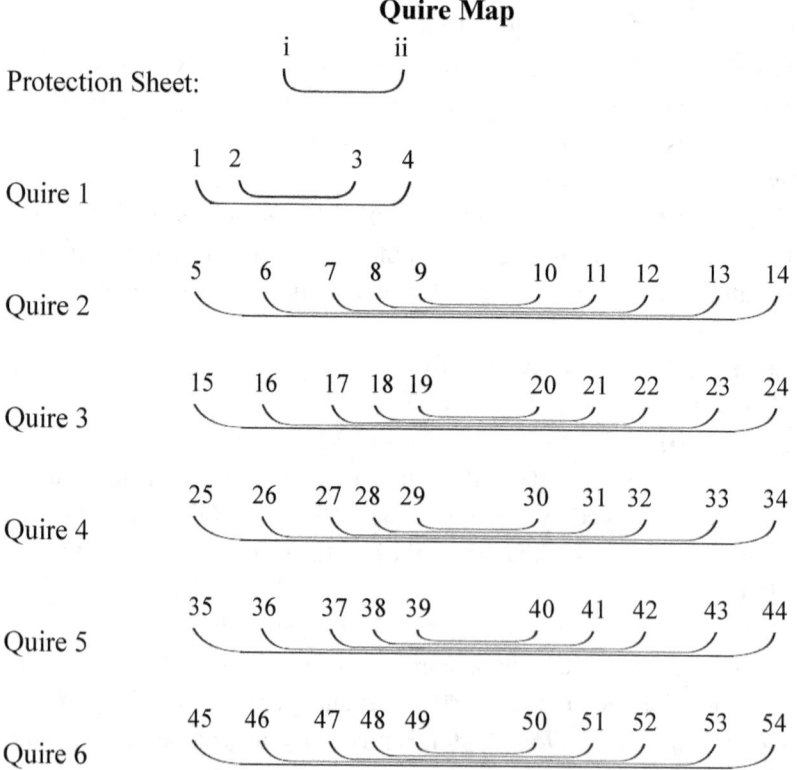

Quire Map

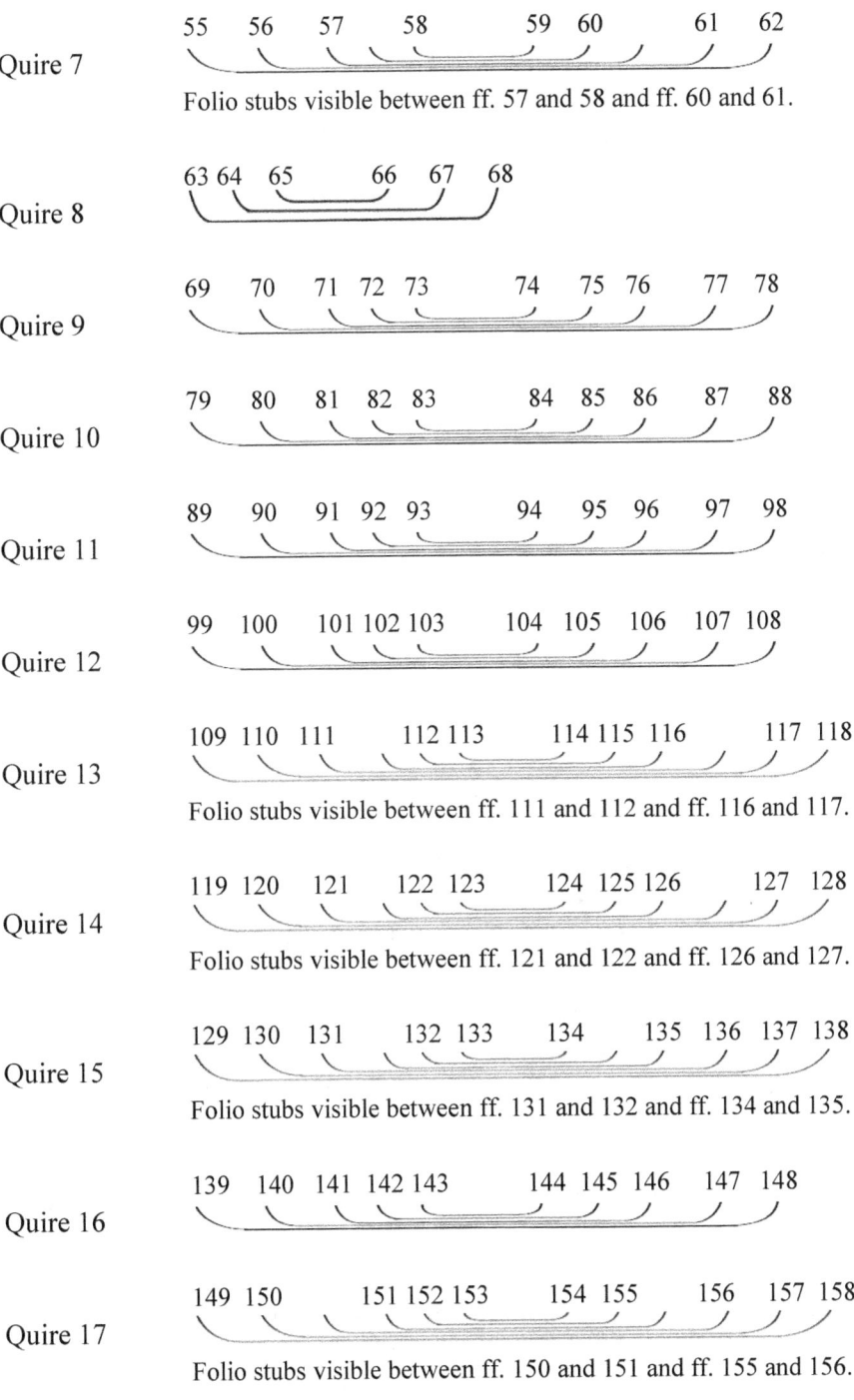

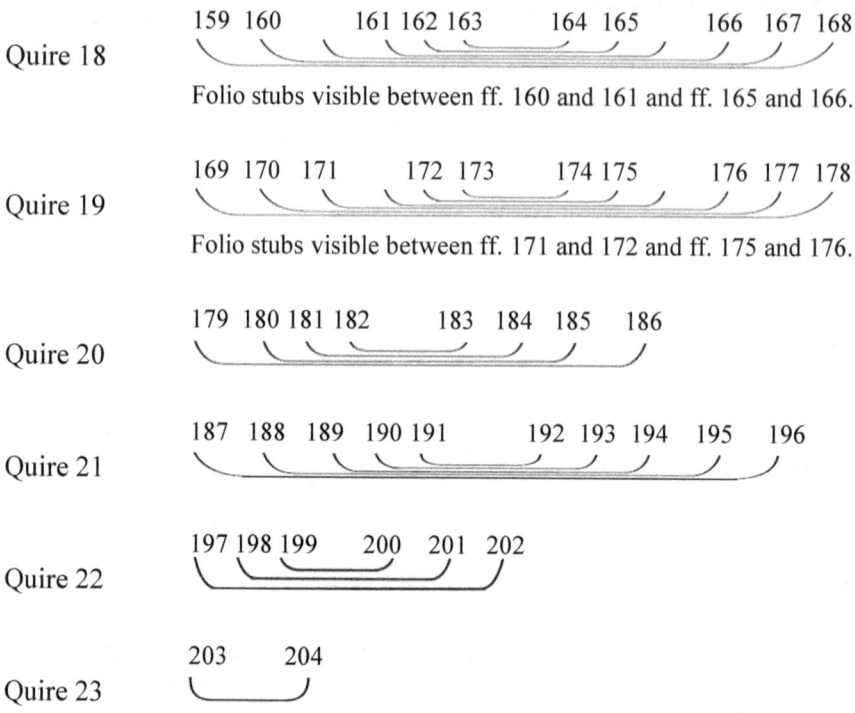

Quire 18: 159 160 | 161 162 163 | 164 165 | 166 167 168
Folio stubs visible between ff. 160 and 161 and ff. 165 and 166.

Quire 19: 169 170 171 | 172 173 | 174 175 | 176 177 178
Folio stubs visible between ff. 171 and 172 and ff. 175 and 176.

Quire 20: 179 180 181 182 | 183 184 185 186

Quire 21: 187 188 189 190 191 | 192 193 194 195 196

Quire 22: 197 198 199 | 200 201 202

Quire 23: 203 204

MYS 22 – EMIP 622
Abbreviated Antiphonary for the year, ድጓ፡, Mə'raf Chants, ምዕራፍ፡, School Chants, copied from EMIP 89

This manuscript is identical in content and layout with EMIP 89 (see Getatchew, et. al., *Catalogue*, volume 1: 231–234), from which it was, apparently, copied.

Parchment, 234 x 200 x 67mm, four Coptic chain stitches attached with bridle attachments to rough-hewn boards of the traditional wood, quarter bound with leather, protection sheet + 12 full quires, ii + 122 folios, top margin 27 mm, bottom margin 55–62 mm, fore edge margin 24–28 mm, gutter margin 8 mm, ff. 1r–78r three columns, ff. 78v– 121v in two columns (even though the parchment has been scored for three columns through f. 89v), 26 lines, Gə῾əz, late-nineteenth century.

Quire descriptions: protection sheet and quires 1–6 and 8–10 balanced; quires 7 and 11–12 adjusted balanced. Navigation system: marginal notation throughout, some of which may be overlooked text.

Major Works:
1. Ff. 1r–77v: Abbreviated Antiphonary for the year, *Dəggʷa*, ድጓ፧. Published in Ethiopia, መጽሐፈ፡ ድጓ፡ ቅዱስ፡ ያሬድ፡ የደረሰው፡ (Addis Ababa: Bərhanənna Sälam Press, 1959 EC), and see now, Kay Kaufman Shelemay and Peter Jeffery, eds., *Ethiopian Christian Religious Chant: An Anthology* (Madison WI: A-R Editions, Inc., 1993–1997); *Introduction*, Volume I (1993); *Performance*, Volume 2 (1994); and *History of Ethiopian Chant*, Volume 3 (1997). Manuscript begins with a table of contents on f. 1r:

በስመ ፡ ሥሉስ ፡ ቅዱስ ፡ አብ ፡ ወወልድ ፡ ወመንፈስ ፡ ቅዱስ ፡ ጸሐፍነ ፡
ዙእቱ ፡ መሥዋዕቱ ፡ ለእግዚአብሔር ፡ ምድር ፡ በምልዓ ፡
ወእግዚአብሔር ፡ ነግሠ ፡ ይትባረክ ፡ አርያም ፡ ወመ ፡ ዘአምላኪየ ፡
ወአርባዕት ፡ ዕዝል ፡ ወይእዜ ፡ ማኅሌት ፡ ወስብሐተ ፡ ነግህ ፡ ፫ ፡ ወሰላም ፡
ዘበዓላት ፡ ወዘሰናብት ፡ ዘመፀው ፡ ወዘፀደይ ፡ ዘክረምት ፡ ወዘሐጋይ ፡
ዘይፌጽም ፡ ጥንቀቀ ፡ ለለአውራሁ ፡ ወለለሰንበቱ ፡ ወዘለለኮሉ ፡ በዓላት ፡
ዘተሠርዓ ፡ በምድር ፡ ለወልደ ፡ አብ በሥምረቱ ፡ ፥ . . .

   a. Ff. 1r–46v: Season beginning with John the Baptist.
   b. Ff. 47r–77v: Season beginning with Easter.
   c. Ff. 78r–79r: Index of type of melodies, Anqäṣä Halleta.
2. Ff. 80r–110v: *Mə_raf* chants, ምዕራፍ፧. Velat, *Me_erāf* I, and Velat, *Me_erāf* II; *AṢZ* 103–246.

ምዕራፍ ፡ ዘዮሐን ፡ ወጌና ፡ ቅዱስ ፡ እግዚአብሔር ፡ ቅዱስ ፡ ኃያል ፡
ቅዱስ ፡ ሕያው ፡ ዘኢይመውት ፡ . . . ለእግዚአብሔር ፡ ምድር ፡ በምልዓ ፡
ወውሕቱ ፡ በባሕር ፡ ሣረራ ፡ ም ፡ ወበአፍላጊኒ ፡ ውእቱ ፡ አጽንዓ ፡ . . .

3. Ff. 112r–121v: School Chants, sometimes called የቃል፡ ትምህርት፧, (i.e., memorized learning).
   a. Ff. 112r–114r: *Əzəl Mästägabə*', መስተጋብዕ፧, beginning:

   ዕዝል ፡ መስተጋብዕ ፡ ዘሰኑይ ፡ ወለቡ ፡ ጽራኅየ ፡ ወአጽምዓኒ ፡ ቃለ ፡
   ስእለትየ ፡ ከመ ፡ ወልታ ፡ ሰሙር ፡ ክለልከነ ፡ እግዚኦ ፡ እግዚኦ ፡
   በመዓትክ ፡ ኢትኮሥፈኒ ፡ ወበመቅሠፍትክ ፡ ኢትገሥጸኒ ፡ አንተ ፡
   እግዚኦ ፡ ዕቀበን ፡ ወተማኅፀነነ ፡ እምዛቲ ፡ ትውልድ ፡ ዘለዓለም ፧. . .

   b. Ff. 114r–116r: *Qaləyä aṣmə*`, ቃልየ፡ አጽምዕ፧, beginning:

   ቃልየ ፡ አጽምዕ ፡ እግዚኦ ፡ ሃሌ ፡ ሉያ ፡ ሃሌ ፡ ሉያ ፡ ወለቡ ፡
   ጽራኅየ ፡ ሃሌ ፡ ሉያ ፡ ወአጽምዕኒ ፡ ቃለ ፡ ስእለትየ ፡
   ንጉሥየኒ ፡ ወአምላኪየኒ ፡ ሃሌ ፡ ሉያ ፡ . . .

   c. Ff. 116r–119v: *Səma_ani*, beginning:

   ስምዓኒ ፡ እግዚኦ ፡ ጽሎትየ ፡ ሃሌ ፡ ሃሌ ፡ ሃሌ ፡ ሉያ ፡ ሃሌ ፡ ሉያ ፡
   ሃሌ ፡ ሉያ ፡ ወይብጻሕ ፡ ቅድሜከ ፡ ገዓርየ ፡ ሃሌ ፡ ሃሌ ፡ ሉያ ፡
   ሃሌ ፡ ሉያ ፡ ሃሌ ፡ ሉያ ፡ ሃሌ ፡ ሉያ ፡ ወኢትሚጥ ፡ ገጽከ ፡ እምኔየ ፡

በዕለተ ፡ ምንዳቤየ ፡ አጽምዕ ፡ እዝነከ ፡ ኀቤየ ፡ ሃሌ ፡ ሉያ ፡ አመ ፡
ዕለተ ፡ እጼውዓከ ፡ ፍጡነ ፡ ስምዓኒ ፡ ሃሌ ፡ ሉያ ፡ ለዓለም ፡
ወለዓለመ ፡ ዓለም ፡ ፡ . . .

d. Ff. 119v–121v: *Arəyam*, አርያም፡, beginning:
አርያም ፡ ሃሌ ፡ ሉያ ፡ ለአብ ፡ ሃሌ ፡ ሉያ ፡ ለወልድ ፡ ሃሌ ፡ ሉያ ፡
ወለመንፈስ ፡ ቅዱስ ፡ ቀዳሚ ፡ ዜማ ፡ ግበሩ፡በዐለ ፡ በትፍሥሕት ፡ እስከ ፡
አትርንቲሁ ፡ ለምሥዋዕ ፡ ዛቲ ፡ ፋሲካ ፡ ቀዳሚት ፡ ሕግ ፡ ዮሐንስኒ ፡
ሁሎ ፡ ያጠምቅ ፡ በሄኖን ፡ በሄኖን ፡ በቅሩብ ፡ ሳሌም ፡ በማዕደተ ፡
ዮርዳኖስ ፡ . . .

Notes:
1. Ff. i r(ecto)–ii v(erso), 79v, 111rv and 122v: blank.
2. F. 121v: note of ownership, ―This book belongs to Ab Śəlus, his father's name is Wäldä Dawit Ṭəqä Ḥer, his mother's name is Ǝgzi'abəḥer Awit. He gave it to his son, Estifanos."
3. F. 122r: Pen trial with the name of the scribe(?): ―A good pen, tried by Sunət (?) (the scribe of the book?), his father Bəyä Giyorgis. I, your servant wrote in my hand."
4. Decorative designs: lines of alternating red and black dots are used as section dividers throughout (e.g., ff. 3v, 5r, 7v); multiple full stops are used as section dividers throughout (e.g, ff. 8rv, 10v).
5. The word Mary is rubricated.
6. Scribal intervention: words of text are written interlinearly (ff. 2v, 3v, 6v, 14v, etc.); and in the upper margin with a symbol (⊥) marking the location where the text is to be inserted (ff. 18r, col. 2, line 17; 31r, col. 3, line 23; 64r, col. 2, line 1; 66r, col. 2, line 3; 121v, col. 1, line 15).

Quire Map

Protection Sheet: i, ii

Quire 1: 1, 2, 3, 4, 5, 6, 7, 8, 9, 10

Quire 2: 11, 12, 13, 14, 15, 16, 17, 18, 19, 20, 21, 22

Quire 3: 23, 24, 25, 26, 27, 28, 29, 30, 31, 32, 33, 34

Quire 4: 35, 36, 37, 38, 39, 40, 41, 42, 43, 44, 45, 46

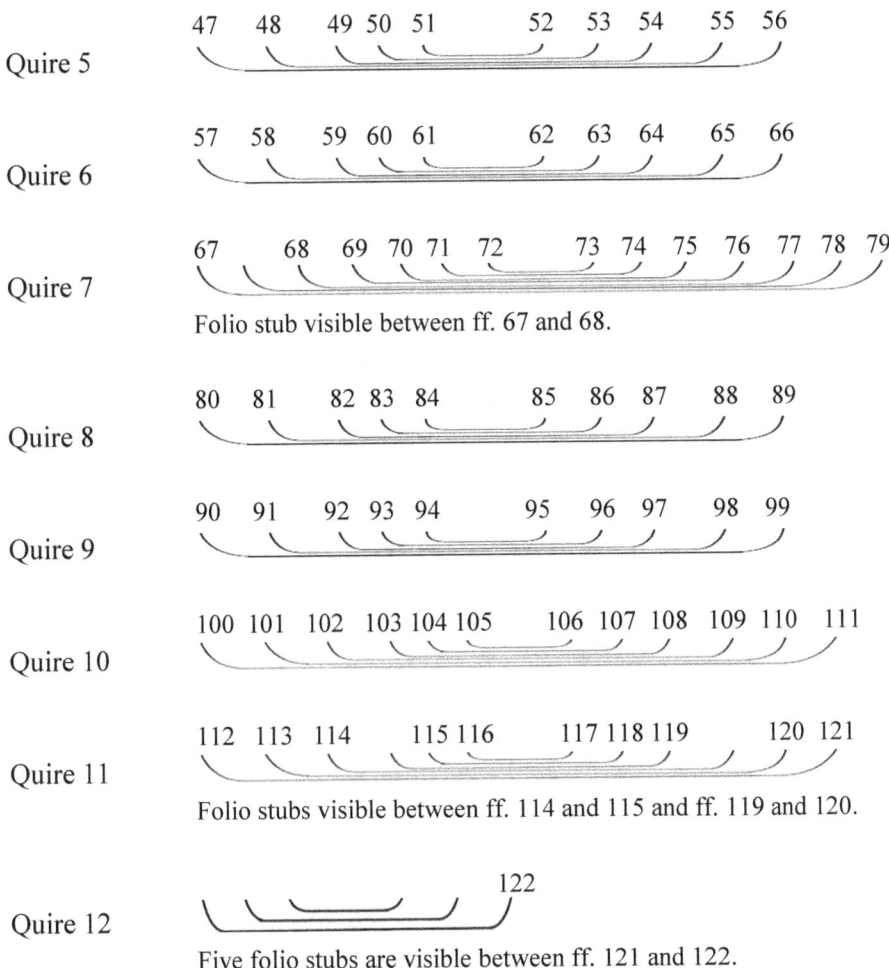

MYS 23 – EMIP 623
Homiliary in Honor of the Monthly Feast of the Archangel Michael, ድርሳነ፡ ሚካኤል፡

Parchment, 265 x 210 x 70 mm, four Coptic chain stitches attached with bridle attachments to rough-hewn boards of the traditional wood, covered with tooled leather and a fabric cover protects the leather, protection sheet + 13 full quires, ii + 91 folios, top margin 22–25 mm, bottom margin 35–40 mm, fore edge margin 23–27 mm, gutter margin 10 mm, ff. 1r–89v two columns, 22–24 lines, Gəʿəz, twentieth century.

Quire descriptions: protection sheet and quires 3–13 balanced; quires 1–2 adjusted balanced.

Major works:
1. Ff. 1r–89r: Homiliary in Honor of the Archangel Michael. Dərsanä Mika'el, ድርሳነ፡ ሚካኤል፡, Published several times in Ethiopia; see for example, *DM* 11–205. See also BL Or. 4849, Strelcyn *BL* 94–7; EMML 1133.
    a. Ff. 1r–10r: Ḫədar.
        (1) Ff. 1r–5v: Homily by Dämatewos, bishop of Alexandria.
        (2) Ff. 6r–7v: Miracle.
        (3) Ff. 7v–9v: Mission of the Archangel to Joshua.
        (4) Ff. 9v–10r: Greeting to the Archangel, *Sälam*.
    b. Ff. 10r–17v: Taḫśaś.
        (1) Ff. 10r–15v: Homily by John, the archbishop.
        (2) Ff. 16rv: Miracle.
        (3) Ff. 16v–17r: Synaxary Entry: Mission of the Archangel to rescue the three holy children.
        (4) F. 17rv: Greeting to the Archangel, *Sälam*.
    c. Ff. 17v–27v: Ṭərr
        (1) Ff. 17v–26r: Homily, author not given.
        (2) Ff. 26v–27r: Miracle.
        (3) F. 27r: Synaxary Entry: Mission of the Archangel to save Jacob from the wrath of Esau.
        (4) F. 27v: Greeting to the Archangel, *Sälam*.
    d. Ff. 27v–32v: Yäkkatit.
        (1) Ff. 27v–31r: Homily, author not given.
        (2) Ff. 31r–32r: Miracle.
        (3) Ff. 32rv: Synaxary Entry: Mission of the Archangel to Samson, the giant.
        (4) F. 32v: Greeting to the Archangel, *Sälam*.
    e. Ff. 33r–49r: Mäggabit.
        (1) Ff. 33r–47v: Homily by the archbishop of Antioch
        (2) Ff. 47v–48v: Miracle.
        (3) F. 48v: Synaxary Entry: Mission of the Archangel to Balaam.
        (4) Ff. 48v–49r: Greeting to the Archangel, *Sälam*.
    f. Ff. 49r–54v: Miyazya.
        (1) Ff. 49r–52v: Homily of Rətu_Haymanot.
        (2) Ff. 52v–54r: Miracle.

(3) F. 54v: Synaxary entries: Mission of the Archangel to the Prophet Jeremiah.
(4) F. 54v: Greeting to the Archangel, *Sälam*.

g. Ff. 55r–58r: Gənbot.
  (1) Ff. 55r–56r: Homily by Yoḥannəs, Bishop of Ethiopia, who came after Bishop Yəsḥaq, on the conflict between the consort of King Arqadewos and John Chrysostom.
  (2) Ff. 56r–57v: Miracle.
  (3) Ff. 57v–58r: Synaxary entry: Mission of the Archangel to Habakkuk.
  (4) F. 58r: Greeting to the Archangel, *Sälam*.

h. Ff. 58r–71r: Säne
  (1) Ff. 58r–63v: Homily by Yoḥannəs, Bishop of Aksum on the family of Astäraniqos and Euphemia.
  (2) Ff. 63v–64v: Miracle.
  (3) Ff. 65r–70v: Synaxary entry: The building of the church of the Archangel in place of a pagan temple in Alexandria.
  (4) Ff. 70v–71r: Greeting to the Archangel, *Sälam*.

i. Ff. 71r–75v: Ḥamle
  (1) Ff. 71r–74v: Homily [by Bishop Yoḥannəs] on the wicked wealthy man whose property was inherited by the son of his poor neighbor.
  (2) Ff. 74v–75r: Miracle.
  (3) Ff. 75rv: Synaxary entry: Mission to the camp of Sennacherib.
  (4) F. 75v: Greeting to the Archangel, *Sälam*.

j. Ff. 76r–79v: Nähase
  (1) Ff. 76r–78v: Homily (anonymous) on the book of the angels that came from Jerusalem.
  (2) Ff. 78v–79r: Miracle.
  (3) Ff. 79rv: Synaxary entry: Mission of the Archangel to the Emperor Constantine.
  (4) F. 79v: Greeting to the Archangel, *Sälam*.

k. Ff. 79v–84v: Mäskäräm.
  (1) Ff. 79v–81v: Homily (anonymous) on not worshipping other gods.
  (2) Ff. 81v and 83r–84v: Miracle. F. 82 is misplaced.
  (3) Ff. 84v: Synaxary entry: Mission to Prophet Isaiah.
  (4) F. 84v: Greeting to the Archangel, *Sälam*.

1. Ff. 84v–89r: Ṭəqəmt.
    (1) Ff. 84v–85v: Homily (anonymous) on the need to make the angels sureties by honoring them.
    (2) Ff. 85v–88v and 82r: Miracle.
    (3) Ff. 82rv: Synaxary entry: Mission to Prophet Samuel.
    (4) Ff. 82v and 89r: Greeting to the Archangel, *Sälam*.
2. Ff. 89rv: Asmat Prayer against disease and demon.

Illumination:
1. Drawing, in pencil, of the Archangel Michael.

Varia:
1. F. ii r(ecto): The days on which the heavens are open to receive prayer.

Notes:
1. Blank: Ff. i rv, ii r(ecto), 10v, 90r, 91v.
2. F. 9v: Original owner: Wäldä Rufa_el. This name has been erased in most places and replaced with that of the secondary owner.
3. F. 1 and *passim*. Secondary owner, in red ink: Wälättä Maryam.
4. F. 90v, bottom in blue ink: scribbles.
5. F. 6v used to have a painting pasted onto the folio. The caption remains: ―How the Jews bound the hands of Jesus and put on him the crown of thorns."
6. Decorative designs: (*ḥaräg*); ff. 9v, 57v, 64v, 71r, 79r, 84v, 89rv (multiple full stops); f. 17v (line of alternating red and black dots).
7. The words Michael and Mary are rubricated.
8. Numbered quires: quires 2 and 6–12.
9. Scribal intervention: erasure markings are visible (f. 62r); text has been removed (e.g., f. 16r).

Quire Map

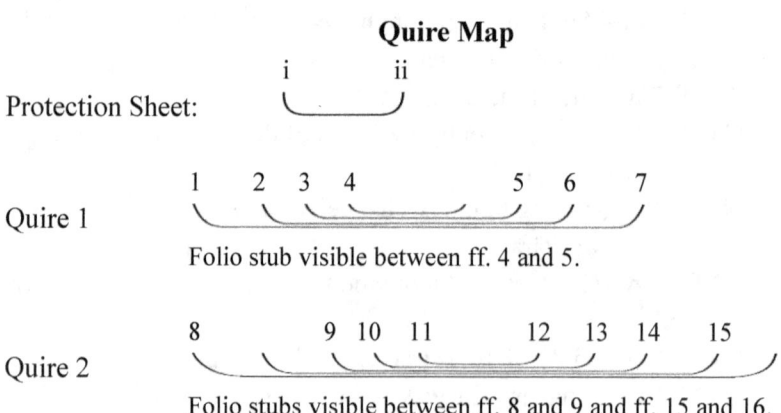

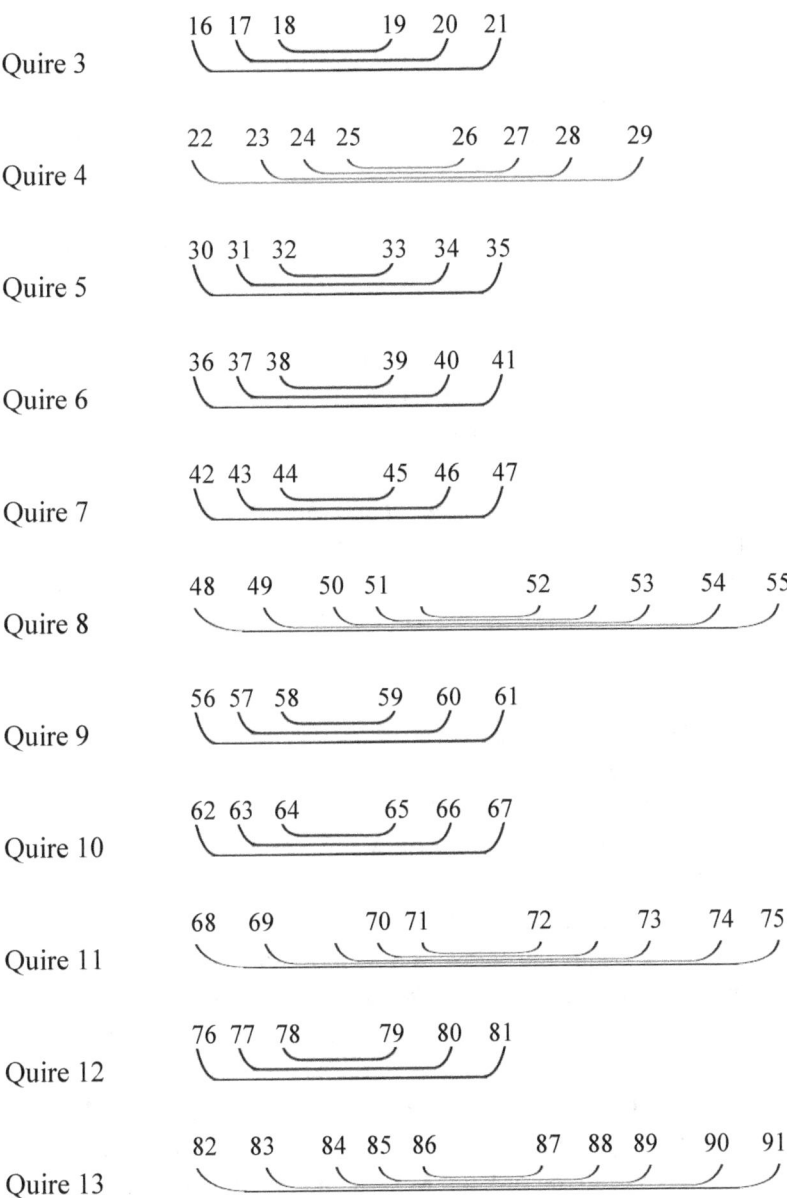

MYS 24 – EMIP 624
Acts of Gäbrä Mänfäs Qəddus, ገድለ፡ ገብረ፡ መንፈስ፡ ቅዱስ፡, and
Miracles of Gäbrä Mänfäs Qəddus, ተአምረ፡ ገብረ፡ መንፈስ፡ ቅዱስ፡
Parchment, 210 x 140 x 75 mm, four Coptic chain stitches attached with bridle attachments to rough-hewn boards of the traditional wood,

protection quire + 18 full quires, iv + 179 folios, top margin 20 mm, bottom margin 44 mm, fore edge margin 15 mm, gutter margin 13 mm, ff. 1r–179r two columns, 17 lines, Gə_əz, twentieth century.

Quire descriptions: protection quire and quires 1–15 and 17–18 balanced; quire 16 adjusted balanced.

Major Works:
1. Ff. 1r–131r: Acts of Gäbrä Mänfäs Qəddus, *Gädlä Gäbrä Mänfäs Qəddus*, ገድለ፡ ገብረ፡ መንፈስ፡ ቅዱስ፡, arranged for the days of the week. See, Paolo Marrassini, *Vita Omelia Miracoli del Santo Gabra Manfas Qeddus*, CSCO 107 and 108 (Louvain, 2003).

    በስመ ፡ እግዚአብሔር ፡ አብ ፡ ዘኢይትዌለጥ ፡ አምሀላዌሁ ፡ ወበስመ ፡ እግዚአብሔር ፡ ወልድ ፡ ዘኢይትፈለጥ ፡ እምሕፅን ፡ አቡሁ ፡ ወበስመ ፡ እግዚአብሔር ፡ መንፈስ ፡ ቅዱስ ፡ መነፈስ ፡ ጥበብ ፡ ጸራቅሊጦስ ፡ ናዛዜ ፡ ኵሉ ፡ . . . ገድል ፡ ለቅዱስ ፡ ወለብፁዕ ፡ አቡነ ፡ ገብረ ፡ መንፈስ ፡ ቅዱስ ፡ ጽሙድ ፡ መስተጋድል ፡ ኮከበ ፡ ገዳም ፡ ዘዝኩር ፡ ክብሩ ፡ ወርዕስናሁ ፡ ሠናይ ፡ ወብፁዕ ፡ ወኔር ፡ አቡነ ፡ ገብረ ፡ መንፈስ ፡ ቅዱስ ፡ ገዳማዊ ፡ ዘሠረቀ ፡ አምሀገረ ፡ ንኒሳ ፡ አምፀዳለ መትሕተ ፡ ምድር ፡ ወአምደቡብ ፡ ግብፅ ፡ . . .

    a. Ff. 1r–21r: [Reading for Monday.]
    b. Ff. 21v–42v: Reading for Tuesday.
    c. Ff. 42v–68v: Reading for Wednesday.
    d. Ff. 68v–87r: Reading for Thursday.
    e. Ff. 87v–110r: Reading for Friday.
    f. Ff. 110r–122r: Reading for Saturday.
    g. Ff. 122r–131r: Reading for Sunday.

2. Ff. 131r–179r: Eighteen Miracles of Gäbrä Mänfas Qəddus, *Tä'ammərä Gäbrä Mänfas Qəddus* ተአምረ፡ ገብረ፡ መንፈስ፡ ቅዱስ፡, partially arranged for the days of the week; sections have been delineated with numbers

    a. Ff. 131r–135v: Miracle One, designated as Reading for Monday. How Səmə_on and Aqəlesya went to the church to pray about a child; how an icon of Saint Mary spoke to Aqəlesya about having a child and how Aqəlesya conceived Gäbrä Mänfas Qəddus that very night; how she gave birth to a child and how he fled to the desert when he was three years old.

    b. Ff. 135v–140r: Miracle Two, designated as Reading for Tuesday. How Gäbrä Mänfas Qəddus was sent to Gibeon by the Lord and how the wild animals were subdued by him; how Satan tried to attack him in the form of a wild beast and how Gäbrä

Mänfas Qəddus defeated him; how the people of Gibeon attacked him but how God comforted him; how our Lord commanded him to go to Ethiopia.

c. Ff. 140r–142v: Miracle Three. How Satan tempted Gäbrä Mänfas Qəddus in the form of an elder; how Satan advised him to abandon his ascetic life and go to his father's house; how an angel of God comforted him and fed him with bread from heaven.

d. Ff. 142v–147r: Miracle Four. How the Lord told Gäbrä Mänfas Qəddus that his hair would be a garment for him; how bishop Abraham ordained him and gave him monastic orders; how he visited the holy land: Bethlehem, Nazareth, Galilee, Jordon, Mount Olives, Mount Tabor and Golgotha.

e. Ff. 147r–150r: Miracle Five. How Gäbrä Mänfas Qəddus came to Ethiopia; how he arrived at Axum; how he met King Lalibela; how the king begged him to stay with him and how he wanted to stay at Mount Cəqʷala; how Gäbrä Mänfas Qəddus died in Cəqʷala; and how the angels took his body to heaven.

f. Ff. 150r–152v: Miracle Six. How a certain monk who led a sinful life heard the reading of the Acts of Gäbrä Mänfas Qəddus and the covenant the Lord had given to him; how the monk decided to make a feast on the memorial of saint Gäbrä Mänfas Qəddus; how, when the monk was killed by bandits, the angel of darkness took him to God, but Gäbrä Mänfas Qəddus interceded to save the monk from hell.

g. Ff. 152v–154r: Miracle Seven. How a certain demon-possessed woman went to a priest and asked him to pray for her; how the priest led her to observe a feast day for Gäbrä Mänfas Qəddus; how Gäbrä Mänfas Qəddus came on the night of the feast day of *Mäggabit*, rebuked the demon and healed the woman.

h. Ff. 154r–155r: Miracle Eight. How a certain widow who observed the feast of Gäbrä Mänfas Qəddus met two bandits on the road; how they took the grain she carried for the feast; how the other bandits took her to the forest to defile her; and how a lion came to rescue her when she cried to Gäbrä Mänfas Qəddus.

i. Ff. 155r–157r: Miracle Nine. How a certain woman was an adulteress, a Sabbath breaker and giver of false oaths; how God sent a big snake to her and it went inside her and ate whatever she ate and whenever she did not eat, the snake ate part of her body; how she prayed to Gäbrä Mänfas Qəddus, made a feast day for him and how he healed her and cast out the snake.

j. Ff. 157r–160r: Miracle Ten. How a certain nun conceived through adultery; how she asked Gäbrä Mänfas Qəddus to save her from this disgrace; how, upon leaving the church she met a barren woman who wanted to conceive; how the saint interceded on behalf of her with Jesus and instructed her to go to the church and lick the covering of the book of Gäbrä Mänfas Qəddus; how she did so and how the barren woman touched the covering and how the fetus transferred from the nun to the barren woman.

k. Ff. 160rv: Miracle Eleven. How a certain man was on his way to the church during the feast of Gäbrä Mänfas Qəddus and a bird took his baptismal necklace of yarn (ማቶብ); how the man beseeched the bird by the power of Gäbrä Mänfas Qəddus; and how, when he returned from the church, the bird was dead and the scarf was there (EMIP 153, ff. 48v–49v).

l. Ff. 160v–163v: Miracle Twelve. How the child of a certain woman who observed the feast day of Gäbrä Mänfas Qəddus was killed, along with six friends, when they were playing; how Gäbrä Mänfas Qəddus determined to raise him from the dead because of the faithful observance of his feast day by the boy's mother; and how the boy was brought back to life and the people of the city determined to observe the feast day of Gäbrä Mänfas Qəddus with renewed fervor and how, when they entered the church, they found the other children, raised from the dead and holding candles.

m. Ff. 163v–164r: Miracle Thirteen. How a certain woman took a dead son to the monastery of Gäbrä Mänfas Qəddus and put him on the community's cooking pot and how the child was raised from the dead.

n. Ff. 164r–167v: Miracle Fourteen. How a certain wealthy man asked a guest in his house, "what can I do to be righteous?" how the man told him to observe the feast days of the saints and martyrs; how the martyrs came one at a time and asked the wealthy man to observe only their feast, how the saints, with Gäbrä Mänfas Qəddus, came to the wealthy man, gave him bread of heaven and told him that he should be devoted only to them, warning him that the martyrs would kill him; how the man agreed, and how, when he died and when the saints were arguing over who would take the soul of the wealthy man, Gäbrä Mänfas Qəddus came, shocked the area with lightening, and took the soul of the wealthy man.

o. Ff. 167v–171r: Miracle Fifteen. How a poor man denied God because of his poverty; how Satan came to him and showed him a stone of gold and asked for his allegiance and promised him wealth; how the man denied God and the Virgin Mary, the apostles and prophets but not Gäbrä Mänfas Qəddus and how, when he died, Gäbrä Mänfas Qəddus took his soul to heaven.

p. Ff. 171r–172v: Miracle Sixteen. How a certain man took a lamb and a cow for the feast day of Gäbrä Mänfas Qəddus; how he met a lion and a tiger on the road; how he fled from the place, leaving the cow and the lamb; how Gäbrä Mänfas Qəddus ordered the lion to protect the lamb and the cow and to take them to the church on his feast day.

q. Ff. 172v–174r: Miracle Seventeen. How a certain man stole a rooster from a poor man who was devoted to Gäbrä Mänfas Qəddus; how the man slaughtered and ate the rooster, but how the rooster cried from the stomach of the man and how the thief died and at his burial place people continued to hear the cry of the rooster and how the rooster came forth from the stomach of the dead man.

r. Ff. 174r–179r: Miracle Eighteen. How the wild beasts cried at the death of Gäbrä Mänfas Qəddus; and how the Father, Son, Holy Spirit, the twenty four elders, the four beasts who carry the throne of God, angels, archangels, apostles, prophets, and martyrs all came to receive his soul.

Notes:
1. Ff. i r(ecto), ii r(ecto)–iii r(ecto), iv v(erso) and 179v: blank.
2. F. i v(erso): Pen trial, Trinitarian formula.
3. F. iii v(erso): Pen trial: "A good pen, the scribe tried the pen" (two times), upside down in relation to the rest of the book.
4. F. iv r(ecto): Pen trial, Trinitarian formula.
5. Ff. 68r and *passim*: owner's name, Gäbrä Iyasus.
6. Ff. 68rv and *passim*: name of the scribe, Wäldä Maryam.
7. F. 178v: name of another scribe, Täklä Maryam.
8. Decorative designs: ff. 87r, 131r (multiple full stops and a line of alternating red and black dots)
9. The words God, Gäbrä Mänfäs Qəddus, Gabriel, Mary, John and Jesus Christ are rubricated.

108 · *Catalog of the Manuscripts*

10. Numbered quires: quires 2–15.
11. Scribal intervention: words of text are written interlinearly (ff. 3r, 7v, 9v, 11r, 12rv, etc.); and lines of text are written interlinearly (f. 12v); and in the upper margin with a symbol (⊥) marking the location where the text is to be inserted (ff. 2r, col. 1, line 7; 2v, col. 1, line 7; 96v, col. 2, line 3; 101r, col. 2, line 3; 155v, col. 2, line 14; 159v, col. 2, line 3), and in another case where the symbol (⊥) is used interlinearly (f. 21v, col. 2, line 6; 90v, col. 1, line 15; 92r, col. 2, line 10; 103v, col. 2, line 6; 140v, col. 2, line 7; 146v, col. 1, line 10; 178r, col. 1, line 6; 178v, col. 1, line 7); erasure markings are visible (ff. 142v, 145v, 146v, 147v, etc.); text has been removed (e.g., ff. 147r, 169v).

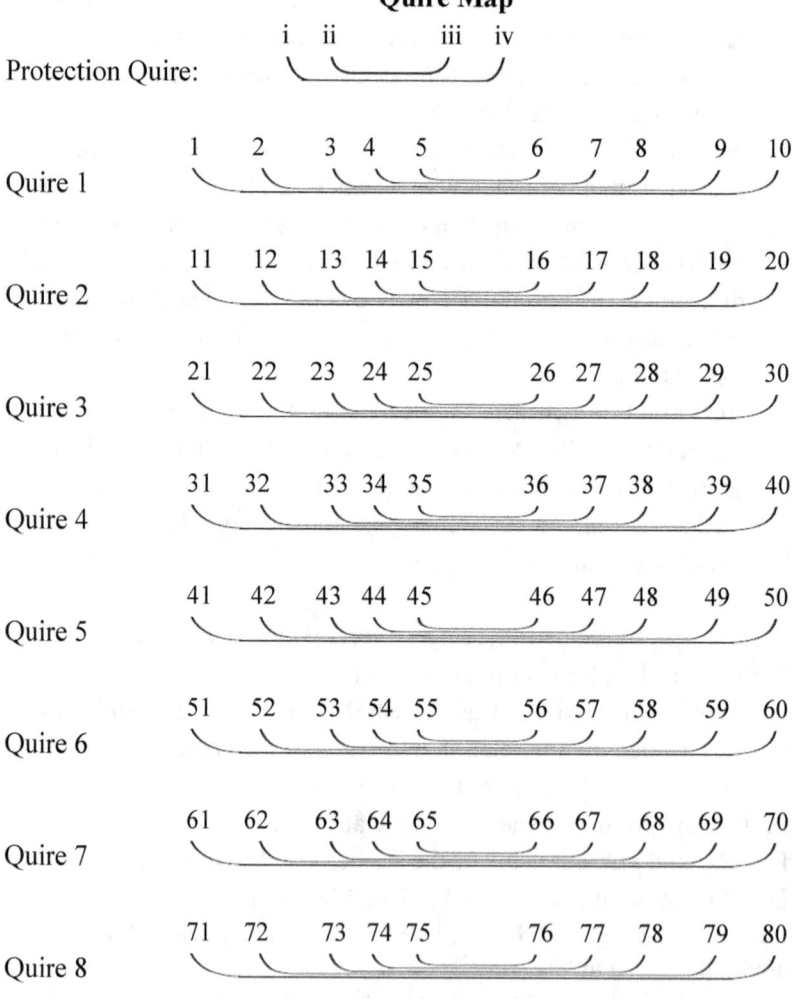

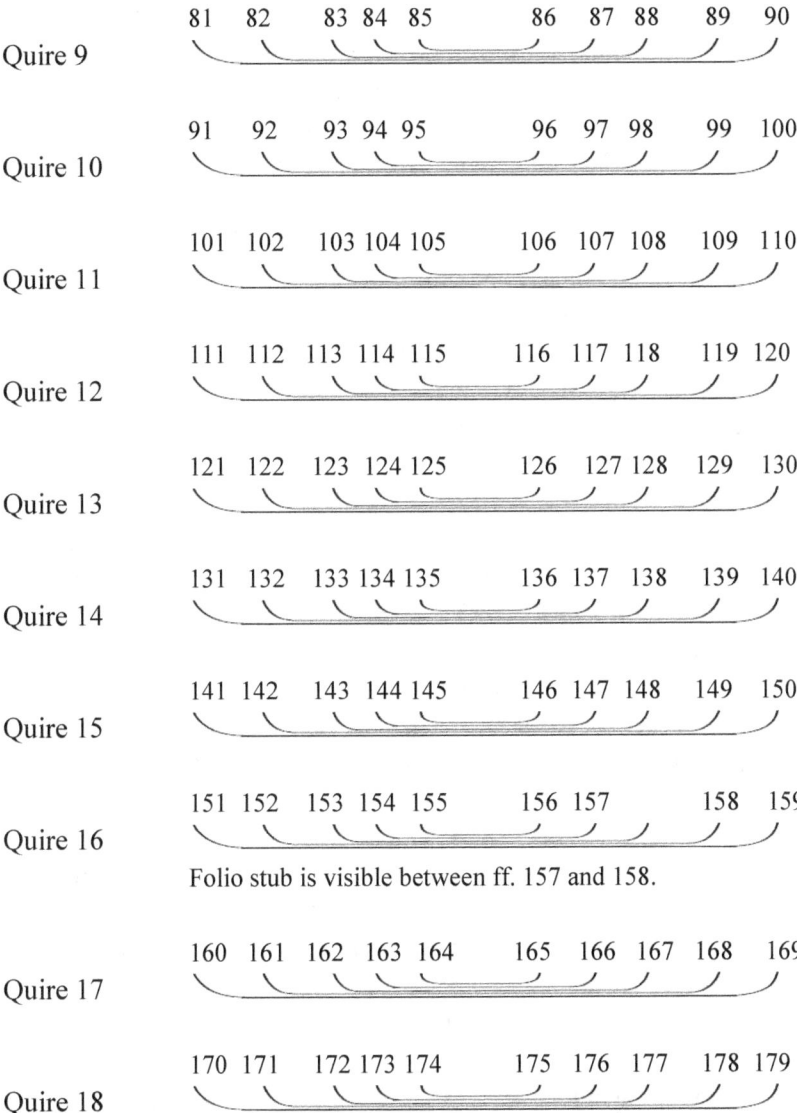

Folio stub is visible between ff. 157 and 158.

MYS 25 – EMIP 625
Pentateuch (Genesis through Deuteronomy), አምስቱ፡ ብሔረ፡ ኦሪት፡, with marginal mnemonics and commentaries

Paper and parchment, 325 x 262 x 38 mm, four Coptic chain stitches attached with bridle attachments to a material for the covers that cannot be seen in the images, covered with tooled leather in the traditional form, protection sheet + 8 full quires, ii + 150 folios, top margin 28–32 mm, bottom margin 40 mm, fore edge margin 15–20 mm, gutter margin 15 mm, ff. 1r–149r three columns, 33–36 lines, Gə_əz, twentieth century.

Quire descriptions: protection sheet and quires 1–2, 4–5 and 7–8 balanced; quires 3 and 6 adjusted balanced. Navigation system: marginal notation throughout, some of which may be overlooked text.

Major Works:
1. Ff. 1r–149r: Orit with marginal mnemonics for the Andemta traditional commentary, and other, extensive commentaries. For the text of Orit, see Dillmann *BVTA* and *DAP*.
   a. F. ii v(erso), columns 1 and 2: Introduction to Genesis, incomplete, (a discussion about whether India, China, Greece and Rome have the Law).
      ኦሪት ፡ ማለት ፡ ዜና ፡ ዘፍጥረት ፡ ማለት ፡ ነው ፡ ቦ ፡ ሕግ፡ ስምዕ ፡ ሥርሃት ፡ ብርሃን ፡ መጽሐት ፡ ማ ፡ ከዚሁ ፡ ይገባል ፡ ቦ ፡ መጽሐት ፡ የአይን ፡ ጉድፍ ፡ የጥርስ ፡ እድፍ ፡ እንዲያሳይ ፡ ጽድቅና ፡ ኃጢአት ፡ ታሳ ፡ በተራራ ፡ ትመስላለች ፡ በተራራ ፡ ያለ ፡ ሰው ፡ ጬንጬውን ፡ ግጬውን ፡ እንዲያይ ፡ ኦሪትም ፡ ዓለም ፡ ከተፈጠረ ፡ እስከ ፡ ምጽአት ፡ የሚደረገውን ፡ ያሳውቃልና ፡ . . .
   b. Ff. 1r–35r: Genesis, ኦሪት፡ ዘልደት፡, with marginal mnemonics.
      ኦሪት ፡ ዘልደት ፡ በቀዳሚ ፡ ገብረ ፡ እግዚአብሔር ፡ ሰማየ ፡ ወምድረ ፡ ምድርስ ፡ ሀለወት ፡ እራቃ ፡ ወኢታስተርኢ ፡ ወኢኮነት ፡ ድሉተ ፡ ወጽልመት ፡ መልእክተ ፡ ቀላይ፡
   c. Ff. 35r–63v: Exodus, ኦሪት፡ ዘወጽት፡, with marginal mnemonics.
      ኦሪት ፡ ዘጻዓት ፡ ዝ ፡ ውእቱ ፡ አስማቲሆሙ ፡ ለደቂቀ ፡ እስራኤል ፡ እለ ፡ ቦኡ ፡ ብሔረ ፡ ግብጽ ፡ ምስለ ፡ ያዕቆብ ፡ አቡሆሙ ፡ ብእሲ ፡ ብእሲ ፡ ወቤቱ ፡ ወቦኡ ፡ ሮቤል ፡ ወስምያን ፡ ሌዊ ፡ ወይሁዳ ፡ ይሳኮር ፡ ወዛብሎን ፡ . . .
   d. Ff. 63v–84r: Leviticus, ኦሪት፡ ዘሌዋውያን፡, with marginal mnemonics.
      ወጸውያ ፡ እግዚአብሔር ፡ ለሙሴ ፡ ወተናገር ፡ እምውስተ ፡ ደብተራ ፡ ዘመርጡል ፡ ወይቤሎ ፡ በሎሙ ፡ ለደቂቀ ፡ እስራኤል ፡ ወአይድዖሙ ፡ እመቦ ፡ ዘአብእ ፡ ብእሲ ፡ . . .
   e. Ff. 84r–113v: Numbers, ኦሪት፡ ዘኍልቍ፡, with marginal mnemonics.
      ኦሪት ፡ ዘኍልቍ ፡ ወነበቦ ፡ እግዚአብሔር ፡ ለሙሴ ፡ በገዳም ፡ ዘሲና ፡ በውስተ ፡ ደብተራ ፡ ዘመርጡል ፡ አሙ ፡ ርእሰ ፡ ሠርቅ ፡ ካልዕ ፡ ወርኅ ፡ በካልእ ፡ ዓመት ፡ እምዘ ፡ ወጽኡ ፡ እምድረ ፡ ግብጽ ፡ ወይቤሎ ፡ አንዙ ፡ እምጥንቱ ፡ ወኍለቍዎሙ ፡ ለኮሉ ፡ ተዓይን ፡ ደቂቀ ፡ እሿል ፡ . . .

f. Ff. 113v–116v: Commentary on the Farewell Speech of Moses, in Amharic.
ወእምከመ ፡ ፈጸምክ ፡ አሥራተ ፡ ኩሉ ፡ አሥተ ፡ አሥራቱን ፡ ሁሉ ፡ አውጥተህ ፡ ከፈጸምክ ፡ በኋላ ፡ ና ፡ ተላላፊ ፡ ነው ፡ አመ ፡ ዳግመ ፡ ትኤሥር ፡ ከአሥሩ ፡ አንድ ፡ ከአወጣህ ፡ በኋላ ፡ ዳግመኛ ፡ . . .

g. Ff. 119r–147r: Deuteronomy, ኦሪት፡ ዘዳግም፡, with marginal mnemonics.
ኦሪት ፡ ዘዳግም ፡ ዝንቱ ፡ ውእቱ ፡ ነገር ፡ ዘነገሮሙ ፡ ሙሴ ፡ ለኩሉ ፡ ጀኤል ፡ በማዕደተ ፡ ዮርዳኖስ ፡ በመንገለ ፡ አረቢሃ ፡ በጎበ ፡ ባሕረ ፡ ኤርትራ ፡ በማዕከለ ፡ ኤርትራ ፡ . . .

h. Ff. 147r–149r: Commentary on the Tabernacle, in Amharic.
ወግበር ፡ ግብረ ፡ ምእናም ፡ በመሀን ፡ ሥራ ፡ ኪሩቤልን ፡ ሥራ ፡ አለው ፡ እንሀ ፡ ብሎታል ፡ በቀኝ ፡ ፩ ፡ አዕማድ ፡ በግራ ፡ ፩ ፡ አአማድ ፡ አቁሚል ፡ . . .

Miniatures:
1. F. i v(erso): Aaron. Caption: Rod of Aaron
2. F. 149v: and f. 150r: The parting of the Red Sea. Turbans identify the Levites, Miriam holds and beats a drum, and Michael (traditionally) assists with the parting of the Sea.

Notes:
1. F. ii r(ecto): blank.
2. Decorative designs: ff. 63r, 98r, 112r, 147r (multiple full stops).
3. Numbered quires: quire 3.
4. Scribal intervention: words of text are written interlinearly (ff. 1rv, 2rv, 3r, 4r, etc.); and lines of text are written interlinearly (ff. 1r, 5v, 8r, 16r, 24r, etc.); erasure markings are visible (ff. 18rv, 19v, 20v, etc.); text has been removed (e.g., ff. 2r, 4r, 16r).

Quire Map

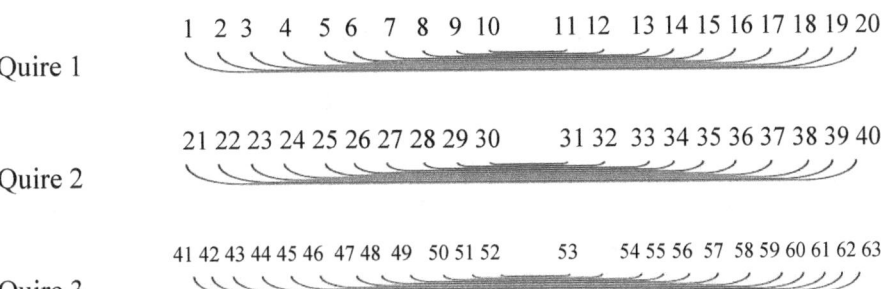

Protection Quire: i ii
Folio i r(ecto) is glued to the inside of the front cover.

Quire 1: 1 2 3 4 5 6 7 8 9 10 11 12 13 14 15 16 17 18 19 20

Quire 2: 21 22 23 24 25 26 27 28 29 30 31 32 33 34 35 36 37 38 39 40

Quire 3: 41 42 43 44 45 46 47 48 49 50 51 52 53 54 55 56 57 58 59 60 61 62 63

Folio stub is visible between ff. 53 and 54.

Quire 4: 64 65 66 67 68 69 70 71 72 73 | 74 75 76 77 78 79 80 81 82 83

Quire 5: 84 85 86 87 88 89 90 91 92 93 | 94 95 96 97 98 99 100 101 102 103

Quire 6: 104 105 106 107 108 109 110 111 | 112 113 114 115 116 117 118

Folio stub is visible between ff. 118 and 119.

Quire 7: 119 120 121 122 123 124 125 126 127 128 | 129 130 131 132 133 134 135 136 137 138

Quire 8: 139 140 141 142 143 144 | 145 146 147 148 149 150

F. 150 v(erso) is glued to the inside of the back cover.

MYS 26 – EMIP 626
Anaphora of Our Lady Mary ascribed to Cyriacus of Bəhənsa, ቅዳሴ፡ ማርያም፡, God of the Luminaries, እግዚአብሔር፡ ዘብርሃናት፡, Prayer of the Covenant, ጸሎተ፡ ኪዳን፡, "For the Sake of Peaceful Holy Things," በእንተ፡ ቅድሳት፡ ሰላማዊት፡, Mystagogia, Anaphora of Our Lord, ቅዳሴ፡ እግዚእ፡, Lamentations of the Virgin

Parchment, 119 x 88 x 44 mm, four Coptic chain stitches attached with bridle attachments to rough-hewn boards of the traditional wood (as far as we can tell), covered with tooled leather that is protected by a linen cover, headband and tailband, protection sheet + 11 full quires, ii + 94 folios, top margin 12 mm, bottom margin 21 mm, fore edge margin 15 mm, gutter margin 9 mm, ff. 1r–93r one column, 14 lines, Gə_əz, early-twentieth century (ff. 2v and *passim* mention *Abba* Peṭros (IV, 1881–1921) and Matewos (1843–1926). Double-slip *maḥdär*.

Quire descriptions: protection sheet and quires 1–3, 5–8 and 10–11 balanced; quires 4 and 9 adjusted balanced.

Major Works:
1. Ff. 1r–31r: Anaphora of Mary attributed to Cyriacus of Bəhənsa, Qəddase Maryam G^wäs'a, ቅዳሴ፡ ማርያም፡. See Ernst

Hammerschmidt, *Studies in the Ethiopic Anaphoras*, 2nd ed, (Stuttgart, 1987). EMIP 27.

ጉሥዓ ፡ ልብየ ፡ ቃለ ፡ ሠናየ ፡ ጉሥዓ ፡ ልብየ ፡ ቃለ ፡ ሠናየ ፡ ጉሥዓ ፡ ልብየ ፡ ቃለ ፡ ሠናየ ፡ ወእን ፡ አየድዕ ፡ ቅዳሴሃ ፡ ለማርያም ፡ . . .

2. Ff. 31r–36r: God of the Luminaries, *Əgzi'abḥer zä-bərhanat*, እግዚአብሔር፡ ዘብርሃናት፡. Chaîne, *Répertoire* 363; EMML 4001 (10: 1); and Princeton Ethiopic 13, ff. 44r–46r. See also, *EA* 2: 249; and *Säbattu Kidanat, Qəddase Maryam, Mälkə'a Guba'e*. Addis Ababa: Täsfa Press, 1959 EC, 38ff. *MG59* 38ff; *MQ51* 199–200; Daoud-Mersie, *Liturgy* 244–5; Sebastian Euringer, "Die äthiopische Anaphora des hl. Epiphanius Bischofs der Insel Cypern," *OC*, third ser., vol. I (1926) 126–8. EMIP 37, ff. 113r–117v.

እግዚአብሔር ፡ ዘብርሃናት ፡ እግዚአብሔር ፡ ዘሥልጣናት ፡ እግዚአብሔር ፡ ዘአርእስተ ፡ መላእክት ፡ ዘአምታሁት ፡ እኅዞትከ ፡ ኵሎሁ ፡ ለፍጥረት ፡ ንጉሡ ፡ ነገሥት ፡ ወእግዚአ ፡ አጋዕዝት ፡ አምላክ ፡ ቅዱሳን ፡ አቡሁ ፡ ለእግዚእነ ፡ ወአምላክነ ፡ ወመድኃኒነ ፡ ኢየሱስ ፡ ክርስቶስ ፡ . . .

3. Ff. 37r–48r: Prayer of the Covenant, *Ṣälotä Kidan*, ጸሎተ፡ ኪዳን፡. As part of the liturgy, the prayer has been copied and printed many times, e.g. *MQ51* 256–62; *MD59* 602–14; see also *DChr* 46–50; Velat, *Me_erāf* I:1–6; and (tr.) Velat, *Me_erāf* II:170–74; Sebastian Euringer, "Übersetzung der _Preces officii matutini' in Dillmann's _Chrestomathia Aethiopica,'" *Or*, NS, vol. 11 (1942) 333–66; and Daoud-Mersie, *Liturgy* 314–21.

አመጽሐፈ ፡ ኪዳን ፡ ዘነገሮሙ ፡ እግዚእነ ፡ ለአርዳኢሁ ፡ ሃሉ ፡ ወምሕረቱ ፡ የሀሉ ፡ ምስለ ፡ . . . ቅዱስ ፡ እግዚአብሔር ፡ ቅዱስ ፡ ኃያል ፡ ቅዱስ ፡ ሕያው ፡ ዘኢይመውት ፡ . . . ለከ ፡ እግዚኦ ፡ ለገባሬ ፡ ኵሉ ፡ ለዘኢታስተርኢ ፡ አምላክ ፡ ንስፍሕ ፡ ነፍስነ ፡ ወስብሐተ ፡ ዘንግሕ ፡ ንፌኑ ፡ ለከ ፡ እግዚኦ ፡ ለጥበበ ፡ ኵሉ ፡ ኃያል ፡ . . .

4. Ff. 48r–52v: Prayer, "For the sake of the peaceful holy things," በእንተ፡ ቅድሳት፡ ሰላማዊት፡. *MQ51* 26–9; *MG59* 41ff.; Daoud-Mersie, *Liturgy,* 33–7; EMIP 37, ff. 109v–113r.

በእንተ ፡ ቅድሳት ፡ ሰማያውያን ፡ ሰላመ ፡ ናስተበቍዕ ፡ ከመ ፡ እግዚአብሔር ፡ ያስተሳልመን ፡ በሃሀስ ፡ ዚአሁ። አሜን ፡ ኪርያላይሶን ፡ እግዚኦ ፡ ተሣሃለነ ፡ . . .

5. Ff. 52v–61r: Mystagogia, *Təmhərtä Ḫəbu_at*, ትምህርተ፡ ኅቡዓት፡. Hammerschmidt, *Texte* 48–72; Lifchitz, *Textes* 40–52; Velat, *Me_erāf* I:215–7; *MG59* 9ff.

በእንተ ፡ ትምህርተ ፡ ኅቡእት ፡ ቅድመ ፡ ዘትትነገር ፡ አምጽርፔራ ፡
ለምእመናን ፡ ኅቡዓት ፡ ትምህተ ፡ ኅቡዓትስ ፡ ከመዝ ፡ ንግር ፡ ዘቀድመ ፡
ሁሉ ፡ ወይኄሉ ፡ ዘመጽአ ፡ ዘሐመ ፡ ወሞተ ፡ . . .

6. Ff. 61r–72r: Anaphora of Our Lord, *Qəddase Ǝgzi'*, ቅዳሴ፡ እግዚእ፡. See Ernst Hammerschmidt, *Studies in the Ethiopic Anaphoras*, second revised edition, (Stuttgart 1987). EMIP 27.
እመጽሐፈ ፡ ኪዳን ፡ በሰማይ ፡ የሃሉ ፡ ልብክሙ ፡ እወ ፡ የሃሉ ፡ በሰማይ ፡
ልብነ ፡ በእንተ ፡ ስምከ ፡ አጽንዓነ ፡ ወረሰየነ ፡ ድልዋነ ፡ ኢየሱስ ፡
ክርስቶስ ፡ እግዚእነ ፡ ወአምላክነ ፡ . . . ነአኩተከ ፡ አምላክ ፡ ቅዱስ ፡
ፈጻሜ ፡ ነፍስነ ፡ ወሀቤ ፡ ሕይወትነ ፡ ዘኢይማስን ፡ መዝገብ ፡ አቡሁ ፡
ለዋህድ ፡ ወልድከ ፡ መድኃኒነ ፡ ዘይጼኑ ፡ ዘዚአከ ፡ ፈቃደ ፡ እስመ ፡
ፈቀድከ ፡ ከመ ፡ ንድኃን ፡ ብከ ፡ . . .

7. Ff. 72rv: Excerpt from Hymns during communion, –Holy, holy, holy, the Triune".
ቅዱስ ፡ ቅዱስ ፡ ቅዱስ ፡ ሥሉስ ፡ ዘኢይትነገር ፡ ሀቢኒ ፡ ከመ ፡
እንሣእ ፡ ለሕይወት ፡ ዘንተ ፡ ሥጋ ፡ ወደመ ፡ ዘእንበለ ፡ ኩነኒ ፡ ፡ ሀቢኒ ፡
እግበር ፡ ፍሬ ፡ ዘያሥምረከ ፡ . . .

8. F. 72v: Prayer for the owner and scribe.
9. Ff. 73rv: Instructions about the measurement of shadows for the telling of time. Cf. EMIP 187, f. i v(erso).
10. Ff. 75r–92v: Lamentations of the Virgin, ሰቆቃወ፡ ድንግል፡. P. Chrysostome P. Hayoz, *Portrait de Marie. Complainte de la Vierge. Deux poésies éthiopiennes inédites. Texte, traduction, commentaire. Thèse* (Fribourg, Switzerland, 1956); Chaîne, *Répertoire* 268.
በስመ ፡ እግዚአብሔር ፡ ሥሉስ ፡ ሕፀተ ፡ ግጻዌ ፡ ዘአልቦ ፡
ሰቆቃወ ፡ ድንግል ፡ እጽሕፍ ፡ ቀለመ ፡ አንብዕ ፡ በእንጡብጦ ፡
ወይሉ ፡ ወላሁ ፡ ለይበል ፡ ዘእንበ ፡
ከማሃ ፡ ጎዘነ ፡ ወተሰደ ፡ ሰብ ፡ በኮለኔ ፡ ረከቦ ፡
ርእዮ ፡ ለይብኪ ፡ ዓይነ ፡ ልብ ፡ ዘቦ፡

11. F. 93r: Addendum to Lamentations of the Virgin.

Notes:
1. Ff. i r(ecto)-ii v(erso), 36v, 74rv and 93v–94v: blank.
2. F. 2v and *passim*: mentions *Abba* Peṭros (IV, 1881–1921) and Matewos (1843–1926). IV, *Abba*
3. F. 30v and *passim*: owner's name, Wäldä Säma‿ət.
4. F. 36r: name of the scribe, Gäbrä Yoḥannəs.
5. Decorative designs: ff. 31r, 61r, 72rv (line of alternating red and black dots); ff. 36r, 53r (lines of full stops and alternating red and black dots); ff. 48r, 62r (multiple full stops).
6. The words Mary, Peter, Jesus Christ and Holy Spirit, are rubricated.

7. Scribal intervention: words of text are written interlinearly (ff. 9v, 41r); and lines of text are written interlinearly (f. 64r); and in the upper margin with a symbol (⊥) marking the location where the text is to be inserted (f. 85v, line 1); text has been removed (e.g., f. 70r).

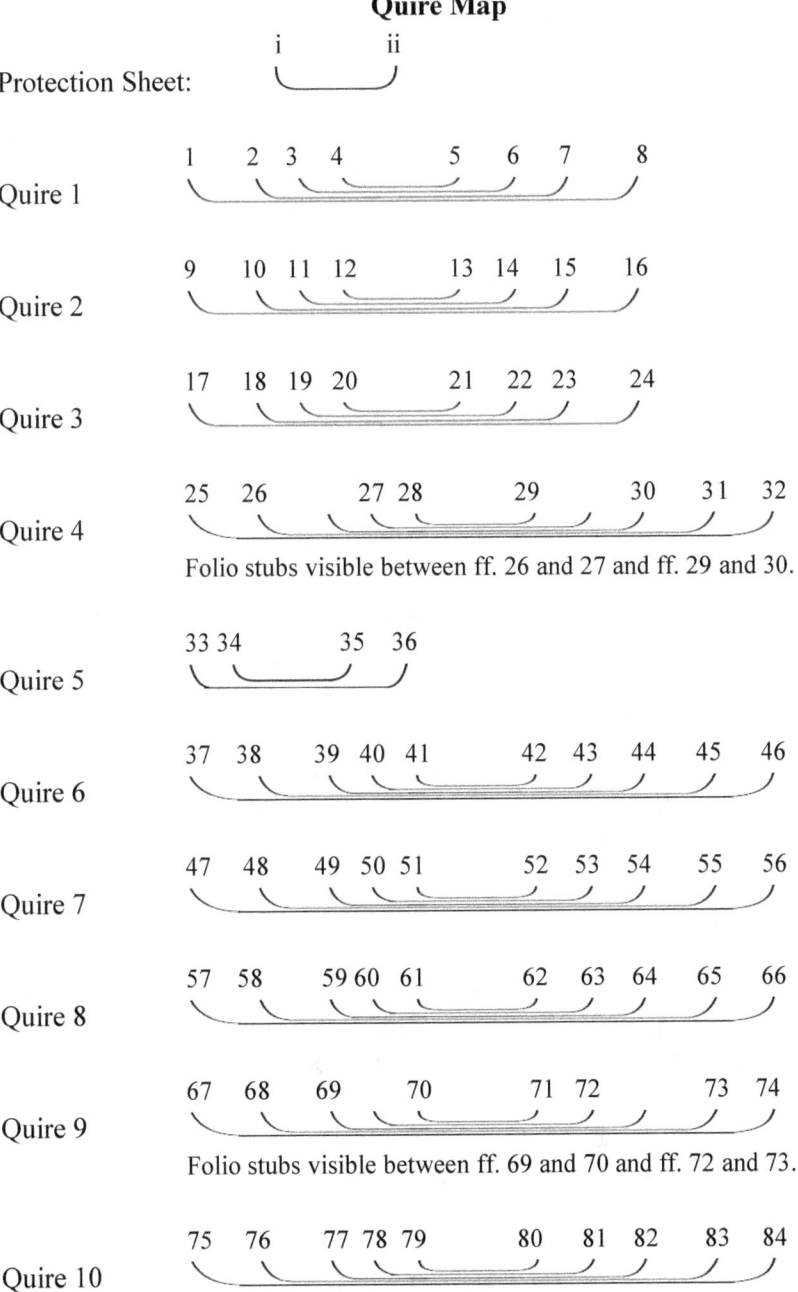

Quire 11   85 86 87 88 89   90 91 92 93 94

MYS 27 – EMIP 627
Sword of the Trinity, ሠይፈ፡ መለኮት፡, and Bandlet of Righteousness, ልፋፈ፡ ጽድቅ፡

Parchment, 114 x 85 x 58 mm, two Coptic chain stitches attached with bridle attachments to rough-hewn boards presumably of the traditional wood, covered with tooled leather, linen is visible between the turn-ins, protection quire + 6 full quires, vi + 44 folios, top margin 13 mm, bottom margin 20 mm, fore edge margin 9 mm, gutter margin 7 mm, ff. 1r–42r one column, 9 lines, Gə_əz, twentieth century.

Quire descriptions: protection quire and quires 1–6 balanced.

Major Works:
1. Ff. 1r–12v: Sword of Divinity, *Säyfä Mäläkot*, ሠይፈ፡ መለኮት፡, Abbadie, *AbbCat* 171, f. 29v; Conti Rossini, *Notice* 104; Abbadie, *AbbCat* 186, f. 104; Conti Rossini, *Notice* 233; Strelcyn, *Lincei* 47, f.88v; EMML 1169, f. 120b, EMIP 33:10.
   በስመ ፡ እግዚአብሔር ፡ ቀዳማዊ ፡ ዘእንበለ ፡ ትማልም ፡ ወማዕከላዊ ፡ ዘእንበለ ፡ ዮም ፡ ወደኃራዊ ፡ ዘእንበለ ፡ ጌሥም ፡ ብሉየ ፡ መዋዕል ፡ ዘእንበለ ፡ ዓም ፡ ገባሬ ፡ ኩሉ ፡ ዘእንበለ ፡ ድካም ፡ . . .

2. Ff. 13r–42r: Bandlet of Righteousness, ልፋፈ፡ ጽድቅ፡ *Ləfafä Ṣədəq*, f. 123r. E. A. Wallis Budge, *The Bandlet of Righteousness* (London: Luzac, 1929); Sebastian Euringer, ―Die Binde der Rechtfertingung (Lefâfa ṣedek)," *Or* NS vol. 9 (1940) 76–96 and 244–59.
   ልፋፈ ፡ ጽድቅ ፡ በስመ ፡ አብ ፡ ወወልድ ፡ . . .ጸሎት ፡ በእንተ ፡ ድጋነት ፡ ነፍስ ፡ ወመጽሐፈ ፡ ሕይወት ፡ ልፋፈ ፡ ጽድቅ ፡ ዘወሐባ ፡ አብ ፡ ለእግዝእትነ ፡ ማርያም ፡ እምቅድመ ፡ ይትወለድ ፡ ክርስቶስ ፡ እምኔሃ ፡...

Notes:
1. Ff. i r(ecto)-vi v(erso) and 42v–44v: blank.
2. Ff. 1v, 4r and *passim*: space was left for a female owner's name (the gender is indicated in the terms, ዕቀባኝ ለአመትክኝ) to be inserted, but it never was.
3. Decorative designs: f. 42r (multiple full stops).
4. The words Jesus Christ, God, Mary, Holy Spirit and other saints are rubricated.

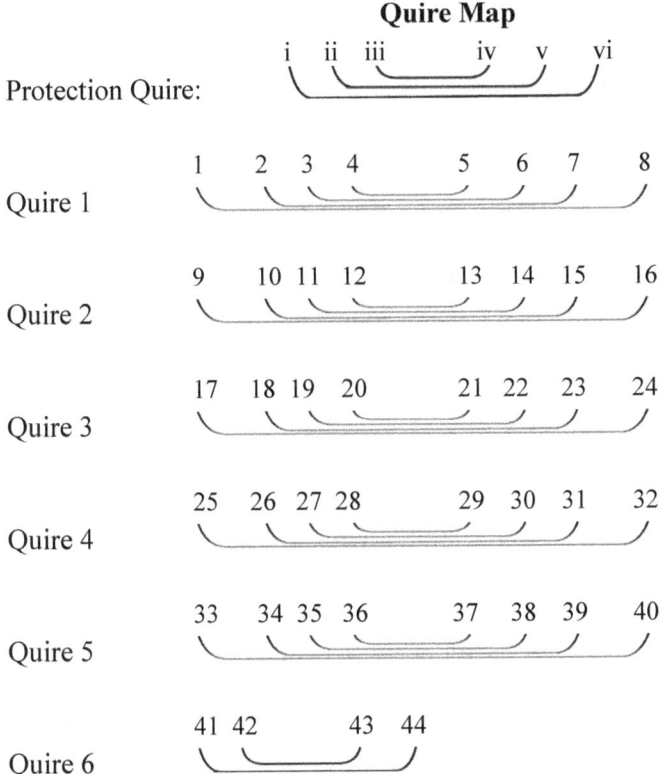

MYS 28 – EMIP 628
Anaphora of Our Lady, ቅዳሴ፡ ማርያም፡, and Image of the Trinity, መልክአ፡ ሥላሴ፡

Parchment, 127 x 88 x 36 mm, three Coptic chain stitches attached with bridle attachments to rough-hewn boards of the traditional wood, covered with tooled leather, protection quire + 8 full quires, iv + 74 folios, top margin 21 mm, bottom margin 36 mm, fore edge margin 20 mm, gutter margin 10 mm, ff. 1r–72v one column, 11 lines, Gǝ_ǝz, 1929–1950 (Ff. 4r and 6r mention *Abba* Qerǝlos).

Quire descriptions: protection quire and quires 1–8 balanced.

Major Works:
1. Ff. 1r–48v: Anaphora of Our Lady Mary, *Qǝddase Maryam Gʷäsʿa*, ቅዳሴ፡ ማርያም፡, arranged by a later hand for the days of the week, Monday (1r and 36v), Tuesday (6v), Wednesday (9v), Thursday (18v), Friday (25v), Saturday (29v), Sabbath (32v).

2. Ff. 51r–71r Image of the Trinity, *Mälk'a Śəllase*, መልክአ፡ ሥላሴ፡. Chaîne, *Répertoire* 20; *MG59* 189ff.
ሰላም ፡ ለህላዌክሙ ፡ ዘይመውእ ፡ ሀላውያት ፡
ለረኪብ ፡ ስሙ ፡ ኅቡዕ ፡ ሰብ ፡ ወጠንኩ ፡ ተምኒተ ፡
እምግብርክሙ ፡ ሥላሴ ፡ አመ ፡ ረክብኩ ፡ አስማተ ፡
መለኮተ ፡ ለለጀ ፡ ዘዚአክሙ ፡ ገጻተ ፡
እንበለ ፡ ትድምርት ፡ አሰሚ ፡ ወአሁብ ፡ ትድምርተ ፡

3. Ff. 71r–72v: Excerpt from Image of the Passion Week, *Mälk_a Ḫämamat*, መልክአ፡ ሕማማት፡ (ሰላም_ታ፡ ዘሰሙ፡ን፡ ሕማማት፡). Chaîne, *Répertoire,* includes this in number 91.
ግናይ ፡ ለክሙ ፡ ሥሉስ ፡ ቅዱስ ፡ ዕሩያን ፡ አካል ፡ ወገጽ ፡
ዘአስተርአይክሙ ፡ እንበለ ፡ ሕፀፅ ፡
[the last line of the first stanza is missing.]

Miniatures:
1. F. i v(erso): a printed card of the Nativity has been pasted onto the folio.
2. F. ii v(erso): a printed card of the Crucifixion with the caption ―Flowers from the Holy Land Placed on the Holy Sepulcher" has been pasted onto the folio.
3. F. iii r(ecto): a printed card of Madonna and Child has been pasted onto the folio.
4. F. iii v(erso): a printed card of the Last Supper has been pasted onto the folio.
5. F. iv v(erso): a printed card of the Holy Family has been pasted onto the folio.
6. F. 49r: a printed card of The Crucifixion has been pasted onto the folio.
7. F. 50r: a printed card of the Striking of the Head has been pasted onto the folio.

Notes:
1. F. 1v: name of the second owner, Abäbä Täklä Ṣadəq, is written over the name of the original owner which is erased. The original owner appears to have been someone with the second name of Abära; cf. f. 73r.
2. F. 4r and 6r: mention *Abba* Qerəlos (2 June 1929–22 October 1950)
3. F. 48v: name of the scribe: Täklä Haymanot.
4. The manuscript has been foliated in Gə_əz numbers by a later hand.
5. F. i r(ecto): ―1938, twentieth of Yäkkatit, at night, he was born."

6. F. ii r(ecto): ―The date Abäbä Čärənät was born was 1917 EC, sixteenth of Mäskäräm on the [feast of] Mercy of the Covenant, at Arero Bedegon. His baptismal name was Täklä Ṣadəq"
7. Ff. iv r(ecto), 49v and 74v: blank.
8. F. 60r: the scribe wrote two mistaken lines, which he then erased, and over which he placed 10 parallel lines per line of text to indicate the error.
9. Ff. 73r: Note of gift of the manuscript: ―On 1941 EC, the first of Mäskäräm this prayer book was given to *Ləj* Abäbä Čärənät from [illegible] Abära.
10. Ff. 73v–74r: erased notes in various hands and inks.
11. Decorative designs: ff. 1r, 51r, 71r (ornate, colorful *ḥarägs*); f. 48v (lines of red and black dots); ff. 60r, 72v (multiple full stops).
12. The workmanship, quality of parchment, tooled leather, trimmed paste downs and, especially, the colorful *ḥärags*, point to the government scriptorium as the place of production for this codex.
13. The word Mary is rubricated.
14. Scribal intervention: words of text are written interlinearly (ff. 51v, 52r, and 54r).

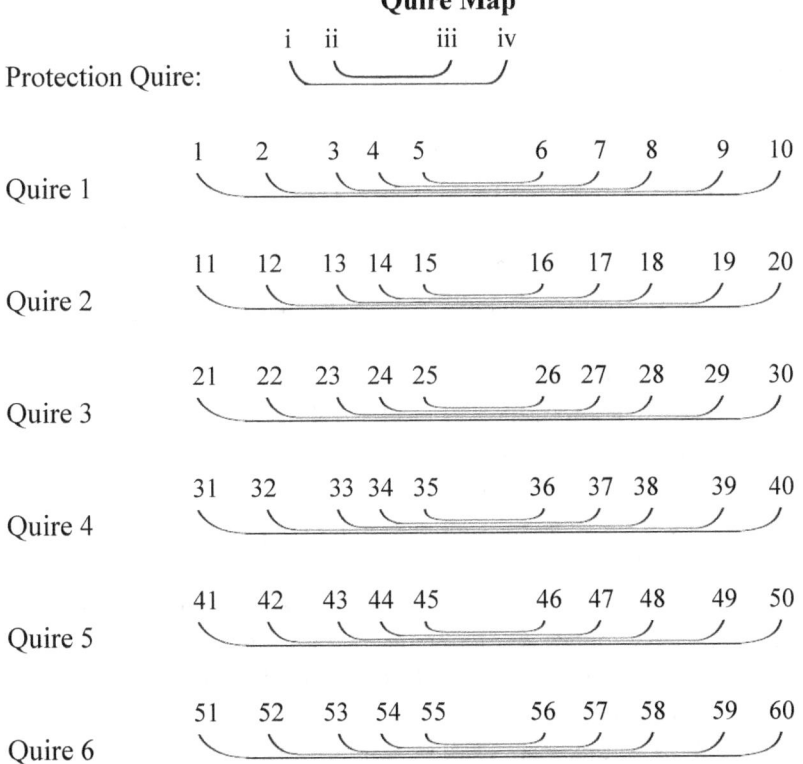

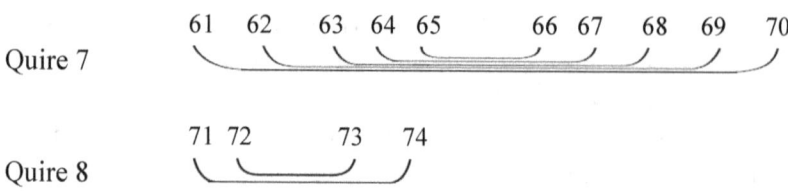

MYS 29 – EMIP 629
Liturgy for the Dedication of a Church, ጸሎተ፡ ቡራኬ፡ ዘቅዳሴ፡ ቤተ፡ ክርስቲያን፡

Parchment, 162 x 112 x 36 mm, two Coptic chain stitches attached with bridle attachments to boards, covered with untooled leather, linen is visible between the turn-ins, protection quire + 9 full quires, iii + 70 folios, top margin 16 mm, bottom margin 35 mm, fore edge margin 24 mm, gutter margin 6 mm, ff. 1r–68r one column, 12 lines, Gə_əz, twentieth century.

Quire descriptions: quires 1–2, 4, 6–7 and 9 balanced; protection quire and quires 3, 5 and 8 adjusted balanced.

Major Works:
1. Ff. 1r–68r: Liturgy for the Dedication of a Church, ጸሎተ፡ ቡራኬ፡ ዘቅዳሴ፡ ቤተ፡ ክርስቲያን፡.
   በስመ ፡ አብ ፡ ወወልድ ፡ . . . እጽሕፍ ፡ ሥርዓተ ፡ ቤተ ፡ ክርስቲያን ፡ አመ ፡ ቅዳሴሃ ፡ ወሶበ ፡ ታነሥእ ፡ ታቦተ ፡ ምስለ ፡ ኵሎሙ ፡ አደር ፡ ምራ ፡ በጀ ፡ አርእዩን ፡ ፍኖቶ ፡ ወንሑር ፡ ቤተ ፡ እስመ ፡ እምጽዮን ፡ ይወጽእ ፡ ሕግ ፡ ወቃለ ፡ እግዚአብሔር ፡ እምኢየሩሳሌም ፡ . . .
   a. Ff. 1r–8r: Instruction and Prayer when the ark is brought to the church.
   b. Ff. 8r–11v: Reading from Hebrews 9:1–15.
   c. F. 11v: Reading (usually sung) from three lines of a Psalm (məsəbak), Ps 45:4–5 (LXX).
   d. Ff 12r–13v. Reading from Gospel of John 10:22–30.
   e. Ff. 13v–18r: Prayer and hymns from Dəgg^{w}a.
   f. Ff. 18rv: Reading from Psalms 64:1–2
   g. Ff. 18v–20r: Reading from Gospel of Matthew 16:13–19.
   h. Ff. 20rv: Supplication and hymns from Dəgg^{w}a.
   i. Ff. 20v–44v: Reading at the East Side of the Church—from 2 Chronicles chapters 5, 6, and 7.
   j. F. 44v: Reading from Psalm 77:68b-69 (LXX).

k. F. 44v–45v: Reading from Luke 6: 47–49.
l. F. 45v–46r: Hymn from Dəggʷa.
m. Ff. 46r–47v: Reading from 2 Ezra (= Ezra) 1:1–5.
n. Ff. 47v–50r: Reading from Revelation 4:1–11.
o. Ff. 50r–52v Continued reading from Revelation 11:19–12:10.
p. Ff. 52v–53r: Reading from Psalm 131:13–14a (LXX).
q. Ff. 53r–54v: Reading from Gospel of John 10:1–10.
r. Ff. 54v–55r: Prayer and Hymns from Dəggʷa.
s. Ff. 55r–59r: Reading by the Qomos Priest[15].
t. Ff. 59r–60v(?): Hymns at the Closing of the Door of the Church.
u. Ff. 61r(?)–66r: Reading from 1 Kings 8:22–40.
v. Ff. 66r–68r: Concluding Hymn and Prayer.

Notes:
1. Ff. i r(ecto)–iii v(erso) and 68v–70v: blank.
2. Decorative designs: ff. 8r, 67r, 68r (multiple full stops).
3. The words Mary, God and Christ are rubricated. Occasionally the word for God is rubricated with alternating red and black letters (f. 6v, 11v, 16v, 17r, 21v, 39v).
4. Numbered quires: quires 2–9.

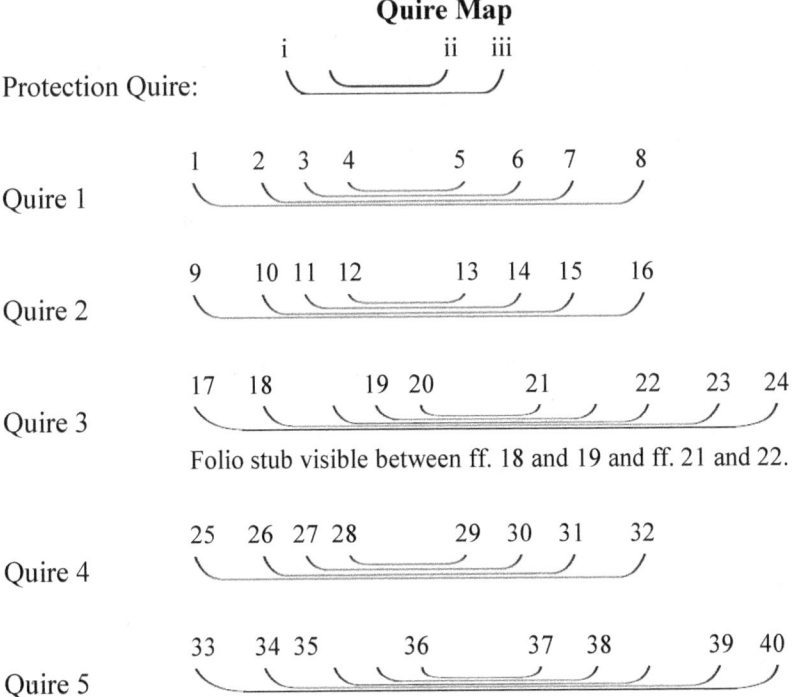

---

[15] i.e., usually a monk, who has been appointed by the bishop to dedicate the church.

Folio stubs visible between ff. 35 and 36 and ff. 38 and 39.

Quire 6: 41 42 43 44 45 46 47 48

Quire 7: 49 50 51 52 53 54 55 56

Quire 8: 57 58 59 60 61 62 63 64

Folio stubs visible between ff. 58 and 59 and ff. 60 and 61.

Quire 9: 65 66 67 68 69 70

MYS 30 – EMIP 630
Synaxarium for the first half of the year, መጽሐፈ፡ ስንክሳር፡

Parchment, 365 x 270 x 105 mm, four Coptic chain stitches attached with bridle attachments to sawn boards of the traditional wood, protection quire + 23 full quires, iii + 165 folios, top margin 27–35 mm, bottom margin 50–70 mm, fore edge margin 34–40 mm, gutter margin 10 mm, ff. 1r–162v three columns, 41–44 lines, Gəʽəz, twentieth century.

Quire descriptions: quires 1, 4–5, 7, 9, 11–17, 19–20 and 22–23 balanced; protection quire and quires 2, 3, 6, 8, 10, 18 and 21 adjusted balanced.

Major Works:
1. Ff. 1r–162v: Synaxarium for the first half of the year, መጽሐፈ፡ ስንክሳር፡. See, E. A. Wallis Budge, *The Book of the Saints of the Ethiopian Church* (Cambridge: Cambridge University Press, 1928). በስመ ፡ አብ ፡ ወወልድ ፡ . . . ንወጥን[16] ፡ በረድኤተ ፡ እግዚአብሔር ፡ ወበሠናይ ፡ ጉብቴ ፡ በጽሒፈ ፡ መጽሐፈ ፡ ስንክሳር ፡ በትርጓሜሁ ፡ ዘቀድሳኖ ፡ አበዊነ ፡ ቅዱሳን ፡ መምህራን ፡ ቤተ ፡ ክርስቲያን ፡ አብ ፡ ክቡር ፡ አባ ፡ ሚካኤል ፡ ኤጲስ ፡ ዘሀገረ ፡ ቡርስ ፡ ወካልእንሂ ፡ አበው ፡ ቅዱሳን ፡ ወክቡራን ፡ እለ ፡ ያስተያብዕዎ ፡ ለዝንቱ ፡ መጽሐፉ ፡ እምነ ፡ ኵሎሙ ፡ ገድላት ፡ በመላእክት ፡ ወነቢያት ፡ ወዘሐዋርያት ፡ ወጻድቃን ፡ ወሰማዕታት ፡ ወሊቃን ፡ ጻጻሳት ፡ ቅዱሳን ፡ ወገዳማውያን ፡ መነኮሳት ፡ ከመ ፡ ይገብሩ ፡ ተዘካሮሙ ፡ . . .

---

[16] ንዌጥን is probably the correct reading.

a. Ff. 1r–26v: Mäskäräm
b. Ff. 27r–52v: Ṭəqəmt
c. Ff. 52v–76r: Ḫədar
d. Ff. 76v–106v: Taḫśaś
e. Ff. 107r–138r: Ṭərr
f. Ff. 138v–162v: Yäkkatit

Notes:
1. Ff. i r(ecto)–iii v(erso) and 163r–165v: blank.
2. F. 162v: The scribe mentions a king by the name of Mäfəqäre Ǝgzi'abḥer I, i.e., ̶t̶h̶e̶ one beloved of God".
3. Decorative designs: multiple full stops used as section dividers throughout (e.g., ff. 20r, 21v).
4. Numbered quires: quires 1–23.
5. Scribal intervention: words of text are written interlinearly (ff. 54r, 126r, 128r, 161v); erasure markings are visible (f. 161r).

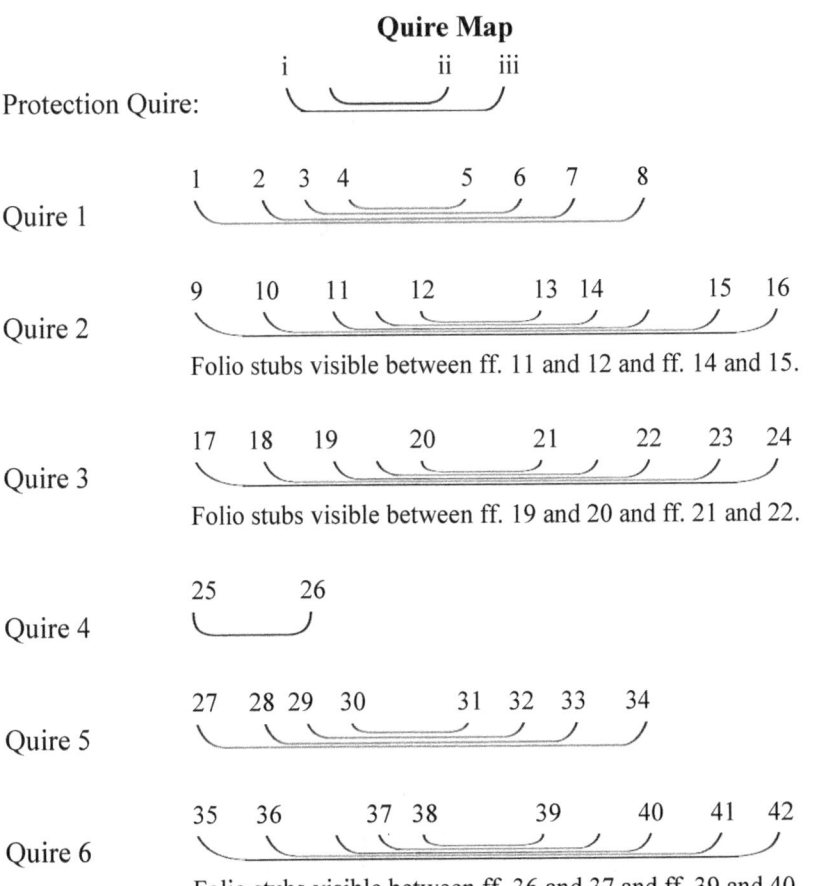

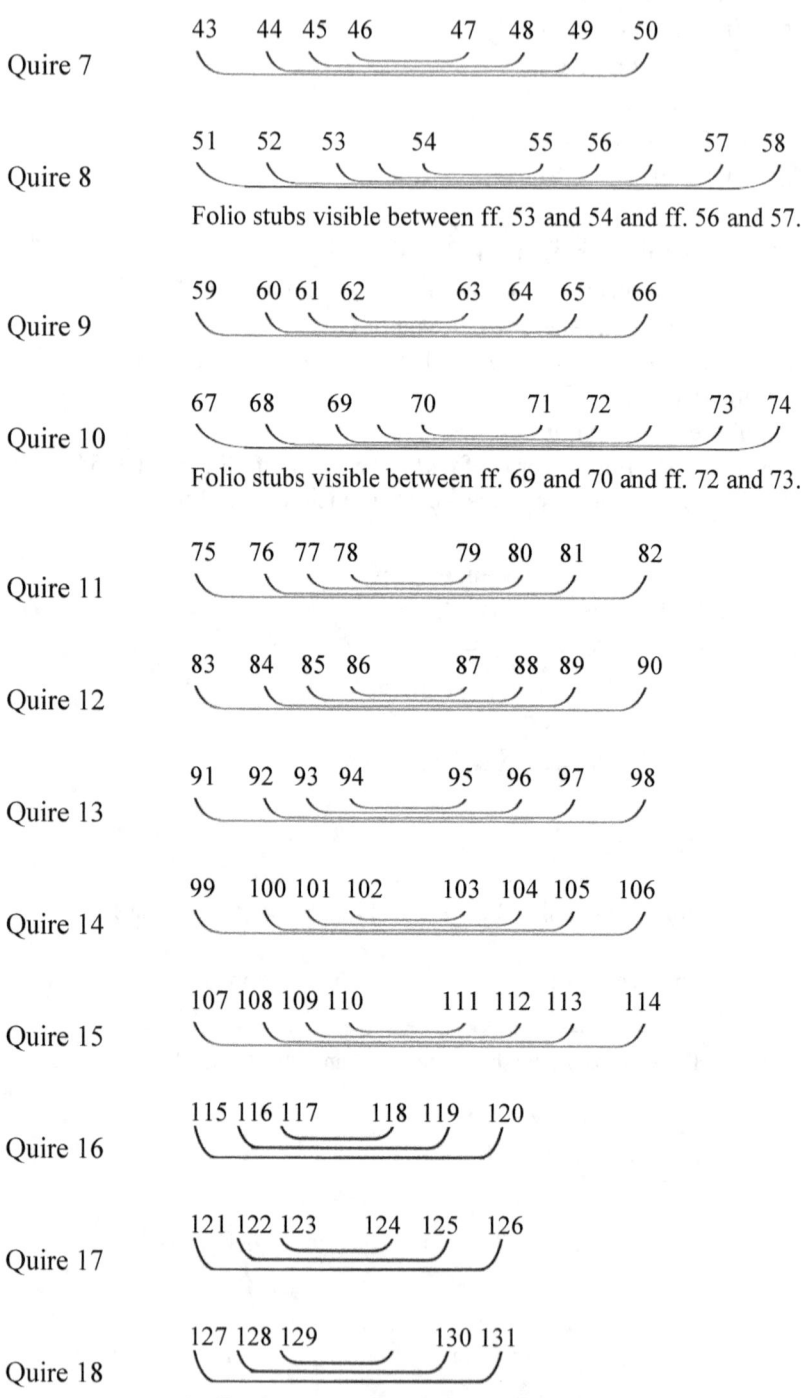

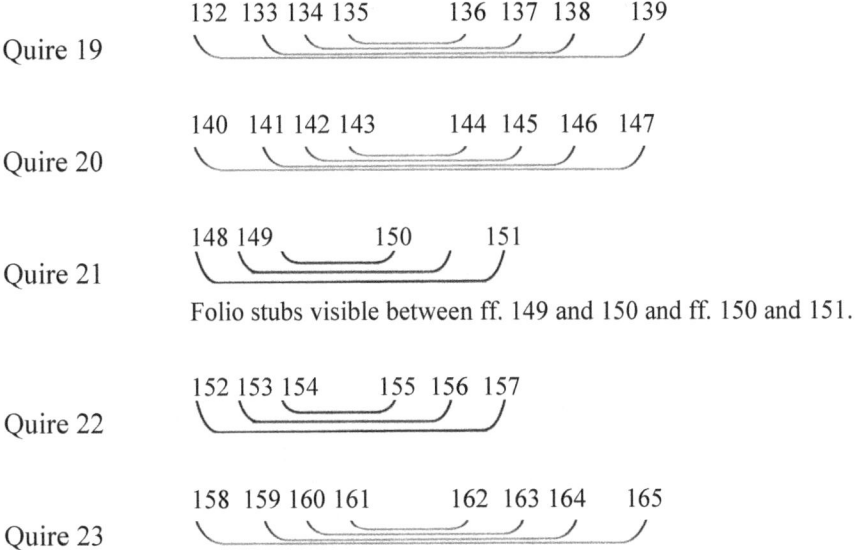

MYS 31 – EMIP 631
Synaxarium for the second half of the year, መጽሐፈ፡ ስንክሳር፡

Parchment, 340 x 260 x 80 mm, four Coptic chain stitches attached with bridle attachments to rough-hewn boards of the traditional wood, covered with tooled leather, protection quire + 17 full quires, ii + 128 folios, top margin 22–28 mm, bottom margin 60 mm, fore edge margin 35–40 mm, gutter margin 10 mm, ff. 1r–128r three columns, 40 lines, Gəʽəz, twentieth century.

Quire descriptions: quires 5–8, 10 and 15–16 balanced; protection quire and quires 1–4, 9, 11–14 and 17 adjusted balanced.

Major Works:
1. Ff. 1r–128r: Synaxarium for the second half of the year. Synaxarium, መጽሐፈ፡ ስንክሳር፡. See, E. A. Wallis Budge, *The Book of the Saints of the Ethiopian Church* (Cambridge: Cambridge University Press, 1928).

በስመ ፡ አብ ፡ ወወልድ ፡ . . . ንዌጥን ፡ በረድኤተ ፡ እግዚአብሔር ፡ ወበሥናይ ፡ ሁብቱ ፡ ወንጽሕፍ ፡ መጽሐፈ ፡ ስንክሳር ፡ ዘሥርዑ ፡ አበዊነ ፡ አባ ፡ ሚካኤል ፡ ኤጲስ ፡ ቆጶስ ፡ ዘሀገረ ፡ አትሪብ ፡ ወመሊክ ፡ ወአባ ፡ ዮሐንስ ፡ ኤጲስ ፡ ቆጶስ ፡ ዘሀገረ ፡ ቡርልስ ፡ ወካልኣን ፡ አበው ፡ መራህራነ ፡ ቤተ ፡ ክርስቲያን ፡ ወውእቱ ፡ ክፍል ፡ ዳግማይ ፡ እመጽሐፈ ፡

ስንክሳር ፡ ዘበትርጓሜሁ ፡ ጉባኤ ፡ ኩሎሙ ፡ ገድላት ፡ ዘሰማዕታት ፡ ወጻድቃን ፡ በረከቶሙ ፡ ወትንብልና ፡ ጸሎቶሙ ፡ . . .

a. Ff. 1r–23v: Mäggabit
b. Ff. 24r–41v: Miyazya
c. Ff. 42r–64v: Gənbot
d. Ff. 65r–86r: Säne
e. Ff. 86r–108r: Ḥamle
f. Ff. 108v–124v: Näḥase
g. Ff. 124v–128r: Ṗagʷame

Notes:
1. Ff. i r(ecto)–ii v(erso) and 128v: blank.
2. Decorative designs: multiple full stops used as section dividers throughout (e.g., ff. 23v, 30r); ff. 23v, 74v, 86r, 108r, 124v, 128r (lines of alternating red and black dots); f. 41v (lines of black dots).
3. Scribal intervention: words of text are written interlinearly (ff. 8r, 105v); erasure markings are visible (ff. 48rv, 78v, 79v, etc.).

Quire Map

Protection Quire: i, ii
Two folio stubs visible between ff. i and ii.

Quire 1: 1 2 3 4 5 6 7 8
Folio stubs visible between ff. 2 and 3 and ff. 5 and 6.

Quire 2: 9 10 11 12 13 14 15 16
Folio stubs visible between ff. 11 and 12 and ff. 14 and 15.

Quire 3: 17 18 19 20 21 22 23
A folio stub is visible between ff. 17 and 18. Two folio stubs are visible between ff. 21 and 22.

Quire 4: 24 25 26 27 28 29 30 31
Folio stubs visible between ff. 26 and 27 and ff. 29 and 30.

Quire 5: 32 33 34 35 36 37 38 39

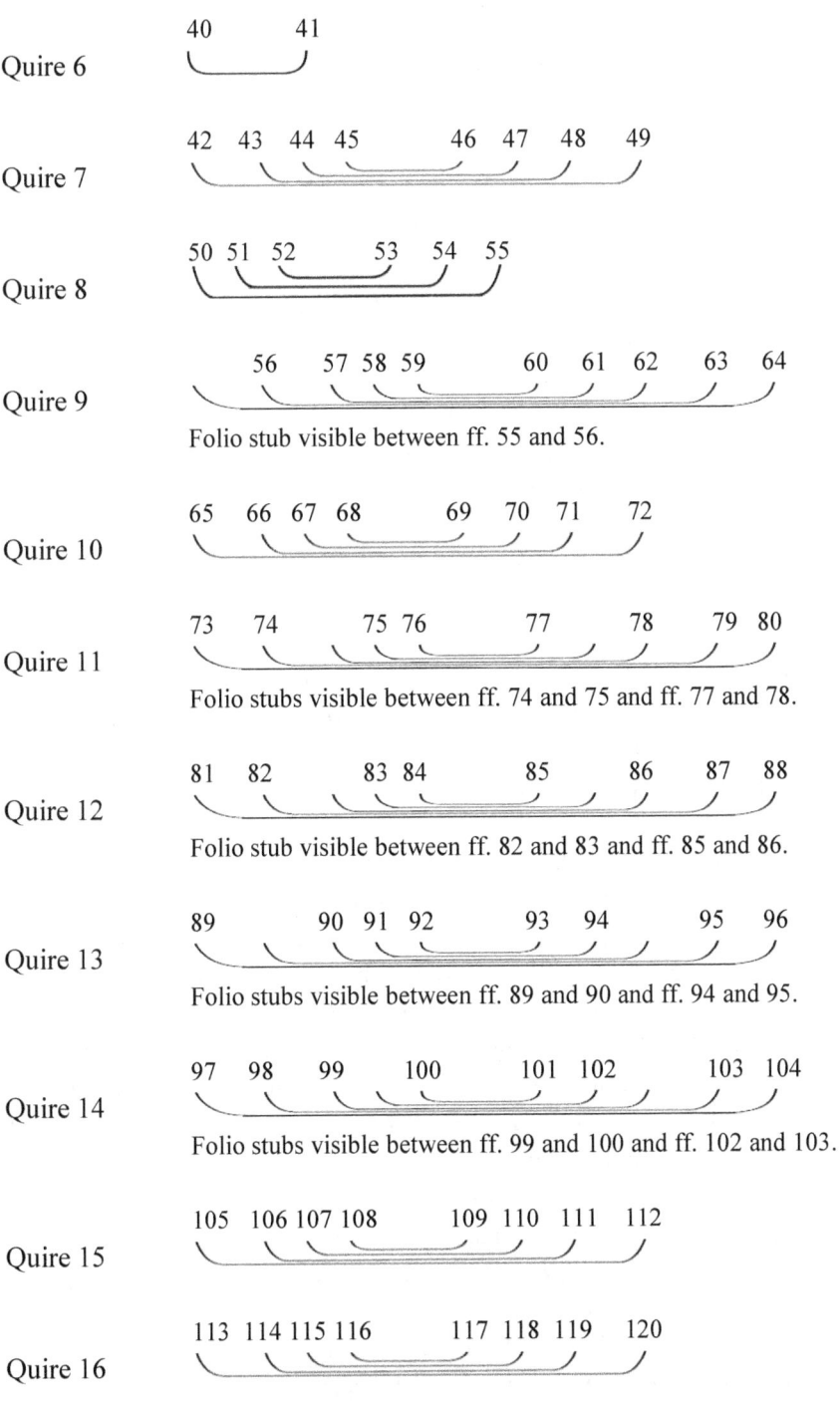

Quire 17   121 122   123 124   125   126 127 128

Folio stubs visible between ff. 122 and 123 and ff. 125 and 126.

MYS 32 – EMIP 632
Missal, መጽሐፍ፡ ቅዳሴ፡

Parchment, 290 x 245 x 87 mm, four Coptic chain stitches attached with bridle attachments to rough-hewn boards of the traditional wood, covered with tooled leather, linen visible between the turn-ins, protection sheet + 15 full quires, ii + 114 folios, top margin 25–30 mm, bottom margin 55–58 mm, fore edge margin 30–35 mm, gutter margin 10–12 mm, ff. 1r–110r two columns, 22–24 lines, Gə_əz, after 1970 (f. 24v mentions the death of *Abuna* Basəlyos in 1970).

Quire descriptions: protection sheet and quires 4–5, 10 and 15 balanced; quires 1–3, 6–9 and 11–14 adjusted balanced.

Major Works:

Ff. 1r–110r: Missal, *Mäṣəhafä Qəddase*, መጽሐፍ፡ ቅዳሴ፡. MQ; Daoud-Mersie, *Liturgy*. For the pertinent references and comments, see Ernst Hammerschmidt, *Studies in the Ethiopic Anaphoras*, 2nd ed. (Stuttgart, 1987). EMIP 27.

1. Ff. 1r–13r: Office Prayers, beginning:
   ሃሌ ፡ ሃሌ ፡ ሉያ ፡ ሃሌ ፡ ሃሌ ፡ ሉያ ፡ ሃሌ ፡ ሉያ ፡ ይእቲ ፡ ማርያም ፡ እምነ ፡ ወእሙ ፡ ለእግዚእን ፡ ሰአሊ ፡ በእንቲአነ ፡ ከመ ፡ ይምሐረነ ፡ ወይስሀለን ፡ ያሥተስሪ ፡ ኂሩቱ ፡ በላዕሌነ፡

   a. Ff. 1r–3v: Prayer of the Covenant, *Ṣälotä Kidan*, ጸሎተ፡ ኪዳን፡. As part of the liturgy, the prayer has been copied and printed many times, e.g. *MQ51* 256–62; *MD59* 602–14; see also *DChr* 46–50; Velat, *Me_erāf* I:1–6; and (tr.) Velat, *Me_erāf* II:170–74; Sebastian Euringer, "Übersetzung der _Preces officii matutini'" in Dillmann's _Chrestomathia Aethiopica,'" *Or*, NS, vol. 11 (1942) 333–66; and Daoud-Mersie, *Liturgy* 314–21.
   b. Ff. 3v–4r: Litany for the evening prayer.
   c. Ff. 4r–6r: Supplications, *Mästäbq^{w}u_ə*.
   d. Ff. 6r–8v: *Liṭon*, ሊጦን፡, for the days of the weeks, including for Holy Saturday.
   e. Ff. 8v: Supplication for the Departed, *Bä'ntä _əlä Nomu*.
   f. Ff. 8v–9v: Supplication for the Departed, *Əgzi'ə Ḥəyawan*.

g. Ff. 9v–10r: Prayer for the Gospel Readings during the Night Hours, *Zätəvelo Lä-fəqʷurəkä Yoḥännəs*
h. F. 10r: Supplication for Saint Mary, *Längəstä Kʷulənä*.
i. Ff. 10rv: Supplication for the Cross, *Lä_əṣ Qədus Mäsqäl*.
j. Ff. 10v–13r: Supplications titled ዘይነግሥን. Velat, *Me_erāf* I:23–29; *MQ51* 277–84.

2. Ff. 13r–34v: Ordinary of the Mass, *Śərə`atä Qədase*.
በስመ ፡ አብ ፡ ወወልድ ፡ . . . እመቦ ፡ ሊቀ ፡ ጳጳሳት ፡ አው ፡ ኤጲስ ፡ ቆጳሳት ፡ አው ፡ ቀሲስ ፡ አው ፡ ዲያቆን ፡ ዘኢተምሕረ ፡ ወኢያዓመረ ፡ መጽሐፈ ፡ ኪዳን ፡ እስከ ፡ ፍጻሜሁ ፡ ወሲኖዶስ ፡ ወዲድስቅልያ ፡ ወሥርዓተ ፡ ቤተ ፡ ክርስቲያን ፡ ወኩሉ ፡ ሕግጋቲሃ ፡ ዘያበጽሕ ፡ ኀበ ፡ ፍኖት ፡ ፍኖተ ፡ ሕይወተ ፡ ኢይባዕ ፡ ለግብረ ፡ ተልዕኮ ፡ ቤተ ፡ ክርስቲያን፡...

3. Ff. 35r–43v: Anaphora of the Apostles, *Qədase Ḥawaryat*, ቅዳሴ፡ ሐዋርያት፡.
4. Ff. 43v–46v: Anaphora of Our Lord, *QədaseƎgzi'ə*, ቅዳሴ፡ እግዚእ፡.
5. Ff. 46v–54r: Anaphora of Mary attributed to Cyriacus of Bəhənsa, *Qəddase Maryam Gʷäs'a*, ቅዳሴ፡ ማርያም፡.
6. Ff. 54v–61r: Anaphora of John, Son of Thunder, *Qədase Yoḥannəs Wäldä Nägʷädəgʷad*, ቅዳሴ፡ ዮሐንስ፡ ወልደ፡ ነጎድጓድ፡.
7. Ff. 61r–63v: Anaphora of Dioscorus, *Qədase Diyosəqoros*, ቅዳሴ፡ ዲዮስቆሮስ፡.
8. Ff. 63v–70r: Anaphora of the 318 Orthodox Fathers, *Qədase za-Śäläsətu Mə_ət*, ቅዳሴ፡ ዘሠለስቱ፡ ምዕት፡.
9. Ff. 70r–78r: Anaphora of Athanasius, *Qədase Atənatewos*, ቅዳሴ፡ አትናቴዎስ፡.
10. Ff. 78r–82v: Anaphora of Jacob of Serugh, *QədaseYa'əkob Z-Śərug*, ቅዳሴ፡ ያዕብ፡ ዘሥሩግ፡.
11. Ff. 83r–87r: Anaphora of John Chrysostom, *Qədase Yoḥannəs Afä Wärq Nahu Nəvenu*, ቅዳሴ፡ ዮሐንስ፡ አፈወርቅ፡.
12. Ff. 87v–92r: Anaphora of Gregory, brother of Basil, *Qədase Gorəgorəyos*, ቅዳሴ፡ ጎርጎርዮስ፡ እኍወ፡ ባስልዮስ፡, *Ǯḫəwä Basləyos*.
13. Ff. 92r–96r: Anaphora of Epiphanius, *Qədase Epifanəyos*, ቅዳሴ፡ ኤጲፋንዮስ፡.
14. Ff. 96r–100v: Anaphora of Cyril, *Qədase Qerəlos*, ቅዳሴ፡ ቄርሎስ፡.
15. Ff. 101r–103r: Anaphora of Gregory, the second, *Qədase Gorəgorəyos Kalə_*, ቅዳሴ፡ ጎርጎርዮስ፡ ካልዕ፡, also known as Anaphora of Gregory, the Wonder Worker, *Qədase Gorəgorəyos, Gäbare mänkərat*, ቅዳሴ፡ ጎርጎርዮስ፡ ገባሬ፡ መንክራት፡.

16. Ff. 103r–110r: Anaphora of Basil, *Qədase Basləyos*, ቅዳሴ፡ ባስልዮስ፡.

Notes:
1. Ff. i r(ecto)-ii v(erso) and 110v–114v: blank.
2. Decorative designs: ff. 34v, 61r, 63v, 70r, 78r, 82v, 91v, 96r, 100v, 103r, 110r (multiple full stops); f. 54r (lines of red dots).
3. F. 23r: mentions Archbishop Luqas (bishop of Arusi province and who died 18 November 1992).
4. F. 24v: May God give rest to the soul of *Abuna* Basəlyos (died 1970).
5. F. 35r: mentions Bishops Luqas and Peṭros
6. The word Mary is rubricated.
7. F. 50r: Columetric layout in alternating red and black letters of the Trinitarian formula.
8. Numbered quires: quires 2–10, 12 and 14.
9. Scribal intervention: words of text are written interlinearly (ff. 1v, 2rv, 4rv, etc.).

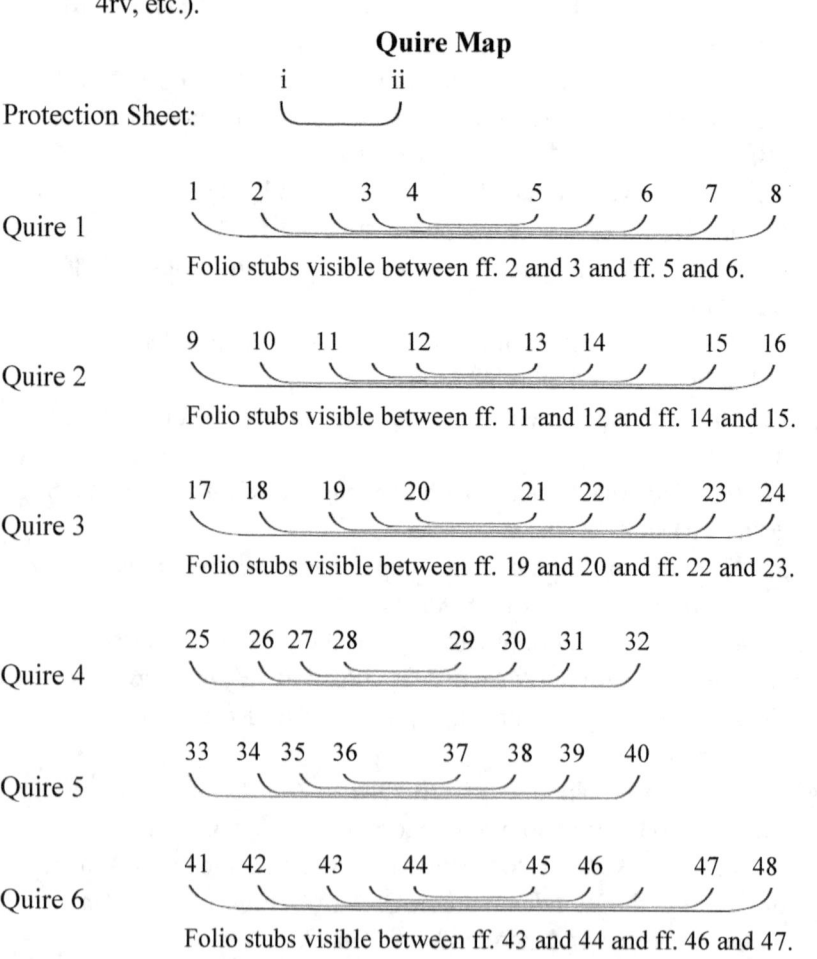

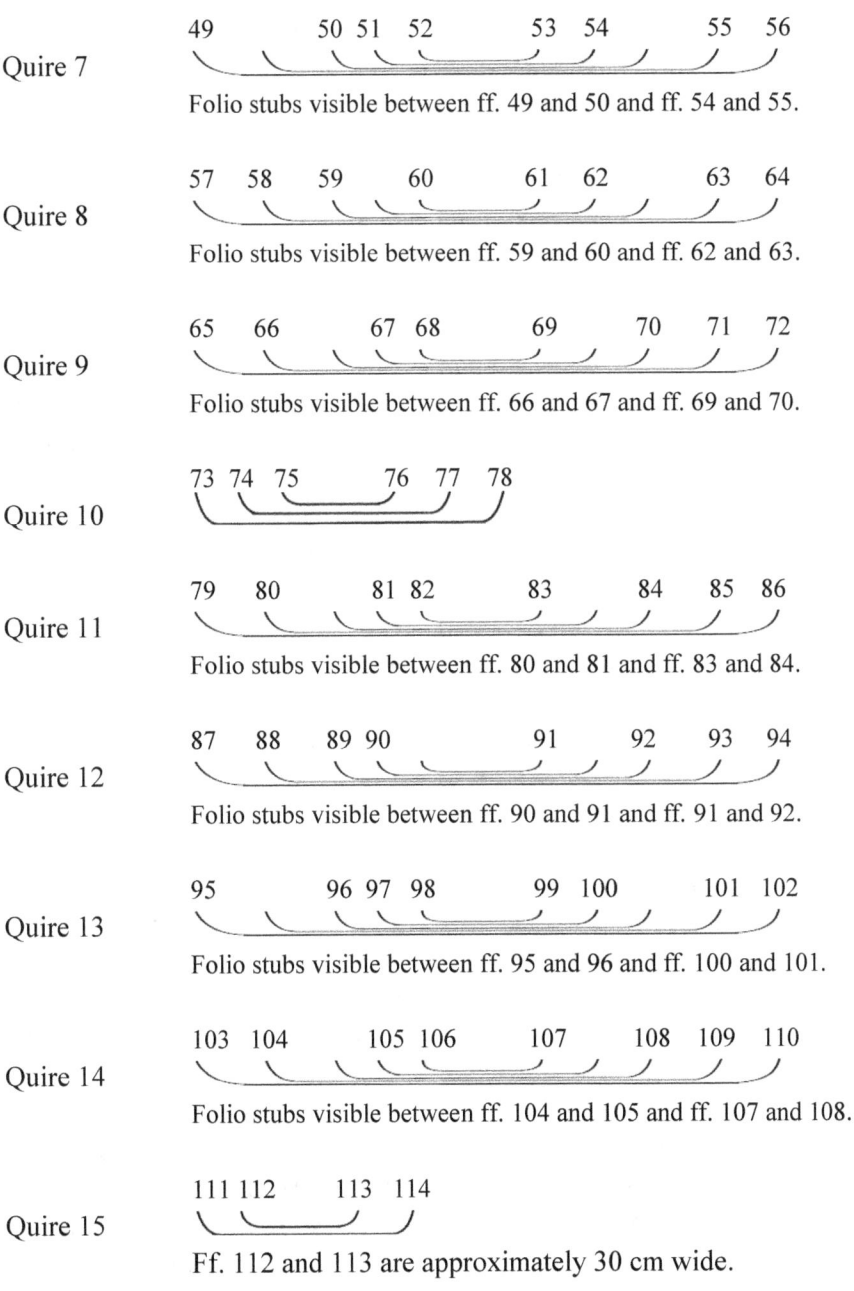

MYS 33 – EMIP 633
Acts, Epistles of Paul, Romans-Hebrews

Parchment, 280 x 238 x 65 mm, four Coptic chain stitches attached with bridle attachments to a front rough-hewn board and a back sawn board of the traditional wood, 12 full quires, ii + 98 folios, top margin 30–35 mm, bottom margin 45–50 mm, fore edge margin 33 mm, gutter margin 15–17 mm, ff. 1r–97r three columns, 26 lines, Gəʿəz, late-eighteenth / early-nineteenth century.

Quire descriptions: quires 2–3 and 6–12 balanced; quires 1, 4 and 5 unbalanced.

Major Works:

Ff. Acts and the Pauline Epistles. See Petrus Aethiops, *Testamentum Novum cum epistula Pauli ad Hebraeos* (Rome, 1548), and *Epistulae XIII divi Pauli* (Rome, 1549).

1. Ff. 2r–25r: Book of Acts from 7:52 through the end. See Curt Niccum, ―The Book of Acts in Ethiopic (with critical text and apparatus) and its relation to the Greek textual tradition," unpublished dissertation, Universtiy of Notre Dame, 2000.
2. Ff. 25r–34r: Introductions to the Pauline Epistles explaining the reasons for writing, beginning:
    a. Ff. 25r–27r: Introduction to the Book of Romans.
    ምክንያተ ፡ ጸሒፎቱ ፡ ለጻውሎስ ፡ ሐዋርያ ፡ መጽሐፈ ፡ መልእክት ፡ ኀበ ፡ ሰብአ ፡ ሮሜ ፡ በእንተ ፡ ተናፍቆ ፡ ወጋዕዝ ፡ ዘኮነ ፡ ማእከሌሆሙ ፡ እስመ ፡ በሀገረ ፡ ሮሜ ፡ ነበሩ ፡ እምቀዳሚ ፡ አይሁድ ፡ ምስለ ፡ አሕዛብ ፡ ኀቡረ። ወሰበ ፡ በጽሐ ፡ ጴጥሮስ ፡ ኀቤሆሙ ፡ ወሰበከ ፡ ሎሙ ፡ በሰሙ ፡ ለኢየሱስ ፡ ክርስቶስ ፡ አምኑ ፡ ወተጠመቁ ፡ ወጸንዑ ፡ ክልኤሆሙ ፡ በሃይማኖት ፡ ወነበሩ ፡ በሰላም ፡ ወፍቅር ፡ ብዙኀ ፡ መዋዕለ ፡ ወሰበ ፡ ሐረ ፡ ጴጥሮስ ፡ እምኔሆሙ ፡ ወቦአ ፡ ተናፍቆ ፡ ወጋዕዝ ፡ ማእከሌሆሙ ፡ . . .
    b. Ff. 27r–28r: Introduction to 1 Corinthians.
    ምክንያተ ፡ መልእክት ፡ ቀዳማዊ ፡ ኀበ ፡ ሰብአ ፡ ቆሮንቶስ ፡ እምጻውሎስ ፡ ሐዋርያ ፡ ኀበ ፡ ሰብአ ፡ ቆሮንቶስ ፡ ኮነ ፡ በውስቴታ ፡ ብዙኅ ፡ ምክንያተ ፡ ነገር ፡ ወእምኔሆሙ ፡ አርአየ ፡ እንዘ ፡ ያቀድም ፡ አእኮቶ ፡ ለእግዚአብሔር ፡ በእንተ ፡ ኩሉ ፡ ጸጋ ፡ ዘተውህበሙ ፡ . . .
    c. Ff. 28rv: Introduction to 2 Corinthians.
    ምክንያተ ፡ መልእክቱስ ፡ ኀበ ሰብአ ፡ ቆሮንቶስ ፡ ኮነ ፡ እምውስታ ፡ ብዙኅ ፡ ምክንያተ ፡ ነገር ፡ ወተወክፎ ፡ ለመልእክቱ ፡ ቀዳማዊ ፡

ተከዙ ፡ ፈድፋደ ፡ እንዘ ፡ ይኔስሑ ፡ እምኃጢአቶሙ ፡ ለእለ ፡
ይነሥኡ ፡ መዓርገ ፡ ዚመቶሙ ፡ መምህራን ፡ ወኃዘኑ ፡...

d. F. 28v: Introduction to Galatians.
ምክንያተ ፡ ጽሒፈቱ ፡ ለጳውሎስ ፡ ሐዋርያ ፡ ነበ ፡ ሰብአ ፡
ገላትያ ፡ ኮነ ፡ በእንተ ፡ ቢጽ ፡ ሐሳውያን ፡ ገላትያኒ ፡ አሐቲ ፡
መከፈልት ፡ እምዮናናውያን ፡ ይእቲ ፡ ወስብአ ፡ እለ ፡ ይነብሩ ፡
ውስቴታ ፡ እሜሃ ፡ ቀዳሚ ፡ በሰብከቱ ፡ ለዝንቱ ፡ ሐዋርያ ፡ አምኑ ፡
. . .

e. Ff. 28v–29r: Introduction to Ephesians.
ምክንያተ ፡ ጽሒፈቱ ፡ ለጳውሎስ ፡ ሐዋርያ ፡ ነበ ፡ ሰብአ ፡
ኤፌሶን ፡ ኮነ ፡ ለአዘክሮ ፡ ብዙኅ ፡ ሀብታት ፡ ዘይትወሀብ ፡
ለምእመናን ፡ እመንገለ ፡ አሜን ፡ ወኤፌሶንኒ ፡ አሐቲ ፡
መከፈልት ፡ እምዮናናውያን ፡ ይእቲ ፡ ወራእስ ፡ አብያተ ፡
ክርስቲያናት ፡ ዘእስያ ፡ በከመ ፡ ኮነ ፡ ቆሮንቶስ ፡ ሊቅተ ፡
አካይያ ፡ ወነብሩ ፡ በውስቴታ ፡ አይሁዳዊ ፡ ወአረሚ ፡ ጋቡሪ ፡
ወጋዳጣን ፡ እምኔሆሙ ፡ አምኑ ፡ ቀዳሚ ፡ በሰብከቱ ፡ ለዮሐንስ ፡
ወንጌላዊ ፡ . . .

f. Ff. 29rv: Introduction to Philippians.
ምክንያተ ፡ ጽሒፈቱ ፡ ለጳውሎስ ፡ ሐዋርያ ፡ ነበ ፡ ሰብአ ፡
ፊልጵስዩስ ፡ ነገር ፡ በእንተ ፡ ቢጽ ፡ ሐሳውያን ፡ ዘበእንቲአሆሙ ፡
አዘዘ ፡ ዝንቱ ፡ ሐዋርያ ፡ በመልእክቱ ፡ ከመ ፡ ኢይወከፍዎሙ ፡
ምእመናን ፡ ወኢይስምዑ ፡ ቃሎሙ ፡ ፡ ...

g. Ff. 29v–30r: Introduction to Colossians.
ወቆላስይስኒ ፡ ሊቅት ፡ በምድረ ፡ እስያ ፡ ወይነብሩ ፡ ውስቴታ ፡
አይሁድ ፡ ወዮናውያን ፡ ጋቡሪ ፡ ወኢርእይዮ ፡ ለጳውሎስ ፡ እስመ ፡
ጎቤሆሙ ፡ ኢበጽሐ ፡ ወባሕቱ ፡ አዘዞሙ ፡ ለአርዳኢሁ ፡ እለ ፡
ይሰመይ ፡ ኤጰፍራ ፡ ወአክርጵስ ፡ ወለደ ፡ ፊልሞና ፡ ከመ ፡
ያጥምቅዎሙ ፡ ወይምህርዎሙ ፡ በሰሙ ፡ ለእግዚእን ፡ . . .

h. Ff. 30rv: Introduction to 1 Thessalonians.
ምክንያተ ፡ ጽሒፈቱ ፡ ለሐዋርያ ፡ ነበ ፡ ሰብአ ፡ ተሰሎንቄ ፡
በእንተ ፡ መከራ ፡ ወምንዳቤ ፡ ብዙኅ ፡ ዘበጽሐ ፡ ላዕለ ፡
ምእመናን ፡ እምነ ፡ አዝማዲሆሙ ፡ እለ ፡ ኢአምኑ ፡ እስመ ፡
ተሰሎንቄስ ፡ አሐቲ ፡ መከፈልት ፡ ይእቲ ፡ እመቄደንያ ፡ ወይነብሩ ፡
ውስቴታ ፡ አይሁድ ፡ ምስለ ፡ አሕዛብ ፡ ጋቡሪ ፡ ወሰብ ፡ በጽሐ ፡
ጳውሎስ ፡ ጎቤሆሙ ፡ . . .

i. F. 30v: Introduction to 2 Thessalonians.
ዘጽሐፈ ፡ ሐዋርያ ፡ መልእክት ፡ ዳግም ፡ ነበ ፡ ሰብአ ፡
ተሰሎንቄ ፡ እስመ ፡ ሰብአ ፡ ተሰሎንቄ ፡ ሰበ ፡ ሰምዕዎ ፡
ለሐዋርያ ፡ በመልእክቱ ፡ ቀዳማዊ ፡ እንዘ ፡ ይብል ፡ ንሕነ ፡

ሕያዋን ፡ እለ ፡ ንተርፍ ፡ አመ ፡ ምጽአተ ፡ እግዚእነ ፡ ንትመሠጥ ፡
በደመና ፡ ከመ ፡ ንትቀበሎ ፡ ለአግዚእነ ፡ ውስተ ፡ አየር ፡
መሰሎሙ ፡ ከመ ፡ ይከውን ፡ ትንሣኤ ፡ ሙታን ፡ በዘመኑ ፡
ለዝንቱ ፡ ሐዋርያ ፡ ወአጠየቆሙ ፡ ። . . .

    j. F. 30v: Introduction to 1 Timothy, incomplete at the end.

ወጽሐፈቱስ ፡ ለሐዋርያ ፡ ኀበ ጢሞቴዎስ ፡ እስመ ፡ ለጢሞቴዎስ ፡
ኃድገ ፡ ቀዳሚ ፡ ዝንቱ ፡ ሐዋርያ ፡ በኤፌሶን ፡ እስመ ፡ የሐውር ፡
መቄዶንያ ፡ ከመ ፡ ይሣይም ፡ ጳጳሳት ፡ ወቀሲሳን ፡ ለለ ፡ አህጉረ ፡
ወጻሕፈ ፡ ሎሙ ፡ እንዘ ፡ ሀሎ ፡ ...

    k. Ff. 31r–33r: Introduction to Hebrews, incomplete at the beginning.

    l. Ff. 33r–34r: Another Introduction to Romans.

መቅድም ፡ ዘመልእክተ ፡ ሮማውያን ፡ ምክንያተ ፡ ተጽሕፎቱስ ፡
ለመልእክተ ፡ ሮማውያን ፡ ኮነ ፡ በእንተ ፡ ግብራት ፡ ብዙኅ ፡
እስመ ፡ ውስተ ፡ ሮሜ ፡ ነበሩ ፡ አይሁድ ፡ ወአረማውያን ፡ ጋብረ ፡
ወክልኤሆሙ ፡ ተወክፉ ፡ አሚነ ፡ ክርስቶስ ፡ ወድኃሬሁ ፡ ተቀሐዉ ፡
በበይናቲሆሙ ፡ ። . . .

3. Ff. 35r–96v: Pauline Epistles, at the end of each book is a conclusion with the messenger and a list of the number of words and chapters in each book.

    a. Ff. 35r–43r: Book of Romans.

    b. Ff. 43rv: Another Introduction to 1 Corinthians.

ወምክንያተ ፡ ጽሒፈ ፡ መልእክቱ ፡ በቀዳሚት ፡ ቆሮንቶስ ፡ ዝ ፡
ውእቱ ፡ እስመ ፡ ይቤ ፡ ሰሎሞን ፡ በተግሣጽ ፡ ነገረ ፡ ጠቢባን ፡
ከመ ፡ ቀኖት ፡ ወዲዮናስዮስኒ ፡ አርያስ ፡ ፋጎስ ፡ ይቤ ፡
መልእክት ፡ እለ ፡ ቅሩባት ፡ ኀበ ፡ እግዚአብሔር ፡ የአምሩ ፡
ፈቃደ ፡ ዚአሁ ፡ እስመ ፡ ለሊሁ ፡ ይስእል ፡ አአምሮተ ፡
በአልባቢሆሙ ፡ ። . . .

    c. Ff. 43v–53v: 1 Corinthians.

    d. F. 53v: Another Introduction to 2 Corinthians.

ምክንያተ ፡ ተጽሕፈቱስ ፡ ዳግማይ ፡ ኀበ ፡ ሰብአ ፡ ቆሮንቶስ ፡
እንብርተ ፡ ፈቃዱ ፡ መልእክት ፡ እስመ ፡ ለመልእክቱ ፡ ቀዳሚት ፡
አምኔሆሙ ፡ በዘተወክፉ ፡ ፍጡነ ፡ ወዐ ፡ ዘተሐሰየ ፡ በተአዝዞቶሙ ፡
ለሐሳውያን ፡ ሐዋርያን ፡ በዘባቲ ፡ ምክንያት ፡ ጸሐፈ ፡ ሎሙ ፡...

    e. F. 53v–60r: 2 Corinthians.

    f. F. 60r: Another Introduction to Galatians.

ምክንያተ ፡ ጽሕፈቱስ ፡ ለገላትያ ፡ እስመ ፡ ገላትያስ ፡ አሐቲ ፡
መክፈልት ፡ ይእቲ ፡ እምዮናውያን ፡ ወይእቲ ፡ ተወክፈት ፡
ሃይማኖት ፡ እምጳውሎስ ፡ ወእምድኃረ ፡ ተፈልጠ ፡ እምኔሃ ፡

ሐዋርያ ፡ ተሐይጠት ፡ በሐሳውያን ፡ ሐዋርያት ፡ እለ ፡ ይብሉ ፡
ዘእንበለ ፡ ዓቂበ ፡ ሕገ ኦሪት ፡ ወግዝረት ፡ ኢይበቁዓክሙ ፡
ለመንግሥተ ፡ ሰማያት ፡ ዓቂበ ፡ ወንጌል ፡ ባሕቲቱ ፡ . . .

    g. Ff. 60r–63r: Galatians. See Siegbert Uhlig and Helge Maehlum, *Novum Testamentum aethiopice: die Gefangenschaftsbriefe*, AF 33 (Stuttgart: Steiner, 1993).

    h. Ff. 63r–64r: Another Introduction to Ephesians. The incipit is the same as that in ff. 28v–29r

    i. Ff. 64r–68r: Ephesians. See Siegbert Uhlig and Helge Maehlum, *Novum Testamentum aethiopice: die Gefangenschaftsbriefe*, AF 33 (Stuttgart: Steiner, 1993).

    j. Ff. 68r–71r: Philippians. See Siegbert Uhlig and Helge Maehlum, *Novum Testamentum aethiopice: die Gefangenschaftsbriefe*, AF 33 (Stuttgart: Steiner, 1993).

    k. Ff. 71r–74r: Colossians. See Siegbert Uhlig and Helge Maehlum, *Novum Testamentum aethiopice: die Gefangenschaftsbriefe*, AF 33 (Stuttgart: Steiner, 1993).

    l. Ff. 74r–77r: 1 Thessalonians.

    m. Ff. 77v–79r: 2 Thessalonians.

    n. Ff. 79r–82v: 1 Timothy.

    o. Ff. 82v–85r: 2 Timothy.

    p. Ff. 85r–86v: Titus.

    q. Ff. 86v–87v: Philemon. See Siegbert Uhlig and Helge Maehlum, *Novum Testamentum aethiopice: die Gefangenschaftsbriefe*, AF 33 (Stuttgart: Steiner, 1993).

    r. Ff. 87v–96v: Hebrews.

Varia:
1. Ff. 1rv: Excerpt from the Book of Revelation 18:12–19:16.
2. Ff. 96v–97r: Hymn to Mary, ―Angels Praise her," *Yəweddəsəwwa Mäla'əkt*, ይዌድሰዋ፡ መላእክት፡ ለማርያም፡, written in a different hand. EMML 1593, f. 92a. Chaîne, *Répertoire* 388; *MD59* 519ff.
ይዌድሰዋ ፡ መላእክት ፡ ለማርያም ፡ በውስተ ፡ ውሳጤ ፡ መንጠላእት ፡
ወይብልዋ ፡ በሀኪ ፡ ማርያም ፡ ሀዳሰዬ ፡ ማዕዋ ፡ . . .

Notes:
1. Ff. i r(ecto), ii rv, 34v and 98v: blank.
2. F. i v(erso): the spine strap around the codex is a rejected leaf. The Gəʿəz alphabet is written on the folio. (rejected leaf)
3. A folio appears to be missing between ff. 30 and 31.
4. F. 97v: Curse on anyone who erases from the book.

5. Decorative designs: ff. 25r, 27r, 28rv, 33r, 34r, 43rv, 53v, 60r, 63r, 64r, 71r, 77r, 82v, 85r, 86v, 87v, 96v (full stops and lines of alternating red and black dots).
6. Scribal intervention: words of text are written interlinearly (ff. 64r, 66r, 67v, 68r, 96v); and lines of text are written interlinearly (ff. 56r, 63r, 66v).

Quire Map

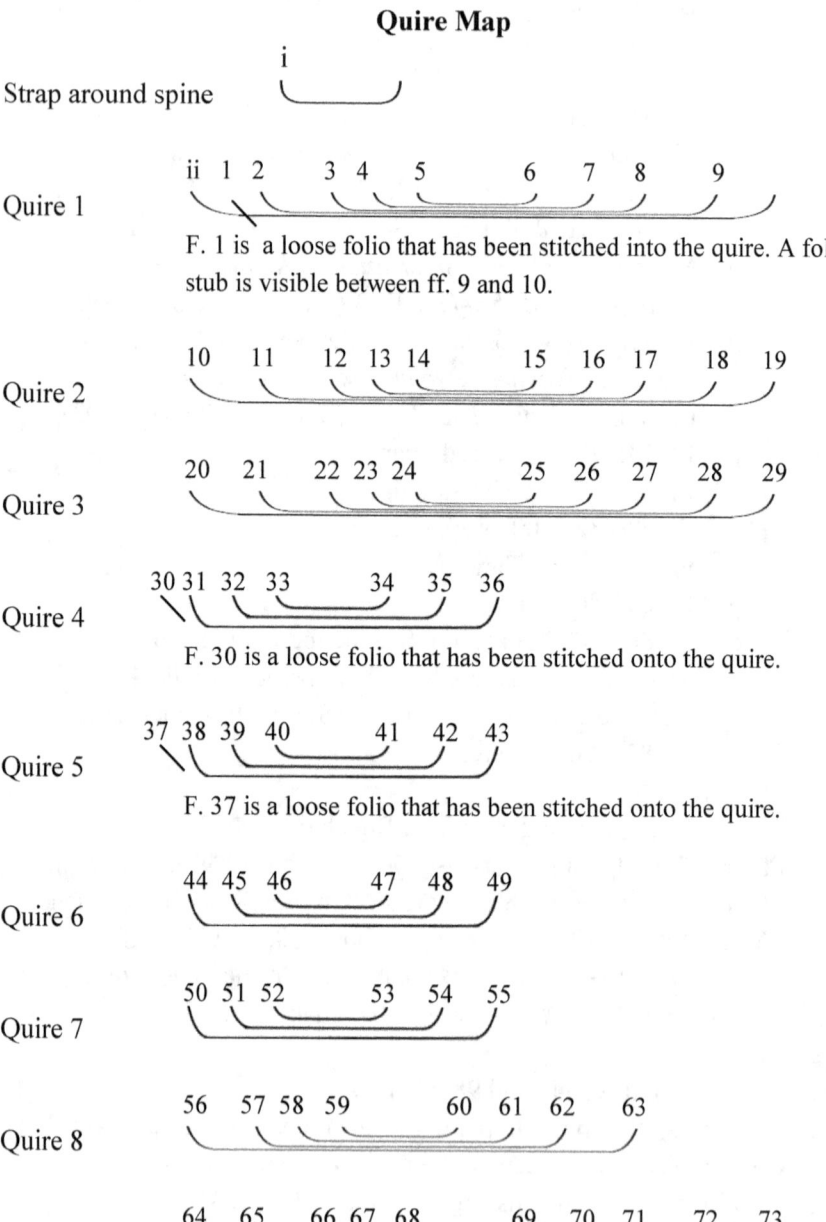

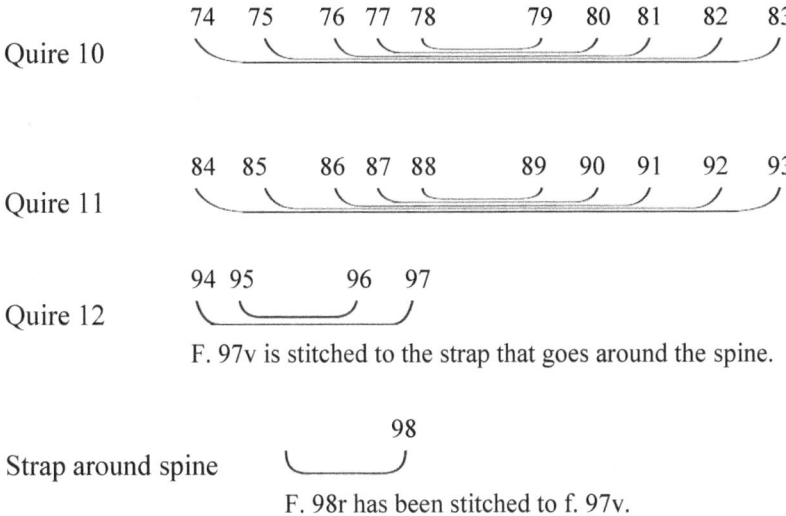

F. 97v is stitched to the strap that goes around the spine.

F. 98r has been stitched to f. 97v.

MYS 34 – EMIP 634
Book of Missal, Text and Commentary, in Gə,əz (the missal) and Amharic (the commentary), መጽሐፈ፡ ቅዳሴ፡ ንባብና፡ ትርጓሜው፡

Parchment, 335 x 282 x 130 mm, four Coptic chain stitches attached with bridle attachments to sawn boards, covered with tooled leather, headband and tailband, protection quire + 30 full quires, vi + 305 folios, top margin 27 mm, bottom margin 40–53 mm, fore edge margin 42–47 mm, gutter margin 15 mm, ff. 1r–301v three columns, 35 lines, Gə_əz and Amharic, dated 1974 EC

Quire descriptions: protection quire and quires 1–29 balanced; quire 30 adjusted balanced.

Major Works:

Ff. 1r–301v: Commentary on the Missal, in Gə_əz (the missal) and Amharic (the commentary). Published in Ethiopia, መጽሐፈ፡ ቅዳሴ፡ ከቅድሞ፡ አባቶች፡ ሲወርድ፡ ሲዋረድ፡ የመጣው፡ ንባብና፡ ትርጓሜው፡ (Addis Ababa: Tənśaʿe, 1988). On the missal itself see, *MQ51*; Daoud-Mersie, *Liturgy*, as well as Ernst Hammerschmidt, *Studies in the Ethiopic Anaphoras*, second revised edition (Stuttgart, 1987); EMIP 27.

1. Ff. 1r–15r: Commentary on Mystagogia, *Tərgʷame Təmhərtä Ḫəbu_at*, ትርጓሜ፡ ትምሕርተ፡ ኅቡዓት፡. See ትርጓሜ፡ ጸሎተ፡ ኪዳን፡, 1–23. For the Mystagogia, see Hammerschmidt, *Aethiopische liturgische*

Texte der Bodleian Library in Oxford, Veröffentlichung 38 (Berlin: Akademie, 1960) 48–72; Lifchitz, *Textes* 40–52; Velat, *Me_erāf* I:215–7; *MG59* 9ff.

በእንተ ፡ ትምህርተ ፡ ኅቡዓት ፡ ቅድመ ፡ ዘትነግር ፡ አምጽርስ ፪ራ ፡ ታሪክ ፡ ጌታ ፡ በሕይወተ ፡ ሥጋ ፡ ሳለ ፡ ያስተማረው ፡ ወንጌል ፡ ይባላል። ከሞተ ፡ ተነሥቶ ፡ ያስተማረው ፡ ኪዳን ፡ ይባላል። በሕይወተ ፡ ሥጋ ፡ ሳለ ፡ ያስተማረው ፡ ወንጌል ፡ መባሉ ፡ ሰለምን ፡ ነው ፡ ቢሉ ፡ ወንጌል ፡ ማለት ፡ ብሥራት ፡ ማለት ፡ ነው። ወንጌል ፡ ብሥራት ፡ ስብከት ፡ ቢል ፡ አንድ ፡ ወገን ፡ ነው። ወንጌል ፡ ቢኃል ፡ በልሳነ ፡ ጽርዕ ፡ ዘበትርጓሜሁ ፡ ስብከት ፡ እንዲል ፡ . . .

2. Ff. 15r–26r: Commentary on Prayer of the Covenant, *Tərgʷame Ṣälotä Kidan*, ጸሎተ፡ ኪዳን፡. See ትርጓሜ፡ ጸሎተ፡ ኪዳን፡, 24–42. As part of the liturgy, the prayer itself has been copied and printed many times, e.g. *MQ51* 256–62; *MD59* 602–14; see also *DChr* 46–50; Velat, *Me_erāf* I:1–6; and (tr.) Velat, *Me_erāf* II:170–74; Sebastian Euringer, ‒Übersetzung der ‗Preces officii matutini' in Dillmann's ‗Chrestomathia Aethiopica,'" *Or*, NS, vol. 11 (1942) 333–66; and Daoud-Mersie, *Liturgy* 314–21.

ኪዳን ፡ ዘነገሀ። መላእክት ፡ ተናግሬውታል ፡ ቢሉ ፡ ለይኩን ፡ ብርሃን ፡ ባለ ፡ ጊዜ ፡ ነውና ፡ ነገሀ ፡ የተመቸ ፡ ዮሴፍና ፡ ኒቆዲሞስ ፡ ተናግሬውታል ፡ ቢሉ ፡ ሞትክኑ ፡ መንሥኢሆሙ ፡ ለምውታን ፡ ደከምክኑ ፡ መጽንዒሆሙ ፡ ለድኩማን ፡ እያሉ ፡ ሲገንዙት ፡ . . .

3. Ff. 26v–34v: Commentary on Supplications, *Tərgʷame Mästäbqʷu_ə*, ትርጓሜ መስተብቁዕ. See ትርጓሜ ፡ ጸሎተ ፡ ኪዳን፡, 43–57.

ጸዋትው ፡ ዘሌሊት ፡ ባስልዮስ ፡ ሥርተ ፡ ቤተ ፡ ክርስቲያንን ፡ ሥርዓተ ፡ ቅዳሴን ፡ ሥርዓተ ፡ ጸሎትን ፡ ተናግሯል ፡ አሥሩን ፡ መስተብቁዕ ፡ ከሲኖዶስ ፡ ዘጠኑን ፡ ኪዳን ፡ ከመጽሐፈ ፡ ኪዳን ፡ አምጥቶ ፡ ተናግሮታል። ምነው ፡ የክፈሉትማ ፡ ሐዋርያት ፡ አይደሉም ፡ ቢሉ ፡ የክፈሉትስ ፡ ሐዋርያት ፡ ናቸው ፡ በጥራዝ ፡ አንድ ፡ ማድረጉን ፡ ሲያይ ፡ ነው ፡ . . .

4. Ff. 35r–41r: Commentary on Litanical Prayer, *Tərgʷame Liṭon*, ትርጓሜ ፡ ሊጦን፡. See ትርጓሜ ፡ ጸሎተ ፡ ኪዳን፡, 57–67.

ሊጦን ፡ ዘነግሕ ፡ ዘሥኑይ ፡ ለባስልዮስ ፡ ሊጥርጊያ ፡ የሚባሉ ፡ መጽሐፍት ፡ አሉት ፡ እስትጉቡዕ ፡ ማለት ፡ ነው ፡ ለጸሎት ፡ ከዚያ ፡ አምጥቶ ፡ ተናግሮታል ፡ ከዚያ ፡ ሰላመጣው ፡ ሊጦን ፡ አለው። ካህናት ፡ በነግሀ ፡ ይጸልያሳና ፡ ዘነግሁ ፡ አለ ፡ በነግሁ ፡ የሚጸልዩት ፡ ጸሎት ፡ ይህ ፡ ነው ፡

5. Ff. 42r–44v: On the History of Liturgy, *Yä-qədase Tərik*, የቅዳሴ፡ ታሪክ፡. See ትርጓሜ፡ ጸሎተ፡ ኪዳን፡, 5–9 (printed after p. 67).

በስመ ፡ አብ ፡ ወወልድ ፡ . . . ጸሎት ፡ ሰብ ፡ ትሰይሞ ፡ ለዓሕል ፡
ወትብል ፡ እግዚአብሔር ፡ አምላክነ። እግዚአብሔር ፡ አዳምን ፡ ከዐ ፡
ባሕርያት ፡ ፈጥሮ ፡ በነፍስ ፡ አክብሮ ፡ በገነት ፡ አኖረው። አዳምም ፡
በገነት ፡ ሲኖር ፡ መካነ ፡ ጸሎት ፡ ለይቶ ፡ ይኖር ፡ ነበር። ኋላ ፡ ግን ፡
ትእዛዙን ፡ ቢያፈርስ ፡ እንግዲህ ፡ በዚህ ፡ ቦታ ፡ መኖር ፡ አይገባህም ፡
ብሎ ፡ አወጣው ፡ . . .

6. Ff. 45r–102r: Commentary on the Ordinary of the Mass, *Tərg^wame Śərə'atä Qədase*, ትርጓሜ፡ ሥርዓተ፡ ቅዳሴ፡. See ትርጓሜ፡ ጸሎተ፡ ኪዳን፡, 10–111.

በስመ ፡ አብ ፡ ወወልድ ፡ . . . በአብ ፡ ስም ፡ አምነን ፡ አብን ፡ ወላዲ ፡
ብለን ፡ በወልድ ፡ ስም ፡ አምነን ፡ ወልድን ፡ ተወላዲ ፡ ብለን ፡ በመንፈስ ፡
ቅዱስ ፡ ስም ፡ አምነን ፡ መንፈስ ፡ ቅዱስን ፡ ሠራኢ ፡ ብለን ፡ ... ሰብ ፡
ትሠይሞ ፡ ለዓሕል ፡ ሐዲስ ፡ ዓሕል ፡ በምታክብርበት ፡ ጊዜ ፡
የምትጸልየውን ፡ ነው። ወትብል ፡ እግዚአብሔር ፡ አምላክነ ፡ ወፀሲ ፡ ሲል ፡
ነው። ስትጸልይም ፡ እግዚአብሔር ፡ አምላክ ፡ ብለህ ፡ ጸልይ ፡ . . .

7. Ff. 103r–132v: Commentary on Anaphora of the Apostles, *Tərg^wame Qədase Ḥawaryat*, ትርጓሜ፡ ቅዳሴ፡ ሐዋርያት፡. See ትርጓሜ፡ ጸሎተ፡ ኪዳን፡, 111–62.

አኩቴተ ፡ ቁርባን ፡ ዘአበዊነ ፡ ሐዋርያት ፡ . . . ታሪክ ፡ ሐዋርያት ፡
ቅዳሴ ፡ የጻፋበት ፡ ምክንያት ፡ መናፍቃን ፡ ሐሳውያን ፡ ሐዋርያት ፡ ነን ፡
እያሉ ፡ መጽሐፍ ፡ እየጻፉ ፡ ዙረው ፡ እያስተማሩ ፡ የዋሃን ፡ ሰዎችን ፡
አሳቱ ፡ ሕገ ፡ ቤተ ፡ ክርስቲያን ፡ ለወጡ ፡ በዚህ ፡ ምክንያት ፡ በርም ፡
ጉባዔ ፡ አደረጉ ፡ . . .

8. Ff. 133r–143v: Commentary on Anaphora of Our Lord, *Tərg^wame Qəddase Əgzi'*, ትርጓሜ፡ ቅዳሴ፡ እግዚእ፡. See ትርጓሜ፡ ጸሎተ፡ ኪዳን፡, 163–81.

የቅዳሴ ፡ እግዚእ ፡ ታሪክ ፡ ምዕራፍ ፡ ፪ ፡ አመጽሐፈ ፡ ኪዳን ፡ ዘነገረሙ ፡
. . . ጌታ ፡ በሕይወተ ፡ ሥጋ ፡ ሳለ ፡ ያስተማረው ፡ ኪዳን ፡ ይባላል ፡...
በሰማይ ፡ የሃሉ ፡ ልብክሙ ፡ ከሰባቱ ፡ ኪዳናት ፡ አንዱ ፡ ይህ ፡ ነው።
የጀቱን ፡ ምክንያቱን ፡ በየደጇ ፡ ይናገራል ፡ የዚሁ ፡ የንጉሥ ፡ ሎሌ ፡
ብለህ ፡ እንዳለፈው ፡ አትት ፡ . . .

9. Ff. 144r–160r: Commentary on Anaphora of John, Son of Thunder, *Tərg^wame Qədase Yoḥannəs Wäldä Näg^wädəg'ad*, ትርጓሜ፡ ቅዳሴ፡ ዮሐንስ፡ ወልደ፡ ነጐድጓድ፡. See ትርጓሜ፡ ጸሎተ፡ ኪዳን፡, 182–211.

አኩቴተ ፡ ቁርባን ፡ ዘዮሐንስ ፡ ወልደ ፡ ነጐድጓድ ፡ . . . ዮሐንስ ፡
ማለት ፡ ርኅራኄ ፡ ወዋህል ፡ ፍሥሐ ፡ ወኃዌት ፡ ማለት ፡ ነው። ፍሥሐ ፡
ወኃዌት ፡ አለ ፡ ቅብጥ ፡ ትፍሥሕት ፡ መንፈስ ፡ ቅዱስን ፡ አስጥቶ ፡ ደስ ፡
ያሰኛናል። ርኅራኄ ፡ ወዋህል ፡ አለ ፡ በጸጋ ፡ ዘነሣእክሙ ፡ በከንቱ ፡ ሀቡ ፡
ባለው ፡ ጸንቶ ፡ ያስተምራናል። ወልደ ፡ ነጐድጓድ ፡ ነባቤ ፡ መለኮት ፡

ማለት ፡ ነው፡ ቀዳሚሁ ፡ ቃል ፡ ብሎ ፡ አንድነትን ፡ ሶስትነትን ፡ አምልቶ ፡
አስፍቶ ፡ ስለተናገረ ፡ . . .

10. Ff. 161r–198r: Commentary on Anaphora of Mary attributed to
    Cyriacus of Bəhənsa, *Tərgʷame Qəddase Maryam Gʷäsʿa*, ትርጓሜ፡
    ቅዳሴ፡ ማርያም፡. See ትርጓሜ፡ ጸሎተ፡ ኪዳን፡, 212–70.
    አኰቴተ ፡ ቁርባን ፡ ዘእግዝእትን ፡ ማርያም ፡ ድንግል ፡ ወላዲተ ፡ አምላክ ፡
    ዘደረሰ ፡ በመንፈስ ፡ ቅዱስ ፡ አባ ፡ ሕርያቆስ ፡ ኤጲስ ፡ ቆጶስ ፡ ዘሀገረ ፡
    ብህንሳ ፡ . . . ሕርያቆስ ፡ ማለት ፡ ጕሩይ ፡ ማለት ፡ ነው። ለሹመት ፡
    መርጠው ታልና። አንድም ፡ ረቂቅ ፡ ማለት ፡ ነው ፡ ምሥጢረ ፡ ሥላሴን ፡
    ይናገራልና ፡ ሊቃውንት ፡ ምሥጢረ ፡ ሥላሴን ፡ የማይናገር ፡ የለም ፡
    ብሎ ፡ ከሁሉ ፡ ይልቅ ፡ እሱ ፡ አምልቶ ፡ አስፍቶ ፡ ይናገራልና፡. . .

11. Ff. 198r–201r: History and Commentary on the Nicaean Creed,
    Tərgʷame Ṣälotä Haymanot, ትርጓሜ፡ ጸሎተ፡ ሃይማኖት፡. See ትርጓሜ፡
    ጸሎተ፡ ኪዳን፡, 271–76.
    የቆስጠንጢኖስ ፡ ብሔረ ፡ ሙላዱ ፡ ጥንት ፡ ነገዱ ፡ ወዴት ፡ ነው ፡ ቢሉ ፡
    እናቱ ፡ አይሁዳዊት ፡ የሮሐ ፡ ሰው ፡ አባቱ ፡ አረማዊ ፡ የበራንጥያ ፡ ሰው ፡
    ናቸው ፡ እናቱ ፡ አይሁዳዊት ፡ አባቱ ፡ አረማዊ ፡ ከሆኑ ፡ እንደምን ፡
    ተገናኙ ፡ ቢሉ ፡ ምክንያቱን ፡ ይናገሩታል ፡. . . ነአምን ፡ በ፩ ፡ አምላክ ፡
    በባሕርይ ፡ በሕልውና ፡ ከወልድ ፡ ከመንፈስ ፡ ቅዱስ ፡ ጋር ፡ አንድ ፡
    አምላክ ፡ በሚሆን ፡ እግዚአብሔር ፡ አብ። በእግዚአብሔር ፡ አብ ፡
    እናምናለን ። አኃዜ ፡ ኵሉ ፡ ገባሬ ፡ ሰማያት ፡ ወምድር ፡ ሁሉን ፡ የሚገዛ ፡
    አንድም ፡ ሁሉን ፡ የፈጠረ ፡ እግዚአ ፡ አኃዜ ፡ ኵሉ ፡ ዓለም ፡ አንዲል ፡
    ሁሉን ፡ እንደጥና ፡ እንደ ፡ ዕንቁላል ፡ በመሐል ፡ እጁ ፡ የያዘ ፡. . .

12. Ff. 201r–217r: Commentary on Anaphora of the 318 Orthodox
    Fathers, *Tərgʷame Qədase za-Śäläsətu Məʾət*, ትርጓሜ፡ ቅዳሴ፡ ሠለስቱ፡
    ምዕት፡. See ትርጓሜ፡ ጸሎተ፡ ኪዳን፡, 276–306.
    አኰቴተ ፡ ቁርባን ፡ ዘ፫፻፲ወ፰ ፡ ርቱዓን ፡ ሃይማኖት ፡. . . ቆስጠንጢኖስ ፡
    መክስምያኖስን ፡ ድል ፡ ነስቶስ ፡ ሮም ፡ ገባ ፡ ዘመክስምያኖስ ፡ ዕልው ፡
    ድጓሬ ፡ ኃልቀ ፡ እድሜ ፡ ቆስጠንጢኖስ ፡ ቦአ ፡ ወነግሠ ፡ በሮሜ ፡ አንዳለ ፡
    ደራሲ ፡ የገባስ ፡ አንጸኪያ ፡ ነው ፡ አንድ ፡ አድርጎ ፡ ስለገዛ ፡ ሮም ፡
    አለ ፡ በአንጸኪያ ፡ ያሉ ፡ ምእመናን ፡ የመስቀሉን ፡ የጥናውን ፡ የጻሕሉን ፡
    ሰባሪ ፡ የልብሱን ፡ ቅዳጅ ፡ ይዘው ፡ መስቀል ፡ ኃይልን ፡ መስቀል ፡ ጽንዕን ፡
    መስቀል ፡ መግሬ ፡ ዐር ፡ መስቀል ፡ መዋዒ ፡ ዐር ፡ እያሉ ፡
    ተቀብለው ታል ፡. . .

13. Ff. 217v–232v: Commentary on Anaphora of Athanasius, *Tərgʷame
    Qədase Atənatewos*, ትርጓሜ፡ ቅዳሴ፡ አትናቴዎስ፡. See ትርጓሜ፡ ጸሎተ፡
    ኪዳን፡, 306–35.
    አኰቴተ ፡ ቁርባን ፡ ዘቅዱስ ፡ አትናቴያስ ፡ ሊቀ ፡ ጳጳሳት ፡ ዘሀገረ ፡
    እስክንድር ፡ . . . አትናቴያስ ፡ ማለት ፡ ሕይወት ፡ ዘኢይመውት ፡ ማለት ፡

ነው ፡ ይህ ፡ ጥንት ፡ ሰሙ ፡ ነው ፡ ወበእንተ ፡ አእምሮተ ፡ ይእቲ ፡
ሕይወት ፡ ረከበ ፡ ሰመ ፡ ዘይሄሉ ፡ ለዓለም ፡ እንዲል። አንድም ፡ በዓለ ፡
ነቅዕ ፡ ዓቢይ ፡ ማለት ፡ ነው ፤ ሰለ ፡ ትምህርቱ ፡ ብዛት ፡ አንድም ፡ በቁሙ ፡
ውሃ ፡ ማለት ፡ ነው። ያ ፡ ውሃ ፡ በዚያም ፡ በዚያም ፡ ሄደ ፡ አትክልትን ፡
አዝርእትን ፡ ከይብስት ፡ ወደ ፡ ልምላሜ ፡ እንዲያደርስ ፡ እርሱም ፡
በትምህርቱ ፡ በተአምራቱ ፡ ብዙ ፡ ምዕመናንን ፡ ይጠቅማልና ፡ . . .

14. Ff. 233r–246r: Commentary on Anaphora of Basil, *Tərgʷame Qəddase Basləyos*, ትርጓሜ፡ ቅዳሴ፡ ባስልዮስ። See ትርጓሜ፡ ጸሎተ፡ ኪዳን፡, 336–60.

አኰቴት ፡ ቀርባን ፡ ዘቅዱስ ፡ ባስልዮስ ፡ . . . ባስልዮስ ፡ ማለት ፡
ማኅቶተ ፡ ቤተ ፡ ክርስቲያን ፡ ማለት ፡ ነው ፡ ብዙ ፡ የቤተ ፡ ክርስቲያን ፡
ሥርዓት ፡ ሠርቷልና ። አንድም ፡ ንጉሥ ፡ ነገሥት ፡ እግዚአብሔር ፡ ማለት ፡
ነው ። ከመ ፡ ዘበእንተ ፡ ትምህርቱ ፡ ያረብሀ ፡ መንግሥተ ፡ ሰማያት ፡
ተሰምየ ፡ በሰመ ፡ መንግሥት ፡ እንዲል ፡ ባስልኤል ፡ ማለት ፡ ንጉሥ ፡
ማለት ፡ እንዲ ፡ ሆነ ። . . .

15. Ff. 246v–256r: Commentary on Anaphora of Gregory, brother of Basil, *Tərgʷame Qəddase Gorəgorəyos Ḫhəwä Basləyos*, ትርጓሜ፡ ቅዳሴ፡ ጎርጎርዮስ እኁሁ። ባስልዮስ። See ትርጓሜ፡ ጸሎተ፡ ኪዳን፡, 360–78.

ይዳ ፡ ጸልዩ ፡ በእንተ ፡ አበዊነ ፡ ጻጻሳት ፡ ወአበዊነ ፡ ኤጲስ ፡ ቀጾሳት ፡
ወአበዊነ ፡ ቀሳውስት ፡ በሰማይ ፡ የሃሉ ፡ ልብክሙ ፡ ባለው ፡ የገባ ፡ ነው።
ስለ ፡ አባቶቻችን ፡ ስለ ፡ ሊቃነ ፡ ጻጻሳት ፡ ስለ ፡ ጻጻሳት ፡ ስለ ፡ ኤጲስ ፡
ቀጶሳት ፡ ስለ ፡ ቀሳውስት ፡ ወአሐዊነ ፡ ዲያቆናት ፡ ስለ ፡ ወንድሞቻችን ፡
ዲያቆናት ። ጸልዩ ፡ ውሉደ ፡ ዛቲ ፡ ቤተ ፡ ክርስቲያን ፡ በቤተ ፡ ክርስቲያን ፡
ያላችሁ ፡ ምዕመናን ፡ ጸልዩ። አንድም ፡ በእንተ ፡ መሐይምናን ፡
ወመሐይምንት ። ጸልዩ ፡ በእንተ ፡ መሐይምናን ፡ ወመሐይምንት ፡ ውሉደ ፡
ዛቲ ፡ ቤተ ፡ ክርስቲያን ፡ ብለህ ፡ ግጠም ፡ በቤተ ፡ ክርስቲያን ፡ ሰላሉ ፡
. . .

16. Ff. 256v–266r: Commentary on Anaphora of Epiphanius, *Tərgʷame Qəddase Epifanəyos*, ትርጓሜ፡ ቅዳሴ፡ ኤጲፋንዮስ። See ትርጓሜ፡ ጸሎተ፡ ኪዳን፡, 379–97.

አኰቴተ ፡ ቀርባን ፡ ዘቅዱስ ፡ ኤጲፋንዮስ ፡ ኤጲስ ፡ ቆጶስ ፡ ዘደሴት ፡
ቆጵሮስ ፡ . . . ኤጲፋንዮስ ፡ ማለት ፡ ከዛቲ ፡ አርኃዊ ፡ አስተርእዮ ፡
ማለት ፡ ነው ። ኤጲፋንያን ፡ ዘውቱ ፡ በዓለ ፡ አስተርእዮ ፡ እንዲለው።
ወኮነ ፡ አበዊሁ ፡ አይሁዳውያን ፡ ይላል ፡ አባት ፡ እናቱ ፡ አይሁድ ፡ ናቸው ፡
ካንድ ፡ አህያ ፡ በቀር ፡ የሌላቸው ፡ ድሆች ፡ ናቸው ፡ ቤቱ ፡ ከቤተ ፡
ክርስቲያን ፡ አጠገብ ፡ ነው። አባቱ ፡ ሲሞት ፡ ለሱ ፡ ለእኅቱ ፡ ለእናቱ ፡
ይረዱበት ፡ ብሎ ፡ አንድ ፡ አህያ ፡ ትቶላቸው ፡ ሞተ ፡ እናቱ ፡ ለተግባር ፡
ልናደርገው ፡ ሽጠህ ፡ አምጣ ፡ ብላ ፡ ሰደደችው ፡ . . .

17. Ff. 266r–274v: Commentary on Anaphora of John Chrysostom, *Tərg^wame Qədase Yohannəs Afä Wärq Nahu Nəvenu*, ትርጓሜ፡ ቅዳሴ፡ ዮሐንስ ፡ አፈ ፡ ወርቅ፤. See ትርጓሜ ፡ ጸሎተ ፡ ኪዳን፤, 397–413.
አኰቴተ ፡ ቁርባን ፡ ዘዮሐንስ ፡ አፈ ፡ ወርቅ ፡ . . . ዮሐንስ ፡ ማለት ፡ ፍስሐ ፡ ወሐዄት ፡ ርኅራኄ ፡ ወዛህል ፡ ማለት ፡ ነው። ሀገሩ ፡ አንጾኪያ ፡ ነው ፡ አባቱ ፡ አስፋኒዶስ ፡ ይባል ። እናቱ ፡ አትናስያ ፡ ትባላለች ። ወኰኑ ፡ እምብዑላኒሃ ፡ ለይእቲ ፡ ሀገር ፡ ይላቸዋል ፡ ባለጸጎች ፡ ነበሩ ፡ አቴና ፡ ወረደ ፡ ጥበብ ፡ ሥጋዊ ፡ ተምር ፡ ከሁሉ ፡ በላይ ፡ ሆነ ፡ ጥበብ ፡ ሥጋዊ ፡ ተምሬ ፡ ከሁሉ ፡ በላይ ፡ እንደሆንሁ ፡ ጥበብ ፡ መንፈሳዊ ፡ ተምሬ ፡ ከሁሉ ፡ በላይ ፡ እሆናለሁ ፡ ብሎ ፡ ባስልዮስ ፡ ከነበረበት ፡ ገዳም ፡ ገባ ፡ . . .

18. Ff. 274v–285r: Commentary on Anaphora of Cyril, *Tərg^wame Qədase Qerəlos*, ትርጓሜ፡ ቅዳሴ፡ ቄርሎስ፤. See ትርጓሜ፡ ጸሎተ፡ ኪዳን፤, 413–32.
አኰቴተ ፡ ቁርባን ፡ ዘቅዱስ ፡ ቄርሎስ ፡ . . . ቄርሎስ ፡ ማለት ፡ ኃያል ፡ ማለት ፡ ነው። ወተጼወው ፡ ቄረ ፡ ሕዝቦሙ ፡ ለሰብአ ፡ ሶርያ ፡ እንዲል ። ኃያላን ፡ ሕዝቦሙ ፡ መኳንንት ፡ ሕዝቦሙ ፡ ሲል ፡ አንድም ፡ አንበሳ ፡ ማለት ፡ ነው ፡ መናፍቃን ፡ ይገሥጻልና ። አንድም ፡ ብዑዕ ፡ ገብር ፡ አምላክ ፡ ማለት ፡ ነው ። አንድም ፡ ሳሩይ ፡ ማለት ፡ ነው፤ አንድም ፡ ዘርዕ ፡ ሠናይ ፡ ማለት ፡ ነው ። አንድም ፡ ጽጌ ፡ ፍሬ ፡ ማለት ፡ ነው ፡ አንድም ፡ መስተገብረ ፡ ምድር ፡ ማለት ፡ ነው ፡ . . .

19. Ff. 285r–293v: Commentary on Anaphora of Jacob of Serugh, *Tərg^wame QədaseYa'əkob Zä-Śərug*, ትርጓሜ፡ ቅዳሴ፡ ያዕቆብ፡ ዘሥሩግ፤. See ትርጓሜ፡ ጸሎተ፡ ኪዳን፤, 432–47.
አኰቴተ ፡ ቁርባን ፡ ዘያዕቆብ ፡ ኤጲስ ፡ ቆጶስ ፡ ዘሥሩግ ፡ . . . ያዕቆብ ፡ ማለት ፡ አኃዚ ፡ አዕቃዪ ፡ ማለት ፡ ነው ፡ የቀደመው ፡ ያዕቆብ ፡ ሰኰና ፡ ኤሳውን ፡ ይዞ እንደ ፡ ተወለደ። አሁም ፡ በትምህርቱ ፡ የመናፍቃንን ፡ ትምህርት ፡ ያስነክላልና ። ያዕብ ፡ ወልደ ፡ ዘብዴዎስ ፡ ያዕቆብ ፡ ወልደ ፡ እልፍዮስ ፡ ያዕቆብ ፡ እኍሁ ፡ ያዕቆብ ፡ ዘአልቦ ፡ ረዳኢ ፡ ያዕቆብ ፡ ዘንጽቢን ፡ ያዕቆብ ፡ ዘገሙድ ፡ ብዙ ፡ ያዕቆብ ፡ አሉና ፡ ከነዚያ ፡ ሲለይ ፡ ዘሥሩግ ፡ ተብሏል። ሥሩግ ፡ የተሾመበት ፡ አገር ፡ ናት ። በጤግሮስና ፡ በኤፍራጥስ ፡ መሃከል ፡ ያለች ፡ አገር ፡ ናት ፤ . . .

20. Ff. 293v–296v: Commentary on Anaphora of Dioscorus, *Tərg^wame Qədase Diyosəqoros*, ትርጓሜ፡ ቅዳሴ፡ ዲዮስቆርስ፤. See ትርጓሜ፡ ጸሎተ፡ ኪዳን፤, 448–54.
አኰቴተ ፡ ቁርባን ፡ ዘቅዱስ ፡ ዲዮስቆርስ ፡ . . . ዲዮስቆርስ ፡ ማለት ፡ ተወካፌ ፡ መከራ ፡ መስቀል ፡ ማለት ፡ ነው ። ትእምርተ ፡ ዲዮስቆርስ ፡ እንዲል ፡ ከጉባኤ ፡ ኒቅያ ፡ እስከ ፡ ጉባኤ ፡ ቁስጥንጥንያ ፡ ሃ፳ ፡ ዓመት ፡ ከጉባኤ ፡ ቁስጥንጥንያ ፡ እስከ ፡ ጉባኤ ፡ ኤፌሶን ፡ ሃ፳ ፡ ዓመት ፡ ያን ፡

ሃጄ ፡ ቢሉ ፡ ይኽን ፡ ሃፊ ፡ ይሏል ፡ ከጉባኤ ፡ ኤፊሶን ፡ አስከ ፡ ጉባኤ ፡
ኬልቄደን ፡ ሸሿ ፡ ዓመት ፡ ነው ። በዚህ ፡ ጊዜ ፡ መርያቅያን ፡ በልዮን ፡
ምክንያት ፡ በኬልቄደን ፡ ጉባኤ ፡ ይሁን ፡ ብሎ ፡ አዋጅ ፡ ነገረ ፡ . . .

21. Ff. 297r–301r: Commentary on Anaphora of Gregory, the Wonder Worker, *Tərgʷame Qədase Gorəgorəyos, Gäbare mänkərat*, ትርጓሜ፡ ቅዳሴ፡ ጎርጎርዮስ፡ ገባሪ፡ መንክራት፡. See ትርጓሜ፡ ጸሎተ፡ ኪዳን፡, 454–62.

አኮቴት ፡ ቁርባን ፡ ዘጎርጎርዮስ ፡. . . ጎርጎርዮስ ፡ ሰመ ፡ ትርጓሜው ፡
እንዳለፈው ፡ ነው ፡ ሀገሩ ፡ ሮም ፡ ነው ፡ በሕፃንነቱ ፡ ብሉይ ፡ ሐዲስ ፡
ተምሯል ፤ ወተዘክረ ፡ ማኀለቆ ፡ ለዝንቱ ፡ ዓለም ፡ ወንብረተ ፡ መንግሥተ ፡
ሰማያት ፡ ዘኢየኀልቅ ፡ ይላል ። ይህ ፡ ዓለም ፡ እንዲያልፍ ፡ የወዲያው ፡
ዓለም ፡ እንደማያልፍ ፡ አውቆ ፡ መንግ ፡ ገዳም ፡ ገባ ፡ ከሄደበት ፡ ገዳም ፡
አንድ ፡ አረጋዊ ፡ ኤኢስ ፡ ቆጾስ ፡ ነበረ ፡ አርዳኝ ፡ ይላዋል ፡ አሱም ፡
አይሆንልኝም ፡ ይላዋ ፡ ውዳሴ ፡ ከንቱ ፡ አይሻምና ፡ ካለበት ፡ ወጥቶ ፡
ዱር ፡ ገባ ፡ ወዲያው ፡ ያ ፡ ኤኢስ ፡ ቆጾስ ፡ ሞተ ፡ ማንን እንጄም ፡
ብለው ፡ ሲጨነቁ ፡ ዒምያ ፡ ለጎርጎርዮስ ፡ ገዳማዊ ፡ የሚል ፡ ቃል ፡
ሰመ ፡ . . .

22. Ff. 301rv: Explanation of the Eucharistic Prayer (*yəräsəyo*, ይረስዮ፡) and the number of times for the blessings and the pointing to the sacrificial elements and circling the altar by the priest. See ትርጓሜ፡ ጸሎተ፡ ኪዳን፡, 462.

ይረስዮ ፡ ያላቸው ፡ ቅዳሴያት ፡ ፰ ፡ ናቸው ፡ ማን ፡ ማናቸው ፡ ቢሉ ፡
ቅዳሴ ፡ ሐዋርያት ፡ ቅዳሴ ፡ እግዚእ ፡ ዮሐንስ ፡ ወልደ ፡ ነጉድጓድ ፡. . .

23. F. 301v: List of the Anaphoras. See ትርጓሜ፡ ጸሎተ፡ ኪዳን፡, 463.

Notes:

1. Ff. i r(ecto)-vi v(erso), 42v, 102v, 160v and 302r–305v: blank.
2. F. 26r: mentions Ḥaylä Śəllase Täfäri Mäkʷonen.
3. F. 301v: Colophon, "This commentary of the book of missal was written in 1974 E.C by *Märige(ta)* Gäbrä Maryam, Wäldä Maryam of Saynt [in Wollo] and Lə_ul Wäldä Rufaʻel." The contents of this manuscript appears to have been copied from the published edition of ትርጓሜ፡ ጸሎተ፡ ኪዳን፡, which was published in 1918.
4. Decorative designs: ff. 1r, 45r, 103r, 133r, 144r, 161r (ornate, colorful *ḥaräg*); multiple full stops are used as section dividers throughout (e.g., ff. 2v, 4r); f. 198r (lines of alternating red and black dots); ff. 201r, 217r, 232v, 246r, 256r, 266r, 274v, 285, 293v, 296v, 301v (full stops connected with red and black dots).
5. Several factors point to the production of this codex in the government scriptorium: fine parchment, trimmed text block, tooled Moroccan leather, headband and tailband, fine workmanship and the multi-colored *ḥarägs*.

144 · Catalog of the Manuscripts

6. Scribal intervention: words of text are written interlinearly (ff. 177r, 223v, 288r); and lines of text are written interlinearly (ff. 103r, 208r, 254r); text has been removed (e.g., ff. 232r, 239v, 241r).

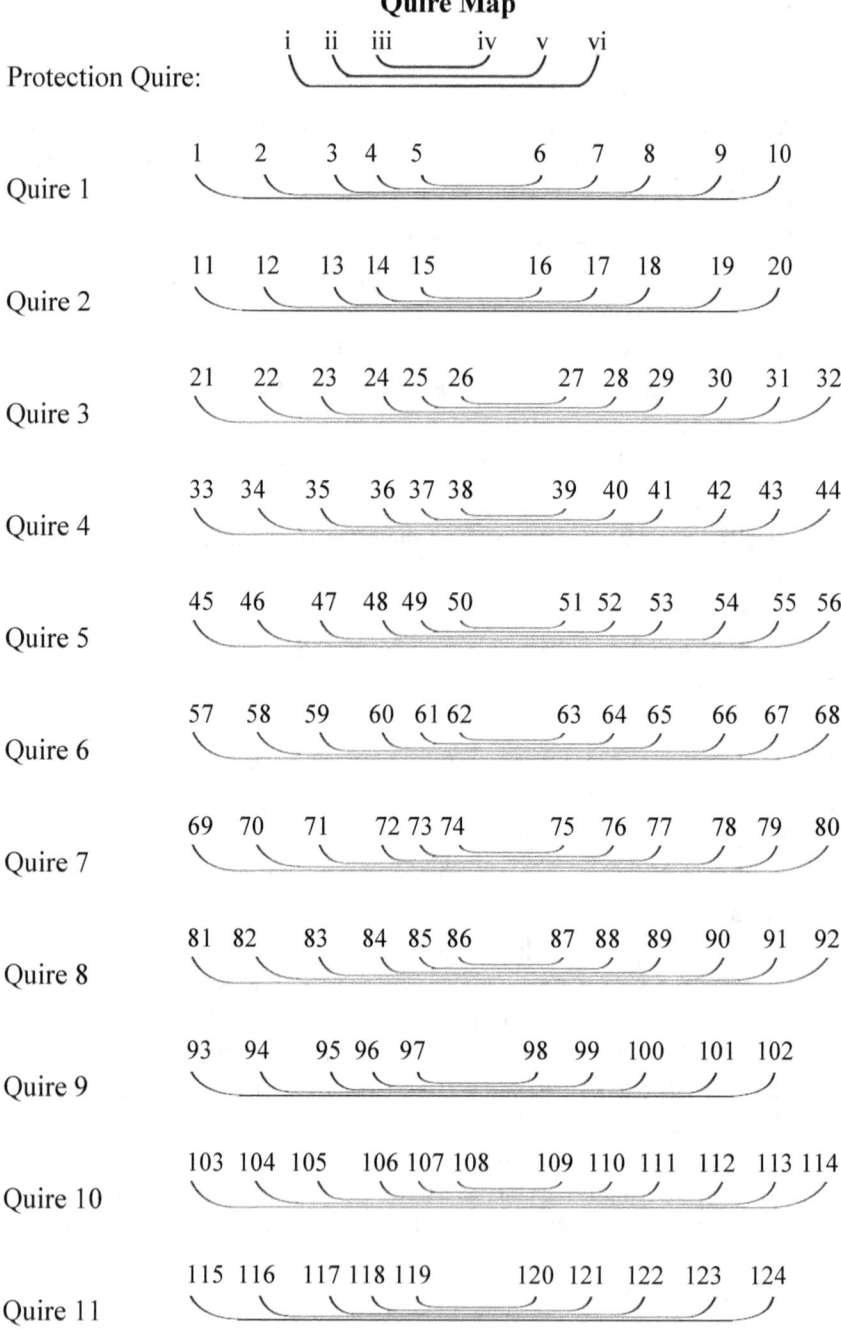

Quire 12: 125 126 127 128 129 130 131 132 133 134

Quire 13: 135 136 137 138 139 140 141 142 143 144

Quire 14: 145 146 147 148 149 150 151 152 153 154

Quire 15: 155 156 157 158 159 160 161 162 163 164

Quire 16: 165 166 167 168 169 170 171 172 173 174

Quire 17: 175 176 177 178 179 180 181 182 183 184

Quire 18: 185 186 187 188 189 190 191 192 193 194

Quire 19: 195 196 197 198 199 200 201 202

Quire 20: 203 204 205 206 207 208 209 210 211 212

Quire 21: 213 214 215 216 217 218 219 220 221 222

Quire 22: 223 224 225 226 227 228 229 230 231 232

Quire 23: 233 234 235 236 237 238 239 240 241 242

Quire 24: 243 244 245 246 247 248 249 250 251 252

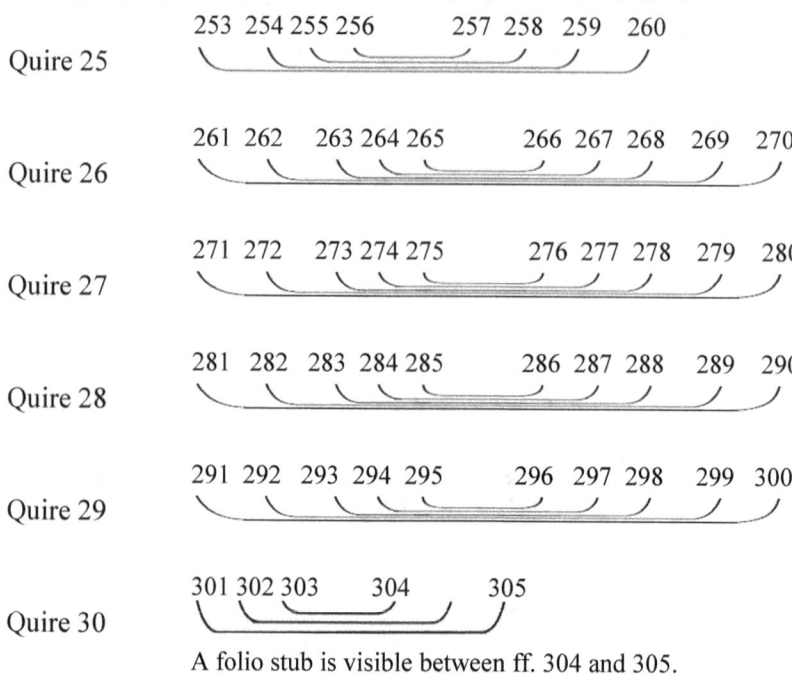

A folio stub is visible between ff. 304 and 305.

MYS 35 – EMIP 635
Faith of the Fathers, ሃይማኖተ፡ አበው፡, Book of Tomar, መጽሐፈ፡ ጦማር፡, and Faith of Jacob Al Baradai, ሃይማኖተ፡ ያዕቆብ፡ አልበራዳኢ፡

Parchment, 360 x 274 x 95 mm, four Coptic chain stitches attached with bridle attachments to rough-hewn boards of the traditional wood, covered with tooled leather, linen visible between the turn-ins, headband and tailband, protection quire + 20 full quires, iii + 160 folios, top margin 33 mm, bottom margin 47 mm, fore edge margin 27 mm, gutter margin 18 mm, ff. 1r–158v three columns, 38–40 lines, Gəʿəz, twentieth century.

Quire descriptions: quires 1–2, 4, 8–9, 13–14, 16 and 18–19 balanced; protection quire and quires 3, 5–7, 10–12, 15, 17 and 20 adjusted balanced. Navigation system: marginal notation throughout.

Major Works:
1. Ff. 1r–133v: Faith of the Fathers, *Haymanotä Abäw*, ሃይማኖተ፡ አበው፡, EMML 1173; Or. 784, Wright, *Catalogue of Ethiopic Manuscripts in the British Museum* (London: British Museum, 1877) CCCXLIV, 232–4; Ṭanasee 11, Ham (Ṭanasee) 1.11 110–114; published under the title *Haymanotä Abäw* (Addis Ababa, 1967 EC).

በሰመ ፡ አብ ፡ ወወልድ ፡ . . . ንዌጥን ፡ በረድኤተ ፡ እግዚአብሔር ፡ ዘቦቱ ፡ መድኃኒት ፡ በጽሒፈ ፡ ሃይማኖተ ፡ አበው ፡ መምህራን ፡ ቅድስት ፡ ቤተ ፡ ክርስቲያን ፡ አሐቲ ፡ ጉባዔ ፡ እንተ ፡ ሐዋርያት ፡ ወነገረ ፡ ሃይማኖተ ፡ ኩሉ ፡ ለለ ፡ ፩፩ ፡ እምኔሆሙ ፡ በእንተ ፡ ቅድስት ፡ ሥላሴ ፡ ዘነበበ ፡ መንፈስ ፡ በልሳናቲሆሙ ፡ ወእሉ ፡ አበው ፡ ሲቲዮሙ ፡ ፩ ፡ መንፈስ ፡ ተናገሩ ፡ ኅቡረ ፡ በእንተ ፡ ቅድስት ፡ ሥላሴ ፡ ወበእንተ ፡ ተዋህዶተ ፡ መለኮት ፡ ወበእንተ ፡ ትሥጉት ፡. . .

a. F. 1r: Introduction, f. 3a;
b. Ff. 1r–2r: Mystagogia, *Təmhərtä Ḫəbu_at*, ትምህርተ፡ ኅቡዓት፡. Hammerschmidt, *Texte* 48–72; Lifchitz, *Textes* 40–52; Velat, *Me_erāf* I: 215–7; *MG59* 9ff. The text here is from the section in Mystagogia called, *Elmäsṭo 'ägeya*.
c. Ff. 2rv: from the Didascalia of the Apostles.
d. Ff. 2v–121r: Testimonies of the Fathers: Irenaeus (f. 2v), Aṭifos (f. 3v), Arkəwos (f. 3v), Dionysius of Areopagus (f. 3v), Ignatius (f. 4r), Gregory the Wonder Worker (f. 4v), Alexander of Alexandria (f. 6r), the 318 Fathers (f. 6r), Athanasius (f. 11r), Basil (f. 20v), Gregory of Nyssa (f. 23r), Felix the Martyr (f. 26v), Hippolytus (f. 27r), Mäṭoligon (f. 30r), Ayokəndyos Bishop of Rome (f. 30v), Sylvester (f. 30v), Naṭalis of Rome (f. 31r), Ephrem the Syrian (f. 31r), Heraclius, (f. 32r), Severius of Elah (i.e., Ashkelon; f. 33v), Afərosyos the Armenian (f. 34r), John, Bishop of Jerusalem (f. 34r), Theodotos of Ankara (f. 35r), Epiphanius of Cyprus (f. 36r), Gregory of Nazianzus (f. 44r), John Chrysostom of Constantinople (f. 46r), Theophilus, archbishop of Alexandria (f. 53v), Cyril of Alexandria (f. 53v), Gregory of Nazianzus (f. 60r), John Chrysostom of Constantinople (f. 62r), Cyril (f. 66r), Severus of Antioch (f. 70v), Cyril (f. 72v), Abəqarils (f. 72v), Farenewos (f. 72v), Severus of Antioch (f. 73v), Jacob of Surug (f. 76r), Benjamin, archbishop of Alexandria (f. 76v), Julius, archbishop of Alexandria (f. 78v), Cyril (f. 80v), Gregory the Theologian (f. 80v), Cyriacus, archbishop of Antioch (f. 81r), Theodotius, archbishop of Antioch (f. 83v), Dionysius (f. 84r), Gabriel, archbishop of Alexandria (f. 85r), Cosmas, bishop of Alexandria (f. 86r), Basil, archbishop of Antioch (f. 86v), [title not given] (f. 89v), Macarius, archbishop of Alexandria (f. 90v), Dionysius (f. 91v), Minas of Alexandria (f. 93v), Dionysius of Antioch (f. 94r), John, archbishop of Antioch (f. 95v), Philotheos,

archbishop of Alexandria (f. 99r), Athanasius, archbishop of Antioch (f. 101v), John, archbishop of Antioch (f. 102v), Zecharius, archbishop of Alexandria (f. 104v), Shenouda, archbishop of Alexandria (f. 106v), Dionysius, archbishop of Antioch (f. 113v), Christodolos, archbishop of Alexandria (f. 114v), John, archbishop of Antioch (f. 118v), Habib, Episcopos of Tikrit (f. 121r), Zacharias Yahya (f. 121r).
   e. Ff. 121v–133v: Anathemas of the Fathers.
2. Ff. 133v–143v: Book of Ṭomar, *Mäṣəḥafä Ṭomar*, መጽሐፈ፡ ጦማር፡. በስመ ፡ አብ ፡ ወወልድ ፡ . . . መጽሐፍ ፡ ዘወረደት ፡ እምሰማይ ፡ ላዕለ ፡ አባ ፡ አትናቴዎስ ፡ በዕለተ ፡ እንድ ፡ ወረደት ፡ ዛቲ ፡ መጽሐፈ ፡ ጦማር ፡ ቦርምያ ፡ በኢየዋሃ ፡ ዓመት ፡ እምዓመተ ፡ እለስክንድርስ ፡ እምአመ ፡ ኃለፈ ፡ ጿወጹ ፡ ወኮነ ፡ ቀዳማይ ፡ ውስተ ፡ ቤተ ፡ ክርስቲያን ፡ በካልዓይ ፡ ቅዱስ ፡ ጴጥሮስ ፡ ወጸውሎስ ፡ አሙንቱ ፡ ጎሩያን ፡ . . .
3. Ff. 143v–144r: Table of Contents of Faith of the Fathers.
4. Ff. 144r–158v: Faith of Jacob Al Baradai, *Haymanotä Yäʾəqob Al Bäradaʿi*, ሃይማኖተ፡ ያዕብ፡ አልበራዳኢ፡. በስመ ፡ አብ ፡ ወወልድ ፡ . . . ንቀድም ፡ በረድኤተ ፡ እግዚአብሔር ፡ ወስመ ፡ ስርሐቱ ፡ በጽሐፈ ፡ ሃይማኖት ፡ ዘቅዱስ ፡ ዓቢይ ፡ ማሪ ፡ ያዕቆብ ፡ አልበራዳኢ ፡ ጸጾሙ ፡ ለያዕቆባውያን ፡ ለሶርያ ፡ ወለቅብጥ ፡ ወለኢትዮጵያ ፡ ወለውእቱ ፡ ኤሲስ ፡ ቆጾስ ፡ ዘሀገረ ፡ ሮሐ ፡ . . .

Notes:
1. The scribe is frequently inaccurate about names, for instance, fusing two names into one (f. 113v).
2. F. i and 160 are pasted beneath the tooled leather.
3. F. 1r and *passim*: owners' names, Fəśəḥ Ḥä Ṣəyon and Niqodimos.
4. F. ii r(ecto)–iii v(erso) and 159rv: blank.
5. Decorative designs: ff. 121r, 124r, 138v (multiple full stops); ff. 124v, 133v, 144r, 158v (line of alternating red and black dots).
6. The word Mary is rubricated.
7. Numbered quires: quires 2–10 numbered on the first folio; quires 11–12, 14–15 and 18–19 are numbered on the verso of the final folio.
8. Scribal intervention: words of text are written interlinearly (ff. 74r, 101r, 130r, 157r); and lines of text are written interlinearly (f. 46r); and in the bottom margin with a symbol (⊥) marking the location where the text is to be inserted ff. 6v, col. 1, line 26); erasure markings are visible (f. 101v); text has been removed (e.g., f. 11v).

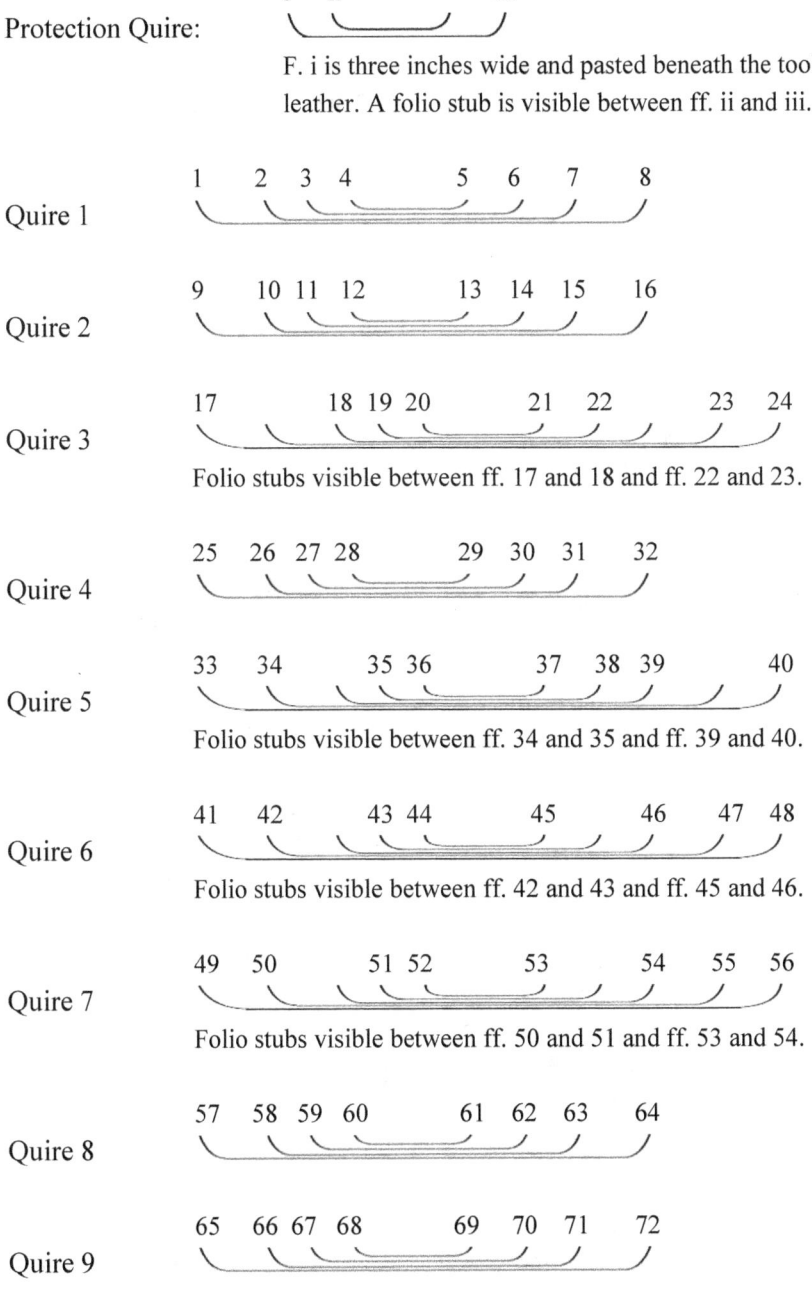

Folio stubs visible between ff. 74 and 75 and ff. 77 and 78.

Quire 11 — 81 82 83 84 85 86 87 88
Folio stubs visible between ff. 82 and 83 and ff. 85 and 86.

Quire 12 — 89 90 91 92 93 94 95 96
Folio stubs visible between ff. 90 and 91 and ff. 93 and 94.

Quire 13 — 97 98 99 100 101 102 103 104

Quire 14 — 105 106 107 108 109 110 111 112

Quire 15 — 113 114 115 116 117 118 119 120
Folio stubs visible between ff. 114 and 115 and ff. 117 and 118.

Quire 16 — 121 122 123 124 125 126 127 128

Quire 17 — 129 130 131 132 133 134 135 136
Folio stubs visible between ff. 131 and 132 and ff. 134 and 135.

Quire 18 — 137 138 139 140 141 142 143 144

Quire 19 — 145 146 147 148 149 150 151 152

Quire 20 — 153 154 155 156 157 158 159 160
F. 160 is three inches wide and pasted beneath the tooled leather. Folio stubs visible between ff. 153 and 154 and ff. 157 and 158.

MYS 36 – EMIP 636
Computus, ባሕረ፧ ሐሳብ፧, Excerpt from Computus, *Abušahər*, አቡሻህር, Computus of Demetrius, *Ḥasab Dəmeṭəros*, ሐሳበ፧ ድሜጥሮስ፧

Parchment, 195 x 150 x 32 mm, four Coptic chain stitches attached with bridle attachments to rough-hewn boards of the traditional wood, protection quire + 7 full quires, ii + 62 folios, top margin 18–22 mm, bottom margin 32–38 mm, fore edge margin 15 mm, gutter margin 10 mm, ff. 1r–57v two columns, 27–28 lines, Gə῾əz, twentieth century.

Quire descriptions: quires 1–5 and 7 balanced; protection quire and quire 6 adjusted balanced.

Major Works:
1. Ff. 1r–41v: Computus, *Bahərä Ḥasab*, ባሕረ፧ ሐሳብ፧, in Amharic. For a detailed study of the computus, see Otto Neugebaur, *Ethiopic Astronomy and Computus*, (Vienna: Verlag der Österreichischen Akademie der Wissenschaften, 1979); and Getatchew Haile (ጌታቸው፡ ኃይሌ), ባሕረ፡ ሐሳብ፡ የዘመን፡ ቆጠራ፡ ቅርሳችን፡ ከታሪክ፡ ማስታወሻ፡ ጋር፤ (Collegeville, Minnesota, 1993 EC).

   በስመ ፡ አብ ፡ ወወልድ፡ . . . ንዌጥን ፡ በረድኤተ ፡ እግዚአብሔር ፡ ጽሒፈ ፡ ባሕረ ፡ ሐሳብ ፡ እግዚአብሔር ፡ እምቅድመ ፡ ዓለም ፡ እንደ ፡ ዛሬ ፡ ሁሉ ፡ በጀት ፡ በ፷ት ፡ ስለ ፡ ክብሩ ፡ በባሕርየ ፡ እንደ ፡ ቀረ ፡ አይቶ ፡ ዓለምን ፡ ልፍጠር ፡ ብሎ ፡ አሰበ ፡ አሰቦም ፡ አልቀረ ፡ ፈጠረ ። ሲፈጥርም ፡ መላእክትና ፡ ሰውን ፡ ሰሙን ፡ ለመቀደስ ፡ ክብሩን ፡ ለመውረስ ፡ ፈጥሮአቸዋል ፡ የቀረውን ፡ ፍጥረት ፡ ግን ፡ ለአንክሮ ፡ ለተዘክሮ ፡ ለምግብ ፡ ሥጋ ፡ ለምግብ ፡ ነፍስ ፡ ፈጠረ ፡ ወኮሉ ፡ ዘፈጥረ ፡ ለመፍቅደ ፡ ነባብያን ፡ ቦ ፡ እምኔሆሙ ፡ ለምህር ፡ ወቦ ፡ እምኔሆሙ ፡ ለተገብር ፡ እንዘ ፡ ኢየኃድግ ፡ ርእሶ ፡ ዘእንበለ ፡ ስማእት፤ . . .

2. Ff. 22r–25v: Excerpt from Computus, *Abušahər*, አቡሻህር፡, attributed, in this manuscript, to John.

   ይህ ፡ መጽሐፍ ፡ አቡሻህር ፡ የተባለ ፡ ዮሐንስ ፡ የጻፈ ፡ መጽሐፍ ፡ ነው ፡ በዚህ ፡ መጽሐፍ ፡ የፀሐይን ፡ የጨረቃን ፡ የከዋክብትን ፡ ነገር ፡ ይናገራሉ ፡ ከጨረቃ ፡ ከዋክብት ፡ አስቀድሞ ፡ የፀሐይን ፡ ነገር ፡ ይናገራሉ ፡ ዓለም ፡ የተፈጠረበት ፡ ዕለት ፡ ዕሁድ ፡ ጥንተ ፡ ዕለት ፡ ዕፀው ፡ የተፈጠሩበት ፡ ዕለት ፡ ሦስት ፡ ጥንተ ፡ ቀመር ፡ ብርሃናት ፡ የተፈጠሩበት ፡ ዕለት ፡ ረቡዕ ፡ ጥንተ ፡ ፀሐይ ፡ ይባላል ። . . .

3. Ff. 25v–27v: The story of how the computus was revealed to Demetrius.

   በስመ ፡ አብ ፡ ወወልድ፡ . . . ንዌጥን ፡ በረድኤተ ፡ እግዚአብሔር ፡ ይኽ ፡ መጽሐፍ ፡ መርህ ፡ እውራን ፡ ባሕረ ፡ አሳብ ፡ ይባላል ፡ እውራን ፡ የተባሉ ፡ ሰዎች ፡ ናቸው ፡ አላዋቆችን ፡ ያሳውቃልና ፡

እንድም ፡ ዕውራን ፡ የተባሉ ፡ አዝማን ፡ ናቸው ፡ ያልታወቁትን ፡
አዝማን ፡ የሚያሳውቅ ፡ ስለሆነ፡ . . .

4. Ff. 28r–41v: Series of calendar tables, ሥንጠሬኽ፡, arranged in columns: computation cycle (_awədä qämär, i.e., according to the 532–year cycle), cycle of epact (_awədä abäqte, i.e., according to the 19–year cycle), birth of epact (lədätä abäqte), Pag^{w}ame (the 13th month), cycle of the year (_awədä _amät, i.e., according to the 365–day solar cycle or the 354–day lunar cycle), feast of John (_əlätä Yoḥannəs), solar epact (ṭəntyon), epact (abäqte), feast of trumpets (mäṭqə_, i.e., Jewish New Year), nights from the new moon (śärqä. lelit, i.e., from the beginning of month), fasting of the Jews (ṣomä ayhud), unleavened bread (mäṣälät, i.e., Passover), nights from the new moon (śärqä. lelit), fasting of Nineveh (Nänäwe), Lent (bäʿatä ṣom, lit., beginning of the fast), Day of Passover (_əlätä fəśh), nights from the new moon (śärqä. lelit), Easter (fasika).

5. Ff. 42r–56v: Computus of Demetrius, patriarch of Alexandria (189–232), Ḥasab Dəmeṭaros, ሐሳበ፡ ድሜጥሮስ፡, making computations from the creation of the world up to the end of the world, in Gəʿəz.
በስመ ፡ አብ ፡ ወወልድ፡ . . . ንቀድም ፡ በረድኤት ፡ እግዚአብሔር ፡ ዜና ፡ አርአስተ ፡ ሐሳብ ፡ እምፍጥረተ ፡ ዓለም ፡ እስከ ፡ ተፍጻሜተ ፡ ዓለም ፡ ወነገሩኒ ፡ በእንተ ፡ ምሥጢረ ፡ አቅማር ፡ ወግብረ ፡ ዓመታት ፡ ወክፍለ ፡ ሰንበታት ፡ ወሱባኤሆሙ ፡ ወኢዮቤላት ፡ ወዑደተ ፡ እንድቅትዮን ፡ ወክፍለ ፡ ጸጉሜን ፡ ወሐሳበ ፡ ሰማይ ፡ ወሐሳበ ፡ ምድር ፡ ወሐሳበ ፡ ፀሐይ ፡ ዘይትበሀል ፡ አበቅቴ ፡ ፀሐይ ፡ ወአበቅቴ ፡ ወርህ ፡ ወዕለተ ፡ መጥቀዕ፡ . . .

6. Ff. 57rv: Names of the months, Asəmatä Awəraḥ, አስማተ፡ አውራኅ፡, in Egyptian, Coptic, Afərəngi (French), Islamic (Arabic), Hebrew, Rome (Latin), Syriac, Greek, and Arabic.

Miniatures:
1. F. 58r: Map of the earth in concentric boxes, organized around the cardinal points. Ocean surrounds the whole. East (at the top) is the place for the righteous (moving toward center) ocean, desert, land with snow, paradise for the righteous, the creation with people. North (at the left) is the land of the living and Sheol. South (at the right) is the land of the blessed. West (at the bottom) is the place for sinners.
2. F. 61r: Diagram of the path of the Zodiac through the heavens from East (bottom) to West (top) for the months of Ṭərr (left) and Yäkkatit (right).

3. F. 61r: Diagram of the path of the Zodiac through the heavens from East (bottom) to West (top) for the months of Mäggabit (left) and Miyazya (right).
4. F. 61r: Diagram of the path of the Zodiac through the heavens from East (bottom) to West (top) for the months of Gənbot (left) and Säne (right).

Notes:
1. Ff. i r(ecto)–ii v(erso), 58v–60v and 62v: blank.
2. F. 22r: note of authorship: ―This book, which is called Abu šahər, is written by John, and tells about the computus of the sun and moon and stars."
3. Decorative designs: ff. 22r, 52r (a line of alternating red and black dots); f. 25v (multiple full stops).
4. Scribal intervention: words of text are written interlinearly (ff. 1v, 2rv, 3r, 4r, etc.); and in the upper margin with a symbol (⊥) marking the location where the text is to be inserted (ff. 4r, col. 2, line 11; 4v, col. 1, line 7; 5v, col. 1, line 7; 6r, col. 1, line 11; 7r, col. 2, line 3; 7v, col. 1, line 16), and in another case where the symbol (⊤) is used (ff. 7v, 20r, 23r, 43r); erasure markings are visible (f. 19v).

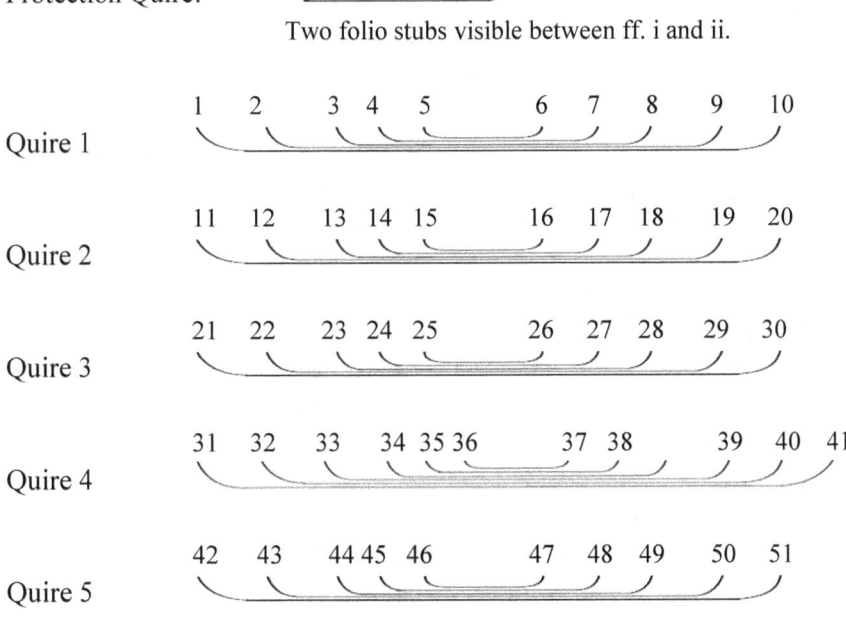

154 · *Catalog of the Manuscripts*

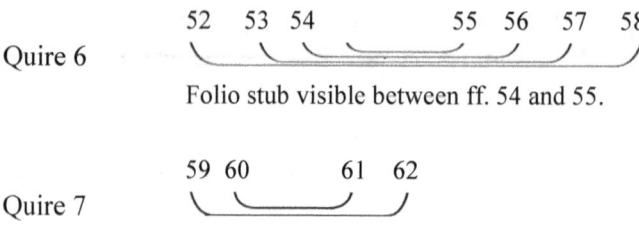

Quire 6

Folio stub visible between ff. 54 and 55.

Quire 7

MYS 37 – EMIP 637
Antiphonary for the Fast of Lent, ጾመ፟ ድጓ፟

Parchment, 170 x 126 x 55 mm, four Coptic chain stitches attached with bridle attachments to rough-hewn boards of the traditional wood, covered with tooled leather, linen is visible between the turn-ins, protection quire + 13 full quires, iv + 125 folios, top margin 17 mm, bottom margin 30 mm, fore edge margin 10 mm, gutter margin 7 mm, ff. 1r–122r two columns, 19 lines, Gə_əz, twentieth century. Single-slip *maḥdär*.

Quire descriptions: protection quire and quires 1–10 and 12 balanced; quires 11 and 13 adjusted balanced. Navigation system: marginal notation throughout.

Major Works:

Ff. 1r–122r: Antiphonary for the Fast of Lent, *Ṣomä Dəggʷa*, ጾሙ፡ ድጓ፡. EMML 1135; Bernard Velat, *Ṣom Deggua. Antiphonaire du carême. Quatre premières semaines*, PO 32.1–2 (1966) and 32.3–4 (1969); and *AṢZ* 1–101, and see now, Kay Kaufman Shelemay and Peter Jeffery, eds, *Ethiopian Christian Religious Chant: An Anthology* (Madison, WI: A-R Editions, Inc., 1993–1997); *Introduction*, Volume I (1993); *Performance*, Volume 2 (1994); and *History of Ethiopian Chant*, Volume 3 (1997). The text begins:
ናሁ ፡ ወጠንኩ ፡ ጽሒፈ ፡ ጾመ ፡ ድጓ ፡ በሥምረተ ፡ እግዚአብሔር ፡ አሜን ፡ በመሕትወ ፡ ድራሬ ፡ ጾም ፡ በጀ ፡ ዘወረደ ፡ እምላዕሉ ፡ አይሁድ ፡ ሰቀሉ ፡ ወሚመ ፡ ኢያእምሩ ፡ እግዚአ ፡ ኩሉ ፡ ዘያሐዩ ፡ በቃሉ ፡ ...

1. Ff. 1r–18v: First Week, *Maḥtəwä drarä ṣom*, መኅትወ፡ ድራሬ፡ ጾም፡. ዘወረደ፡ እምላዕሉ፡ አይሁድ፡ ሰቀሉ፡ ወሚመ፡ ኢያእምሩ፡ . . .

2. Ff. 18v–31r: Second Week, *Qəddəst*, ቅድስት፡. ዛቲ፡ ዕለት፡ ቅድስት፡ ይእቲ፡

3. Ff. 31r–45v: Third Week, *Məkʷrab*, ምኩራብ፡. በዕለተ፡ ሰንበት፡ ቦአ፡ ኢየሱስ፡ ምኩራብ፡ አይሁድ፡ . . .

4. Ff. 45v–58v: Fourth Week, *Mäzagʷu*, መጋጉዕ. ውእቱ፡ እግዚእ፡ ለሰንበት፡ ወአቡሃ፡ ለምሕረት፡

5. Ff. 58v–72v: Fifth Week, *Däbrä Zäyt*, ደብረ፡ ዘይት፡, Sunday through Friday.
   እንዘ፡ ይነብር፡ እግዚእነ፡ ውስተ፡ ደብረ፡ ዘይት፡ ወይቤሎሙ፡ ለአርዳኢሁ፡ ዑቁኬ፡
6. Ff. 72v–81r: Collection of Hymns for the Lent Season
   a. Ff. 72v–73r: Hymn for the apostle Mathias, *Matəyas ḥäwarəya*, ማትያስ፡ ሐዋርያ፡, to be sung on the eighth of Mäggabit.
   b. Ff. 73r–74v: Hymn for the feast of the Cross, zä-Mäsqäl, ዘመስቀል፡, to be sung on the tenth of Mäggabit.
   c. Ff. 74v–75r: Hymn for the feast of the forty martyrs, *Arba Ḫära sämay*, ፵፡ ሐራ፡ ሰማይ፡, to be sung on the 13th of Mäggabit.
   d. Ff. 75rv: Hymn for Tewoqərṭos, *zä-Tewoqərṭos*, ዘቴዎቅርጦስ፡, to be sung on the sixteenth of Mäggabit.
   e. Ff. 75v–78r: Hymn for the Feast of Saint Mary, *Bä_alä Ǝgzəʾətənä Maryam*, በዓለ፡ እግዝእትነ፡ ማርያም፡, to be sung on the 21st of Mäggabit.
   f. Ff. 78r–81r: Hymn for the Feast of the Conception of Our Lord, *Təsbə_ət lä-Ǝgziʾəna*, ትስብዕቱ፡ ለእግዚእነ፡, to be sung on the twenty-ninth of Mäggabit.
7. Ff. 81rv: Fifth Week, *Däbrä Zäyt*, ዕዝል፡ ደብረ፡ ዘይት፡ ዘቀዳሚት፡, Saturday.
8. Ff. 81v–92v: Sixth Week, *Gäbr ḫer*, ገብር፡ ኄር፡.
   ገብር፡ ኄር፡ ወገብር፡ ምእመን፡ ገብር፡ ዘአስመር፡ ለአግዚሁ፡
9. Ff. 92v–104v: Seventh Week, *Niqodimos*, ኒቆዲሞስ፡.
   ወሀሎ፡ ፩፡ ብእሲ፡ እምፈሪሳውያን፡ ዘስሙ፡ ኒቆዲሞስ፡ ዘሐረ፡ ኀቤሁ፡
10. Ff. 104v–118v: Eighth Week—Passion Week, *Sämunä Ḫəmamat*, ሰሙነ፡ ሕማማት፡.
    a. Ff. 104v–110v: Palm Sunday, *Hośa_na*.
       በዕምርት፡ ዕለት፡ በዓልነ፡ ንፍሑ፡ ቀርነ፡ በጽዮን፡ ወስብኩ፡ . . .
    b. Ff. 110v–116v: Instructions and hymns for Passion Week.
    c. Ff. 116v–118v: Holy Sunday [*sic*, Saturday].
11. Ff. 118v–122r: Index of Halleluiatic chants, *Anqäṣä halleta*, እንቀጸ፡ ሃሌታ፡. Supplied with musical notation.

Notes:
1. Ff. i r(ecto)–iv v(erso) and 122v–125v: blank.
2. Decorative designs: f. 10r (line of black dots); lines of alternating red and black dots are used as section dividers throughout (e.g., ff. 11v, 12r, 13rv); ff. 22v, 36rv, 67r, 69r (line of red dots); f. 118v (multiple full stops).

3. Numbered quires: quires 2–10.
4. Scribal intervention: words of text are written interlinearly (ff. 6r, 16r, 17r, 20v, 46v, etc.); and in the upper margin with a symbol (⊥) marking the location where the text is to be inserted (ff. 2v, col. 1, line 4; 8v, col. 1, line 2; 11r, col. 1, line 10; 11v, col. 1, line 11; 22v, col. 2, line 15; 26r, col. 1, line 11, etc.), and in another case where the symbol (+) is used (ff. 4v, col. 1, line 6; 6v, col. 1, line 1; 14v, col. 1, line 16; 55v, col. 2, line 4; 58r, col. 1, line 13; 88v, col. 1, line 12, etc.), and in another case where the symbol (+) is corresponding to text in the bottom margin (ff. 21r, col. 2, line 2; 113r, col. 2, line 9) and in another case where the symbol (⊤) is used (f. 100r, col. 1, line 20); erasure markings are visible (ff. 10r, 14v, 17v, 30v, 40r, etc.).

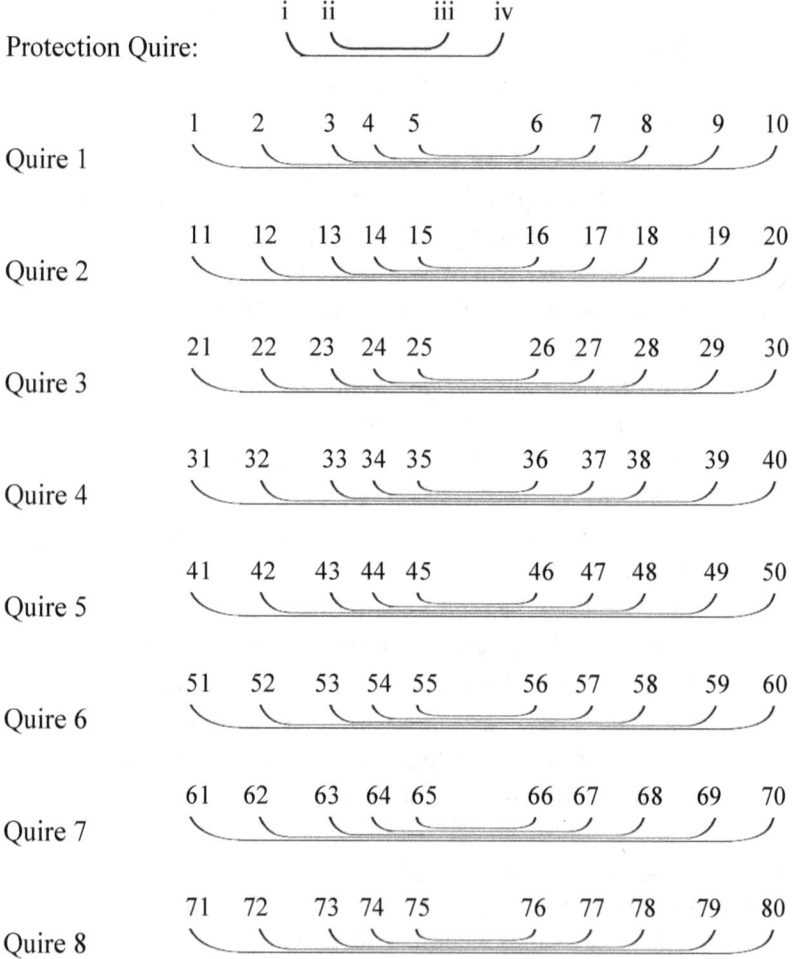

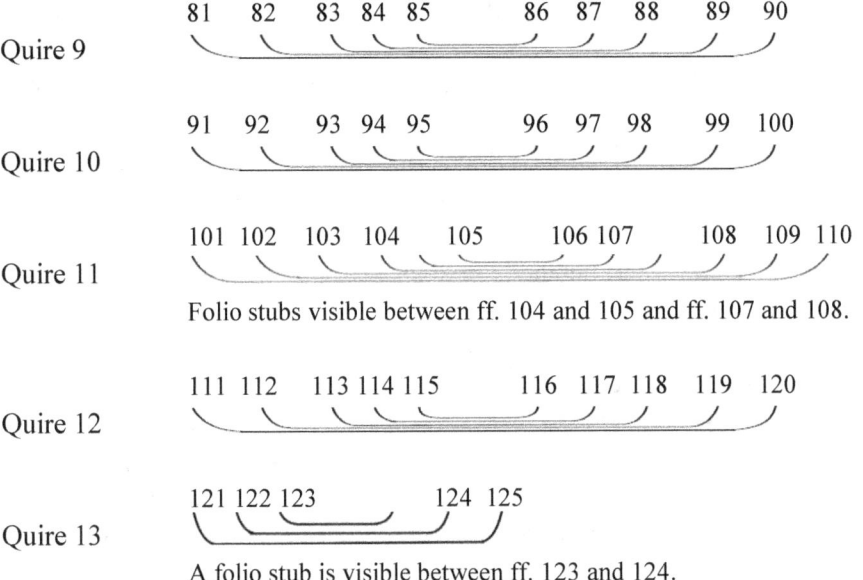

Folio stubs visible between ff. 104 and 105 and ff. 107 and 108.

A folio stub is visible between ff. 123 and 124.

MYS 38 – EMIP 638
Petition and Supplication, ስእለት፡ ወአስተብቁዖት፡, Harp of Praise, አርጋኖነ፡ ውዳሴ፡

Parchment, 253 x 220 x 65 mm, four Coptic chain stitches attached with bridle attachments to rough-hewn boards of the traditional wood, remnants of headband and tailband are visible, protection quire + 21 full quires, i + 165 folios, top margin 35 mm, bottom margin 50 mm, fore edge margin 35 mm, gutter margin 17 mm, ff. 1r–162r two columns, 25 lines, Gəʿəz, late-eighteenth century.

Quire descriptions: quires 1–19 balanced; quires 20 and 21 adjusted balanced; protection quire unbalanced.

Major Works:
1. Ff. 1r–87r: Petition and Supplication, *Səʾälät wä-_asətäbəq^{w}u_ot*, ስእለት፡ ወአስተብቁዖት፡, arranged for the days of the Week. Cf. EMIP 178.
    በስመ ፡ አብ ፡ ወወልድ ፡ . . . ንቤጥን ፡ በረድኤተ ፡ እግዚአብሔር ፡ ጽሒፈ ፡ ስእለት ፡ ወአስተብቁዖት ፡ እንተ ፡ ነበበ ፡ ዛቲ ፡ ቅዱስ ፡ ባስልዮስ ፡ ኤጲስ ፡ ቆጶስ ፡ ዘቂሳርያ ፡ በእንተ ፡ ሱብቄ ፡ ዕለታት ፡ ዘመፍትው ፡ ይጸለይ ፡ ባቲ ፡ ለለኵሉ ፡ ዕለት ፡ . . .
    a. Ff. 1r–11r: Monday, Prayer of Petition of Basil of Caesarea.
    b. Ff. 11r–26v: Tuesday, Prayer of Petition of Ephrem the Syrian.

    c. Ff. 27r–39v: Wednesday, Second Prayer of Petition of Ephrem the Syrian.
    d. Ff. 39v–55v: Thursday, Prayer of Petition collected from Saint John.
    e. Ff. 56r–67v: Friday, Prayer of Petition of *Abba* Sinoda
    f. Ff. 67v–77r: Saturday, Prayer of Petition collected from Coptic Songs by *Abba* Athanasius, archbishop of Alexandria.
    g. Ff. 77r–87r: Sunday, Prayer of Petition of Cyril, archbishop of Alexandria.
2. Ff. 87v–162r: Harp of Praise, *Arganonä Wəddase*, አርጋኖነ፡ ውዳሴ፡, arranged for the days of the week. Pontus Leander, `*Arganona Ueddase nach Handschriften in Uppsala, Berlin, Tübingen und Frankfurt a. M.*, Göteborgs Högskolas Årsskrift 28.3 (Leipzig, 1922). Monday (f. 87v), Tueday (f. 100r), Wednesday (f. 112r), Thursday (f. 125r), Friday (f. 138r), Saturday (149r), Sunday (f. 157r).

በስመ ፡ እግዚአብሔር ፡ ሥሉስ ፡ ዘእንበለ ፡ ፍልጠት ፡ ወአሐዱ ፡ በጽምረት ፡ ጎቡረ ፡ ህላዌ ፡ ዕሩይ ፡ መለኮት ፡ ዘአሐተ ፡ ይሰገድ ፡ እምነ ፡ ሰብእ ፡ ወመላእክት ፡ ንጽሕፍ ፡ እንከ ፡ ዘንተ ፡ መጽሐፈ ፡ ዘይሰመይ ፡ አርጋኖነ ፡ ውዳሴ ፡ ወመስንቆ ፡ መዝሙር ፡ ወዕንዚራ ፡ ስብሐት ፡ ዘአስተብዕየ ፡ ድንግልናየ ፡ ወነጊረ ፡ ዕበያ ፡ ወአክብር ፡ ስማ ፡ ወሰብሐ ፡ ቅድስናሃ ፡ ወግናይ ፡ ለንግሣ ፡ ለቅድስት ፡ ወንጽሕት ፡ ወቡርክት ፡ ማርያም ፡ ዘበዕራይሥጢ ፡ ማርያምድንግል ፡ ወላዲተ ፡ አምላክ ፡ . . .

Miniatures:
    1. F. 162v: crude drawing of a figure.

Varia:
    1. F. i v(erso): Asmat Prayer against Hail, column one is partly destroyed. Cf. *Şälotä bäräd*, ጸሎተ፡ በረድ፡; EMIP 165.
    2. Ff. 163r, column one: Excerpt from a Treatise on the four elements: earth, wind, fire, and water.
    3. Ff. 163r, column two-165v: Collection of Poems to Susənyos
    4. Excerpt from Greetings for the Saints, written on folios from another book, bound into the back of this book. The sheets are written in an eighteenth century hand.

Notes:
    1. Ff. i r(ecto): blank
    2. F. 1r and *passim*: owner, Arsanəyos.
    3. F. 162v: Curse on anyone who steals the book.

4. Decorative designs: multiple full stops are used as section dividers throughout (e.g., ff. 5v, 9r, 11r); ff. 11r, 26v, 67v, 87r, 157r, 162r (line of alternating red and black dots); ff. 39v, 55v, 87r, 100r, 149r (line of full stops between lines of alternating red and black dots).
5. The word Mary is rubricated.
6. Numbered quires: quires 2–11 and 14–19 (with the numbers 3–8).
7. Scribal intervention: words of text are written interlinearly (ff. 58r, 71v, 75r, 93r, 110v, etc.); and lines of text are written interlinearly (ff. 93v, 101v, 108v, 109rv, etc.); and in the upper margin with a symbol (+) marking the location where the text is to be inserted (f. 28r, col. 2, line 7); text has been removed (e.g., f. 25r).

Quire Map

Protection Quire: i

F. i is a loose folio that has been stitched into the front of the quire. Two folio stubs are visible between ff. i and 1.

Quire 1: 1 2 3 4 5 6 7 8

Quire 2: 9 10 11 12 13 14 15 16

Quire 3: 17 18 19 20 21 22 23 24

Quire 4: 25 26 27 28 29 30 31 32

Quire 5: 33 34 35 36 37 38 39 40

Quire 6: 41 42 43 44 45 46 47 48

Quire 7: 49 50 51 52 53 54 55 56

Quire 8: 57 58 59 60 | 61 62 63 64

Quire 9: 65 66 67 68 | 69 70 71 72

Quire 10: 73 74 75 76 | 77 78 79 80

Quire 11: 81 82 83 84 | 85 86 87 88

Quire 12: 89 90 91 92 | 93 94 95 96

Quire 13: 97 98 99 100 | 101 102 103 104

Quire 14: 105 106 107 108 | 109 110 111 112

Quire 15: 113 114 115 116 | 117 118 119 120

Quire 16: 121 122 123 124 | 125 126 127 128

Quire 17: 129 130 131 132 | 133 134 135 136

Quire 18: 137 138 139 140 | 141 142 143 144

Quire 19: 145 146 147 148 | 149 150 151 152

Quire 20: 153 154 155 156 | 157 158 | 159 160

Folio stubs visible between ff. 155 and 156 and ff. 158 and 159.

Quire 21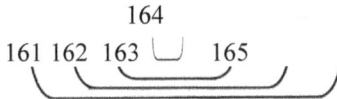

A loose sheet has been placed between ff. 163 and 165. A folio stub is visible between ff. 164 and 165. Two folio stubs follow f. 165.

MYS 39 – EMIP 639
Six Images of Raguel, መልክአ፡ ራጉኤል፡, Asmat Prayers of the Seven Archangels, ድርሳን፡ ዘሰባቱ፡ ሊቃነ፡ መላእክት፡, Image and of John, Son of Thunder, መልክአ፡ ዮሐንስ፡ ወልደ፡ ነጎድጓድ፡ combined with Asmat Prayer, and Image of the Guardian Angel, መልክአ፡ ዐቃቤ፡ መልአክ፡

Parchment, 111 x 83 x 36 mm, four Coptic chain stitches attached with bridle attachments apparently to rough-hewn boards of the traditional wood, covered with tooled leather, headband and tailband, protection quire + 8 full quires, iv + 60 folios, top margin 11 mm, bottom margin 22 mm, fore edge margin 11 mm, gutter margin 6 mm, ff. 1r–57r one column, 15 lines, Gəʽəz, twentieth century.

Quire descriptions: protection quire and quires 1–8 balanced.

Major Works:
1. Ff. 1r–30v: Six Images of Saint Raguel, *Mälk_a Raguʽel*, መልክአ፡ ራጉኤል፡.
    a. Ff. 1r–5v: First Image of Raguel, for Monday.
    ሰላም ፡ ለአብ ፡ ገባሬ ፡ ኩሉ ፡ ፍጥረት ፡
    ለወልድ ፡ ሰላም ፡ ለገሴ ፡ ትስብእት ፡
    ወለመንፈስ ፡ ቅዱስ ሰላም ፡ ወሀቤ ፡ ጿቱ ፡ ሀብታት ፡
    እንዘ ፡ Ρቱ ፡ አካላት ፡ ወኄ ፡ መለኮት ፡
    እምሕፅ ፡ ዘይሠርር ፡ በመዓልት ፡ ወእምግብር ፡ ዘየሐውር ፡ በጽልመት ፡
    በእደ ፡ ቅዱስ ፡ ራጉኤል ፡ መልአክ ፡ ምሕረት ፡
    ዕቀቡኒ ፡ በኩሉ ፡ ጊዜ ፡ ,በኩሉ ፡ ሰዓት ፡ . . .

    በስመ ፡ እግዚአብሔር ፡ ሥሉስ ፡ በገብ ፡ ኩሉ ፡ ውዱስ ፡
    ናሁ ፡ ወጠንኩ ፡ ድርሳነ ፡ ራጉኤል ፡ ርኡስ ፡
    ተወክፍ ፡ ወትረ ፡ ጸሎትየ ፡ ከመ ፡ ጺና ፡ ዕጣን ፡ ቅዱስ ፡
    ዘተወክፍከ ፡ ለዳዊት ፡ ንጉሥ ፡
    b. Ff. 7r–11v: Second Image of Raguel, for Tuesday.
    እዌጥን ፡ አንሰ ፡ ዝክረ ፡ መልክዓቲክ ፡ በአስተሐምሞ ፡
    አኮ ፡ ንስቲተ ፡ ለወድስ ፡ ዳዕሙ ፡ ለፈጻሞ ፡
    ራጉኤል ፡ መልአክ ፡ ቱባ ፡ ቅዳሴ ፡ ዓባሞ ፡

አስተበቍዓከ ፡ ተሀበኒ ፡ መና ፡ ሰማያት ፡ ለጥዕም ፡
ከመ ፡ ዘይስእል ፡ ወልድ ፡ አባሁ ፡ ወእም ፡

- c. Ff. 12r–21v: Third Image of Raguel and Asmat Prayer (ff. 21v), for Wednesday. Chaîne, *Répertoire* 365; *MG59* 357ff.

  እኤውዕ ፡ ስመከ ፡ ወእኢምኃከ ፡ በተድላ ፡
  ራጉኤል ፡ መልአከ ፡ ለዓለም ፡ መስተበቅላ ፡
  እለ ፡ ያንኩረኮሩ ፡ ዘልፈ ፡ ለጠፈረ ፡ ሰማይ ፡ በማዕከላ ፡
  ድጓሪ ፡ ኃላፈ ፡ መዓልት ፡ ለጸልመተ ፡ ሌሊት ፡ በክፍላ ፡
  በሥልጣነ ፡ ቃልከ ፡ ይትኤዘዙ ፡ ከዋክብት ፡ ወዕብላ ፡

- d. Ff. 23r–26r: Fourth Image of Raguel, for Thursday.

  ሰላም ፡ ለዝክረ ፡ ስምከ ፡ ዝክረ ፡ ስመ ፡ አብ ፡ ጉብዓት ፡
  ወሞገሰ ፡ ጌራን ፡ ነገሥት ፡
  ራጉኤል ፡ መልአከ ፡ ወሀቤ ፡ ጔቱ ፡ ህብታት ፡
  ጸግወኒ ፡ ስመ ፡ ዘአስተብርከ ፡ ወስመ ፡ ኬንያ ፡ ኤላት ፡
  እስመ ፡ በጎቡዕ ፡ ስምከ ፡ ይትነሣእ ፡ ምውት፡

- e. Ff. 26v–29r: Fifth Image of Raguel, for Friday.

  ሰላም ፡ ለዝክረ ፡ ስምከ ፡ ወለሥዕርትከ ፡ ኤጤሜሶር ፡
  ምስለ ፡ ርእስከ ፡ ግልድምያሶር ፡
  መፍትሔ ፡ ህብታት ፡ ራጉኤል ፡ ፍልድምያሶር ፡
  በእንተ ፡ ጎቡዕ ፡ ስመ ፡ ለእግዚአብሔር ፡
  ተሀበኒ ፡ ነዓ ፡ ህብታተ ፡ ሰማይ ፡ ወምድር ፡

- f. Ff. 29v–30v: Sixth Image of Raguel, for Saturday.

  ሰላም ፡ ለዝክረ ፡ ስምከ ፡ እምሀሊብ ፡ ዕጉልት ፡ ጥዑም ፡
  ዓዲ ፡ እምወይን ፡ ዘውስተ ፡ ኤደም ፡
  ራጉኤል ፡ ክንፍከ ፡ ዘተሴረየ ፡ በደም ፡
  ሢመከ ፡ ወአልዓልከ ፡ እግእአ ፡ መላእከት ፡ አፍሐም ፡
  መድኃኒተ ፡ ትኩን ፡ ለኩሉ ፡ ዓለም፡

2. Ff. 31r–38r: Asmat Prayers of the Seven Archangels, *Dərsanä Zäsäbatu Liqənä Mäla'kət*, ድርሳን፡ ዘሰባቱ፡ ሊቃነ፡ መላእክት፡

   - a. Ff. 31rv: Asmat Prayer of the Archangel Michael.
   - b. Ff. 32rv: Asmat Prayer of the Archangel Gabriel.
   - c. Ff. 33rv: Asmat Prayer of the Archangel Rufael.
   - d. Ff. 34rv: Asmat Prayer of the Archangel Raguel.
   - e. Ff. 35rv: Asmat Prayer of the Archangel Saquel.
   - f. Ff. 36rv: Asmat Prayer of the Archangel Fanuel.
   - g. Ff. 37rv: Asmat Prayer of the Archangel Afnin.
   - h. F. 38r: Concluding Prayer.

3. F. 48r: Image of John, Son of Thunder, *Mälk_a Yoḥannəs Wäldä Näg^{w}ädəg^{w}ad*, መልክአ፡ ዮሐንስ፡ ወለደ፡ ነጉድጓድ፡.

a. F. 40r: Asmat Prayer on John 1:1–4 as protection against demons and evil people and sorcerers.
b. Ff. 40v–48r: Image of John, Son of Thunder, *Mälk_a Yoḥannəs Wäldä Näg*ʷ*ädəg*ʷ*ad*, መልክአ፡ ዮሐንስ፡ ወልደ፡ ነጉድጓድ፡, combined with the first line from six of the sections of Psalm 118 (each of which begins with a successive Hebrew letter): mem, gimal, zyin samech, vav, and taph and are combined with an *asmat* prayer as protection from an enemy and for gaining wealth.
በስመ ፡ አብ ፡ ወወልድ ፡ . . . ጸሎት ፡ በእንተ ፡ መግረሬ ፡ ፀር ፡ ወመፍትሔ ፡ ሀብት ፡ ዘነገር ፡ እግዚአብሔር ፡ ለዮሐንስ ፡ ወልደ ፡ ነጉድጓድ ፡ እንዘ ፡ ሀሎ ፡ በገነት ፡ ከመ ፡ ይዐቀብ ፡ ሥጋሃ ፡ ለእግዝእትነ ፡ ማርያም ፡ ወላዲተ ፡ አምላክ ፡ እንዘ ፡ ይብል ፡ ያርክ ፡ ያርክ ፡ ያርክ ፡ ከምላድ ፡ ከላዩድ ፡ ሀልክናድ ፡ ሲምኑድ ፡ በቃለ ፡ እሉ ፡ አስማት ፡ ሀበኒ ፡ ሀብተ ፡ ወዛመተ ፡ . . .

4. Ff. 48v–52r: Five Psalms from the Book of Psalms.
5. Ff. 53v–57r: Image of the Guardian Angel, *Mälk_a Aqabe Mälə'ak*, መልክአ፡ ዐቃቤ፡ መልአክ፡. Cf. Chaîne, *Répertoire* 219 and EMML 3706, whose incipits are slightly different.
በስመ ፡ አብ ፡ ወወልድ ፡ ወመንፈስ ፡ ቅዱስ ፡ ፩ ፡ አምላክ ፡ ሠራዪ ፡ ሥነ ፡ ሥርጡ ፡ ሰማይ ፡ ወምድር ፡ ወስእለት ፡ ኮሉ ፡ ሰማዪ ፡ መልአክ ፡ ዑቃቤ ፡ ዘትሬኢ ፡ ወዘኢ.ታስተርኢ ፡ ይትመሳህ ፡ ቅድመ ፡ ገጽየ ፡ ሰይፈ ፡ እዴክ ፡ በላዪ ፡ ዘንተ ፡ ርእዮ ፡ ለይጎፈር ፡ ጸላዪ ፡

Miniatures:
1. F. iv v(erso): The Holy Trinity surrounded by the Four Living Creatures.
2. F. 3r: David and Solomon, based on the text of the image.
3. F. 5r: The four heads of Qerubim, based on the text of the image.
4. F. 5v: Unknown (a winged creature standing between two plants with red flowers).
5. F. 6r: Four serpents. Prayer ―Save me and protect me from the evil ones whose mouth is like the serpent. . . ."
6. F. 6v: Box with X-shape creating four triangular spaces, each with a asmat prayer, e.g., ―Put fear inside the heart of my enemies. . . ― (top).
7. F. 8v: Lamb holding Cross. Caption (reading from inside to outside): ―Behold, the Lamb of God who takes away the sin of the world, Alpha and O[mega], Beta, Iota, Ahəya Šärahya, Jesus Christ, son of

God, Victor and Son of Mary, the Virgin, protect me suffering and perdition, your servant, Ḥaylä Maryam."
8. F. 11r: Box with X-shape creating four triangular spaces, each with a asmat prayer, e.g., "Look upon my prayer for your servant" (top); "Rebuke my enemies and adversaries" (bottom).
9. F. 11v: Two Serpents. Asmat prayer written in a circular flow in the center (from the inside): "Give me deliverance from spear and sword. . . ."
10. F. 22r: Four Serpents: Asmat prayer written in a circular flow in the center (from the inside): "Save me and protect me from the hand of the children of aliens who prepare their mouths as the mouths of serpents. They stretch their bow to do harm."
11. F. 22v: Four Angels in the corners around a box with an X shape. Four texts are at top, bottom, right and left, e.g., bottom: "Rebuke my enemies and adversaries. With this asmat, protect me, your servant Ḥaylä Maryam."
12. F. 25r: Gäbrä Mänfäs Qəddus.
13. F. 26r: The angel Raguel, here called "steward of lights," with wings outstretched, holding sun and moon.
14. F. 27r: The Striking of the Head of Jesus.
15. F. 31r, upper margin: The Angel Michael.
16. F. 32r: The angel Gabriel, with wings outstretched.
17. F. 33r: The angel Rufael, with wings outstretched.
18. F. 34r: The angel Raguel, with wings outstretched.
19. F. 35r: The angel Saquel, with wings outstretched.
20. F. 36r: The angel Fanuel, with wings outstretched.
21. F. 37r: The angel Afnin, with wings outstretched.
22. F. 38v–39r: Madonna and Child. Caption: "Mary, daughter of Hanna and Joakim, rainbow of Patriarch Shem, intercede for your beloved son, Savior of the World. May He visit me from heaven. Your servant and sinner, Ḥaylä Maryam. Amen."
23. F. 39v: John, Son of Thunder.
24. F. 44r: The Crucifixion. Caption (l. to r.): "He said to his mother, ˏbehold, your son.'" "He said to his disciple, ˏbehold, your mother.'"
25. F. 46r: Saint Yarǝd and Saint John. Caption: "How Saint Yarǝd, the Singer, praised Saint John, the Evangelist."

Notes:
1. Ff. i r(ecto)–iv r(ecto), 44v, 46v and 57v–60v: blank.
2. Ff. 1r and *passim*: owner, Ḥaylä Maryam.

3. The arrangement of the codex for reading extends beyond the reading of the Images of Raguel; Sunday (f. 40r), daily (f. 52v).
4. Decorative designs: ff. 1r, 7r, 12r, 23r, 26v, 29v, 40r, 52v (ornate, colorful ḥarägs); ff. 30v, 47v, 50r, 57r (multiple full stops);
5. Columetric layout of text: f. 47v.
6. The words Raguel and Mary are rubricated.
7. Several of the aspects of codicology (leather work, materials, two-toned head band and tail band, and especially the ḥarägs, suggest that this manuscript was produced in or around the Government Scriptorium. At the same time, the use of particle board for the cover boards is interesting.
8. Scribal intervention: words of text are written interlinearly (ff. 2v, 4r, 9v, 10v, 12v, etc.).

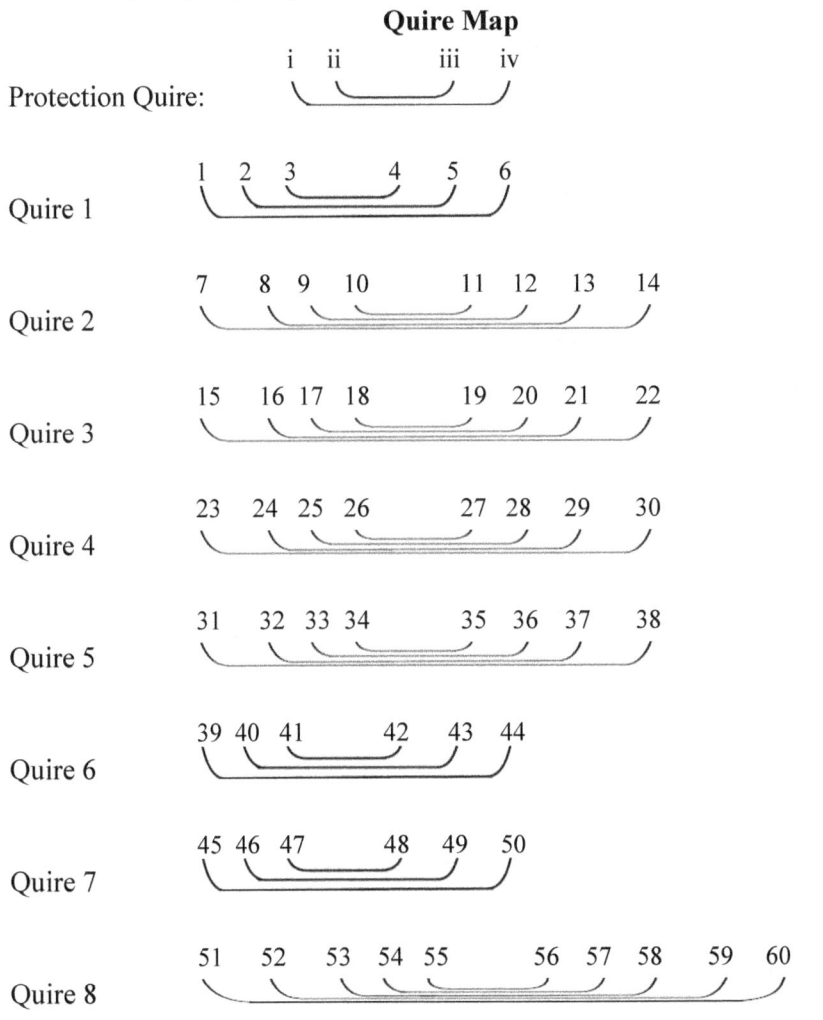

MYS 40 – EMIP 640
Zəmmare Chants, ዝማሬ፤ *Mäwaś'ət* Chants, መዋሥዕት፤

Parchment, 202 x 175 x 53 mm, four Coptic chain stitches attached with bridle attachments to rough-hewn boards of the traditional wood, protection quire + 10 full quires, iv + 95 folios, top margin 10–20 mm, bottom margin 30–40 mm, fore edge margin 11–15 mm, gutter margin 12 mm, ff. 1r–93r three columns, 24–25 lines, Gə̄əz, 1961 EC (= 1967/8, f. 1r).

Quire descriptions: quires 1–10 balanced; protection quire adjusted balanced. Navigation system: marginal notation throughout, some of which may be overlooked text.

Major Works:
1. Ff. 1r–68v: Zəmmare Chants for the entire year, *Zəmmare*, ዝማሬ፤. Cf. *AṢZ* 401–527. F. 68rv includes an index of the chants.
   በስመ ፡ አብ ፡ ወወልድ ፡ . . . ንቴጥን ፡ በረድኤት ፡ እግዚአብሔር ፡ መጽሐፈ ፡ ዝማሬ ፡ አምዮሐንስ ፡ እስከ ፡ ዮሐንስ ፡ ዘይትበሀል ፡ . . . እስመ ፡ ለዓለም ፡ ምሕረቱ ፡ ወተፈነወ ፡ ዮሐንስ ፡ ከመ ፡ ይስብክ ፡ ምጽአት ፡ ለክቡር ፡ መዝሙር ፡ ወከመ ፡ ይስብክ ፡ ጥምቀተ ፡ ለንስሐ ፡ ወለሥርየተ ፡ ኃጢአት ፡ . . .
2. Ff. 69r–93r: *Mäwaś_ət* chants, መዋሥዕት፤, *AṢZ* 529–604.
   መዋሥዕት ፡ አምዮሐንስ ፡ እስከ ፡ ዮሐንስ ፡ እግዚኦ ፡ መኑ ፡ የሐድር ፡ ውስተ ፡ ጽላሎትክ ፡ ዐቢየ ፡ ነቢየ ፡ ዮሐንስሃ ፡ አስአልነ ፡ ያስተምሕር ፡ በእንቲአነ ፡ ሣህልክ ፡ ይኩን ፡ ላዕሌነ ፡ ዘይገብር ፡ ከመዝ ፡ ኢትሐወክ ፡ ለዓለም ፡ . . .

Varia:
1. Ff. ii v(erso)-iii r(ecto): Excerpt from Antiphonary for the Fast of Lent.

Notes:
1. The spine strap was added after the binding of the book was completed. Slots were cut in the parchment in order to be able to slide the strap around the binding.
2. F. i rv, iii v(erso)-iv v(erso) and 94r–95v: blank.
3. F. ii r(ecto): pen trials.
4. F. 1r: The top three lines of text (in red) are written across the three columns.
5. F. 1r: mentions King Ḫaylä Śəllase and bishop *Abba* Basələyos, and the date, 1961 EC = 1967–68.
6. F. 93v: Graduation Certification: Gənbot 17, 1962 EC, given from Mägabe G^{w}angul Mäkonän (the authority) of Zur Aba Ṣərḥa Arəyam

to *Märigeta* Səbḥat Gäbrä Maryam. His two seals in red ink are in the lower margin. Zur Aba Ṣərḥa Arəyam is said to be the most esteemed place to study *Zəmmare* and *Mäwaśə̣t* in Ethiopia.

ግንቦት ፡ ፲፯ ፡ ቀን ፡ ፺፪ ፡ ዓመተ ፡ ምሕረት ፡ ስለዝማሬ ፡ ምስክርነት ፡ ዘተጎረየ ፡ በአምር ፡ ለምሕር ፡ እምነ ፡ ጽርሐ ፡ አርያም ፡ መካነ ፡ ብሔሩ ፡ ለአቡነ ፡ አረጋዊ ፡ ዘነበረ ፡ ባቲ ፡ አቡነ ፡ ያሬድ ፡ እንዘ ፡ ይሜሕር ፡ ...

7. Decorative designs: lines of alternating red and black dots used as section dividers throughout (e.g., ff. 6v, 7rv, 8rv); f. 58r (multiple full stops).
8. Spliced folios: 94.
9. Scribal intervention: words of text are written interlinearly (ff. 1rv, 2rv, 3r, 6r, etc.); and lines of text are written interlinearly (ff. 30v, 47v, 48v); erasure markings are visible (ff. 2v, 27v, 34r, 75v, etc.).

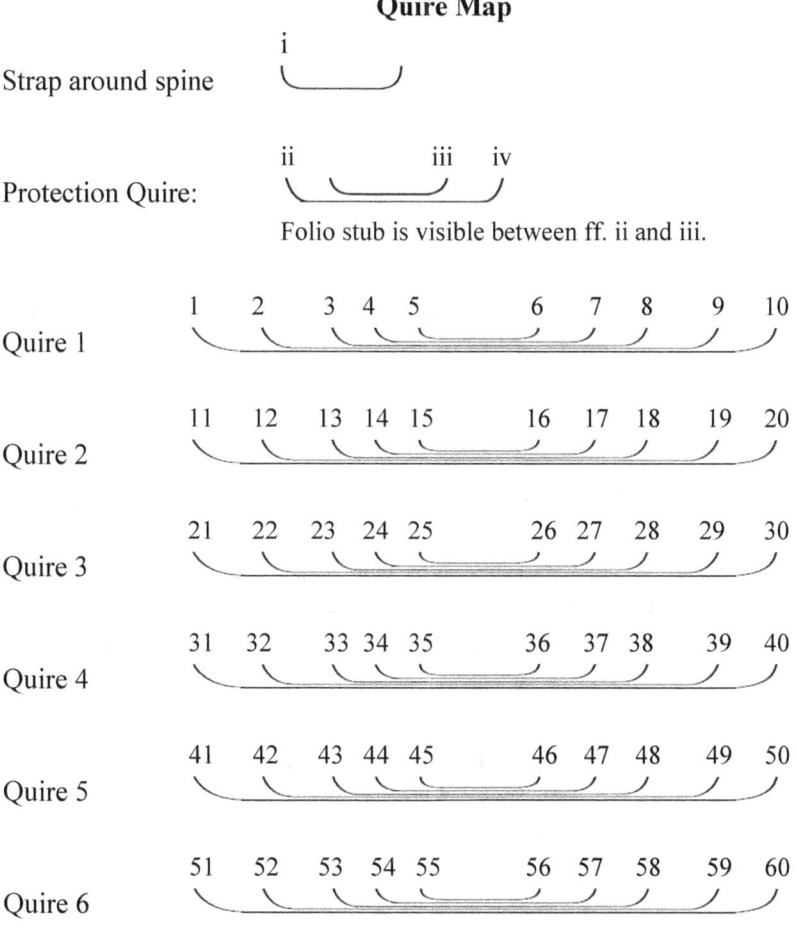

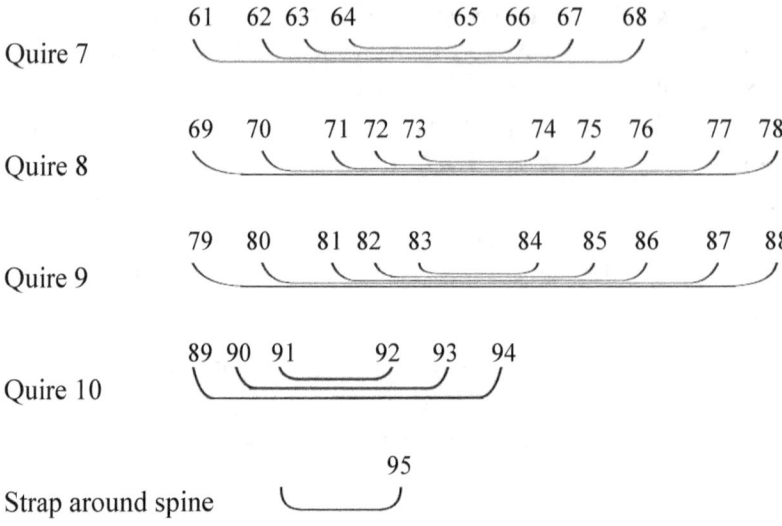

MYS 41 – EMIP 641
Qerəlos, ቄርሎስ፥, Biography of Qerəlos

Parchment, 208 x 172 x 69 mm, four Coptic chain stitches attached with bridle attachments to rough-hewn boards of the traditional wood, protection quire + 15 full quires, iv + 149 folios, top margin 20 mm, bottom margin 41 mm, fore edge margin 21 mm, gutter margin 17 mm, ff. 1r–148v two columns, 24 lines, Gə_əz, early-twentieth century.

Quire descriptions: protection quire and quires 1–14 balanced; quire 15 adjusted balanced.

Major Works:

Ff. 1r–145r: Qerəlos, Theological and Christological Works of Cyril of Alexandria and other church fathers, ቄርሎስ፥. Cf. EMML 4448.

1. Ff. 1r–24r: On the Orthodox Faith (*De recta fide*), *Bä'ntä Haymanot Rət_ət*, በእንተ፥ ርትዕት፥ ሃይማኖት፥, addressed to Emperor Theodosius. Bernd Manuel Weischer, *Qerellos I*, Afrikanische Forschungen 7 (Hamburg: Augustin, 1973).

ነገር ፥ ዘጻሕፈ ፥ ቅዱስ ፥ ቄርሎስ ፥ ሊቀ ፥ ጳጳሳት ፥ ዘእለ ፥ እስክንድርያ ፥ ለቴዎደስዮስ ፥ ንጉሥ ፥ በእንተ ፥ ርትዕት ፥ ሃይማኖት ፥ ዘበእንተ ፥ እግዚእነ ፥ ኢየሱስ ፥ ክርስቶስ ፥ ዘመንገለ ፥ ሱብእ ፥ ክቡር ፥ ወልዑል ፥ ወኢይትአየይ ፥ ምስለ ፥ ካልዕ ፥ በልዕልናሁ ፥ አንትሙ ፥ ኦ ፥ ፍቁራን ፥ ክርስቶስ ፥ ንጉሥ ፥ ወዛመትክሙኒ ፥ ድልው ፥ ወስኑይ ፥ እምነበ ፥ እግዚአብሔር ፥ . . .

2. Ff. 24r–72r: The Beauty of the News, *Sena Zena*, ሰነ፡ ዜና፡, continuation of the *Haymanot Rət_ət*, by Cyril, addressed to Arcadia and Marina.
ሰነ ፡ ዜና ፡ ዘለዓለም ፡ ወምክሁ ፡ ዘቅዱሳት ፡ አብያተ ፡ ክርስቲያናት ፡ ዘመድኅን ፡ ኩልነ ፡ ኢየሱስ ፡ ክርስቶስ ፡ ለሰምዮ ፡ ኩሉ ፡ ሰብእ ፡ በአማን ፡ ኪያክን ፡ ቅዱሳት ፡ ወንጹሐት ፡ መራዕዊሁ ፡ አርቃድያ ፡ ወመሪና ፡ ክልኤ ፡ አሕት ፡ ክቡራት ፡ ወመፍቀርያተ ፡ እግዚአብሔር ፡ ዘበላዕሌክን ፡ ያንጸበርቅ ፡ ብዑድ ፡ ሰነ ፡ ላህይ ፡ ዘአዕይንተ ፡ ልብ፡. . .

3. Ff. 73r–108v: That Christ is One, *Kama aḥadu Krestos*, ከመ አሕዱ ክርስቶስ, by Cyril of Alexandria. Bernd Manuel Weischer, *Qerellos III: Der Dialog —Dass Christus einer ist" des Kyrillos von Alexandrien*, AF 2 (Wiesbaden, Steiner, 1977).
ግጻዌ ፡ ድርሳን ፡ ዘቅዱስ ፡ ቄርሎስ ፡ ሊቀ ፡ ጳጳሳት ፡ ዘእለ ፡ እስክንድርያ ፡ ከመ፬ ፡ ክርስቶስ ፨ ቄርሎስ ፡ ይቤ ፡ ለትምሕርተ ፡ ቅዱሳት ፡ መጻሕፍት ፡ ግሙራ ፡ አልቦ ፡ ዘይጸግቦ ፡ ወኢመኑሂ ፡ ወፈድፋድስ ፡ እለ ፡ ይኄልዩ ፡ ጥበበ ፡ ወአእምሮ ፡ ማኅየዊ ፡ አጥረዩ ፡ ውስተ ፡ አልባቢሆሙ ፡ እስመ ፡ ጽሑፍ ፡ አኮ ፡ በጎብስት ፡ ባሕቲቱ ፡ ዘየሐዩ ፡ ሰብእ ፡ አላ ፡ በኩሉ ፡ ነገር ፡ ዘይወጽእ ፡ እምአፉሁ ፡ ለእግዚአብሔር ፡ እስመ ፡ ስሲተ ፡ ልብ ፡ ቃላቲሁ ፡ ለእግዚአብሔር ፡ ውእቱ ፡ ወጎብስት ፡ መንፈሳዊ ፡ ዘያንዕ ፡ ኃይለ ፡ ሰብእ ፡ በከመ ፡ ጽሑፍ ፡ ውስተ ፡ መዝሙር ፡ ጸላድዮስ ፡ ይቤ ፡ ሠናየ ፡ ትቤ ፡. . .

4. Ff. 109r–110v: Homily by Theodotus of Ancyra. Bernd Manuel Weischer, *Qerellos IV 1: Homilien und Briefe zum Konzil von Ephesos*, AF 4 (Wiesbaden: Steiner, 1979) 42–53.

5. Ff. 110v–111v: Homily by Cyril of Alexandria, Weischer, *ibid.*, 54–61.

6. Ff. 111v–112v: Homily by Severus of Synnada, Weischer, *ibid.*, 62–7.

7. Ff. 112v–114r: Homily by Acacius of Melitene, Weischer, *ibid.*, 68–81.

8. Ff. 114r–115r: Homily by Juvenalius of Jerusalem, Weischer, *ibid.*, 82–7.

9. Ff. 115r–116v: Homily by Cyril of Alexandria, Weicher, *ibid.*, 88–99.

10. Ff. 116v–117v: Homily by Rheginus of Constantinople, Weicher, *ibid.*, 100–7.

11. Ff. 117v–119r: Homily by Cyril of Alexandria, Weicher, *ibid.*, 108–17.

12. Ff. 119rv: Homily by Eusiebius of Heraclea, Weicher, *ibid.*, 117–21.

13. Ff. 119v–121r: Homily by Theodotus of Ancyra, Weicher, *ibid.*, 122–33.
14. Ff. 121rv: Homily by Firmus of Caesarea, Weicher, *ibid.*, 134–37.
15. F. 121v: Epistle of the Synod of Ephesus to John of Antioch, Weicher, *ibid.*, 138–41.
16. F. 122r: Homily by Cyril of Alexandria, Weicher, *ibid.*, 142–5.
17. Ff. 122r–123r: Epistle of John of Antioch to Cyril of Alexandria, Weicher, *ibid.*, 146–53.
18. Ff. 123r–125v: Epistle of Cyril of Alexandria to John of Antioch, Weicher, *ibid.*, 153–69.
19. Ff. 125v–128v: Homily by Epiphanius of Cyprus. Bernd Manuel Weischer, *Qerellos IV 2: Traktate des Epiphanius von Zypern und des Proklos von Kyzikos*, AF 6 (Wiesbaden: Steiner, 1979) 24–47.
20. Ff. 128v–129r: Homily by Epiphanius of Cyprus on the Trinity, Weicher, *ibid.*, 52–8.
21. Ff. 129r–132r: Homily by Proclus of Cyzicus, Weicher, *ibid.*, 64–87.
22. Ff. 132r–137r: Homily by Severianus of Gabala. Bernd Manuel Weischer, *Qerellos IV 3: Traktate des Severianos Von Gabala, Gregorios Thaumaturgus und Kyrillos von Alexandrien*, AF 7 (Wiesbaden: Steiner, 1980) 22–67.
23. Ff. 137rv: The Faith of Gregory Thaumaturgus, Weischer, *ibid.*, 70–7.
24. Ff. 137v–139v: The first homily of Cyril of Alexandria on Melchisedec, Weischer, *ibid.*, 82–97.
25. Ff. 139v–142v: The second homily of Cyril of Alexandria on Melchisedec, Weischer, *ibid.*, 98–117.
26. Ff. 142v–143r: Homily by a Sage on Melchisedec. Bernd Manuel Weischer, "Die äthiopischen Psalmen- und Qerlosfragmente in Evevan/Armenien," OC 53 (1969) 142–3.
27. F. 143r: On the 318 Orthodox Fathers, Weischer, *ibid.*, 143–4.
28. Ff. 143rv: On the Nativity and Life of Our Lord, Weischer, *ibid.*, 144–5.
29. Ff. 143v–145r: Confession of faith, Weischer, *ibid.*, 146.
30. Ff. 145r–148v: Biography of Qerəlos.
    በስመ ፡ አብ ፡ ወወልድ ፡ . . . ንዌጥን ፡ በረድኤተ ፡ እግዚአብሔር ፡ ጽሒፈ ፡ ዜናሁ ፡ ለአብ ፡ ቅዱስ ፡ ወክቡር ፡ ቄርሎስ ፡ ሊቀ ፡ ጳጳሳት ፡ ዘአለ ፡ እስክንድርያ ፡ ወውእቱ ፡ ጉልቆሙ ፡ ለአበው ፡ ሊቃነ ፡ ጳጳሳት ፡ ጀወዐ ፡ ዘተረክቡ ፡ እምጽሐፈ ፡ ስንክሳር ፡ ወእምጽሐፈ ፡ ዮሐንስ ፡ መደብር ፡ ወአቡሻክር ፡ ወእምጽሐፉ ፡ ሊጎርጊስ ፡ ወልደ ፡ አሚድ ፡

እንዘ ፡ እደምር ፡ ዜናሁ ፡ ለቅዱስ ፡ ቴዎፍሎስ ፡ ሊቃነ ፡ ጳጳሳት ፡ ዘአለ ፡
እስክንድርያ ፡ እነዐ ፡ እሙ ፡ ለቄርሎስ ፡ . . .

Varia:
1. F. iv r(ecto)-iv v(erso): Explanation of special words used in Qerəlos.

Notes:
1. F. i r(ecto): Note of attribution: ―Saint Cyril, Archbishop of Alexandria, wrote this treatise to Theodotius."
2. F. i v(erso), ii v(erso), iii v(erso), 72v and 149rv: blank.
3. F. ii r(ecto): Note of attribution: ―Saint Cyril, Archbishop of Alexandria, wrote this treatise to Theodotius" as a pen trial.
4. F. iii r(ecto): six random sentences from the text.
5. The manuscript is replete with marginal notes providing mnemonics for the *andemta* commentary to the work.
6. Decorative designs: multiple full stops are used as section dividers throughout (e.g., ff. 24r, 48r, 52v); f. 148r (line of alternating red and black dots).
7. The word Mary is rubricated.
8. Numbered quires: quires 1–15.
9. Scribal intervention: words of text are written interlinearly (ff. 1v, 2v, 3v, 4v, 8r, etc.); and lines of text are written interlinearly (ff. 13r, 43r); and in the upper margin with a symbol (⊥) marking the location where the text is to be inserted (ff. 1v, col. 2, line 1; 2r, col. 2, line 6; 6v, col. 2, line 13; 7r, col. 1, line 6; 12r, col. 2, line 10; 26v, col. 1, line 19, etc.), and in another case where the symbol (⊤) is used to correspond with text in the bottom margin (f. 37v, col. 2, line 22); erasure markings are visible (ff. 12v, 21v, 28v, 29r, etc.); text has been removed (e.g., ff. 6r, 29r).

Quire Map

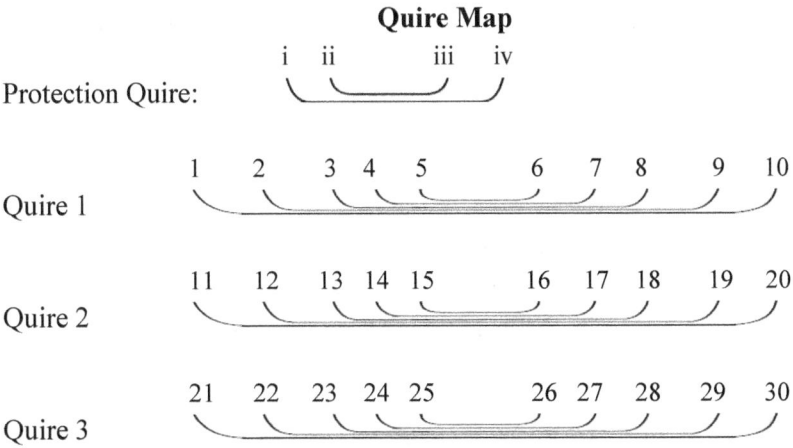

Quire 4: 31 32 33 34 35 36 37 38 39 40

Quire 5: 41 42 43 44 45 46 47 48 49 50

Quire 6: 51 52 53 54 55 56 57 58 59 60

Quire 7: 61 62 63 64 65 66 67 68 69 70

Quire 8: 71 72 73 74 75 76 77 78 79 80

Quire 9: 81 82 83 84 85 86 87 88 89 90

Quire 10: 91 92 93 94 95 96 97 98 99 100

Quire 11: 101 102 103 104 105 106 107 108 109 110

Quire 12: 111 112 113 114 115 116 117 118 119 120

Quire 13: 121 122 123 124 125 126 127 128 129 130

Quire 14: 131 132 133 134 135 136 137 138 139 140

Quire 15: 141 142 143 144 145 146 147 148 149

A folio stub is visible between ff. 143 and 144.

MYS 42 – EMIP 642
Gə‚əz Grammar, ሰዋሰው፡ ግእዝ፡

Parchment, 145 x 95 x 40 mm, four Coptic chain stitches attached with bridle attachments to rough-hewn boards of the traditional wood, protection sheet + 8 full quires, ii + 82 folios, top margin 7 mm, bottom margin 20 mm, fore edge margin 8 mm, gutter margin 5 mm, ff. 1r–75v one column, 24–25 lines, Gə_əz and Amharic, twentieth century. Double-slip *maḥdär*.

Quire descriptions: protection sheet and quires 1–8 balanced.

Major Works:
1. Ff. 1r–75v: Gə_əz Grammar, *Säwasəw*, ሰዋሰው፡ ግእዝ፡.
   በስመ ፡ አብ ፡ ወወልድ ፡ . . . ንቴጥን ፡ ጽሐፈ ፡ ሰዋሰው ፡ በረድኤተ ፡ እግዚአብሔር ፡ ዘሎቱ ፡ ስብሐት ፡ ለዓለም ፡ ዓለም ፡ አሜን ፡ ብሂል ፡ ማለት ፡ ማለት ፡ ነው ፡ ባሕል ፡ ማለት ፡ ማለት ፡ ነው ፡ ብሂሎቱ ፡ ባሕሉ ፡ ማለቱ ፡ ብሂሎታ ፡ ባሕላ ፡ ማለትዋ ፡ ብሂሎቶሙ ፡ ባሕሎሙ ፡ ማለታቸው ፡ ብሂሎቶን ፡ ባህሎን ፡ ማለታቸው ፡ ብሂሎትክ ፡ ባህልክ ፡ ማለትህ ፡ ብሂሎትኪ ፡ ባሕልኪ ፡ ማለትሽ ፡ . . .

Notes:
1. Ff. i r(ecto)-ii v(erso), 53v–54r and 76r–82v: blank.
2. The word Mary is rubricated.
3. Numbered quires: quires 2–8.
4. Scribal intervention: words of text are written interlinearly (f. 1v); erasure markings are visible (ff. 16r, 63r); text has been removed (e.g., ff. 2r, 65v).

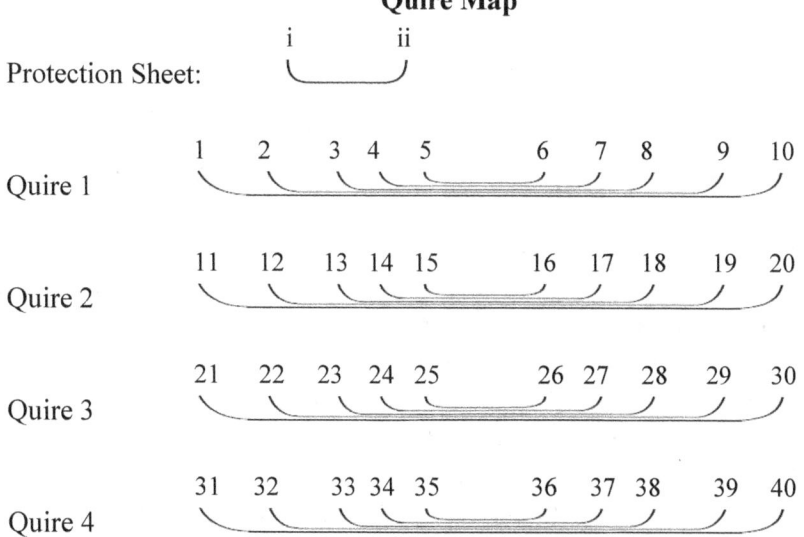

Quire Map

```
Quire 5    41  42  43 44 45      46 47 48  49 50

Quire 6    51 52  53  54 55 56    57 58 59  60 61 62

Quire 7    63  64   65 66 67    68 69 70  71 72

Quire 8    73 74  75 76 77    78 79 80  81 82
```

MYS 43 – EMIP 643
Acts of Gälawədewos (Claudius), ገድሉ፡ ኢያስጣቴዎሱ, Miracles of Gälawədewos (Claudius), ተአምረ፡ ገላውዴዎሱ, Image of Gälawədewos (Claudius), መልክአ፡ ገላውዴዎሱ

Parchment, 285 x 215 x 59 mm, four Coptic chain stitches attached with bridle attachments to rough-hewn boards of the traditional wood, protection quire + 11 full quires, iv + 86 folios, top margin 33 mm, bottom margin 57 mm, fore edge margin 32 mm, gutter margin 12 mm, ff. 1r–85r two columns, 23 lines, Gə_əz, twentieth century.

Quire descriptions: protection quire and quires 1, 3 and 9–10 balanced; quires 2, 4–8 and 11 adjusted balanced.

Major Works:
1. Ff. 1r–53v: Acts of Gälawədewos (Claudius), *Gädlä Gälawədewos*, ገድሉ፡ ገላውዴዎሱ, arranged for the months: Ḥamle (f. 12r), Näḥase (f. 20r), Mäskäräm (f. 29v), Ṭəqəmt (f. 35v), Ḫədar (f. 38r), Taḫśaś (f. 40r), Ṭərr (f. 42v), Yäkkatit (f. 44v), Mäggabit (f. 50v), and Miyazya (f. 52r).
   በስመ ፡ ወወልድ ፡ . . . ድርሳን ፡ ዘነበበ ፡ በእንተ ፡ ቅዱስ ፡ ክቡር ፡ ገላውዴዎስ ፡ ክቡር ፡ አባ በዚአሁ ፡ ያታ ፡ አባ ፡ ቴዎድርስ ፡ ሊቀ ፡ ጳጳሳት ፡ ዘእንጾኪያ ፡ በእንተ ፡ ክብሩ ፡ ለቅዱስ ፡ ጽኑዕ ፡ ወኃያል ፡ ድንግል ፡ ወንጹሕ ፡ መዋዒ ፡ ወመስተጋድል ፡ መልክዓ ፡ መላእክት ፡ …
2. Ff. 53v–79v: Nine Miracles of Gälawədewos (Claudius), *Tä'ammərä Gälawədewos*, ተአምረ፡ ገላውዴዎሱ.
3. Ff. 79v–85r: Image of Gälawədewos (Claudius), *Mälk_a Gälawədewos*, መልክአ፡ ገላውዴዎሱ. Chaîne, *Répertoire* 315.
   ናሁ ፡ ተወጥነ ፡ ለመልክዕከ ፡ ሰላመ ፡

እንዘ ፡ መንፈስ ፡ ቅዱስ ፡ ይረድእ ፡ ወያበጽሕ ፡ እስከ ፡ ተፍጻሜ ፡
ገላውዴዎስ ፡ ዓርከ ፡ መንግሥት ፡ ገላውዴዎስ ፡ ለለጌሠሙ ፡
ዘምስለ ፡ ንግሥከ ፡ ንግሥዉ ፡ ወምስለ ፡ ስምከ ፡ ሰሙ ፡
እስመ ፡ ተሳተፈ ፡ እምርሐይ ፡ ቀዳሙ ፡

Miniatures:
1. F. ii v(erso): Saint Gälawədewos, the Martyr as Equestrian Saint. Caption: ―Saint Gälawədewos, the Martyr" (top); ―Sobä Dayat" (bottom).

Notes:
1. Ff. i r(ecto)-ii r(ecto), iii r(ecto)-iv v(erso) and 85v–86v: blank.
2. Ff. 20r and *passim*: a space has been left to enter the owner's name.
3. Decorative designs: ff. 79rv, 84v (multiple full stops).
4. The word Gälawədewos is rubricated.
5. Numbered quires: quires 2–11.
6. Scribal intervention: words of text are written interlinearly (ff. 59r and 82v).

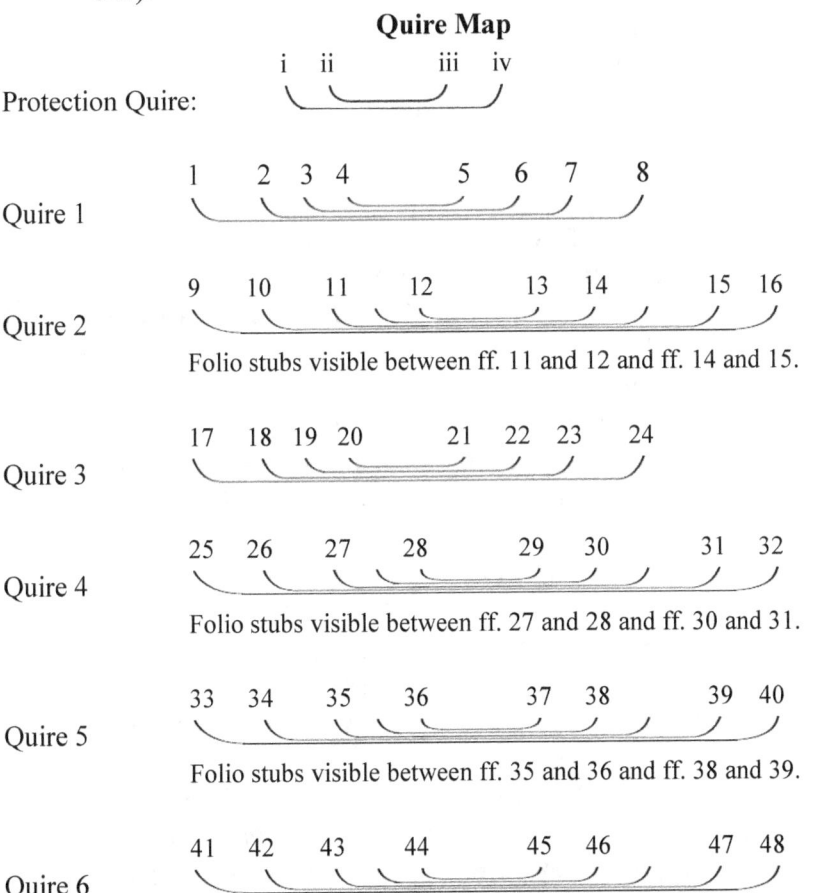

Folio stubs visible between ff. 43 and 44 and ff. 46 and 47.

Quire 7: 49 50 51 52 53 54 55 56

Folio stubs visible between ff. 51 and 52 and ff. 54 and 55.

Quire 8: 57 58 59 60 61 62 63 64

Folio stubs visible between ff. 59 and 60 and ff. 62 and 63.

Quire 9: 65 66 67 68 69 70 71 72

Quire 10: 73 74 75 76 77 78 79 80

Quire 11: 81 82 83 84 85 86

Folio stubs visible between ff. 82 and 83 and ff. 85 and 86.

MYS 44 – EMIP 644
A Theological Critique of Certain Practices of the Orthodox Church, in Amharic, ስለ፣ ኦርቶዶክስ፣ ቤተ፣ ክርስቲያን፣ አንዳንድ፣ ሥርዓቶች፣ የቀረበ፣ ነገረ፣ መለኮታዊ፣ ትችት፣, by *Aläqa* Tayye Gäbrä Maryam

Paper, (no measurements available), bound in a two-ring binder, iii + 451 folios, one column, 37 lines, Gə_əz and Amharic, twentieth century.

Pp. 1–449: A Theological Critique of Certain Practices of the Orthodox Church, ስለ፣ ኦርቶዶክስ፣ ቤተ፣ ክርስቲያን፣ አንዳንድ፣ ሥርዓቶች፣ የቀረበ፣ ነገረ፣ መለኮታዊ፣ ትችት፣, in Amharic

1. Pp. 1–6: Introduction, መቅድም፣.
   የምርመራ ፡ ወራት ፡ መጣች ፡ የፍዳም ፡ ወራት ፡ ደረስች ፡ እስራኤል ፡ ያውቁታል፤ ሆሴዕ ፡ ፱ ፡ ፯፣ ስለዚህ ፡ ስኔች ፡ እቱኮ ፡ እግዚአብሔር ፡ የሚወደውን ፡ አስተውሉ ፡ እንጂ ፡ መርምራችሁ ፡ እግዚአብሔርን ፡ ደስ ፡ ደስ ፡ የሚያሰኝ ፡ ሥራ ፡ ምን ፡ እንደሆነ ፡ ፍሬ ፡ ከሌለው ፡ ከጨለማ ፡ ሥራ ፡ ጋር ፡ አንድ ፡ አትሁኑ ፡ . . .

2. Pp. 6–28: On the Word of God, ስለ፣ እግዚአብሔር፣ ቃል፣.
   ምዕራፍ ፡ ፩ ፡ ስለ ፡ እግዚአብሔር ፡ ቃል ፡ የሚናገሩ ፡ ቃላት ፡ በ፪ ፡ ክፍል ፡ ይከፈላሉ፡ መጀመሪያ ፡ ክፍል ፡ ጥሬ ፡ ንባቡን ፡ በመስማት ፡

ወይም ፡ በማየት ፡ ከሁሉ ፡ ይቅል ፡ አስቀድሞ ፡ እርሱን ፡ መስማትና ፡
ማመን፤ አድርገም ፡ መጋደልና ፡ መጠበቅ ፡ እንደገባ ፡ ይናገራል። ሁለተኛ ፡
ክፍል ፡ ጥሬ ፡ ንባቡን ፡ በመስማት ፡ ወይም ፡ በማየት ፡ ተሰናክለን ፡ ወደ
ስሕተት ፡ ጉድንድ ፡ እንዳንወድቅ ፡ ምሥጢሩን ፡ ጠንቅቀን ፡ መመርመር ፡
ማስተዋል ፡ እንደገባን ፡ ይመክራል ፡ . . .

3. Pp. 28–33: On literal interpretation, ጥሬ፡ ንባቡን፡ ከምሥጢር፡ ጋር፡ ስለማስማማት፡.

4. Pp. 33–42: On the Gospel of Christ, ስለ፡ ክርስቶስ፡ ወንጌል፡.

5. Pp. 42–87: On the Book of Synodos, ስለ፡ መጽሐፈ፡ ሲኖዶስ፡. Beginning:
ስለ ፡ ሲኖዶስ ፡ የሚናገሩ ፡ ቃላት ፡ በስድስት ፡ ክፍል ፡ ይከፈላሉ።
መጀመሪያ ፡ ክፍል ፡ ሐዋርያት ፡ እንዳልጻፉት ፡ የሚያስረዳ ፡ ብዙ ፡
ምስክር ፡ በውስጡ ፡ እንዳለበት ፡ ያሳያል ፡ ሁለተኛ ፡ ክፍል ፡ ከመጻሕፍት ፡
ሐዋርያት ፡ ቃል ፡ ጋር ፡ የማይስማማ ፡ ብዙ ፡ ነገር ፡ እንዳለበት ፡
ይገልጻል። ሶስተኛ ፡ ክፍል ፡ በሲኖዶስ ፡ ሐዋርያት ፡ አዘዙ ፡ ተብሎ ፡
የተጻፈ ፡ ሜሮን ፡ የሚባል ፡ ቅብዓት ፡ ከሐዋርያት ፡ እንዳልታዘዘ ፡ ያሳያል፡...

6. Pp. 87–95: On the Holy Oil Meron, ስለ፡ ሜሮን፡ ቅብዓት፡. Beginning:
ስለሜሮን ፡ ታሪካቸው ፡ የሚል ፡ ሌላ ፡ ነው ፡ ምክንያቱ ፡ ግን ፡ ከአሪት ፡
ዘፀአት ፡ ስለ ፡ ቅብዐ ፡ ቅዱስ ፡ ከተጻፈ ፡ የወሰዱት ፡ ነው። በዚያም ፡
የተጻፈ ፡ ቃል ፡ ስለ ፡ ቅብዐ ፡ ቅዱስ ፡ ይህ ፡ ነው ፡ ወነበቦ ፡
እግዚአብሔር ፡ ለሙሴ ፡ ወይቤሎ ፡ ንሣእ ፡ አፈዋተ ፡ ጽጌ ፡ ዘክርቤ ፡
ቅጽው ፡ ወቀናንሞስ ፡ . . .

7. Pp. 95–98: On the Proper Books for Lectionary Readings in Church, በቤተ፡ ክርስቲያን፡ ሊነበቡ፡ ስለሚገባቸው፡ ቅዱሳት፡ መጻሕፍት፡. Beginning:
ከመጻሕፍት ፡ ቅዱሳት ፡ በቀር ፡ በልብ ፡ ፈጠራ ፡ የተጻፉት ፡ መጻሕፍት ፡
በቤተ ፡ ክርስቲያን ፡ መነበብ ፡ እንዳይባቸው ፡ የሚናገሩ ፡ ቃላት፡ ተስእሎ ፡
በልብ ፡ ፈጠራ ፡ የተጻፉ ፡ መጻሕፍት ፡ በቤተ ፡ ክርስቲያን ፡ መነበብ ፡
እንዳይገባቸው ፡ የሚናገር ፡ መጻሕፍት ፡ ቅዱሳትን ፡ ብቻ ፡ አንብቡ ፡
የሚል ፡ በሲኖዶስ ፡ ምን ፡ ክፍል ፡ ይገኛል ፡ . . .

8. Pp. 98–103: On the Memorial Service for the Dead, ስለ፡ ተዝካር፡. Beginning:
በሲኖዶስ ፡ ተዝካር ፡ እንዳያድን ፡ የሚናገር ፡ ቃል ፡ ተስእሎ ፡ በሲኖዶስ ፡
ተዝካር ፡ እንዲያድን ፡ የሚናገር ፡ በምን ፡ ክፍል ፡ ይገኛል ። ተውጥፖ ፡
በመጀመሪያው ፡ ሲኖዶስ ፡ . . .

9. Pp. 103–132: On the Law of the Kings, ስለ፡ ፍትሐ፡ ነገሥት፡. Beginning:
ከዚህ ፡ ወዲህ ፡ ስለ ፡ ፍትሐ ፡ ነገሥት ፡ ታሪክ ፡ እንመልከት ፡ ምዕራፍ ፡
ጄ ፡ ፩ኛ ፡ በዘክርተ ፡ መጻሕፍት ፡ ስለሚገኙ ፡ ቃላት ፡ ሁለተኛ ፡

በየአናቅጹ ፡ የሰለስቱ ፡ ምዕት ፡ ቀኖና ፡ እንደ ፡ ሌሎች ፡ መጻሕፍት ፡ ሁሉ ፡ በጥቅስ ፡ እንጂ ፡ የመጽሐፉ ፡ መሠረት ፡ አንዳይደለ ፡ . . .

10. Pp. 133–151: On the Book of Ginzet, ስለ፡ መጽሐፈ፡ ግንዘት፡.
Beginning:
ስለ ፡ ግንዘት ፡ የሚናገሩ ፡ ቃላት ፡ በ፩ ፡ ይከፈላሉ ፡ መጀመሪያ ፡ ክፍል ፡ ስለሙታን ፡ ስለሚደረግ ፡ ሥርዓት ፡ ሁሉና ፡ ስለ ፡ ተዝካር ፡ እንዴት ፡ እንደሆነ ፡ ይናገራል ፡ ሁለተኛ ፡ ክፍል ፡ ለዓዕመ ፡ ሮቤል ፡ በሙሴ ፡ ጸሎት ፡ እግዚአብሔር ፡ አስተሠረየለት ፡ ስለማለቱ ፡ ይናገራል። ሶስተኛ ፡ ክፍል ፡ በሕልም ፡ ያባቱን ፡ ሥቃይ ፡ በገሃነም ፡ ስላየ ፡ ኤጲስ ፡ ቆጰስ ፡ ይናገራል ፡ . . .

11. Pp. 151–155: On the Bandlet of Righteousness, ልፋፈ፡ ጽድቅ፡ ስለሚባል፡ ክታብ፡. Beginning:
ልፋፈ ፡ ጽድቅ ፡ ስለሚባል ፡ ክታብ የተጻፈ ፡ ቃል ፡ ከንቱ ፡ እንደሆነ ፡ ያሳያል ፡ ያልነው ፡ ይህ ነው ። በስመ ፡ አብ ፡ ወወልድ ፡ ወመንፈስ ፡ ቅዱስ ፡ ፩ ፡ አምላክ ፡ ጸሎተ ፡ ልፋፈ ፡ ጽድቅ ፡ ዘጽሐፉ ፡ አብ ፡ በእዱ ፡ ወወሀባ ፡ ለእግዝእትነ ፡ ማርያም ፡ እምቅድመ ፡ ይትወለድ ፡ ክርስቶስ ፡ እንተ ፡ ታበውእ ፡ ውስተ ፡ ጸባብ ፡ አንቀጽ ፡ ወትወልድ ፡ ውስተ ፡ መንግሥተ ፡ ሰማያት ፡ መርህ ፡ በጻድቃን ፡ ወዘንተ ነገራ ፡ ክርስቶስ ፡ ለማርያም ፡ እምድኅረ ፡ ተወልደ ፡ . . .

12. Pp. 155–157: The Contradictions in the Book of Ginzät, የግንዘት፡ ቃል፡ እርስ፡ በእርሱ፡ እንዲጣላ፡ የሚያሳይ፡. Beginning:
የግንዘት ፡ ቃል ፡ እርስ ፡ በእርሱ ፡ እንዲጣላ ፡ የሚያሳይ ፡ ይህን ፡ ስለ ፡ ግንዘት ፡ የተነገረ ፡ ነገርን ፡ ሁሉ ፡ ከሕይወት ፡ ቴጥሮት ፡ ዛቲ ፡ መጽሐፍ ፡ ዘወጽአት ፡ እምኢየሩሳሌም ፡ በእንተ ፡ እለ ፡ ኖሙ ፡ ነፍሳተ ፡ ክርስቲያን ፡ ከመ ፡ ትኩን ፡ መድኃኒተ ፡ ለኃጥአን ፡ ወሥርየተ ፡ ለዘማውያን ፡ ይላል ። ነገር ፡ ግን ፡ በፊተ ፡ እንዳሳየን ፡ ከትእዛዛ ፡ እግዚአብሔር ፡ ለወጡ ፡ ረዊያን ፡ በፈቃደ ፡ እግዚአብሔር ፡ ለማይኔዱ ፡ ኃጥአን ፡ . . .

13. Pp. 157–223: On the Acts, Miracles and Homilies of the Saints, ስለ፡ ገድላና፡ ስለ፡ ተአምር፡ ስለ፡ ድርሳንም፡. Beginning:
ስለ ፡ ገድላና ፡ ስለ ፡ ተአምር ፡ ስለ ፡ ድርሳንም ። ስለ ፡ ገድላና ፡ ስለ ፡ ተአምር ፡ ስለ ፡ ድርሳንም ፡ የሚነገሩ ፡ ቃላት ፡ በ፩ ፡ ክፍል ፡ ይከፈላሉ ። መጀመሪያ ፡ ከዚህ ፡ ዓለም ፡ ድካም ፡ ላረፉ ፡ ቅዱሳን ፡ ለሰማዕታት ፡ ለመላእክት ፡ በልመናቸው ፡ ኃጢአተኞችን ፡ ሊያድኑ ፡ እግዚአብሔር ፡ ኪዳን ፡ ሰጥቷቸዋል ፡ ስለማለቱ ፡ ይናገራል ። ሁለተኛው ፡ ክፍል ፡ ነገር ፡ በማስመሰል ፡ ሱን ፡ ለማታለል ፡ በጥብ ፡ በሥጋ ፡ ምክር ፡ ከቃለ ፡ እግዚአብሔር ፡ ጋር ፡ ተቀላቅሎ ፡ እንደተጻፈ ፡ ያሳያል ፡ . . .

14. Pp. 223–239: On the Glory of the Saints, ስለ፡ ቅዱሳን፡ ክብር፡. Beginning:

ሰለ ፡ ቅዱሳን ፡ ክብር ፡ ብዙ ፡ ሰዎች ፡ በክርስቶስ ፡ ሞት ፡ የተገኘውን ፡
መድኃኒት ፡ ፍጹም ፡ ባያስተውሉ ፡ በዚህ ፡ ባለፈው ፡ ምዕራፍ ፡ እንዳሳየነ ፡
የገድልና ፡ የተአምር ፡ የድርሳን ፡ ቃል ፡ ከመጻሕፍት ፡ ቅዱሳት ፡ ቃል ፡ ጋር ፡
የሚጣላ ፡ ትምህርት ፡ ከጉሥዓት ፡ ልብ ፡ የወጣ ፡ ስሕተት ፡ ነው ፡ ብለው ፡
ሰለማይቀበሉ ፡ ከስማየ ፡ ስማያት ፡ ወርደ ፡ ከቅድስት ፡ ድንግል ፡ ተወልደ ፡
ሥጋውን ፡ ቆርሶ ፡ ደሙን ፡ በዕፀ ፡ መስቀል ፡ አፍስሶ ፡ የአዳምን ፡ በደል ፡
በሞቱ ፡ ክሶ ፡ ሱን ፡ ከእግዚአብሔር ፡ ጋር ፡ ያስታረቀ ፡ ከወልደ ፡
እግዚአብሔር ፡ በቀር ፡ ከፍጡር ፡ አንድ ፡ አይገኝም ፡ . . .

15. Pp. 239–359: On the Intercession of the Saints, ሰለ፡ ቅዱሳን፡ ማማለድ፡ እንዴት፡ እንደሆነ፡ የሚያሳይ፡. Beginning:

ሰለ ፡ ቅዱሳን ፡ ማማለድ ፡ እንዴት ፡ እንደሆነ ፡ የሚያሳይ ፡ ቅዱሳን ፡ በዚህ ፡
ዓለም ፡ በሕይወተ ፡ ሥጋ ፡ ሳሉ ፡ ድውያንን ፡ ከሥጋ ፡ ደዌ ፡ ተፈሰሰው ፡
ከነፍስ ፡ ደዌ ፡ ለመፈወስ ፡ መንፈሳዊ ፡ መድኃኒትን ፡ ለመሻት ፡ እንዲጸኑ ፡
ዓላውያን ፡ ወደ ፡ ሃይማኖተ ፡ ክርስቶስ ፡ ተመልሰው ፡ ከዘላለም ፡ ጥፋት ፡
እንዲድኑ ፡ እግዚአብሔርን ፡ እንዲለምኑ ፡ እርሱም ፡ ልመናቸውን ፡
እንዲሰማቸው ፡ እናምናለን ፡ እንጂ ፡ አንክድም ፡፡ ወጸሎተ ፡ ሃይማኖት ፡
ያሐይም ፡ ለድውይ ፡ ወያነሥኦ ፡ እግዚአብሔር ፡ . . .

16. Pp. 359–364: On Scripture, ሰለ፡ መጻሕፍት፡ ቅዱሳት፡. Beginning:

ለነፍስ ፡ ደኅንነት ፡ የሚመክሩ ፡ ለእውነተኛው ፡ መድኃኒት ፡ የሚመስክሩ ፡
በእግዚአብሔር ፡ መንፈስ ፡ የተጻፉ ፡ መጻሕፍት ፡ ቅዱሳት ፡ የተባሉ ፡ ብሎችና ፡
ሐዲሳት ፡ ናቸው ፡ እነርሱም ፡ እሊህ ፡ ናቸው ፡ . . .

17. Pp. 364–397: On the Holy Assembly, ሰለ፡ ቅድስት፡ አንድነት፡. Beginning:

ሰለ ፡ ቅድስት ፡ አንድነት ፡ በዘመነ ፡ ሐዋርያት ፡ ሰለ ፡ ነበሩ ፡ ምእመናን ፡
ቅዱስ ፡ ሉቃስ ፡ በግብረ ፡ ሐዋርያት ፡ ሲናገር ፡ ወኰሎሙ ፡ እለ ፡ አምኑ ፡
ኅቡረ ፡ ይነብሩ ፡ ወድሙር ፡ ኰሉ ፡ ንዋዮሙ ፡ ወጥሪቶሙ ፡ ይሠይጡ ፡
ወይከፍሉ ፡፡ . . .

18. Pp. 397–447: On Religious Divisions, ስለመለያየት፡ በሃይማኖት፡ ምክንያት፡. Beginning:

ስለመለያየት ፡ በሃይማኖት ፡ ምክንያት ፡ ሃይማኖት ፡ ማለት ፡ ሥላሴን ፡
በባሕርያቸው ፡ ለማወቅ ፡ መራቀቅ ፡ በምሥጢረ ፡ ሥላሴ ፡ መመራመርና ፡
በውቀት ፡ በፍልስፍና ፡ መጥለቅ ፡ አይደለም ፡ ሥላሴን ፡ በባሕርያቸው ፡
ለማወቅ ፡ ተራቅ ምሥጢረ ፡ ሥጋዌን ፡ በፍልስፍና ፡ ተመራምር ፡ ጠንቅቆ ፡
ያወቀ ፡ ካሁኑ ፡ ቀደም ፡ የነበረ ፡ አሁንም ፡ ያለ ፡ እንግዲህም ፡ የሚመጣ ፡
ሥጋ ፡ ከለበሰ ፡ አንድ ፡ አይገኝም ፡፡ . . .

19. Pp. 447–449: Conclusion, ማጠቃለያ፡.

Notes:

1. *Aläqa* Tayye (also spelled Taye) Gabra Maryam (1858–1924) was an Ethiopian scholar and teacher. He wrote five books, among them a

Geez Grammar (published by the Swedish Mission at Minkwillo, Eritrea, in 1897). He was a preacher in Monkolu for about 20 years and drew the attention of Emperor Menilek II who commissioned him to write a history of Ethiopia. But the Emperor also had to protect Tayye from the clergy of the church, many of whom considered Tayye a heretic. Around 1905, Menilek sent Tayye to Germany for four years at the request of Kaiser Wilhelm II who had asked for a scholar who could catalogue Ethiopian manuscripts and teach Gə_əz. He worked with Germany's Dr. Eugene Mittwoch to publish a set of Ethiopian folk songs in 1907. After Menilek's decline he was imprisoned, but eventually reinstated as a scholar and published a social history of Ethiopia in 1922. The entry in the list of biographies, ብላቴን፡ ጌታ፡ ማኅተሙ፡ ሥላሴ፡ ወልደ፡ መስቀል፡ ቼ፡ በሰው፡,[17] says this about *Aleqa* Tayye: ―Native of Bägemdər. In addition to mastering our country's church education, he was educated abroad. He expended great energy in order to write down the entire history of Ethiopia and produced many books. In order to acknowledge his learning and to say, ―He knows; Let him speak; Let him tell the story; Let him present the argument," he was named ―*Abba* Yəbäl" [which means Knowledgeable Father]. *Aleqa* Tayye was praised for his scholarship and his work became his memorial in history."[18]

2. The manuscript is written in black and red ink on lined paper, held in a two-ring binder. After three pages of front matter, the main work begins and the pages are numbered throughout in Amharic.
3. F. ii: Yellow card with the following typewritten in red ink: ―This manuscript belongs to Dr. F. B. Hylander and is deposited with Yemissrach Dimts Literature Programme. It is to be returned to Rev. M. Lundgren, Mekane Yesus Church Headquarters. Tel. 17220."

---

[17] published in *JES* 7.2 (1969) 195ff.
[18] This entry was translated from the Amharic. For more on Tayye, see, Bairu Tafla, ―Aaqa Tayye Gabra-Maryam," *The Encyclopaedia Africana Dictionary of African Biography, volume one: Ethiopia-Ghana*, ed. Keith Irvine and L. H. Ofosu-Appiah (New York: Reference, 1997). For his work with music in Ethiopia, see, Simeneh Betreyohannes ―Scholarship on Ethiopian Music: Past, Present and Future Prospects" *African Study Monographs*, Supp 41 (2010) 19–34, esp. 21.

MYS 45 – EMIP 645
Acts of Märqorewos, ገድለ፡ መርቆሬዎስ፡, Miracles of Märqorewos, ተአምረ፡ መርቆሬዎስ፡, Image of Märqorewos, መልክአ፡ መርቆሬዎስ፡

Parchment, 223 x 168 x 47 mm, four Coptic chain stitches attached with bridle attachments to rough-hewn boards of the traditional wood, protection quire + 11 full quires, iii + 84 folios, top margin 26 mm, bottom margin 47 mm, fore edge margin 27 mm, gutter margin 11 mm, ff. 1r–82v two columns, 19 lines, Gə_əz, twentieth century.

Quire descriptions: quires 1–3, 5 and 8–11 balanced; protection quire and quires 4 and 6–7 adjusted balanced.

Major Works:
1. Ff. 1r–41r: Acts of Märqorewos (Mercurius), *Gädlä Märqorewos*, ገድለ፡ መርቆሬዎስ፡, divided into sections: Section 1 (f. 1r), section 2 (f. 14r), section 3 (f. 16r), section 4 (f. 22r), section 5 (f. 31v), section 6 (f. 36r).
   በስመ ፡ አብ ፡ ወወልድ ፡ . . . ወኮነ ፡ በመዋዕለ ፡ ዳኬዎስ ፡ ንጉስ ፡ ዘሮሜ ፡ ተወለደ ፡ ሕጻን ፡ ዘስሙ ፡ ፒሉፓደር ፡ ዘበትርጓሜሁ ፡ መርቆሬዎስ ፡ ብሂል ፡ ስም ፡ አቡሁ ፡ አሮስ ፡ ወስመ ፡ እምሔዉ ፡ ሳዳሮስ ፡ ወጀኤሆሙ ፡ አላውያን ፡ ነዓዊያነ ፡ አራዊት ፡ ወእምከመ ፡ አጎዙ ፡ ይወስዱ ፡ ለነገሥት ፡ ወለመኳንንት ፡ ወለመሳፍንት ፡ ወይውህብዎሙ ፡ ዓስቦሙ ፡ . . .

2. Ff. 42r–77v: Twenty-three Miracles of Märqorewos (Mercurius), *Täʿamməra Märqorewos*, ተአምረ፡ መርቆሬዎስ፡
   በስመ ፡ አብ ፡ ወወልድ ፡. . . ናሁ ፡ እንከ ፡ ንጽሕፍ ፡ ዜና ፡ ተአምሪሁ ፡ ለቅዱስ ፡ መርቆሬዎስ ፡ ብዑዓዊ ፡ ዘገብረ ፡ እምድኅረ ፡ ሞቱ ፡ . . .

3. Ff. 78r–82v: Image of Märqorewos, (Mercurius), *Mälk_a Märqorewos*, መልክአ፡ መርቆሬዎስ፡.
   ሰላም ፡ ለዝክረ ፡ ስምከ ፡ ገብረ ፡ ኢየሱስ ፡ ብሂል ፡ ወለሥዕርተ ፡ ርእስከ ፡ ዐሊም ፡ ዘቆናዝሊሁ ፡ ፍቱል ፡ መርቆሬዎስ ፡ ስማዕት ፡ ገባሬ ፡ ተአምር ፡ ወኃይል ፡ ለዮሐንስ ፡ ፍና ፡ ድኂን ፡ ከመ ፡ መራኅከ ፡ በሐቅል ፡ ምርሒኒ ፡ ለወልድክ ፡ ፍና ፡ ጽድቅ ፡ ወሣህል ፡

Notes:
1. Ff. i r(ecto)–iii v(erso), 41v and 83r–84v: blank.
2. Decorative designs: f. 1r (*ḥaräg*); ff. 16r, 21v, 77v, 82v (line of alternating red and black dots and full stops); ff. 44r, 52v, 56v, 61r (multiple full stops).
3. F. 44v and *passim*: a space was left for an owner's name.
4. F. 77v: colophon: "finished in the year of Luke the Evangelist, 1971 EC in the month of Ṭəqəmt by the peace of God the Father, Amen."

5. The words Marqorios, Michael and Mary are rubricated.
6. Numbered quires: quires 2–11.
7. Scribal intervention: words of text are written interlinearly (ff. 28r, 35r, 67r, 70v); erasure markings are visible (f. 10r).

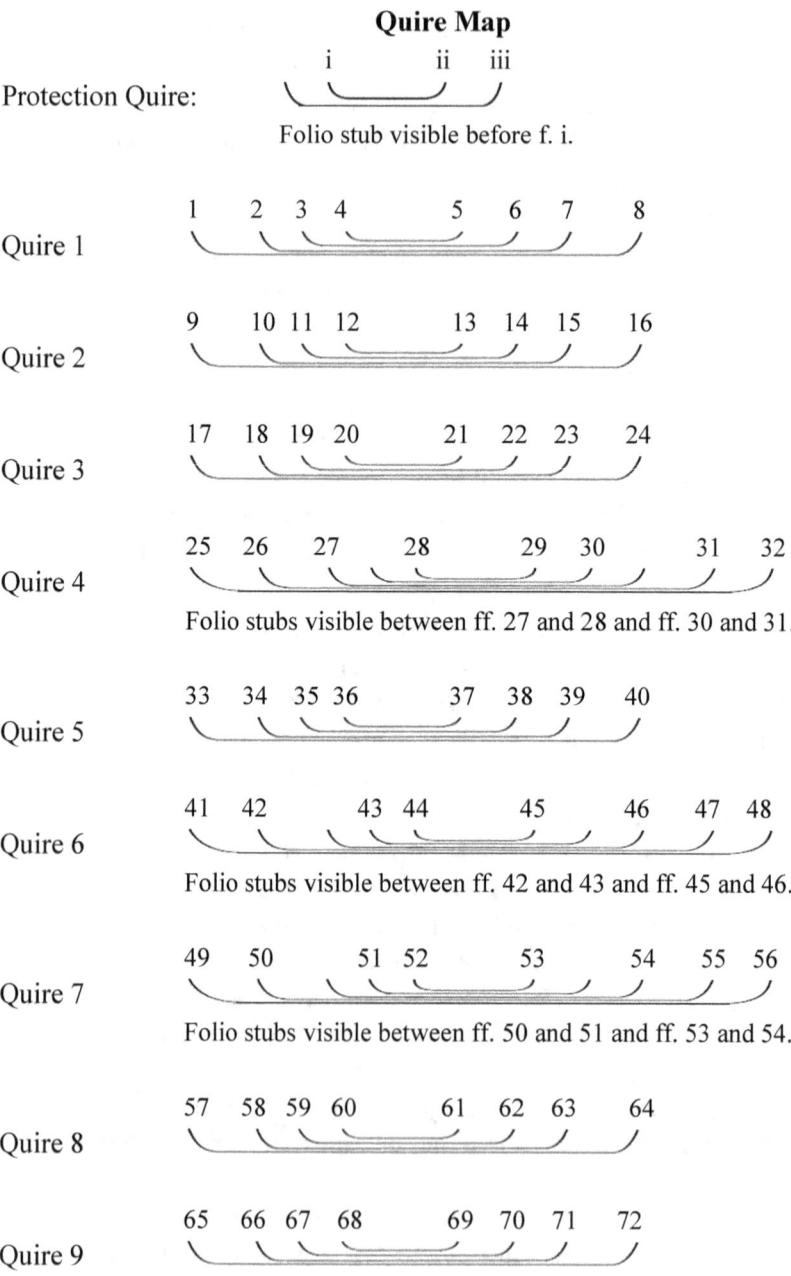

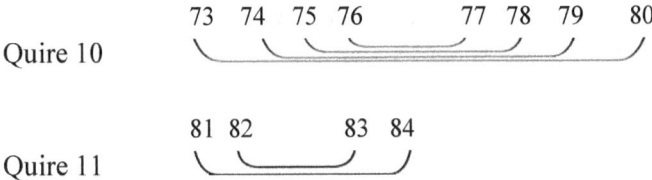

MYS 46 – EMIP 646
Five Pillars of Mystery, አምስቱ፡ አዕማደ፡ ምሥጢር፡, Commentary on the Ten Commandments, in Amharic

Parchment, 214 x 137 x 58 mm, four Coptic chain stitches attached with bridle attachments to rough-hewn boards of the traditional wood, protection sheet + 10 full quires, iii + 92 folios, top margin 17 mm, bottom margin 32 mm, fore edge margin 15 mm, gutter margin 12 mm, ff. 1r–90r one column, 25 lines, Gə_əz and Amharic, twentieth century. Double-slip *maḥdär*.

Quire descriptions: protection sheet and quires 1–8 and 10 balanced; quire 9 adjusted balanced. Navigation system: red yarn is sewn into the fore edge of ff. 17 and 60 to mark content.

Major Works:

Ff. 1r–36v: Five Pillars of Mystery, *Aməstu A_əmadä Məsṭir*, አምስቱ፡ አዕማደ፡ ምሥጢር፡. The basic work is an Amharic explanation of the teachings of the Church, widely copied, e. g. EMML 1648, f. 16a; EMML 1815; see also ፬ቱ አዕማደ፡ ምሥጢር፡ (Addis Ababa: Täsfa Press, 1952 EC). In what follows, the commentaries are not a usual part of the Five Pillars.

በስመ ፡ አብ ፡ ወወልድ ፡ . . . ሦስቱን ፡ ስም ፡ ሦስቱን አካል ፡ አንድ ፡ አምላክ ፡ ብለን ፡ አምነን፡ በሦስትነቱ ፡ በአንድነቱ ፡ ተማዕነን ፡ ሰይጣንን ፡ ከደን ፡ ዓዕማደ ፡ ምስጢርን ፡ እንናገርለን፡

1. Ff. 1r–36v: Mystery of the Trinity, *Məsṭir Śəllase*, ምሥጢረ፡ ሥላሴ፡, with commentary and warnings.

   ምስጢረ ፡ ሥላሴ ፡ እንደት ፡ ነው ፡ ቢሉ ፡ ከዓለም ፡ በፊት ፡ ከዓለም ፡ በኋላ ፡ ሥላሴ ፡ መብለጥ ፡ መበላጥ ፡ መቅደም ፡ መቀዳደም ፡ መከታል ፡ መከታተል ፡ ሣይኖርባቸው ፡ ዘለዓለም ፡ ትክክል ፡ ሆነው ፡ ይኖራሉ ፡ . . .

2. Ff. 44r–51v: Mystery of the Incarnation, *Mə śṭir Śəgawe*, ምሥጢረ፡ ሥጋዌ፡.

   በስመ ፡ አብ ፡ ወወልድ ፡ ምስጢረ ፡ ሥጋዌ ፡ ወልድን ፡ እንናገርለን ፡ ምስጢረ ፡ ሥጋዌ ፡ ወልድ ፡ እንደት ፡ ቢሉ ፡ ነው ፡ አዳም ፡ በተፈጠረ ፡ በ፯ ፡ ዓመት ፡ በምክረ ፡ ከይሲ ፡ አምላክነትን ፡ ሲፈልግ ፡ ቴዕስ ፡ በለን ፡

በበላ ፡ ጊዜ ፡ ሥላሴ ፡ ወኮነ ፡ አዳም ፡ ከመጀ ፡ ንሕነ ፡ አሉ ፡ ያን ፡ ጊዜ ፡ ተጀመረ ፡ . . .

3. Ff. 52r–54v: Mystery of the Baptism, *Mə śṭir Ṭəmqät*, ምሥጢረ፡ ጥምቀት፡.

በስመ ፡ አብ ፡ ወወልድ ፡ . . . ምስጢረ ፡ ጥምቀትን ፡ እንናገራለን፨ ጌታችን ፡ ከአመቤታችን ፡ በተወለደ ፡ በ፵ ፡ ዓመት ፡ በመንፈቅ ፡ ሌሊት ፡ በዮርዳኖስ ፡ ተጠመቀ፨ ስለምን ፡ ተጠመቀ ፡ ቢሉ ፡ እናንተም ፡ በውሃ ፡ ተጠመቁ ፡ ብትጠመቁ ፡ ከሥላሴ ፡ የአጋ ፡ ልጅነትን ፡ ታገኛላችሁ ፡ ቄጸል በለስን ፡ በመብላት ፡ የሄደ ፡ ልጅነታችሁ ፡ ይመለሰላችኋል ፡ መንግሥተ ፡ ሰማያት ፡ ትገባላችሁ ፡ ሲል ፡ ተጠመቀ ፡ . . .

4. Ff. 55v–57v: Mystery of Holy Communion, *Mə śṭir Qurəban*, ምሥጢረ፡ ቁርባን፡.

በስመ ፡ አብ ፡ ወወልድ ፡ . . . ምስጢረ ፡ ቁርባንን ፡ እንነገራለን ፨ በጾሎተ ፡ ሐሙስ ፡ ለድራር ፡ ከአመጡለት ፡ የሥንዴ ፡ ኅብስት ፡ ከአመጡለት ፡ ወይን ፡ ነገ ፡ የሚፈተት ፡ ሥጋዬ ፡ የሚፈስስ ፡ ደሜ ፡ ይህ ፡ ነው ፡ ብሎ ፡ ለሐዋርያት ፡ ሠጣቸው ፡ ተመገቡ ፡ መጠምሙ ፡ አምድኃረ ፡ ተደሩ ፡ ይላል ፨

5. Ff. 58r–60v: The Thirteen Stations of the Cross, አሥራ ሣስቱ ሕማማተ መስቀል, in Amharic.

በስመ ፡ አብ ፡ ወወልድ ፡ . . . አሥራ ፡ ሣስቱን ፡ ሕማማተ ፡ መስቀልን ፡ የጌታችንን ፡ ትንሣኤ ፡ እንናገራለን ፨ አሥራ ፡ ሣስቱ ፡ ሕማማተ ፡ መስቀል ፡ ማን ፡ ማን ፡ ናቸው ፡ ቢሉ ፡ አንድ ፡ ነውር ፡ ኃጢአት ፡ በደል ፡ ሳይገኝበት ፡ ጌታችን ፡ እንደ ፡ ሌባ ፡ የግርንግሪት ፡ አሠሩት ፡...

6. Ff. 60v–65v: Mystery of the Resurrection of the Dead, *Mə śṭir Tənśa'e Mutan*, ምሥጢረ፡ ትንሣኤ፡ ሙታን፡.

በስመ ፡ አብ ፡ ወወልድ ፡ . . . የአኛን ፡ ትንሣኤ ፡ እንናገራለን፨ ይህ ፡ ኩሉ ፡ ሰው ፡ ጢስ ፡ ታይቶ ፡ እንደ ፡ ሚጠፋ ፡ ታይቶ ፡ ይጠፋል ፡ ከጠፋም ፡ አይመለስም ፡ በእዚህ ፡ ዓለም ፡ ቢበላ ፡ ቢጠጣ ፡ ቢሽለም ፡ ቢገዛ ፡ ፃዕረ ፡ ሞት ፡ በመጣ ፡ ጊዜ ፡ እንድ ፡ ቀን ፡ የበላሁ ፡ የጠጣሁ ፡ የሞገስኩ ፡ የገዛሁ ፡ አይመሰለውም ፡ . . .

7. Ff. 66r–86v: Commentary on the Ten Commandments, in Amharic.

በስመ ፡ አብ ፡ ወወልድ ፡. . . አሥርቱን ፡ ቃላተ ፡ ያሪትን ፡ እንናገራለን ፡ እንዱ ፡ ኢታምልክ ፡ ባዕደ ፡ አምላክ ፡ ዘእንበሌየ ፡ ብሎ ፡ እግዚአብሔር ፡ አዘዘው ፡ የአዳምን ፡ ልጅ ፡ ሁሉ ፡ በእግዚአብሔር ፡ ብቻ ፡ ማምለክ ፡ እንዴት ፡ ነው ፡ ቢሉ ፡ ያለእግዚአብሔር ፡ በቀር ፡ የሚሠጥ ፡ የሚነሣ ፡ የሚገል ፡ የሚያድን ፡ ሌላ ፡ ፈጣሪ ፡ ባድ ፡ አምላክ ፡ እንደሌለ ፡ መማር ፡ ማወቅ ፡ ነው ፡ . . .

8. Ff. 86v–90r: Mystery of Baptism, second version, *Mə śṭir Ṭəmqät*, ምሥጢረ፡ ጥምቀት፡.

ምስጢሬ ፡ ጥምቀት ፡. . . እኛን ፡ ከክፉ ፡ ጠላታችን ፡ ለማዳን ፡ ከሰማየ ፡
ሰማያት ፡ ወርደ ፡ ያለ ፡ ሰው ፡ ዘር0 ፡ ከቅድስት ፡ ከንጽሕት ፡ ድንግል ፡
ሥጋችን ፡ ለብሶ ፡ ተዋህደ ፡ በለት ፡ ድንግልና ፡ ተወልደ ፡ ከኃጢአት ፡
በቀር ፡ እንደ ፡ እኛ ፡ ፍጹም ፡ ሰው ፡ ጎኖ ፡ ከውኃ ፡ ከመንፈስ ፡ ቅዱስ ፡
ያልተወለደ ፡ መንግሥት ፡ ሰማያትን ፡ መግባት ፡ አይቻለውም ፡ : . . .

Miniatures:
1. F. 38r: crude drawing of a figure with arms upraised, in pencil.
2. F. 39v: The Holy Trinity.
3. F. 40r: The Crucifixion.
4. F. 41r: Saint George and the Dragon.
5. F. 41v: Madonna and Child.

Varia:
1. Ff. i v(erso)-ii v(erso): Explanation of the Islamic teaching on Jesus and Mary, የክርስቲያኖች፡ እና፡ የሰላሞች፡ ሃይማኖት፡ ጥያቄ፡, in Amharic.
2. F. iii v(erso), lines 1–15: Blessings for the one who follows this faith and consequences for the one who rejects this faith with a testimony to its power.
3. Ff. 37r–38r: Greeting to the archangel Fanuel, Chaîne, *Répertoire* 49.
   በሰመ ፡ አብ ፡ . . . ጸሎት ፡ በእንተ ፡ አአምን ፡ በ፫ ፡ አካላት ፡ ሰላም ፡
   ለከ ፡ ሰዳዬ ፡ ሰይጣናት ፡ ፋ ። ለእግዚአብሔር ፡ አምጽርሁ ፡ ከመ ፡
   ኢይሰክዬ ፡ ሰብአ ፡ አለይኔሰሁ ፡ ለጌጋይ ፡ ዘዘዚአሁ ፡ : . . .
4. F. 38v: Instructions about the measurement of shadows for the telling of time for the whole year. Cf. EMIP 187, f. i v(erso), and MYS 26, ff. 73rv.
5. F. 43r: Excerpt from the Mystery of the Incarnation.

Notes:
1. Ff. i r(ecto), iii r(ecto), 39r, 40v, 42rv, 43v and 90v: blank.
2. F. iii v(erso), lines 16–19: note of donation of the book to Ṣata Mikaʻel church.
3. F. iii v(erso), lines 20–25: Note on the Prophet Mohammad and his wives. ―Mohammad lived 550 years after the apostles. What he took by himself 15 legal wives and 11 concubines. They said that those he put in hidden places are without number. But for his people he commanded four wives."
4. Ff. 91rv: Amharic alphabet and numbers.
5. F. 92r: Arabic phrases (written in Amharic characters) and Amharic translation, in blue ink.
6. F. 92v: excerpt from the Gospel, in pencil, illegible.

7. Decorative designs: ff. 1r, 44r, 52r, 60v, 66r (*ḫaräg*); f. 54v (line of alternating red and black dots).
8. The word Mary is rubricated.
9. Numbered quires: quires 1–4 and 6–10 (numbered 5–9).
10. Scribal intervention: words of text are written interlinearly (ff. 1rv, 2r, 3r, 4r, 5v, etc.); and lines of text are written interlinearly (f. 89r); and in the bottom margin with a symbol (⊤) marking the location where the text is to be inserted (ff. 3v, line 11; 5v, line 25; 22r, line 24; 22v, line 24; 26r, line 22; 34v, line 14, etc.), and in the upper margin where the symbol (⊥) is used (ff. 7v, line 3; 13r, line 7; 13v, line 2; 15r, line 5; 16r, line 2; 18r, line 11, etc.), and in another case where the symbol (⊣) is used (ff. 11v, line 1; 14r, line 2; 14v, line 1; 17r, line 1; 17v, line 5); erasure markings are visible (ff. 3v, 4r, 5r, 6v, etc.); text has been removed (e.g., ff. 18r, 19r, 59v).

Quire Map

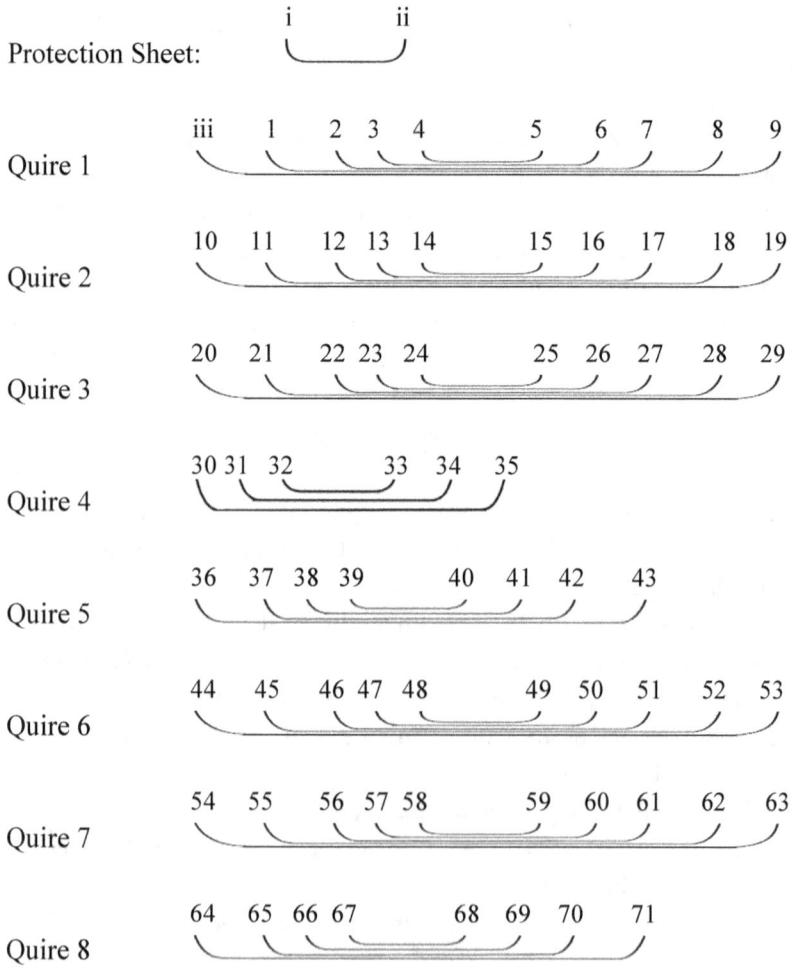

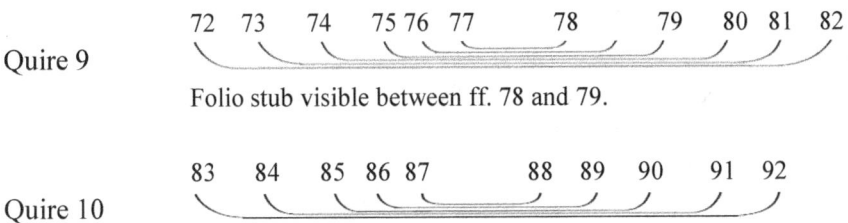

Quire 9

Folio stub visible between ff. 78 and 79.

Quire 10

MYS 47 – EMIP 647
Acts of Saint George, ገድለ፡ ጊዮርጊስ፡, Miracles of Saint George, ተአምረ፡ ጊዮርጊስ፡

Parchment, 293 x 230 x 87 mm, four Coptic chain stitches attached with bridle attachments apparently to rough-hewn boards of the traditional wood, protection sheet + 14 full quires, ii + 109 folios, top margin 25 mm, bottom margin 55–60 mm, fore edge margin 28 mm, gutter margin 10 mm, ff. 1r–108v two columns, 26–27 lines, Gəʽəz, twentieth century.

Quire descriptions: protection sheet and quires 1–4, 6–10 and 12–13 balanced; quires 5, 11 and 14 adjusted balanced.

Major Works:
1. Ff. 1r–47r: Acts of Saint George, *Gädlä Giyorgis*, ገድለ፡ ጊዮርጊስ፡. arranged for some of the months: Ḥamle (f. 14r), Mäskäräm (f. 21r), and Ṭərr (f. 37v).

   በስመ ፡ አብ ፡ ወወልድ ፡ . . . ድርሳን ፡ ዘደረሰ ፡ አብ ፡ ብፁዕ ፡ ወክቡር ፡ አባ ፡ ቴዎደስዮስ ፡ ኤጲስ ፡ ቆጶስ ፡ ዘዐንቆራ ፡ እምአድያመ ፡ ገብላት ፡ በዕለት ፡ ተዝካሩ ፡ ለፀሐየ ፡ ጽድቅ ፡ ክቡር ፡ ኮከበ ፡ ጽባሕ ፡ ብሩህ ፡ ወዕዱል ፡ ኃይሎሙ ፡ ለገድላውያን ፡ ፈረሳዊ ፡ እንተ ፡ ክርስቶስ ፡ ንጉሥ ፡ ግሩም ፡ ኃያል ፡ መዋዒ ፡ ትሩፈ ፡ ገድል ፡ ቅዱስ ፡ ማር ፡ ጊዮርጊስ ፡ ሰማዕት ፡ እምሱብእ ፡ ልዳ ፡ ወእምአድያም ፡ ፍልስጥኤም ፡ . . .

2. Ff. 49r–108v: Seventy-Nine Miracles of Saint George, *Täʽammärä Giyorgis*, ተአምረ፡ ጊዮርጊስ፡. Victor Arras, *Miraculorum S. Georgii Megalomartyris collectio altera*, CSCO 138; SA 31 (1953); E. A. Wallis Budge, *George of Lydda* (London, 1930).

   በስመ ፡ አብ ፡ ወወልድ ፡ . . . ንጽሐፍ ፡ ኃይለ ፡ ወተአምረ ፡ ዘገብረ ፡ እግዚአብሔር ፡ ለስማዕት ፡ ቅዱስ ፡ ጊዮርጊስ ፡ እምድኅረ ፡ ፈጸመ ፡ ስምዑ ፡ ወአጽኡ ፡ ሥጋሁ ፡ ውስት ፡ ልዳ ፡ ወሐነፁ ፡ ቤተ ፡ ክርስቲያን ፡ ወአንበሩ ፡ ሥጋሁ ፡ ቅዱስ ፡ ውስቴታ ፡ ወቀደሰዋ ፡ አመ ፡ ፪ ፡ ለወርኃ ፡ ኅዳር ፡ ወቀደሰ ፡ አባ ፡ ቴዎፍሎስ ፡ ሊቀ ፡ ጳጳሳት ፡

ወኤጲስ ፡ ቆጰሳት ፡ በዝንቱ ፡ ኃይል ፡ ወተአምር ፡ ወስብሐት ፡ ዘአርኃየ ፡
እግዚአብሔር ፡ እግዚእ ፡ ለሰማዕት ፡ . . .

Notes:
1. Ff. i r(ecto)-ii v(erso), 47v–48v and 109rv: blank.
2. Ff. 78r and *passim*: a space was left for the owner's name.
3. Decorative designs: f. 14r (line of red dots); multiple full stops are used as section dividers throughout (e.g., ff. 16v, 21r, 28v).
4. The word George is rubricated.
5. Numbered quires: quires 2–6 and 8–13 (numbered 9–14).
6. Scribal intervention: words of text are written interlinearly (ff. 1v, 11v, 24r, 29v, 41r, etc.); and lines of text are written interlinearly (ff. 39v, 49v, 51v); and in the upper margin with a symbol marking the location where the text is to be inserted (ff. 67v, col. 1); erasure markings are visible (ff. 34r, 70v); text has been removed (e.g., ff. 15r, 66v).

Quire Map

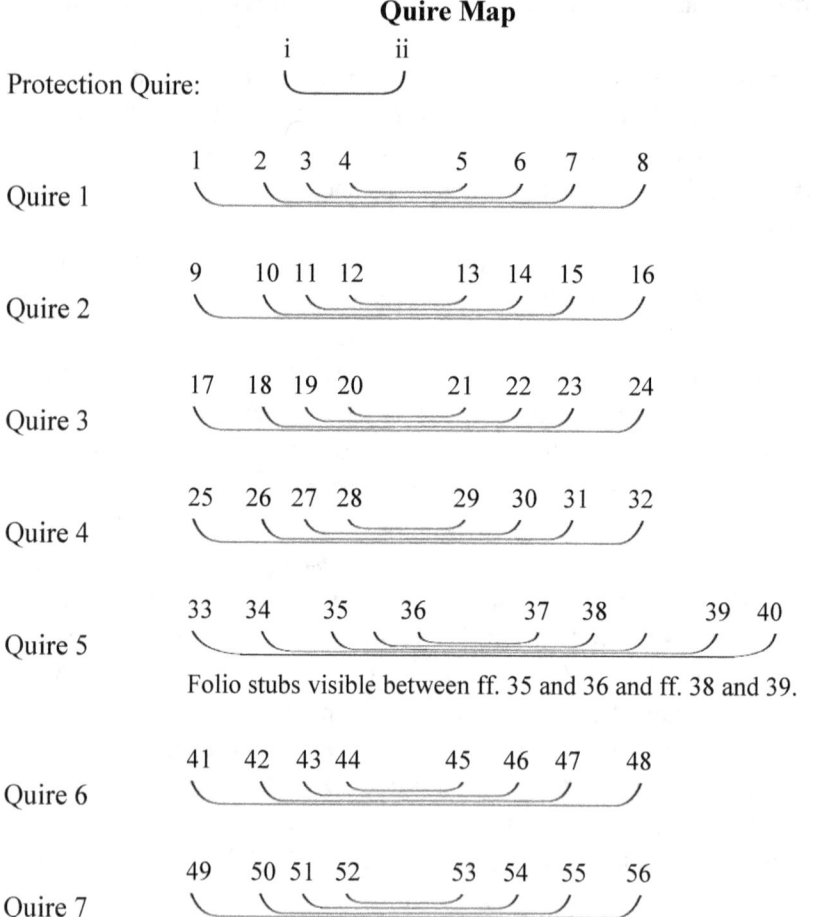

Folio stubs visible between ff. 35 and 36 and ff. 38 and 39.

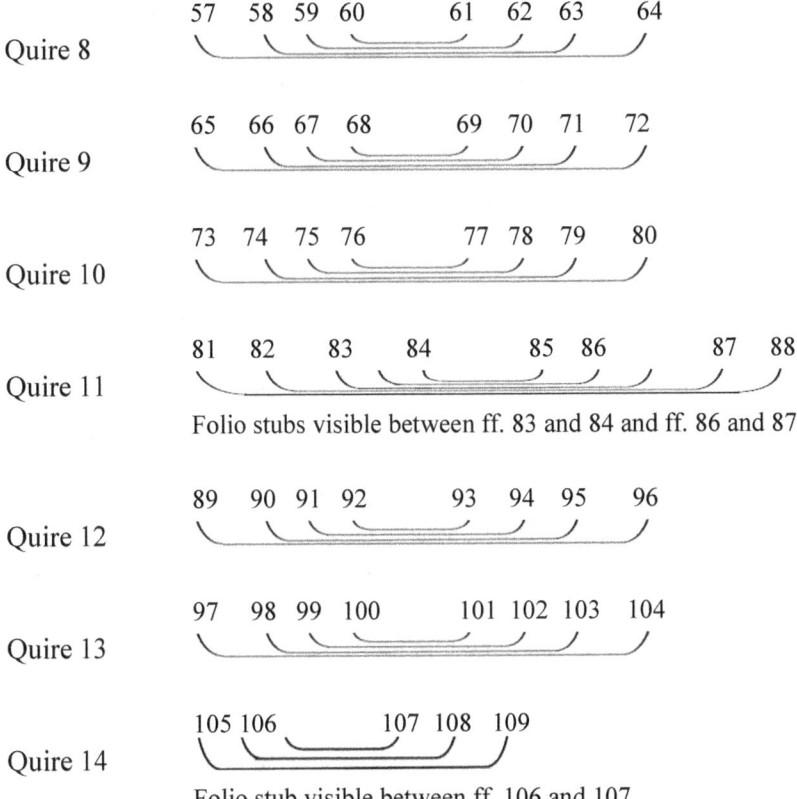

Folio stubs visible between ff. 83 and 84 and ff. 86 and 87.

Folio stub visible between ff. 106 and 107.

MYS 48 – EMIP 648
Thirty-four Miracles of Mary, ተአምረ፡ ማርያም፡, and Nine Miracles of Jesus, ተአምረ፡ ኢየሱስ፡

Parchment, 247 x 185 x 38 mm, four Coptic chain stitches attached with bridle attachments to rough-hewn boards of the traditional wood, protection sheet + 7 full quires, ii + 50 folios, top margin 25 mm, bottom margin 55 mm, fore edge margin 30 mm, gutter margin 10 mm, ff. 1r–48v two columns, 21 lines, Gəʽəz, twentieth century.

Quire descriptions: protection sheet and quires 1–3, 5 and 7 balanced; quires 4 and 6 adjusted balanced.

Major Works:
1. Ff. 1r–31v: Miracles of Mary, *Täʽammərä Maryam*, ተአምረ፡ ማርያም፡. The standard works on the miracles of Mary are Cerulli, *Maria*, and Budge, *Mary*.

a. Ff. 1r–4v: Extended version of Introductory Rite from *Mu_allaqa*. Cf. Budge, *Mary* xlvi-liv.
b. Ff. 4v–31v: Thirty-four Miracles of Mary.
   1. Ff. 4v–5v: How the Virgin Mary spoke from her picture to a devout worshipper and said to him, "Blessed art thou among men" (Budge, II; MYS 1, f. 171v; Princeton 20, ff. 41v–42r; Princeton 23, ff. 28v–29v; Princeton 41, ff. 54v; Princeton 43, ff. 8rv; Princeton 46, ff. 10v–11r).
   2. Ff. 5v–6v: How an aged Jew of Akhmim, who had spent his whole life in ministering in a church of the Virgin Mary, fell down one day during the service and broke his back, and how the Virgin Mary touched his backbone and made it whole, and made him to stand by her on the right-hand side of the altar (Budge, III; MYS 1, ff. 6v–7r).
   3. Ff. 6v–7r: How the scribe Damianus used to write the name of the Virgin Mary in gold and colored paints, and how the Virgin appeared to him when dying, and took his soul to Paradise and showed him his name inscribed upon a pillar of gold (Budge, IV; MYS 1, ff. 7rv; Princeton Ethiopic MS 41, ff. 55v–56r)
   4. Ff. 7r–8r: How [Abbas,] Bishop of Rome, cut off his hand which had been kissed by a woman when he was celebrating the Eucharist, and how the Virgin Mary rejoined it to his arm (Budge, V; MYS 1, ff. 7v–8r; Princeton Ethiopic MS 41, ff. 55rv).
   5. Ff. 8rv: How two women called Juliana and Barbara, went on a pilgrimage to Jerusalem, were attached by robbers who stole their provisions; and how, when the thieves tried to eat them, the Virgin Mary turned the bread into stones upon which the thieves broke their teeth; and how the thieves repented and restored twofold what they had stolen from the women, when the Virgin Mary had healed their wounded mouths and mended their broken teeth (Budge, XI; MYS 1, ff. 11rv; Princeton Ethiopic MS 41, ff. 60v–61r).
   6. Ff. 8v–9v: How three Arabs set sail for Rif, and were overtaken by a storm which sank their boat and hurled them into the water; how two of them appealed to the Virgin Mary for help, and were saved by her, whilst the third, who jeered at their prayers and called upon Muhammad the Prophet,

was swallowed up by a crocodile; and how the men who were saved paid their vow and sent a camel-load of dates to the Monastery of Kalman, where there was a church dedicated to the Virgin Mary (Budge, XII; MYS 1, ff. 11v–12r; Princeton Ethiopic MS 41, ff. 61r–62r).

7. Ff. 9v–10v: How the Virgin Mary removed a Monastery near Jericho from the site on which it had been built in the desert to the side of a running stream; and how the removal was effected by night whilst the monks were sleeping (Budge, XIII; MYS 1, ff. 12rv; Princeton Ethiopic MS 41, ff. 62rv).

8. Ff. 10v–11r: How the Virgin delivered from devils the soul of a scribe who was engaged in writing a copy of the Book of her Miracles. This scribe had a brother who had sinned, but not knowing him they seized the innocent man and tried to carry him off to hell (Budge, XVIII; MYS 1, f. 15r Princeton Ethiopic MS 41, ff. 66v–67v).

9. Ff. 11r–12r: How the Virgin Mary delivered from prison a certain man called ―George the New" who had been condemned to suffer by the judges, and how she healed the wound in his head which had been inflicted by those who beat him (Budge, XIX; MYS 1, ff.15rv; Princeton Ethiopic MS 41, ff. 67v–68r).

10. Ff. 12rv: How the Virgin Mary cleansed Bishop Mercurius of his leprosy by touching his body with her hand (Budge, XXIII; MYS 1, ff. 17rv; Princeton Ethiopic MS 41, ff. 70v–71r).

11. Ff. 12v–13v: How the Virgin Mary used to appear in person in the church at Ḥärtärom, and how she healed the broken foot of a woman therein (Budge, XXIV; MYS 1, ff. 17v–18r; Princeton Ethiopic MS 41, ff. 73v–74v).

12. Ff. 13v–14v: How the Virgin Mary received the soul of Barok, a dissolute man who worshipped her, and took it to Paradise (Budge, XXVI; MYS 1, ff. 19rv; Princeton Ethiopic MS 41, ff. 85v–86v).

13. Ff. 14v–15v: How the Virgin Mary received the soul of Anastasius, a deacon of Rome, who addressed the ―Five Gaudes" to her at all times, and took it to Paradise (Budge,

XXVII; MYS 1, ff. 19v–20r; Princeton Ethiopic MS 41, ff. 84r–85r).

14. Ff. 15v–16r: How a certain man used to put fifty roses on the icon of the Virgin Mary and how, when roses were out of season he would recite fifty Hail Mary's instead; and how fifty roses sprang from his grave three months after he died with their roots springing from his heart (MYS 1, f. 161r; cf. Budge, X and Princeton 8, ff. 39r–41r; Princeton 23, ff. 31r–34v; Princeton 41, ff. 59r–60v; Princeton 43, ff. 30v–32v; Princeton 46, ff. 16r–17r; Princeton 47, ff. 39r–42r).

15. Ff. 16rv: How a priest who loved his children and wife became a monk and promised to the Virgin Mary to serve her throughout his life; how he fell into sin, became mad, and, in the end, turned to the Virgin Mary to save him.

16. Ff. 16v–17r: How the Virgin Mary made a stream to reverse its course and water to run uphill in order to assist a laundry man (Budge, XXXVI; MYS 1, f. 149v; Princeton 41, f. 54r; Princeton 8, ff. 43rv).

17. Ff. 17r–18r: How the Virgin Mary appeared to a certain sick man and commanded him to stay at the gate of the church during her fasting season and how she healed him on the feast day of her assumption to heaven (MYS 1, ff. 149rv).

18. Ff. 18r–19r: How the Virgin Mary revealed a vision of the departed saints of the monastery of Asqeṭəs to the monks who were praying there (MYS 1, f. 156v; Princeton 41, ff. 155v–156r).

19. Ff. 19rv: How the Virgin Mary removed a Monastery near Jericho from the site on which it had been built in the desert to the side of a running stream; and how the removal was effected by night whilst the monks were sleeping (above ff. 9v–10v; Budge, XIII; MYS 1, ff. 12rv; Princeton Ethiopic MS 41, ff. 62rv).

20. Ff. 19v–20v: How a certain woman was bereft of her nine children; how the Virgin Mary appeared to her and promised three children who would become priests; how she conceived three children who became priests and presided at her funeral (MYS 1, ff. 24v–25r; Princeton Ethiopic MS 41, ff. 76v–77r).

21. Ff. 20v–21r: How the Virgin Mary gave food to a certain poor beggar to be able to share with a guest (MYS 1, ff. 159v–160r).
22. Ff. 21r–22r: How the Virgin Mary received the gift of a certain woman who was forbidden to fast by her husband (MYS 1, ff. 172v–173v; cf. MYS 1, ff. 148v–149r; Budge, XCIX; Princeton 20, ff. 6rv; Princeton 43, ff. 58r–61r).
23. Ff. 22r–23r: How the Virgin Mary saved a certain nun who died before she finished her penitence and how she appeared to the Abbess and told her how the Virgin Mary saved her (MYS 1, f. 174r; Princeton 20, ff. 28r–29v).
24. Ff. 23r–24r: How the Virgin Mary appeared to a certain nun and commanded her to continue reciting the Hail Mary (MYS 1, f. 31v; Princeton Ethiopic 41, ff. 96rv).
25. Ff. 24rv: How the Virgin Mary saved a certain man from being killed by his enemies, until he had confessed his sins to a priest.
26. Ff. 24v–26r: How the Virgin Mary appeared a certain deacon who was sick and how she took him into paradise (MYS 1, ff. 87rv; Princeton Ethiopic 8, ff. 14v–17v).
27. Ff. 26r–27r: How the Virgin Mary saved the soul of an evil, wealthy man who had gained his wealth by taking the property of other people, but who nonetheless was devoted to the Virgin Mary; how the Virgin Mary appeared to the wife of this man and commanded her to commemorate her feast days.
28. Ff. 27r–28r: How the Virgin Mary saved the robber's soul from judgment because he drank from water that sprang from her feet (MYS 1, ff. 146rv; Princeton 20, ff. 5rv).
29. Ff. 28rv: How the Virgin Mary appeared to the abbot of Asqetəs when he was afraid of demons (MYS 1, ff. 83rv).
30. Ff. 28v–29v: How the Virgin Mary appeared to a monk and promised to take his soul to Paradise after three days (cf. MYS 1, ff. 87rv; Princeton Ethiopic 8, ff. 14v–17v; and cf. MYS 1, ff. 171v–172r; Budge, XXVII; Princeton 20, ff. 81rv; Princeton 41, ff. 84r–85r; Princeton 43, ff. 6v–8r; Princeton 43, ff. 50v–51v; Princeton 46, ff. 27v–28r; Princeton 47, ff. 80v–81r).

31. F. 29v: How the Virgin Mary appeared to an adulterous woman who was in prison awaiting her punishment by stoning, incomplete at the end (a folio or a full sheet appears to be missing).
32. F. 30r: an unknown Miracle of Mary, incomplete at the beginning (only six lines are visible). It is possible that these are the final lines of the miracle that begins on f. 29v.
33. Ff. 30r–31r: How the Virgin Mary described to Anthony of Q^{w}usq^{w}am the future glory of that place (cf. MYS 1, f. 83v; Princeton Ethiopic 20, ff. 85v–86v; Princeton Ethiopic 46, ff. 49v–50v).
34. Ff. 31rv: Ff. 83v–84r: How the Virgin Mary blessed the Monastery of Q^{w}usq^{w}am with its people and animals and how she anointed them again (MYS 1, ff. 83v–84r and the references in the miracle just above).

2. Ff. 33r–48v: Nine Miracles of Jesus, *Tä'ammərä Iyyäsus*, ተአምረ፡ ኢየሱስ፡. Stefan Strelcyn, *Catalogue of Ethiopian Manuscripts in the British Library* (London: British Library, 1978) 19–21, entry 16 = Or. 8824; S. Grébaut, *Les Miracles de Jésus*, PO 12.4 (Paris, 1919); and M. Chaîne, *Liber Nativitatis Mariae*, in CSCO 1.7 (Paris, 1909), 13–16.

   a. Ff. 33r–35r: First Miracle: On the conception of Jesus: 1) how Mary was presented to the temple; 2) the Annunciation; 3) how Jesus was conceived and how Mary was subjected to the ancient Israelites' test of the Water of the Curse (Grébaut, *Miracles of Jesus*, I:577–583; EMML 2180, f. 16a; EMIP 347, ff. 4r–9v).
   b. Ff. 35r–37r: Second Miracle: On the Virginity of Mary: 1) The birth of Jesus; 2) how the hand of the midwife Salome was completely dry; 3) how Mary cured the hand of Salome by putting the hand of Jesus on Solome's hand, 4) how Jesus declared that his mother was the Virgin predicted by Isaiah (Grébaut, *Miracles of Jesus*, I:583–589; EMML 2180, f. 26a; EMIP 347, ff. 9v–11r).
   c. Ff. 37r–38r: Third Miracle: On the Baptism of Jesus (cf. EMML 2180, f. 85b; Grébaut, Jésus III, 841ff; EMIP 347, ff. 42v–44r).
   d. Ff. 38r–39v: Fourth Miracle: The wedding at Cana of Galilee (EMML 2180, f. 90b; EMIP 347, ff. 45v–46r).

e. Ff. 40r–41r: Fifth Miracle: Jesus' comments on his second coming.
f. Ff. 41r–43v: Sixth Miracle: Jesus' triumphal Entry into Jerusalem on the donkey and how the children of Jerusalem praised him when they saw light on him; how the Jews became angry because of the praise of the children and how Jesus rebuked them.
g. Ff. 44r–45v: Seventh Miracle: The Crucifixion of Jesus; how he was crucified and how the soldier thrust a spear into his side; how Joseph of Arimathea requested the body from Pilate and how Joseph and Nicodemus prepared the body for burial.
h. Ff. 45v–47r: Eighth Miracle: The Resurrection: How Christ rose from the dead and how many others were raised and went to Jerusalem and preached about Jesus Christ (EMML 2180, f. 144a; EMIP 347, ff. 78v–79v).
i. Ff. 47r–48v: Ninth Miracle: The Ascension: How Jesus gathered the disciples at Däbrä Zäyt, promised the Holy Spirit and ascended to heaven (cf. EMML 2180, f. 159b).

Notes:
1. Ff. i r(ecto)-ii v(erso), 32rv and 49r–50v: blank.
2. Decorative designs: ff. 3v, 12v, 31r, 37r, 38r (multiple full stops), f. 48v (line of alternating red and black dots).
3. The words Mary and Jesus Christ are rubricated.

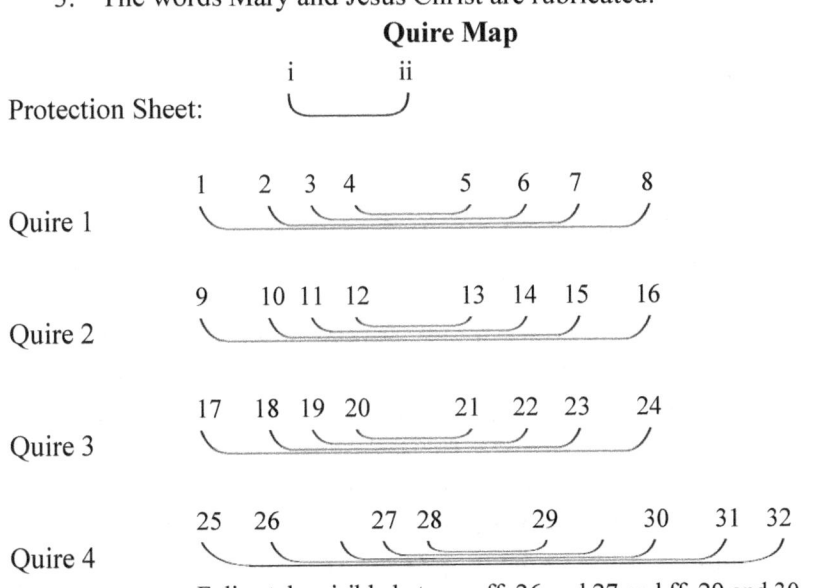

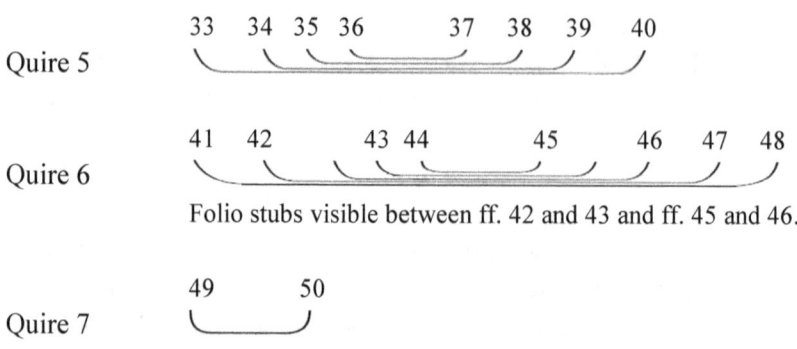

Folio stubs visible between ff. 42 and 43 and ff. 45 and 46.

MYS 49 – EMIP 649
Andemta Commentary on the Epistles of Paul, ትርጓሜ፡ ጳውሎስ፡, Notes on the Stars, On the Life of Jesus, in Amharic

Paper, 214 x 168 x 54 mm, four Coptic chain stitches attached with bridle attachments to pieces of plywood, protection quire + 14 full quires, x + 424 folios, top margin 12 mm, bottom margin 22 mm, fore edge margin 10 mm, gutter margin 12 mm, ff. 1r–408r two columns, 21 lines, Amharic, twentieth century.

Quire descriptions: protection quire and quires 1–14 balanced.

Major Works:

Ff. 1r–406r: Andemta Commentary on the Epistles of Paul, Yä-Qəddus *Pawəlos Mäṣəḥaf Nəbabu Känätərg^wamew*, የቅዱስ፡ ጳውሎስ፡ መጽሐፍ፡ ንባቡ፡ ከነትርጓሜው፡. See, የቅዱስ፡ ጳውሎስ፡ መጽሐፍ፡ ንባቡ፡ ከነትርጓሜው፡, *Book of Saint Paul: Text with its Commentary* (Addis Ababa: Tənśa'e zä-Guba'e Publishing House, second edtion, 1988 EC).

1. Ff. 1r–95v: Romans
    a. Ff. 1r–10v: Introduction
    መልእክት ፡ ቀዳማዊ ፡ ንበ ፡ ሰብአ ፡ ሮሜ ፡ ይች ፡ ሀገር ፡ ቅድመ ፡ ማየ ፡ አይን ፡ አርስጣሚሊስ ፡ ትባል ፡ ነበረ ፡ በሕላ ፡ ውሉደ ፡ ከይተም ፡ ቢሰፍሩባት ፡ ከይተም ፡ ተብላላች ።። ቀጥሎ ፡ እንጋሉስ ፡ የሚባል ፡ ነገሠባት ፡ በእንጋሉስ ፡ አጥልያ ፡ ተብላች ፡ ቀጥሎ ፡ ሮምሉስ ፡ ሮማኖስ ፡ የሚባሉ ፡ ሁለት ፡ ወንድማማች ፡ ነገሡውባታል ፡ በርምሉስ ሮም ፡ በርማኖስ ፡ ሮሜ ፡ ርምያ ፡ ተብላች ፡ . . .
    b. Ff. 10v–95v: Text and Commentary on Romans
    እምጳውሎስ ፡ ገብሩ ፡ ወሐዋርያሁ ፡ ለኢየሱስ ፡ ክርስቶስ ፡ ሳውል ፡ አላለም ፡ ጳውሎስ ፡ አለ ፡ ሳውል ፡ ማለት ፡ ዘዐውቅ ፡ ፈዳዬ ፡ ዐዳ ፡

ውሁብ ፡ ሀብት ፡ እግዚአብሔር ፡ ማለት ፡ ነው ፡ ሳውል ፡ በብሉይ ፡
የወጣለት ፡ ስሙ ፡ ነው ፡ ሳውል ፡ የተባልሁባት ፡ ሕግ ፡ አለፈች ፡
ጳውሎስ ፡ የተባልሁባት ፡ ሕግ ፡ አታልፍም ፡ ሲል ፡ ጳውሎስ ፡ አለ ፡ ...

2. Ff. 96r–174r: 1 Corinthians
   a. Ff. 96r–96v: Introduction
      በስመ ፡ አብ ፡ ወወልድ ፡ . . . ንዌጥን ፡ በረድኤተ ፡ እግዚአብሔር ፡
      ጽሒፈ ፡ ትርጓሜ ፡ መልእክታቲሁ ፡ ለጳውሎስ ፡ ረድኤተ ፡ ጸሎቱ ፡
      የሃሉ ፡ ምስሌን ፡ ለዓለም ፡ ዓለም ፡ አሜን። መልእክት ፡ ቀዳማዊ ፡
      ኀበ ፡ ሰብአ ፡ ቆሮንቶስ ፡ ሁለተኛ ፡ ይደፋልና ፡ ቀዳማዊ ፡ አለ ፡
      በመላዉ ፡ አካደያ ፡ ትባላለች ፡ ቆሮንቶስ ፡ መዲናይቱ ፡ ናት ፡
      በመቄደንያ ፡ ፊልጵስዮስ ፡ እንዳለች ፡ . . .
   b. Ff. 97r–174r: Text and Commentary on 1 Corinthians
      በፈቃደ ፡ እግዚአብሔር ፡ ጳንቺ ፡ ብገኝ ፡ ሰውን ፡ በፈቃደ ፡
      እግዚአብሔር ፡ አጻና ፡ ዘንድ ፡ ኢየሱስ ፡ ክርስቶስ ፡ ከሸመኝ ፡ ከኔ ፡
      ከጳውሎስ ፡ እሱ ፡ ሿሚ ፡ እኔ ፡ ተሿሚ ፡ ምን ፡ አገናኘተን ፡ ከሱ ፡
      ታነጻጽሩናላችሁ ፡ ለማለት ፡ እንዲህ ፡ አለ ፡ ከወንድማችን ፡
      ከሶስቴንስ ፡ የተላከ ፡ በጽሑፈት ፡ በድርስት ፡ አግዞት ፡ አይደለም ፡
      ስለ ፡ ትሕትና ፡ ያነሳዋል ፡ እንጂ ፡ . . .

3. Ff. 174r–212r: 2 Corinthians.
   a. Ff. 174rv: Introduction
      ሁለተኛ ፡ ይጽፍላቸዋል ፡ በፊልጵስዮስ ፡ ሁኖ ፡ ቲቶን ፡ ጠይቀሃቸው ፡
      ና ፡ ብሎ ፡ ላከው ፡ እነ ፡ ዘጳውሎስ ፡ እነ ፡ ዘአጵሎስ ፡ እነ ፡ ዘኬፋ ፡
      ማለትን ፡ ትተው ፡ እነ ፡ ዘክርስቶስ ፡ ሲሉ ፡ ያባቱን ፡ ሚስት ፡
      የቀማውን ፡ የመምሩን ፡ ሹመት ፡ የወሰደውን ፡ ለይተው ፡ ለአስተዋጽኦ ፡
      ሲተጉ ፡ ለምግባር ፡ ለትሩፋት ፡ ሲፈካከሩ ፡ አግኝቷቸዋል ፡ . . .
   b. Ff. 174v–212r: Text and Commentary on 2 Corinthians
      ቸር ፡ አላችሁ፤ የጌታችን ፡ የኢየሱስ ፡ ክርስቶስ ፡ ጸጋው ፡
      ይደረግላችሁ ፡ የፍሕም ፡ ተስፋው ፡ ባሌቤት ፡ ልጅ ፡ ከአባቱ ፡
      እንዲገን ፡ ምህረትም ፡ ከእርሱ ፡ ትገኝለች ፡ የጌታችን ፡ የኢየሱስ ፡
      የባህርይ ፡ አባቱ ፡ እግዚአብሔር ፡ አብ ፡ ይክበር ፡ ይመስገን ፡ . . .

4. Ff. 212r–232v: Galatians.
   a. Ff. 212r–213r: Introduction
      ገላትያ ፡ ምድረ ፡ ጽርዕ ፡ ናት ፡ ቁጽሯ ፡ ግን ፡ ከጌቱ ፡ ዮናናውያን ፡
      አይደለም ፡ ቅዱስ ፡ ጳውሎስ ፡ ከዚህ ፡ ገብቶ ፡ ጌታ ፡ ከእንስ ፡
      ጀምሮ ፡ ያደረገውን ፡ ተአምራት ፡ ያስተማረውን ፡ ትምህርት ፡
      የሰራውን ፡ ምግባር ፡ ትሩፋት ፡ አስተማራቸው ፡ . . .
   b. Ff. 213r–232v: Text and Commentary on Galatians
      ቸር ፡ አላችሁ፤ የባታችን ፡ የእግዚአብሔር ፡ አብ ፡ የጌታችን ፡
      የኢየሱስ ፡ ክርስቶስ ፡ ጸጋው ፡ ይደረግላችሁ፤ የኛን ፡ ኃጢአት ፡

ማስተሥረይ ፡ ራሱን ፡ ለሕማም ፡ ለሞት ፡ አሳልፎ ፡ የሰጠ፤ በፍቅረ ፡ ንዋይ ፡ ከሚቃወም ፡ ከፈቃደ ፡ ሥጋ ፡ በፈ ፡ (በፈቃደ ፡ ከሚቃወም ፡) ከፈቃደ ፡ ሰይጣን ፡ ያድነን ፡ ዘንድ ፡ ባዐታችን ፡ በእግዚአብሔር ፡ አብ ፡ ፈቃድ ፡ . . .

5. Ff. 232v–251v: Ephesians. Siegbert Uhlig and Helge Maehlum, *Novum Testamentum aethiopice: die Gefangenschaftsbriefe*, AF 33 (Stuttgart: Franz Steiner Verlag, 1993).
   a. Ff. 232v–233r: Introduction
   መልእክት ፡ ገበ ፡ ሰብአ ፡ ኤፌሶን ፡ ኤፌሶን ፡ ምድረ ፡ ጽርዕ ፡ ናት ፡ ቁጽራም ፡ ከጃ ፡ ዮናናውያን ፡ ነው ፤ ቅዱስ ፡ ጳውሎስ ፡ ከዚሀ ፡ ገብቶ ፡ ጌታ ፡ ያደረገውን ፡ ተአምራት ፡ ያስተማረውን ፡ ትምህት ፡ ያሰራውን ፡ ግምባር ፡ ትሩፋት ፡ አስተማራቸው ፡ ከአምልኮተ ፡ ጣዖት ፡ ወደ ፡ አምልኮተ ፡ እግዚአብሔር ፡ ከገቢረ ፡ ኃጢአት ፡ ወደ ፡ ገቢረ ጽድቅ ፡ ተመለሱ ፡ አመኑ ፡ ተጠመቁ ፡ . . .
   b. Ff. 233r–251v: Text and Commentary on Ephesians
   በፈቃደ ፡ እግዚአብሔር ፡ ጸንቼ ፡ ብገኝ ፡ ሰውን ፡ በፈቃደ ፡ እግዚአብሔር ፡ አጸና ፡ ዘንድ ፡ ኢየሱስ ፡ ስክርስቶስ ፡ ከሾመኝ ፡ ከኔ ፡ ለሱ ፡ አካል ፡ ሕዋስ ፡ ብልት ፡ ማህደር ፡ ቤተ ፡ ሰብእ ፡ እሆን ፡ ዘንድ ፡ ዘንድ ፡ አለም ፡ ሳይፈ(ጠ)ር ፡ እንደመረጠን ፡ መጠን፤ ዘባረከን ፡ ቦ ፡ ስርስቱ ፡ ለጉልቱ ፡ ከጸውሎስ ፡ . . .

6. Ff. 251v–264r: Philippians. Siegbert Uhlig and Helge Maehlum, *Novum Testamentum aethiopice: die Gefangenschaftsbriefe*, AF 33 (Stuttgart: Franz Steiner Verlag, 1993).
   a. Ff. 251v–252r: Introduction
   መልእክት ፡ ገበ ፡ ሰብአ ፡ ፊልጽስዩስ ፡ ፊልጽስዮስ ፡ በመቄደንያ ፡ ውስጥ ፡ ያለች ፡ አገር ፡ ናት ፤ በአካይ ፡ ቆርንቶስ ፡ እንዳለች ፡ ቅዱስ ፡ ጳውሎስ ፡ ከዚሀ ፡ ገብቶ ፡ ብለህ ፡ እንዳለፈው ፡ ተርክ ፡ . . .
   b. Ff. 252r–264r: Text and Commentary on Philippians
   የክርስቶስ ፡ ተገዥ ፡ ከምሆን ፡ ከኔ ፡ ከጸውሎስ ፡ ከጢሞቴዎስ ፡ የተላክ ፡ በጽፈትም ፡ በድር ፡ እግ ፡ ያይደለ ፡ ለኩሉ ፡ ቅዱሳን ፡ በክርስቶስ ፡ አምነው ፡ ከኢአማንያን ፡ ለተለዩ ፡ ከኃጢአት ፡ ለነጹ ፡ ከንደት ፡ ለከበሩ ፡ ንውዳን ፡ ክቡራን ፡ ለሚሆኑ ፡ በፈልጽስዮስ ፡ ላሉ ፡ ለምዕመናን ፡ . . .

7. Ff. 264v–275v: Colossians. Siegbert Uhlig and Helge Maehlum, *Novum Testamentum aethiopice: die Gefangenschaftsbriefe*, AF 33 (Stuttgart: Franz Steiner Verlag, 1993).
   a. Ff. 264v–265r: Introduction
   መልእክት ፡ ገበ ፡ ሰብአ ፡ ቄላስይስ፤ ቄላስይስ ፡ በመቄደንያ ፡ ፊልጽስዩስ ፡ ባጠገብ ፡ ያለች ፡ አገር ፡ ናት፤ በጐደር ፡ ባጠገብ ፡

እንፍራንዝ ፤ እንዳለች፤ ቅዱስ ፡ ጳውሎስ ፡ ከዚሀ ፡ አልገባም፤ ኢጻፍራስን ፡ ጂሞ ፡ ሰደላቸዋል ፡ እሱ ፡ ከዚሀ ፡ ገብቶ ፡ ጌታ ፡ ከዕን ፡ ሰ ፡ ጅምር ፡ ያደረገውን ፡ ተአምራት ፡ ያስተማረውን ፡ ትምህርት ፡ የሰራውን ፡ ምግባር ፡ ትሩፋት ፡ አስተማራቸው ፡ . . .

   b. Ff. 265r–275v: Text and Commentary on Colossians

በፈቃደ ፡ እግዚአብሔር ፡ ጸንቼ ፡ ብገኝ ፡ ሰውን ፡ በፈቃደ ፡ እግዚአብሔር ፡ አጸና ፡ ዘንድ ፡ ኢየሱስ ፡ ክርስቶስ ፡ ከሸመኛ ፡ ከኔ ፡ ከጳውሎስ ፡ የተላከ ፤ ሐተታ ፡ እንዳለፈው ፤ በክርስቶስ ፡ በቄላስይስ ፡ ላሉ ፡ ንዑዳን ፡ ክቡራን ፡ ለሚሆኑ ፡ ለወንድሞቻችን ፡ ይድረሳቸው ፡ ነአኮቶ ፡ ዘልፈ ፡ በናንት ፡ ምክንያት ፡ የጌታችን ፡ የኢየሱስ ፡ ክርስቶስ ፡ የባሕርይ ፡ አባቱን ፡ እግዚአብሔርን ፡ እናመሰግነዋለን ፡...

8. Ff. 275v–276v: Notes on the Stars in their courses through the seasons.

ለከዋክብትም፡ አስገዛቸው፤ ማነን፡ ቢሉ፡ ዓመቱን፡ ፬፡ አድርጎ፡ አስገዛቸው፤ ይህስ፡ እንደምን፡ ነው፡ ቢሉ፡ ፬፡ ሊቃነ፡ ከዋክብት፡ አሉ፡ . . .

9. Ff. 276v–286v: Continuation of Commentary on Epistles of Paul: 1 Thessalonians.

   a. Ff. 276v–277r: Introduction

ይች ፡ ተሰሎንቄ ፡ በመቄደንያ ፡ በፊልጵስዩስና ፡ በአካይያ ፡ ቆሮንቶስ ፡ መካከል ፡ ያለች ፡ ሀገር ፡ ናት ፡ አሪንጊና ፡ ቢፀባባ ፡ መካከል ፡ ደራ ፡ እንዳለ ፡ ቅዱስ ፡ ጳውሎስ ፡ ከዚሀ ፡ ገብቶስ ፡ ጌታ ፡ ከዕንስ ፡ ጅምር ፡ ያደረገውን ፡ ተአምራት ፡ ፈጽሞ ፡ ቢነግራቸው ፡ እኩሌቶቹ ፡ አምነዋል ፡ እኩሌቶቹ ፡ አናምንም ፡ ብለዋል ፡ ያላመኑት ፡ የሚጣሉት ፡ ቢሆን ፡ ያመኑት ፡ በሌሊት ፡ አውጥተው ፡ ሰደውታል ፡ ቢርያ ፡ ገብቶ ፡ ያስተምር ፡ ጀመረ ፡ . . .

   b. Ff. 277r–286v: Text and Commentary on 1 Thessalonians

ከኔ ፡ ጳውሎስ ፡ ከጢሞቴዎስ ፡ ከስልዋኖስ ፡ የተላከ ፡ ባባታችን ፡ በእግዚአብሔር ፡ አብ ፡ በጌታችን ፡ በኢየሱስ ፡ ክርስቶስ ፡ አምነው ፡ በተሰሎንቄ ፡ ላሉ ፡ ምዕመናን ፡ ይድረሳቸው ፤ በጽሕፈት ፡ በድርስት ፡ አግዛውት ፡ አይደለም ፡ ስለ ፡ ትሕትና ፡ ያነሣላቸዋል ፡ እንጂ ፤ ቸር ፡ አላችሁ ፤ . . .

10. Ff. 286v–291v: 2 Thessalonians.

   a. Ff. 286v–287r: Introduction

መልእክት ፡ ካልዕት ፡ ኀበ ፡ ሰብአ ፡ ተሰሎንቄ ፡ ሁለተኛ ፡ ይጽፍላቸዋል ፤ በቀዳማዊ ፡ ተሰሎንቄ ፡ ንሕነ ፡ ሕያዋን ፡ እለ ፡ ንተርፍ ፡ ኢ.ንበጽሐሙ ፡ ለምውታን ፡ ሲል ፡ ስምተው ፡ ምጽአት ፡ በጳውሎስ ፡ ዘመን ፡ ይደርጋል ፡ ብለዋል፤ ስለዚሀ ፡ ይጽፋል፡...

   b. Ff. 287r–291v: Text and Commentary on 2 Thessalonians

ከጵውሉስ ፡ ከጢሞቴ ፡ ከሰልዋ ፡ የተላከ ፡ ክታብ ፡ ባባታችን ፡ በአግ
አብ ፡ በጌታችን ፡ በኢ ፡ ክር ፡ አምነው ፡ በተሰሉንቄ ፡ ላሉ ፡ ምዕ
ትድረስ ፡ የቀረውን ፡ እንዳለፈው ፡ በል ፤ ወንድሞቻችን ፡ በናንት ፡
ምክንያት ፡ እግዚአብሔርን ፡ . . .

11. Ff. 292r–306r: 1 Timothy.
   a. Ff. 292rv: Introduction
      መልእክት ፡ ጳውሉስ ፡ ቀዳማዊ ፡ ኀበ ፡ ጢሞቴዎስ ፡ ይህ ፡
      ጢሞቴዎስ ፡ አባቱ ፡ አረማዊ ፡ ነው ፤ ወአቡሁስ ፡ አረማዊ ፡ ውእቱ ፡
      እንዲል ፤ እናቱ ፡ ግን ፡ ጥንቱንም ፡ አይሁዳዊት ፡ ናት ፤ ነበረች ፤
      በሗላም ፡ በጳውሉስ ፡ ስብከት ፡ አምናለች ፤ ተጠምቃለች፤ ወእሙሰ ፡
      አይሁዳዊት ፡ ወአምነት ፡ እንዲ ፤ ሀገሩ ፡ ልስጥራን ፡ ነው ፤ . . .
   b. Ff. 292v–306r: Text and Commentary on 1 Timothy
      መድኃኒታችን ፡ እግዚአብሔር ፡ ተስፋችን ፡ ኢየሱስ ፡ ክርስቶስ ፡
      ሐሩ ፡ ወመሐሩ ፡ ባለው ፡ ትእዛዝ ፡ ቦ ፡ በትእዛዘ ፡ እግዚአብ ፡
      ኢየሱስ ፡ ክርስ ፡ መድኃኒ ፡ ወተስፋን ፡ መድኃኒታችን ፡ ተስፋችን ፡
      እግዚ ፡ ኢየሱ ፡ ክር ፡ ሐሩ ፡ ወመሐሩ ፡ ባለው ፤ ትእዛዝ ፡ ኢየሱስ ፡
      ክር ፡ ከሾመኝ ፡ ከኔ ፡ ከጳውሉስ ፡ የተላከ ፡ ክታብ፡...

12. Ff. 306r–315v: 2 Timothy.
   a. Ff. 306rv: Introduction
      መልእክት ፡ ካልዕት ፡ ኀበ ፡ ጢሞቴዎስ ፡ ሁለተኛ ፡ ይጸፋልና ፤ ካልዕት ፡
      አለ ፤ ከዚህም ፡ ዓላውያን ፡ መክሩ ፡ አጸንተውበታል፤ መከራውን ፡
      ታግሦ ፡ ቢያስተምራቸው ፡ ምዕመናን ፡ ልባቸው ፡ ፈዘ ፡ ጆራቸው ፡
      ደንዝዞ ፡ ትምህርቱን ፡ አንቀበለውም ፡ ብለዋል፤ እኔ ፡ ምን ፡ አግደኝ ፡
      ጌታ ፡ በወንጌል ፡ አስመ ፡ ውስተ ፡ ቤተ ፡ አቡየ ፡ ብዙኃ ፡ ማኀደር ፡
      ወምዕራፍ ፡ ቦቱ ፡ ይላል ፡ በመምርነት ፡ መግባት ፡ ቢቀርብኝ ፡
      በተባህትም ፡ እገባለሁ ፡ . . .
   b. Ff. 306v–315v: Text and Commentary on 2 Timothy
      በፈቃደ ፡ እግዚአብሔር ፡ በኢየሱስ ፡ ክርስቶስ ፡ በሚሆን ፡ ደንነት ፡
      አለኝታ ፡ ጸንቼ ፡ ብገኝ ፡ ሰውን ፡ በፈቃደ ፡ እግ ፡ አጸናለት ፡ ዘንድ፤
      ኢየሱስ ፡ ክርስቶስ ፡ ከሾመኝ ፡ ከኔ ፡ ከኔ ፡ ከጳውሉስ ፡ የተላከ ፡
      ክታብ ፡ በሃይማ ፡ ጸንቶ ፡ ምግባር ፡ ትሩ ፡ ሲሰራ ፡ ቢገኝ ፡
      ለምወደው ፡ ለምወልደው ፡ ልጄ ፡ ለጢሞቴዎስ ፡ ይድረስለት ፡
      የቀረውን ፡ እንዳለፈው ፡ . . .

13. Ff. 315v–321r: Titus.
   a. Ff. 315v–316r: Introduction
      መልእክት ፡ ኀበ ፡ ቲቶ ፡ ይህ ፡ ቲቶ ፡ ሀገሩ ፡ ቀርጤስ ፡ ነው ፡
      ዓረማዊ ፡ ነው ፤ ቅዱስ ፡ ጳውሉስ ፡ ሲያስተምር ፡ ከዚህ ፡ ደረስ ፡ በገ ፡
      ብላቴንቱን ፡ አይቶ ፡ እንዲያሳው ፡ እንዲፈጸምለት ፡ አውቆ ፡
      አስክትሎታል ፤ ሲያስክትለውም ፡ ሳይገዝር ፡ አስክትሎታል ፤ ወቲቶስ ፡

ዘምስሌያ ፡ እንዝ ፡ አረማዊ ፡ ውእቱ ፡ ኢያገበርክዎ ፡ ይትገዘር ፡ እንዲል ፡ . . .

b. Ff. 316r–321r: Text and Commentary on Titus

ኢየሱስ ፡ ክርስቶስ ፡ ከሾመኝ ፡ የኢየሱስ ፡ ክርስቶስ ፡ ተገኘ ፡ ከምሆን ፡ ከኔ ፡ ከጳውሎስ ፡ የተላክ ፡ ክብ፤ በአብርሃም ፡ በይስሐቅ ፡ በያዕቆብ ፡ በነቢያት ፡ በሐዋርያት ፡ ሃይማኖት ፡ ጸንቼ ፡ ብገኝ ፡ በሦስትነቴ ፡ ጸንቶ ፡ ያለ ፤ነቱን ፡ ባንድነቱ ፡ ጸንቶ ፡ ያለ ፡ . . .

14. Ff. 321r–324v: Philemon. Siegbert Uhlig and Helge Maehlum, *Novum Testamentum aethiopice: die Gefangenschaftsbriefe*, AF 33 (Stuttgart: Franz Steiner Verlag, 1993).

    a. Ff. 321r–322r: Introduction

    መልእክት ፡ ኀበ ፡ ፊልሞና፤ ይህ ፡ ፊልሞና ፡ ባለጸጋ ፡ ነው ፡ በቅዱስ ፡ ጳውሎስ ፡ ስብከት ፡ አምኗል ፡ አናሲሞስ ፡ ባሪ ፡ ነበረው ፡ እርሱ ፡ ሲያምን ፡ አላመነም ፡ የአምነት ፡ ነገር ፡ ፬ ፡ ጊዜ ፡ አይሆንምና ፡ ቦ ፡ እሱ ፡ መጽቶ ፡ ስለ ፡ ለተልዕኮ ፡ ወጽቶ ፡ ነበረና ፡ ከሄደበት ፡ ገንዘብ ፡ ጠፍት ፡ የሚከፍለው ፡ አጋ ፡ ማን ፡ ባስታረቀኝ ፡ ሲል ፡ . . .

    b. Ff. 322r–324v: Text and Commentary on Philemon

    የኢየሱስ ፡ ክርስቶስ ፡ እስሩ ፡ ከምሆን ፡ ከኔ ፡ ከጳውሎስ ፡ የተላክ ፤ ከወንድማችን ፡ ከጢሞቴ ፡ የተላክ ፡ ክታብ ፤ በድርሰት ፡ በጽሕፈት ፡ አግዞት ፡ አይደለም ፤ ስለ ፡ ትሕትና ፡ ያነሣዋል ፡ እንጂ ፤ በስራ ፡ . . .

15. Ff. 324v–405v: Hebrews.

    a. Ff. 324v–327r: Introduction

    መልእክት ፡ ኀበ ፡ ዕብራውያን ፤ ዕብራውያን ፡ ማለት ፡ ፈላስያን ፡ ማለት ፡ ነው ፡ አባቶቻቸው ፡ ከከላውዴዎን ፡ ወደካራን ፡ ከካራን ፡ ወደከነዓን ፡ ፈልሰዋልና ፡ ቦ ፡ ዓዳውያን ፡ ፈልግ ፡ ማለት ፡ ነው ፡ አባቶቻቸው ፡ ገብሩን ፡ ፈርሩን ፡ ተሻግረው ፡ መጸተዋልና፤ ቦ ፡ ባባታቸው ፡ በኤበር ፡ ዕብራውያን ፡ ተብለዋል ፤ ባባት ፡ ስም ፡ መጸራትም ፡ ልማድ ፡ ነው ፤ በፋሬስ ፡ ፈረሳውያን ፡ በሳደቅ ፡ ሰዱቃውያን ፡ በይሁዳ ፡ አይሁድ ፡ እንደተባሉ ፡ ቦ ፡ ቁንቁቸው ፡ ዕብራይስጥ ፡ ነው ፡ ስለዚህ ፡ ዕብራውያን ፡ ተብለዋል ፡ ይህስ ፡ እንዳይሆን ፡ ቁንቁ ፡ በሰው ፡ ይጸራል ፡ እንጂ ፡ ሰው ፡ በቁንቁ ፡ አይጸራም ፡ ብሎ ፡ ክቀደመው ፡ ይገባል ፡ . . .

    b. Ff. 327r–405v: Text and Commentary on Hebrews

    ከጥንት ፡ ጀምሮ ፡ እግዚአብሔር ፡ በነቢያት ፡ አድሮ ፡ ለአባቶቻችን ፡ ነገረ ፡ በምሳሌ ፡ በመስበ ፡ ወርቅ ፡ በተቅዋም ፡ ወርቅ ፡ በማዕጠንት ፡ ወርቅ ፡ በበትረ ፡ አሮን ፡ እንበ ፡ ምሳሌ ፡ በዘፈቀደ ፡ ታይቶ ፡ ቦ ፡ ብቡዙን ፡ ነገር ፡ ብ፮ ፡ ቃላት ፡ ወበብዙን ፡ መክፈ ፡ ወነበ ፡ ባለው ፡ ቦ ፡ በብዙን ፡ ጉብራ ፡ አምሳል ፡ ጉብራ ፡ ትንቢት ፡ ወነገርነኒ ፡ ከመ ፡

ሕገን ፡ ወከመ ፡ ሥርዑ ፡ ዘውስተ ፡ ምድር ፡ ዕምዕት ፡ ይአቲ ፡ ጽጌ ፡
አስተርአየ ፡ ምድርኒ ፡ ትሁብ ፡ ፍሬሃ ፡ ናሁ ፡ ድንግል ፡ እለመ ፡
አምኔኪ ፡ ይወጽእ ፡ ንጉሥ ፡ ባለው ፡ . . .

16. Ff. 405v–406r: Numbers of words for each book of the Epistles of Paul.

ዘቀዳማዊ ፡ ቆርንቶስ ፡ ቃሉ ፡ ፫፻፶ ፡ ምዕራፉ ፡ ፲፱ ፡ ወትርጓሜሁ ፡ ሧ ፡...

17. Ff. 406r–408r: On the Life of Jesus: from his conception through the sending of the Holy Spirit to the disciples.

ጌታ ፡ አምቅድመ ፡ ዓለም ፡ በልብ ፡ የመከረውን ፡ በቃል ፡ የተናገረውን ፡
ለመፈጸም ፡ ሰው ፡ ሆነ ሰው ፡ ሁኖም ፡ ሕግ ፡ ጠባያዊ ፡ ሕግ ፡
መጽሐፋዊ ፡ ሲፈጸም ፡ አደገ ፡ ሕግ ፡ ጠባያዊስ ፡ እንደምን ፡ ነው ፡
ቢሉ ፡ በየጥቂቱ ፡ ማደግ ፡ ነው ፡ ልህቀ ፡ በበሕቅ ፡ እንዘ ፡ ይትኤዘዝ ፡
ለአዝማዲሁ ፡ እንተ ፡ ይአቲ ፡ እመ ፡ እንዲል ፡ . . .

Notes:

1. F. i r(ecto): note of purchase. –$80.00 bought for MYS 7/5/76."
2. F. i v(erso)-vii v(erso), viii v(erso)-ix r(ecto), 408v–416v, 417v–423r and 424r: blank.
3. F. viii r(ecto): letter of application to *Ato* Takälä Täfäma, Ṭərr 16, 1966 EC, written upside down.
4. F. ix v(erso)-x v(erso): Amharic language and math exercises, written upside down, in blue ink.
5. F. 417r: Note on the year of enthronement of Ethiopian kings.
6. F. 423v: Note on the Italian language.
7. F. 424v: Note of ownership, written upside down: –This book belongs to Mänkər Fänta.
8. Decorative designs: ff. 18r, 25v, 30r, 36v, 40v, 49r, 51v, 58r, 66r, 70v, 79v, 84v, 89v, 104r, 109v, 128r, 135v, 141v, 148r, 154v, 159v, 163r, 168r, 174r, 179v, 184v, 190v, 199v, 207r, 212r, 225r, 232v, 238r, 243v, 251v, 258r, 264v, 271r, 275v, 276v, 283v, 286v, 291v, 292r, 298v, 306r, 310v, 315v, 321r, 324v, 331r, 340v, 346r, 352v, 360v, 380r, 388v, 400v, 406r (line of alternating red and black dots); ff. 115v, 120v, 324v (multiple full stops).
9. The words Mary and Jesus Christ are rubricated.
10. Numbered quires: quires 2–14.
11. Scribal intervention: words of text are written interlinearly (ff. 5v, 7r, 10v, 11rv, etc.); and lines of text are written interlinearly (ff. 5v, 10v, 11r, 12r, 14r, etc.); and in the bottom margin with a symbol (+) marking the location where the text is to be inserted (ff. 18v, col. 1, line 6; 19r, col. 1, line 1; 19v, col. 2, line 17; 20r, col. 2, line 2; 21r, col. 1, line 19; 21r, col. 2, line 1, etc.), and interlinearly where the symbol (⊥) is used (ff. 39v, col. 1, line 14; 60v, col. 1, line 5; 75v, col. 2, line 3;

76v, col. 2, line 5; 77r, col. 1, line 20; 85r, col. 1, line 3, etc.), and the symbol (⊥) is occasionally used with interlinear insertions (e.g., ff. 32v, col. 2, line 5; 287v, col. 1, line 9) as well as marking the location of text in the upper margin (f. 80v, col. 1, line 17); erasure markings are visible (ff. 6v, 7r, 9r, 16r, etc.); text has been removed (e.g., ff. 161r, 178r, 190r).

Quire Map

Protection Quire: i-x (balanced).

Quire 1: ff. 1–24 (balanced).

Quire 2: ff. 25–40 (balanced).

Quire 3: ff. 41–72 (balanced).

Quire 4: ff. 73–104 (balanced).

Quire 5: ff. 105–136 (balanced).

Quire 6: ff. 137–168 (balanced).

Quire 7: ff. 169–200 (balanced).

Quire 8: ff. 201–232 (balanced).

Quire 9: ff. 233–264 (balanced).

Quire 10: ff. 265–296 (balanced).

Quire 11: ff. 297–328 (balanced).

Quire 12: ff. 329–360 (balanced).

Quire 13: ff. 361–392 (balanced).

Quire 14: ff. 393–424 (balanced).

MYS 50 – EMIP 650

Acts of Krəstos Śämra, ገድለ፡ ክርስቶስ፡ ሠምራ፡

Parchment, 155 x 127 x 28 mm, four Coptic chain stitches attached with bridle attachments to a manufactured particle board, spine and corners are covered in untooled leather, headband and tailband, protection quire + 9 full quires, iv + 92 folios, top margin 20 mm, bottom margin 35 mm, fore edge margin 23 mm, gutter margin 11 mm, ff. 1r–89r one column, 10 lines, Gə_əz, twentieth century. Double-slip *maḥdär*.

Quire descriptions: quires 1–9 balanced; protection quire adjusted balanced.

Major Works:
1. Ff. 1r–67v: Acts of Krəstos Śämra, *Gädlä Kərəstos Śämra*, ገድለ፡ ክርስቶስ፡ ሠምራ፡, in Gə_əz and Amharic. Enrico Cerulli, *Atti Di Krestos Samrā*, CSCO AE 33/ 34 (Louvain: Peeters, 1956); Dennis Nosnitsin, "Krəstos Śämra," *EA* 3, 443–45.
   በስመ ፡ አብ ፡ ወወልድ ፡ . . . ንጽሐፍ ፡ ዝክረ ፡ ውዳሴሃ ፡ ለእምነ ፡ ክርስቶስ ፡ ሠምራ ፡ ዘወሐባ ፡ ኪዳን ፡ እግዚእን ፡ ኢየሱስ ፡ ክርስቶስ ፡ ንጉሡ ፡ ሰማይ ፡ ወምድር ፡ ወሀለወት ፡ አሐቲ ፡ ሀገር ፡ እምአህጉረ ፡ ሸዋ ፡ ሀገረ ፡ ሙላዳ ፡ ለእምነ ፡ ክርስቶስ ፡ ሠምራ ፡ ሀገረ ፡ ቡልጋ ፡ ቅዱሴ ፡ ቅድስት ፡ ወንበሩ ፡ አቡሃ ፡ ወእማ ፡ ጌራን ፡ ወፈራህያን ፡ እግዚአብሔር ፡ ወወላዲ ፡ ወለተ ፡ ሳሪት ፡ . . .

2. Ff. 68r–74r: Three Miracles of Krəstos Śämra, *Tä'amərä Kərəstos Śämra*, ተአምረ፡ ክርስቶስ፡ ሠምራ፡.
   a. Ff. 68r–70v: First Miracle: On the death of Krəstos Śämra: How a certain monk named Isaac found the body of our mother, Krəstos Śämra; how he vowed to stay there with her body until he died, and how he died after forty days.
   b. Ff. 70v–72v: Second Miracle: How Krəstos Śämra spoke to Filipos when she died.
   c. Ff. 72v–74r: Third Miracle: How the Virgin Mary appeared to our mother, Krəstos Śämra.

3. Ff. 74v–89r: Image of Krəstos Śämra, *Mäləkə'a Kərəstos Śämra*, መልክአ፡ ክርስቶስ፡ ሠምራ፡, beginning:
   ሰላም ፡ ለዝክረ ፡ ስምኪ ፡ ለክርስቶስ ፡ ሥምረቱ ፡
   እንዘ ፡ ይብል ፡ ካሀን እንተ ፡ አንበሮ ፡ አምጥንቱ ፡
   ሥምረት ፡ ክርስቶስ ፡ ሠምራ ፡ እስመ ፡ ኢየሐጽጽኪ ፡ ለለዕለቱ ፡
   ተረክበ ፡ ፍካሬሁ ፡ ለንባበ ፡ ስምኪ ፡ ዝንቱ ፡
   ለኩሉስ ፡ ተንብዮ ፡ ፍካሬ ፡ አልቦቱ ፡ . . .

Miniatures:
1. F. iii v(erso): Krəstos Śamra, her maid, and her child on the maid's back, on their way to Däbrä Libanos monastery.
2. F. iv r(ecto): Heart of Jesus (from catholic tradition).
3. F. iv v(erso). Krəstos Śamra, when she went in the river and stood in the middle of the river for a long time and prayed. When she prayed the fish passed through her body.

Notes:
1. F. 66v, 68r and *passim*: name of original owner: Wälätä Ṣadəq.
2. F. 67v: Colophon: "This book was written in the reign of King Haylä Śəllase (2 April 1930–12 September 1974)." The scribe's name is: Gäbrä Ḥəywät.
3. F. 1r, 33r, 74v, and 89r, bottom margin in blue ink: name of later owner *Abba* Gäbrä Ḥəywät.
4. F. 89r: other names in blue ink: Wälätä Iyäsus and Ḥirutä Śəllase.
5. F. 90v, in blue ink: *Abba* Gäbrä Ḥəywät was born 1879 EC The war of Sägäle was on 1911 EC [October 1916 A.D., war between the forces of King Mikael, father of *Ləj* Iyasu, and the forces of the central government, let by Shoan aristocrats].
6. F. 92v, in blue ink: Wälätä Bərhan.
7. Blank pages: Ff. i r(ecto)-iii r(ecto), 89v, 90r, 91r–92r.
8. Decorative designs: f. 1r (*ḥaräg*).
9. The words God, Michael, Krestos Samra, Gabriel, Jesus and Mary are rubricated.
10. Scribal intervention: words of text are written interlinearly (ff. 16v, 29v, 31v, 32v, 72v); text has been removed (e.g., f. 83r).
11. In places, (e.g., f. 57r), the ink is flaking off of the parchment. In places, (e.g., f. 47v), a later hand has attempted to retrace letters in blue ink or pencil.

Quire Map

Protection Quire: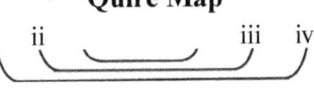

Two folio stubs visible between ff. ii and iii.

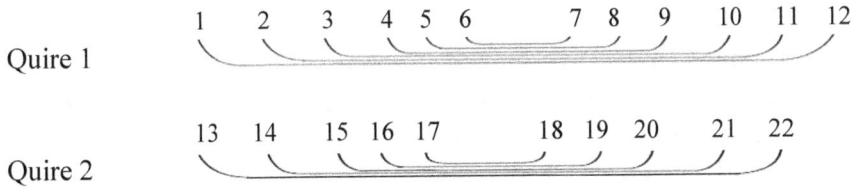

Quire 3: 23 24 25 26 27 28 29 30 31 32

Quire 4: 33 34 35 36 37 38 39 40 41 42

Quire 5: 43 44 45 46 47 48 49 50 51 52 53 54

Quire 6: 55 56 57 58 59 60 61 62 63 64

Quire 7: 65 66 67 68 69 70 71 72 73 74

Quire 8: 75 76 77 78 79 80 81 82 83 84

Quire 9: 85 86 87 88 89 90 91 92

MYS 51 – EMIP 651
Sword of the Trinity, ሠይፈ፡ ሥላሴ፡,
Image of the Trinity, መልክአ፡ ሥላሴ፡

Parchment, 164 x 116 x 32 mm, four Coptic chain stitches attached with bridle attachments to rough-hewn boards of the traditional wood, protection quire + 10 full quires, vi + 98 folios, top margin 21 mm, bottom margin 41 mm, fore edge margin 19 mm, gutter margin 11 mm, ff. 1r–96r two columns, 14 lines, Gǝʿǝz, Sane 10, 1961 EC (= 17 June 1969).

Quire descriptions: protection quire and quires 1–10 balanced.

Major Works:
1. Ff. 1r–82r: Sword of the Trinity, *Säyfä Śǝllase*, ሠይፈ፡ ሥላሴ፡. Arranged for days of the week. Abbadie, *AbbCat* 244, f. 13r, Conti Rossini, *Notice* 106; Strelcyn, *Lincei* 53 and 62; EMML 1170 and EMIP 7. See ሰይፈኝ ሥላሴኛኛ ወመልክአ ሥላሴኛ ዘደረሰኝ አባኝ ስብሐትኝ ለአብኝኛ (Addis Ababa: Täsfa Press, 1947 EC).

በሰመ ፡ አብ ፡ ወወልድ ፡ . . . ተማኅፅንኩ ፡ ብክሙ ፡ አብ ፡ ወወልድ ፡
ወመንፈስ ፡ ቅዱስ ፡ እነ ፡ ኃጥእ ፡ በከመ ፡ አተውክሙ ፡ ቤተ ፡ አብርሃም ፡
ከማሁ ፡ አእትውኒ ፡ ውስተ ፡ መንበርክሙ ፡ . . .

   a. Ff. 1r–7v: Daily readings.
   b. Ff. 8r–13r: Introduction.
   c. Ff. 13r–21v: Monday.
   d. Ff. 22r–32v: Tuesday.
   e. Ff. 33r–42r: Wednesday.
   f. Ff. 42v–51v: Thursday.
   g. Ff. 52r–63v: Friday.
   h. Ff. 64r–71v: Saturday.
   i. Ff. 72r–82r: Sunday.
2. Ff. 83r–95v: Image of the Trinity, *Mälk'a Śəllase,* Image of the Trinity, መልክአ፡ ሥላሴ፡. Chaîne, *Répertoire* 20; *MG59* 189ff. or no. 189.
   ሰላም ፡ ለሀላዌክሙ ፡ ዘይመውዕ ፡ ሀላዊያት ፡
   ለረኪበ ፡ ስሙ ፡ ኅቡእ ፡ አመ ፡ ወጠንኩ ፡ ተምኔት ፡
   እምግብርክሙ ፡ ሥላሴ ፡ ሰብ ፡ ረክብኩ ፡ አስማተ ፡
   መለኮተ ፡ ለለ ፡ አሐዱ ፡ ዘዚአክሙ ፡ ገጻተ ፡
   እንበለ ፡ ትድምርት ፡ እስሚ ፡ ወእሁብ ፡ ትድምርተ ፡ . . .

Notes:
1. Several lines of evidence point to the conclusion that this manuscript was produced in the government scriptorium.
2. Ff. 95v–96r: Colophon: ╫ is finished Sane 10, 1961 EC. The scribe is Mäkʷonən Mäqʷuriya. His baptismal name is Täklä Ṣadəq. His native land is Mänz, the exact place is Giyorgis."
   ተፈጸመ ፡ ሰኔ ፡ ፲፬ ፡ ቀን ፡ ፲፱፻፷፩ዓ ፡ ምሕረት ፡ ጸሐፊሁ ፡ መኰንን ፡
   መኰሪያ ፡ ወስመ ፡ ጥምቀቱ ፡ ተክለ ፡ ጻድቅ ፡ ብሔረ ፡ ሙላዴ ፡ መንዝ ፡
   ክፍለ ፡ ሀገሩ ፡ ዋካ ፡ ጊዮርጊስ፡
3. Ff. i r(ecto)–vi v(erso), 82v, 96v–98v: blank.
4. Decorative designs: ff. 1r, 13r, 22r, 33r, 42v, 52r, 64r, 72r, 83r (colorful, ornate *ḥarägs*); ff. 17r, 19v, 21v, 24r, 27r, 31v, 32v, 42r, 51r, 63v, 80r (multiple full stops).
5. The words God and Mary are rubricated.
6. Page numbers on ff. 1v–31r.
7. Scribal intervention: words of text are written interlinearly (ff. 49v, 88v); text has been removed (e.g., f. 89r).

Quire Map

Protection Quire: i ii iii iv v vi

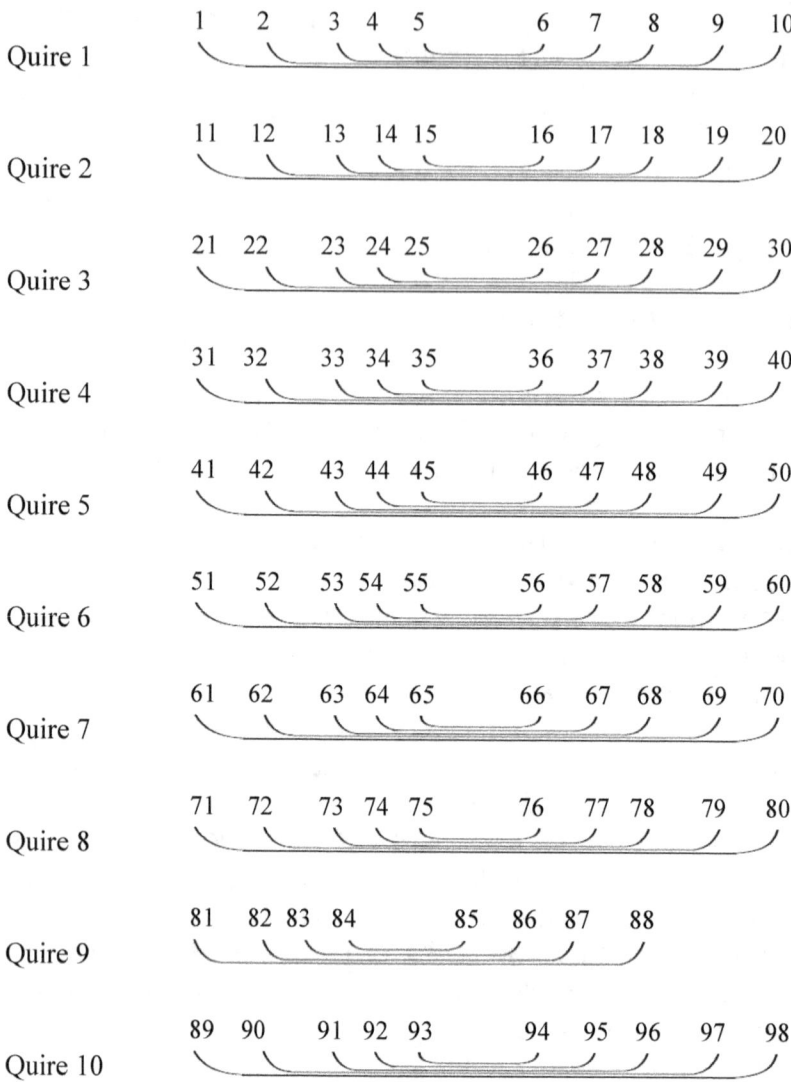

MYS 52 – EMIP 652
Sword of the Trinity, variant form, ሠይፈ፡ ሥላሴ፡

Parchment, 150 x 110 x 43 mm, four Coptic chain stitches attached with bridle attachments to rough-hewn boards of the traditional wood, protection sheet + 6 full quires, ii + 70 folios, top margin 10 mm, bottom margin 35 mm, fore edge margin 15 mm, gutter margin 7 mm, ff. 1r–68r two columns, 13 lines, Gəʿəz, twentieth century.

Quire descriptions: protection sheet balanced; quires 1–6 adjusted balanced.

Major Works:
1. Ff. 1r–68r: Sword of the Trinity, *Säyfä Śəllase*, ሠይፈ፡ ሥላሴ፡. Arranged for days of the week (Monday 1r, Tuesday 12r, Wednesday 21v, Thursday 34r, Friday 38v, Saturday 49v, Sunday 61r). Abbadie, *AbbCat* 244, f. 13r; Conti Rossini, *Notice* 106; Strelcyn, *Lincei* 53 and 62; EMML 1170 and EMIP 7. See ሰይፈኝ ሥላሴኝኛ መመልክእ ሥላሴኝ ዘደረሰኝ አባኝ ስብሐትኝ ለአብኝኛ (Addis Ababa: Täsfa Press, 1947 EC). This copy of Sword of the Trinity contains a variant form at ff. 49v–68r, containing the Asmat prayer of the prophet Moses.

በስመ ፡ አብ ፡ ወወልድ ፡ . . . በስመ ፡ አብ ፡ ወወልድ ፡ ወመንፈስ ፡ ቅዱስ ፡ እትመሐፀን። በስመ ፡ አብ ፡ ወወልድ ፡ ወመንፈስ ፡ ቅዱስ ፡ አዓትብ ፡ ገጽየ ፡ በምዕዛረ ፡ ገጹ ፡ ለእግዚአብሔር ፡ ዘኢያንቃዕደወ ፡ ገበ ፡ ካልእ ፡ አዓትብ ፡ አዕይንትየ ፡ በምዕዛረ ፡ አዕይቲሁ ፡ ለእግዚአብሔር ፡ ዘያርዕድ ፡ ገበ ፡ ነጸረ ፡ . . .

Incipit at 49v:

በስመ ፡ አብ ፡ . . . ንነግረክሙ ፡ በዘድኅነ ፡ ሙሴ ፡ እምእደሁ ፡ ለፈርዖን ፡ በጸሎቱ ፡ ወበአስተብቁዖቱ ፡ ለሙሴ ፡ ዘወሀቦ ፡ ለሙሴ ፡ እግዚአብሔር ፡ መግረሬ ፡ ዐር ፡ ወረደ ፡ ገብርኤል ፡ ወይቤሎ ፡ ኢትፍራህ ፡ ሙሴ ፡ ተሰምዓ ፡ ጸሎት ፡ ገበ ፡ እግዚአብሔር። ነጋ ፡ አርግ ፡ ውስተ ፡ ደብረ ፡ ሲና ፡ . . .

Varia:
1. Ff. i rv: Excerpt from Gospel of John, chapter 3.

Notes:
1. Blank: ff. ii rv and 68v–70v.
2. Ff. 21v and *passim*: owner, Gäbrä Maryam.
3. Decorative designs: ff. 4v, 38v, 61r, 68r (multiple full stops).
4. The words Jesus, God, Mary, Michael and Gabriel are rubricated.
5. Numbered quires: quires 2 and 4.
6. The inside back cover has a large niche carved out, presumably for a mirror.

Quire Map

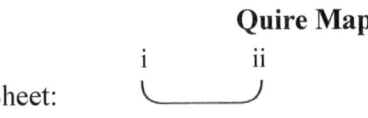

Folio stubs are visible between ff. 2 and 3, ff. 4 and 5, ff. 7 and 8, and ff. 11 and 12.

Quire 2: 13 14 15 16 17 18 19 20 21 22 23 24

Folio stubs visible between ff. 13 and 14, ff. 17 and 18, ff. 20 and 21 and ff. 22 and 23.

Quire 3: 25 26 27 28 29 30 31 32 33 34 35 36

Folio stubs visible between ff. 25 and 26 and ff. 34 and 35.

Quire 4: 37 38 39 40 41 42 43 44 45 46 47 48

Folio stubs visible between ff. 38 and 39 and ff. 45 and 46.

Quire 5: 49 50 51 52 53 54 55 56 57 58 59 60

Folio stubs visible between ff. 50 and 51 and ff. 57 and 58.

Quire 6: 61 62 63 64 65 66 67 68 69 70

Folio stubs visible between ff. 61 and 62 and ff. 68 and 69.

MYS 53 – EMIP 653
Computus, Book of the Mystery of Heaven and Earth, መጽሐፈ፡ ምሥጢረ፡ ሰማይ፡ ወምድር፡, Faith of Jacob Al Baradai, ሃይማኖተ፡ ያዕቆብ፡ አልበራዳኢ፡

Parchment, 213 x 190 x 45 mm, four Coptic chain stitches attached with bridle attachments to rough-hewn boards of the traditional wood, protection quire + 8 full quires, ii + 79 folios, top margin 23–26 mm, bottom margin 42–47 mm, fore edge margin 27–30 mm, gutter margin 12 mm, ff. 13r– two columns, 21 lines, Gəʿəz, eighteenth century.

Quire descriptions: quires 1 and 5–6 balanced; protection quire and quires 4 and 7–8 adjusted balanced; quires 2–3 unbalanced.

Major Works:
1. F. 1r: Chart of the orbit and windows of the stars.   Top (from left to right): month of the year (in pairs). Second row: doors of the stars

(Hebrew months). Four corners of box: Matthew and Euphrates (top left), Mark and Gihon (bottom left), Luke and Tigress (top right), John and Pishon (lit., Efeson, bottom right). Left to right at top of box (i.e., from Matthew to Luke): ―from the right side of the eastern door comes out cold, frost, snow, and dryness;" ―from the center of the door will come fair weather, rain, seed, peace, dew, and life;" ―from the left side of the door comes destruction, dryness, death, and Perdition." From Luke to John (upper right to lower right of the box): ―from southeast or right door comes out wind, strong winds called *nətug*, dryness, destruction, heat and Perdition;" ―from the center door comes out fragrance, dew, rain, peace and life;" ―from the left door comes out dew, rain, locust, and destruction." From Mark to John (written upside down and left to right along the bottom of the box): ―from the left door comes dryness, destruction, heat, and Perdition;:" ―from the center door comes dew, rain, blessing, and peace;" ―from the right door of the west comes dew, snow, cold, and frost." From Matthew to Mark (from upper left to lower left): ―from left door comes dew, rain, locust, and destruction;" ―from the center door comes fair (weather), life, rain, dew, and peace;" ―from the northeast [*sic*, northwest] of the right door comes clouds, cold, snow, rain, dew, and locust." Central box (clockwise from upper center): ―east, southeast, south, southwest, west, northwest, north, northeast." The center of the box: ―Sun."

2. F. 1v: Chart of käntəros, cycle of a quarter of a year, interval of two minutes. Neugebaur, *Ethiopic Astronomy and Computus*, 178, says that ―käntəros indicates 1/30." Along the bottom of the chart is written ―30 units" six times. Along the right side of the chart are listed the hours from one through twelve. The red lines indicate the käntəros for each hour. Along the top of the chart: ―Säne, Ḥamle, sixth door, Gənbot, Näḥase, fifth door, Miyazya, Mäskäräm, fourth door, Ṭəqəmt, Mäggabit, third door, Ḥədar, Yäkkatit, second door, Taḥśaś, Ṭərr, first door." Left side: ―Fifteen käntəros for a month."

3. Ff. 2r–10v, left column: Series of calendar tables with historical events, ending with the death of King Susənyos (1606–1632).

4. Ff. 10v, right column–11r: three charts with measurements of the shadows of the hours, arranged by month. Red ink: the hour; black ink: the measurement. Final column on 11r says, ―For Pag^{w}ame do as Näḥase."

5. Ff. 11v–12r: Computation tables of the Epact and Solar Cycle of the year, with leap year.
6. Ff. 13r–66r: Book of the Mystery of Heaven and Earth, *mäṣəḥafä məṣṭirä sämay wä-mədr*, መጽሐፈ፡ ምሥጢረ፡ ሰማይ፡ ወምድር፡ Edited by J. Perruchon, "Le livre des mysteres du ciel et de la terre," PO 1 (1947) 1–96, (with French translation), and by E. Wallis Budge, *The Book of the Mysteries of Heaven and Earth*, London 1935 (with an English translation). See EMML 2161. Organized with titles in the upper margins: about the creation of Sunday (f. 14r), about the creation of Monday (f. 15r), about the creation of Tuesday (f. 15r), about the creation of Wednesday (16r), about the creation of Thursday (16r), about the creation of Friday (f. 16v), about the creation of Saturday (f. 17v), about Adam (18r), about Enoch and his ten seven-year cycles (lit. Sabbaths, f. 18v), about Noah and the ark (f. 19v), about Abraham (f. 20r), about Isaac (f. 21r), about Jacob (f. 21r), about Joseph (f. 21v), about Moses and the Passover lamb (f. 21v), about the Tabernacle (f. 22r), about the five vestments of Aaron (f. 22v), about the twelve leaders (lit. angels) of the gentiles (f. 24r), about the ark of Moses, the ten commandments and the virginity of Mary (f. 26r), about Joshua (f. 26r), about David (f. 26v), about the Trinity (f. 27r), about Paradise (f. 27v), about the seven heavens (f. 28r), about the creation of earth (f. 29v), about the Fall of Satan and his fight with Michael (f. 30v), about the majesty of Satan (f. 31r), about Tuesday (f. 31r), about birds who were conceived through the sun (f. 31v), about the creation of Adam and his honor (f. 32r), about how Saint Michael brought souls from Sheol (f. 33r), about how Satan deceived Eve (f. 33v), about how the fallen angels showed the secret of heaven to (the children of) men (f. 34v), about the children of Seth and their relatives (f. 35r), about the children of Cain who came to Ethiopia (f. 35v), about the early prophets, Enoch, his father, Yared, and his mother, Barika, Noah and his father, Lamech, and his mother, Bitols (f. 36v), about the children of Yared (f. 37r), about the circumcision of Abraham (f. 37r), about the fourteen trees that Enoch saw (f. 37v), about the journey of Israel to Egypt (f. 38r), about the appointing of the priest with oil (f. 38r), about the soul of a person (f. 39r), about the tabernacle and all of its utensils (f. 39v), about the temple Ezekiel saw and its Mystery (f. 43v), about the praise of Aaron (f. 45r), about the measurement *gomor* and the tree called *kamon* (f. 45v), about the word of God (f.

45v), about the sacrifice of the Torah (f. 45v), about the kings that Daniel saw (f. 48v), about the vineyard which was planted around the tabernacle (f. 52r), about the seven feasts and the red heifer (f. 52r), about the words of prophets about Christ (f. 52v), about the fathers and mothers of the prophets (f. 62r), about kings whose names are written in Clement (f. 65r).
7. Ff. 66r–68v: Mystery of the Resurrection of the Dead (from the Five Pillars).
8. Ff. 69r–76v: Faith of Jacob Al Baradai, ሃይማኖተ፡ ያዕቆብ፡ አልበራዳኢ፡
9. Ff. 76v–77r: The Ten Commandments.
10. F. 77v: List of the Alexandrian Popes.
11. Ff. 78r: Excerpt from commentary by John Chrysostom on Matthew's note about Mary not knowing Joseph until the birth of Jesus.

Miniatures:
1. F. ii v(erso): chart, in pencil, of the cardinal points of the compass and their division: East (top), West (bottom), North (left), South (right).

Varia:
1. F. ii rv: the shortest form of the Baḥərä Ḥasab, recited by the priest on the New Year.

Notes:
1. Front cover has been repaired with a piece of modern board attached to the remaining piece of rough-hewn board.
2. F. i r(ecto): pen trial (top), and incomplete Trinitarian formula pen trial.
3. Ff. i v(erso), 12v and 78v–79r: blank.
4. F. 77v: note of ownership: ―This book belongs to *Aläqa* Ḥəruy, that is, Kidanä Maryam.
5. F. 78r: pen trial on introduction to a miracle of Mary.
6. F. 79v: note of items lent to other people.
7. Decorative designs: ff. 14r, 15r, 17v, 21v, 26v, 32r, 36v, 37v, 38r, 41v, 42r, 58v, 64v, 66r, 68r, 76v, 77v, 78r (multiple full stops); black lines are used as section dividers throughout (e.g., ff. 16r, 18r); ff. 27r, 29r, 61r (line of alternating red and black dots).
8. The word Mary is rubricated.
9. Scribal intervention: words of text are written interlinearly (ff. 13rv, 14v, 15r, 17rv, etc.); and lines of text are written interlinearly (ff. 30v, 46r, 62rv, 64r, 68v, etc.); and in the upper margin with a symbol (⊥) marking the location where the text is to be inserted (ff. 36v, col. 2, line

214 · *Catalog of the Manuscripts*

17; 62r, col. 1, line 7; 68v, col. 1, line 7); text has been removed (e.g., f. 72r).

Quire Map

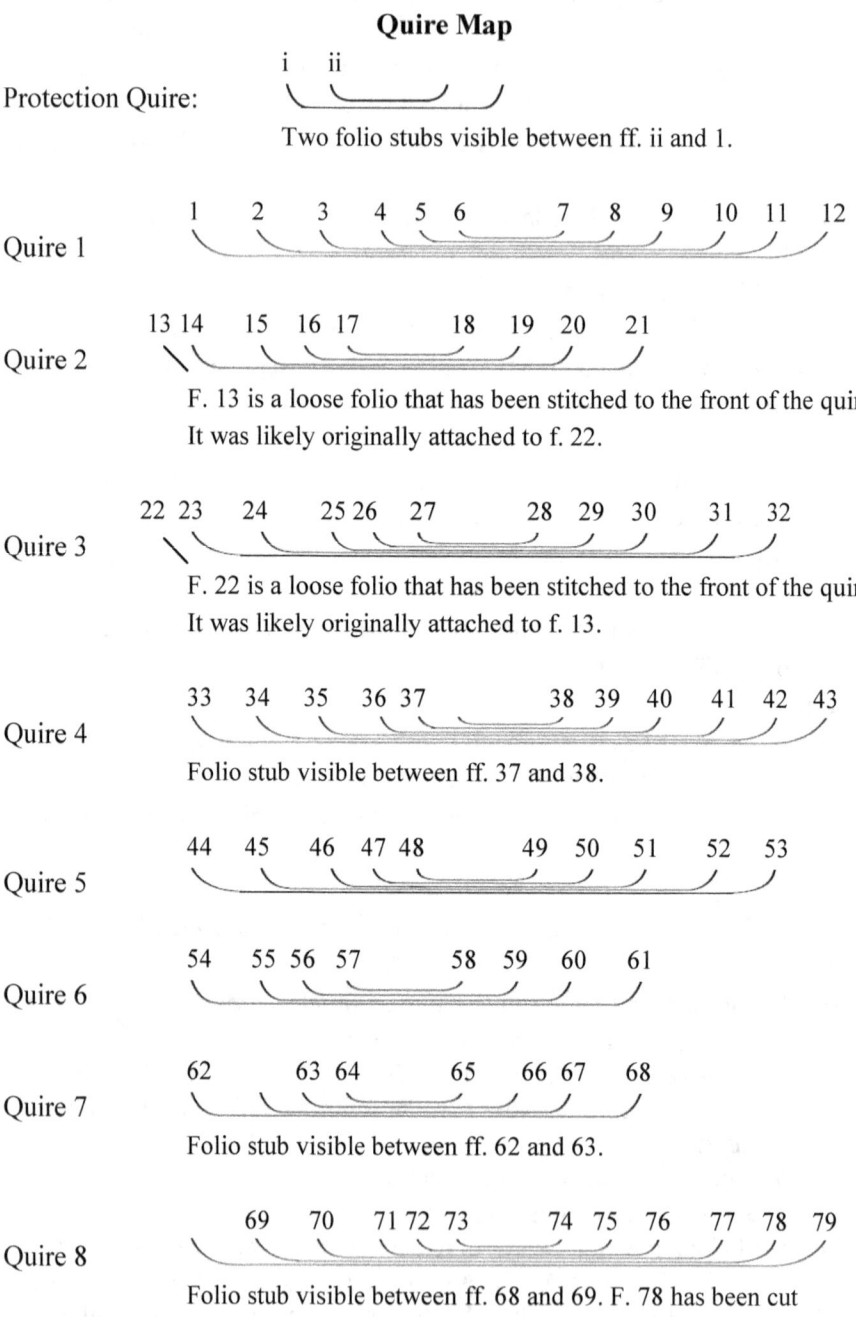

Protection Quire: i, ii
Two folio stubs visible between ff. ii and 1.

Quire 1: 1, 2, 3, 4, 5, 6, 7, 8, 9, 10, 11, 12

Quire 2: 13, 14, 15, 16, 17, 18, 19, 20, 21
F. 13 is a loose folio that has been stitched to the front of the quire. It was likely originally attached to f. 22.

Quire 3: 22, 23, 24, 25, 26, 27, 28, 29, 30, 31, 32
F. 22 is a loose folio that has been stitched to the front of the quire. It was likely originally attached to f. 13.

Quire 4: 33, 34, 35, 36, 37, 38, 39, 40, 41, 42, 43
Folio stub visible between ff. 37 and 38.

Quire 5: 44, 45, 46, 47, 48, 49, 50, 51, 52, 53

Quire 6: 54, 55, 56, 57, 58, 59, 60, 61

Quire 7: 62, 63, 64, 65, 66, 67, 68
Folio stub visible between ff. 62 and 63.

Quire 8: 69, 70, 71, 72, 73, 74, 75, 76, 77, 78, 79
Folio stub visible between ff. 68 and 69. F. 78 has been cut so that only the column nearest the gutter remains.

MYS 54 – EMIP 654
The Delamarter Codex of Jubilees, መጽሐፈ፡ ኩፋሌ፡, and the Minor Prophets Hosea, ሆሴዕ, Amos, ዘአሞጽ, and Micah, ዘሚክያስ

Parchment, 183 x 175 x 48 mm, no covers remain and the codex has been arranged in disorder, 55 folios, top margin 21 mm, bottom margin 36 mm, fore edge margin 27 mm, gutter margin mm, ff. 1r–55v two columns, 24 lines, Gəʾəz, late-fifteenth / early-sixteenth century.

Regarding Jubilees, መጽሐፈ፡ ኩፋሌ፡, cf. James C. VanderKam, *The Book of Jubilees*, CSCO 510/511; SA 87/88 (Louvain: Peeters, 1989).

Regarding Hosea, ሆሴዕ, cf. Hans Ferdinand Fuhs, *Die Äthiopische Übersetzung des Propheten Hosea*, BBB 38 (Bonn: Hanstein, 1971).

Regarding Amos, ዘአሞጽ, cf. F. M. Esteves Pereira, *O livro do profeta Amós e a sua versão etiópica*, Separata de Boletin do Segunda Classe 11 (Academia das sciêncas de Lisboa: Coimbra, 1917).

Regarding Micah, ዘሚክያስ, cf. Hans Ferdinand Fuhs, *Die Äthiopische Übersetzung des Propheten Micha*, BBB 28 (Bonn: Hanstein, 1968).

In its current state of disorder the content of the folios is as follows:
Ff. 1rv: Jubilees 15:3–19
Ff. 2rv: Hosea 14:4–9; Amos 1:1–9
Ff. 3rv: Amos 1:9–2:10
Ff. 4rv: Jubilees 49:1–11
Ff. 5rv: Hosea 11:8b–13:2a
Ff. 6rv: Hosea 9:5–10:5a
Ff. 7rv: Jubilees 43:21–44:12
Ff. 8rv: Amos 2:10–3:12a
Ff. 9rv: Amos 3:12b–4:10a
Ff. 10rv: Jubilees 31:3–16a
Ff. 11rv: Jubilees 31:16b–28a
Ff. 12rv: Jubilees 26:27–27:6
Ff. 13rv: Jubilees 27:6–21
Ff. 14rv: Jubilees 27:21–28:6
Ff. 15rv: Jubilees 28:6–19 (through, —. .and Jacob went in again. . .")
Ff. 16rv: Jubilees 30:17–31:2
Ff. 17rv: Jubilees 28:19–29:2
Ff. 18rv: Amos 8:7–9:6 (through, —. .the one who builds his upper chamber in the heavens")
Ff. 19rv: Amos 9:6–15; Micah 1:1–5 (through, —what is the. . .")
Ff. 20rv: Micah 6:11–7:12a
Ff. 21rv: Jubilees 43:7–21

Ff. 22rv: Jubilees 23:11–20
Ff. 23rv: Jubilees 21:4b-13a
Ff. 24rv: Jubilees 42:4–20a
Ff. 25rv: Jubilees 37:19b-38:8
Ff. 26:vr: (folio is reversed) Micah 1:5–2:3
Ff. 27rv: Hosea 13:2–14:3
Ff. 28rv: Jubilees 34:7b-20a
Ff. 29rv: Jubilees 34:20b-35:10a
Ff. 30rv: Jubilees 35:10b-20b
Ff. 31rv: Jubilees 35:20b-36:4b
Ff. 32rv: Jubilees 32:9a-21b (through, ".. .do not dwell here")
Ff. 33rv: Jubilees 38:8b-39:5b
Ff. 34rv: Jubilees 39:5b-39:18b
Ff. 35rv: Jubilees 39:18b-40:11b (through, ".. .the chief cook.")
Ff. 36rv: Jubilees 40:11b-16b (through, ".. .and when")
Ff. 37rv: Jubilees 40:16b-42:3 (through "that he might give them")
Ff. 38rv: Jubilees 42:20a-43:7b
Ff. 39rv: Jubilees 44:13a-34b (through, ".. .and the children of Israel buried)
Ff. 40rv: Jubilees 44:34b-45:13b (through, ".. .and he died in the fourth")
Ff. 41rv: Jubilees 31:21b-32:9a
Ff. 42rv: Jubilees 45:14a-46:9 (through, "all the bones of the children of Jacob except")
Ff. 43rv: Jubilees 46:9–47:9 (through, "taught you writing")
Ff. 44rv: Jubilees 47:9–48:9a (through, "and Prince Mastema stood up")
Ff. 45rv: Jubilees 48:9b-49:1 (through, ".. .eat it by night")
Ff. 46rv: Jubilees 49:20b-50:8a (through, "and the man")
Ff. 47rv: Jubilees 50:8b-13 (through the end of the book)
Ff. 48rv: Hosea 2:2–15b (through, "land of Egypt")
Ff. 49rv: Hosea 2:16–4:3 (through, ".. .even the fish")
Ff. 50rv: Hosea 4:3–5:3 (through, "played the whore; Israel")
Ff. 51rv: Hosea 5:3–6:8 (through, "Gilead is the city of")
Ff. 52rv: Hosea 6:9–7:16 (through, "that which does not prophet")
Ff. 53rv: Hosea 7:16–9:4 (end)
Ff. 54r–55v: excerpt from Gate of Light, in a nineteenth century hand.

Summary of the contents when reorganized:
- Jubilees 15:3–19; 21:4b-13a; 23:11–20; 26:27–29:2; 30:17–32:21b; 34:7b-36:4b; 37:19b-50:13.
- Hosea 2:2–10:5a; 11:8b-14:9.
- Amos 1:1–4:10a; 8:7–9:15.
- Micah 1:1–2:3; 6:11–7:12a.

Geometric Designs:
1. F. 13r: small, woven geometric pattern.
2. F. 19r: small, woven geometric pattern.
3. F. 53v: small, woven geometric pattern.

Notes:
1. This manuscript was originally digitized as EMIP 430, Addis Dealers' Project 30.
2. F. 29v: text written above and below col. 1:
3. F. 38v: text below col. 1:
4. Decorative designs: f. 36v (red and black lines); ff. 46r, 51v (line of red dots).
5. Scribal intervention: words of text are written interlinearly (ff. 47v, 54v); text has been erased and replaced (1v, 11r, 12r, 13r, 14v, 15r, 18r, 19r).
6. Provenance: For $300 Steve Delamarter purchased the codex from a dealer in Addis Ababa in June of 2010 and donated it to the Mekane Yesus Seminary.

Quire Map

This codex is disbound and in obvious disorder. It is not possible to determine a quire map of its original construction.

List of the Manuscripts

MYS 1/EMIP 601: Three Hundred Seventy-One Miracles of Mary, ተአምረ፡ ማርያም፡

MYS 2/EMIP 602: Printed Reproduction of the Ḥaylä Śǝllase Bible, in Amharic and Gǝ_ǝz, መጽሐፍ፡ ቅዱስ፡ (በግዕዝና፡ በአማርኛ፡ የተጻፈ፡), volume 1, Genesis through Esther.

MYS 3/EMIP 603: Printed Reproduction of the Ḥaylä Śǝllase Bible, in Amharic and Gǝ_ǝz, መጽሐፍ፡ ቅዱስ፡ (በግዕዝና፡ በአማርኛ፡ የተጻፈ፡), volume 2, Psalms and New Testament

MYS 4/EMIP 604: Printed Reproduction of the Ḥaylä Śǝllase Bible, in Amharic and Gǝ_ǝz, መጽሐፍ፡ ቅዱስ፡ (በግዕዝና፡ በአማርኛ፡ የተጻፈ፡), volume 3, Apocrypha. A gift from Ḥaylä Śǝllase himself.

MYS 5/EMIP 605: Fifty-Eight Miracles of Jesus, ተአምረ፡ ኢየሱስ፡

MYS 6/EMIP 606: Images of Mary, መልክአ፡ ማርያም፡, Michael, መልክአ፡ ሚካኤል፡, Gabriel, መልክአ ገብርኤል፡, and Saint George, መልክአ፡ ጊዮርጊስ፡, Hymn to Saint George, –Θ, who is quick for help," አ፡ ፍጡነ፡ ረድኤት፡

MYS 7/EMIP 607: Canticle of the Flower, ማሕሌተ፡ ጽጌ፡

MYS 8/EMIP 608, Yä-Aba Jale Ziq Chants, የአባ፡ ጃሌ፡ ዚቅ፡

MYS 9/EMIP 609: Ziq Chants, መጽሐፈ፡ ዚቅ፡

MYS 10/EMIP 610: Ziq Chants, መጽሐፈ፡ ዚቅ፡

MYS 11/EMIP 611: Homiliary in Honor of the Monthly Feast of the Archangel Michael, ድርሳነ፡ ሚካኤል፡, Asmat Prayer for the Archangel Michael, Images of Michael, መልክአ፡ ሚካኤል፡, and Gabriel, መልክአ ገብርኤል፡

MYS 12/EMIP 612: Homiliary in Honor of the Monthly Feast of the Archangel Michael, ድርሳነ፡ ሚካኤል፡

MYS 13/EMIP 613: Image of John the Baptist, መልክአ፡ ዮሐንስ፡ መጥምቅ፡, God Reigns, ነግሠ፡, Images of Gäbrä Mänfas Qǝddus, መልክአ፡ ገብረ፡ መንፈስ፡ ቅዱስ፡, Saint George, መልክአ፡ ጊዮርጊስ፡, Michael, መልክአ፡ ሚካኤል፡, and Gabriel, መልክአ ገብርኤል፡

MYS 14/EMIP 614: Sword of Trinity, ሠይፈ፡ ሥላሴ፡, and Book of Disciples

MYS 15/EMIP 615: Penitential Prayers, Book of Confession, መጽሐፈ፡ ኑዛዜ፡

MYS 16/EMIP 616: Prayer of the Covenant, ጸሎተ፡ ኪዳን፡, Supplications, መስተብቍዕ፡, God of the Luminaries, እግዚአብሔር፡ ዘብርሃናት፡, Mystagogia, ትምህርተ፡ ኅቡዓት፡, Prayer against the Tongue of People, ልሳነ፡ ሰብእ፡, Asmat Prayers of the Seven Archangels, ድርሳን፡ ዘሰባቱ፡ ሊቃነ፡ መላእክት፡, Asmat Prayers, Prayers, Net of Solomon, መርበብተ፡ ሰሎሞን፡, Prayer of Mary at Golgotha, ጸሎተ፡ እግዝእትነ፡ ማርያም፡ ዘሰኔ፡ ጎልጎታ፡, Image of Fanuel, መልክአ፡ ፋኑኤል፡, Anaphora of Mary,

ቅዳሴ፡ ማርያም፡, Sword of Divinity, ሠይፈ፡ መለኮት፡, and Litanies, ሊጦን፡

MYS 17/EMIP 617: Acts of Gäbrä Krestos, ገድለ፡ ገብረ፡ ክርስቶስ፡

MYS 18/EMIP 618: Mere_af Chants, ምዕራፍ፡

MYS 19/EMIP 619: Horologium for the Daytime Hours, ሰዓታት፡ ዘመዓልት፡, One Miracle of Mary, ተአምረ፡ ማርያም፡, Readings from Scripture, and One Miracle of Jesus, ተአምረ፡ ኢየሱስ፡

MYS 20/EMIP 620: Lectionary from the Four Gospels, መጽሐፈ፡ ግጻዌ፡

MYS 21/EMIP 621: Dəggwa for the whole year, ድጓ፡, EMML 1256

MYS 22/EMIP 622: Abbreviated Antiphonary for the year, ድጓ፡, Mə_raf Chants, ምዕራፍ፡, School Chants, copied from EMIP 89

MYS 23/EMIP 623: Homiliary in Honor of the Monthly Feast of the Archangel Michael, ድርሳነ፡ ሚካኤል፡

MYS 24/EMIP 624: Acts of Gäbrä Mänfäs Qəddus, ገድለ፡ ገብረ፡ መንፈስ፡ ቅዱስ፡, and Miracles of Gäbrä Mänfäs Qəddus, ተአምረ፡ ገብረ፡ መንፈስ፡ ቅዱስ፡

MYS 25/EMIP 625: Pentateuch (Genesis through Deuteronomy), አምስቱ፡ ብሔረ፡ ኦሪት፡, with marginal notes and commentaries

MYS 26/EMIP 626: Anaphora of Our Lady Mary ascribed to Cyriacus of Bəhənsa, ቅዳሴ፡ ማርያም፡, God of the Luminaries, Prayer of the Covenant, ጸሎተ፡ ኪዳን፡, "For the Sake of Peaceful Holy Things," በእንተ፡ ቅድሳት፡ ሰላማዊት፡, Mystagogia, ትምህርተ፡ ኅቡዓት፡, Anaphora of Our Lord, ቅዳሴ፡ እግዚእ፡, Lamentations of the Virgin

MYS 27/EMIP 627: Sword of the Trinity, ሠይፈ፡ መለኮት፡, and Bandlet of Righteousness, ልፋፈ፡ ጽድቅ፡

MYS 28/EMIP 628: Anaphora of Our Lady, ቅዳሴ፡ ማርያም፡, and Image of the Trinity, መልክአ፡ ሥላሴ፡

MYS 29/EMIP 629: Liturgy for the Dedication of a Church, ጸሎተ፡ ቡራኬ፡ ዘቅዳሴ፡ ቤተ፡ ክርስቲያን፡

MYS 30/EMIP 630: Synaxarium for the first half of the year, መጽሐፈ፡ ስንክሳር፡

MYS 31/EMIP 631: Synaxarium for the second half of the year, መጽሐፈ፡ ስንክሳር፡

MYS 32/EMIP 632: Missal, መጽሐፍ፡ ቅዳሴ፡

MYS 33/EMIP 633: Acts and Epistles of Paul (Romans through Hebrews), ጳውሎስ፡

MYS 34/EMIP 634: Book of Missal, Text and Commentary, in Gə_əz (the missal) and Amharic (the commentary), መጽሐፈ፡ ቅዳሴ፡ ንባቡና፡ ትርጓሜው፡

MYS 35/EMIP 635: Faith of the Fathers, ሃይማኖተ፡ አበው፡, Book of Tomar, መጽሐፈ፡ ጦማር፡, and Faith of Jacob Al Baradai, ሃይማኖተ፡ ያዕቆብ፡ አልበራዳኢ፡

MYS 36/EMIP 636: Computus, ባሕረ፡ ሐሳብ፡, Excerpt from Computus, *Abušahər*, አቡሻሁር, Computus of Demetrius, *Ḥasab Dəmeṭəros*, ሐሳበ፡ ድሜጥሮስ፡

MYS 37/EMIP 637: Antiphonary for the Fast of Lent, ጾመ፡ ድጓ፡

MYS 38/EMIP 638: Petition and Supplication, ስእለት፡ ወአስተብቍዖት፡, Harp of Praise, አርጋኖነ፡ ውዳሴ፡

MYS 39/EMIP 639: Six Images of Raguel, መልክአ፡ ሩጉኤል፡, Asmat Prayers of the Seven Archangels, ድርሳን፡ ዘሰባቱ፡ ሊቃነ፡ መላእክት፡, Image and of John, Son of Thunder, መልክአ፡ ዮሐንስ፡ ወልደ፡ ነጉድጓድ፡ combined with Asmat Prayer, and Image of the Guardian Angel, መልክአ፡ ዐቃቤ፡ መልአክ፡

MYS 40/EMIP 640: Zəmmare Chants, ዝማሬ፡, *Mäwaś̱ət* chants, መዋሥዕት፡

MYS 41/EMIP 641: Qerəlos, ቄርሎስ፡, Biography of Qerəlos

MYS 42/EMIP 642: Gə_əz Grammar, ሰዋስወ፡ ግእዝ፡

MYS 43/EMIP 643: Acts of Gälawədewos (Claudius), ገድለ፡ ኤያስጣቴዎስ፡, Miracles of Gälawədewos (Claudius), ተአምረ፡ ገላውዴዎስ፡, Image of Gälawədewos (Claudius), መልክአ፡ ገላውዴዎስ፡

MYS 44/EMIP 644: A Theological Critique of Certain Practices of the Orthodox Church, in Amharic, ስለ፡ ኦርቶደክስ፡ ቤተ፡ ክርስቲያን፡ አንዳንድ፡ ሥርዓቶች፡ የቀረቡ፡ ነገረ፡ መለኮታዊ፡ ትችት፡, by *Aläqa* Tayye Gäbrä Maryam

MYS 45/EMIP 645: Acts of Märqorewos, ገድለ፡ መርቆሬዎስ፡, Miracles of Märqorewos, ተአምረ፡ መርቆሬዎስ፡, Image of Märqorewos, መልክአ፡ መርቆሬዎስ፡

MYS 46/EMIP 646: Five Pillars of Mystery, አምስቱ፡ አዕማደ፡ ምሥጢር፡, Commentary on the Ten Commandments, in Amharic

MYS 47/EMIP 647: Acts of Saint George, ገድለ፡ ጊዮርጊስ፡, Miracles of Saint George, ተአምረ፡ ጊዮርጊስ፡

MYS 48/EMIP 648: Thirty-three Miracles of Mary, ተአምረ፡ ማርያም፡, and Nine Miracles of Jesus, ተአምረ፡ ኢየሱስ፡

MYS 49/EMIP 649: Andemta Commentary on the Epistles of Paul, ትርጓሜ፡ ጳውሎስ፡, Notes on the Stars, On the Life of Jesus, in Amharic

MYS 50/EMIP 650: Acts of Krəstos Sämra, ገድለ፡ ክርስቶስ፡ ሥምራ፡

MYS 51/EMIP 651: Sword of the Trinity, ሠይፈ፡ ሥላሴ፡, Image of the Trinity, መልክአ፡ ሥላሴ፡

MYS 52/EMIP 652: Sword of the Trinity, variant form, ሠይፈ፡ ሥላሴ፡

MYS 53/EMIP 653: Computus, Book of the Mystery of Heaven and Earth, መጽሐፈ፡ ምሥጢረ፡ ሰማይ፡ ወምድር፡, Faith of Jacob Al Baradai, ሃይማኖተ፡ ያዕቆብ፡ አልበራዳኢ፡

MYS 54/EMIP 654: The Delamarter Codex of Jubilees, መጽሐፈ፡ ኩፋሌ፡, and the Minor Prophets Hosea, ዘሆሴዕ, Amos, ዘአሞጽ, and Micah, ዘሚክያስ

List of Dated or Datable Manuscripts

1881–1921 (probably in the early-twentieth century; ff. 2v and *passim* mention *Abba* Peṭros [IV, 1881–1921] and Matewos [1843–1926]) : MYS 26.

1929–1950 (Ff. 4r and 6r mention *Abba* Qerəlos): MYS 28

1934/35: MYS 2, 3, and 4.

21 May 1937–29 July 1939: MYS 16

12 June 1947–1950 (= Sane 5, 1939 EC [f. 5a], Miyazya 28, 1941 EC [f. 201b], and 1942 EC [f. 128r]): MYS 21

17 June 1969 (= Sane 10, 1961 EC): MYS 51

1967/8 (= 1961 EC, f. 1r): MYS 40.

After 1970 (f. 24v mentions the death of *Abuna* Basəlyos in 1970): MYS 32

1981/2 (= 1974 E.C): MYS 34

List of Undated Manuscripts

15th Century
    15th century: MYS 54

18th Century
    18th century: MYS 53
    Late 18th century: MYS 38
    18th/19th century: MYS 33

19th Century
    Late 19th century: MYS 22

20th Century
    Early 20th century: MYS 11, 13, 14, and 41
    20th century: MYS 1, 5, 6, 7, 8, 9, 10, 12, 15, 17, 18, 19, 20, 23, 24, 25, 27, 29, 30, 31, 35, 36, 37, 39, 42, 43, 45, 46, 47, 48, 49, 50, and 52

Bibliography

NB: Western scholars are listed alphabetically by last name then first name; Ethiopian scholars are listed in the traditional manner, by first name.

Abbadie, Antoine d'. *Catalogue raisonné de manuscrits éthiopiens appartenant à Antoine d'Abbadie*, Paris, 1859.
Ammestu Ṣawatewa Zemawočč, አምስቱ፡ ጸዋትው፡ ዜማዎች፡፡ እነርሱም፤ ፩ኛ – ጸመ፡ ድጓ፤ ፪ኛ – ምዕራፍ፤ ፫ኛ – ዚቅ፤ መዝሙር፤ እሰመ፡ ለዓለም፤ ፬ኛ – ዝማሬ፤ ፭ኛ – ምዋሥዕት፡፡ Addis Ababa: Bərhanənna Sälam Press, 1965 EC.
Arras, Victor. *Miraculorum S. Georgii Megalomartyris collectio altera*. CSCO 138 (= SA 31). Louvain: Peeters, 1953.
Aethiops, Petrus, ed. *Testamentum Novum cum epistula Pauli ad Hebraeos*. Rome, 1548.
———. *Epistulae XIII divi Pauli*. Rome, 1549.
Bahru Zewde. *A History of Modern Ethiopia, 1855–1991*. 2nd edition. Eastern Africa Studies. Ohio: Ohio University Press; Addis Ababa: Addis Ababa University Press, 2001.
Bairu Tafla. *A Chronicle of Emperor Yoḥannes IV (1872–89)*. AF 1. Wiesbaden: Steiner, 1977.
Basset, René. *Les Apocryphes éthiopiens traduits en français. I–XI*. Paris: Bibliotheque de la Haute Science, 1893–1909.
Betreyohannes, Simeneh. "Scholarship on Ethiopian Music: Past, Present and Future Prospects." *African Study Monographs* Supp 41 (2010) 19–34.
Beyene, Yaqob. *Giyorgis di Sagla. Il libro del mistero (Mashafa Mestir)*, CSCO EA 97 and 98. Louvain: Peeters, 1993.
Bezold, Carl. "The Ordinary Canon of the Mass according to the Use of the Coptic Church." In *The Greek Liturgies Chiefly from Oriental Authorities*, edited by Charles Anthony Swainson, 347–95. Cambridge: Cambridge University Press, 1871.
Boyd, J. Oscar. *The Octateuch in Ethiopic According to the Text of the Paris Codex, with the variants of five other manuscripts, Part I, Genesis*. Leiden: Brill, 1909.
Brock, Sebastian. *St. Ephrem the Syrian: Hymns on Paradise*. New York: Saint Vladimir's Seminary, 1990.

Budge, E. A. Wallis. *Legend of Our Lady Mary the Perpetual Virgin and Her Mother Ḥannâ*. London: The Medici Society, 1922.
———. Wallis. *The Book of the Saints of the Ethiopian Church*. Cambridge: Cambridge University Press, 1928.
———. *The Bandlet of Righteousness. An Ethiopian Book of the Dead. The Ethiopic Text of the Lefâfaf Ṣedeḳ in Facsimile from Two Manuscripts in the B.M., edited with an English Translation*. London: Luzac, 1929.
———. *George of Lydda. The Patron Saint of England. A Study of the cults of Saint George in Ethiopia*. London: Oxford University Press, 1930.
———. *One Hundred and Ten Miracles of Our Lady Mary*. London: Oxford University Press, 1933.
Book of Saint Paul: Text with its Commentary (የቅዱስ፡ ጳውሎስ፡ መጽሐፍ፡ ንባቡ፡ ከነትርጓሜው፡). 2nd edtion. Addis Ababa: Tənśaʿe zä-Gubaʿe Publishing House, 1988 EC.
Catalogue of Manuscripts Microfilmed by the UNESCO Mobile Microfilm Unit in Addis Ababa and Gojjam Province. Addis Ababa: Ministry of Education and Fine Arts, 1970.
Cerulli, Enrico. *Il libro etiopico dei Miracoli di Maria e le sue fonti nelle letterature del medio evo latino*. SO 1. Rome: Bardi, 1943.
———. *Atti Di Krestos Samrā*. CSCO, SA 33 and 34. Louvain: Peeters, 1956.
Chaîne, Marius. "Repertoire des Salam et Malkeʿe contenus dans les manuscrits thiopiens des bibliothèques d'Europe." *ROC* 18 (1913) 183–203, 337–57.
Conti Rossini, Carlo. "Manoscritti ed opera abissine in Europa" In *Rendiconti della Reale Accademia dei Lincei. Classe di scienze morali, storiche e filologiche*, 5, 8 (1899) 606–37.
———. *Acta Yared et Pantalewon*. CSCO 26/27; SA 9/10. Leipzig: Harrassowitz, 1904.
———. *Vitae sanctorum indigenarum. I. Acta S. Walatta Peṭros. II. Miracula S. Zara-Buruk*. CSCO 68 SA 25. Rome, 1912.
———. "Notice sur les manuscrits thiopiens de la collection d'Abbadie." *JA* 10.15 (1912) 551–78 [I]; 20 (1913) 5–72, 449–94 [II]; 11.2 (1913) 5–64 [III]; 5 (1915) 189–238, 447–93 [IV]; reprinted. Paris, 1914.
Crummey, Donald. "The Ethiopian Orthodox *Täwahedo* Church." In *The Cambridge History of Christianity, Volume 5: Eastern Christianity*, edited by M. Angold. Cambridge: Cambridge University Press, 2006.

Daoud, Marcos, and H. E. Blatta Marsie Hazen. *The Liturgy of the Ethiopian Church*. Cairo: Egyptian Book Press, 1959.

Delamarter, Steve. "Catalogues and Digitization for Previously Uncatalogued Ethiopian Manuscripts in the United States." In *Proceedings of the Sixteenth International Conference of Ethiopian Studies*. Forthcoming.

———. "More Ethiopian Manuscripts in North America." *SBL Forums*, November, 2007. Online: http://www.sbl-site.org/publications/article.aspx?ArticleId=736.

———. "The SGD Digital Collection: Previously Unknown and Uncatalogued Ethiopian Manuscripts in North America." *SBL Forums*, February 2007. Online:http://www.sbl-site.org/Article.aspx?ArticleId=622.

Delamarter, Steve, and Demeke Berhane. *A Catalogue of Previously Uncatalogued Ethiopic Manuscripts in England: Twenty-Three Manuscripts in the Bodleian, Cambridge University and John Rylands University Libraries and in a Private Collection*. JSSSup 21 Oxford: Oxford University Press on behalf of the University of Manchester, 2007.

Delamarter, Steve and Melaku Terefe. *Ethiopian Scribal Practice 1: Plates for the Catalogue of the Ethiopic Manuscript Imaging Project (Companion to EMIP Catalogue 1)*. EMTS 2. Eugene, OR: Pickwick, 2009.

Dərsanä Mikaʾel. ድርሳነ፡ ሚካኤል፡ ወድርሳነ፡ ሩፋኤል፡፡ መልክእ፡ ሚካኤል፡ ወመልክእ፡ ሩፋኤል፡፡ ዘአኅተሞ፡ ተስፋ፡ ገብረ፡ ሥላሴ፡ ዘብሔረ፡ ቡልጋ፡፡ = *Dərsanä Mikaʾel wä-Dərsanä Rufaʾel. Mälkəʾa Mikaʾel wä- Mälkəʾa Rufaʾel. zä-aḥətämo Täsfa Gäbrä Śəllase zä-bəḥerä Bulga*. Addis Ababa: Artistik Press, 1940 EC.

Dillmann, Augustus. *Catalogus codicum manuscritorum qui in Museo Britannico asservantur. Volume III, Codices Aethiopici*. London: British Museum, 1847.

———. *Chrestomathia Aethiopica*. Leipzig: Weigel, 1866.

Dobberahn, Friedrich Erich. "Der äthiopische Ritus." In *Liturgie im Angesicht des Todes: Judentum und Ostkirchen*, edited by Hansjakob Becker and Herman Ühlein, Band 1: *Texte und Kommentare*, 137–316; plates 9 and 10. Mainz: Saint Ottilien, 1996.

———. "Der äthiopische Begräbnisritus." In *Liturgie im Angesicht des Todes: Judentum und Ostkirchen*, edited by Hansjakob Becker and Herman Ühlein, Band 1: *Texte und Kommentare*, 657–84; and Band

2: *Übersetzungen, Anhänge und Register*, 1397–432. PL 9 and 10. Mainz: Saint Ottilien, 1996.

Euringer, Sebastian. "Ein abessinisches Amulet mit Liedern zu Ehren der Heiligen Gabra Manfas Qeddus, Johannes und Kyros." *ZS* 3 (1924) 116–35.

———. "Das Netz Salomons." *ZS* 6 (1928) 76–100, 179–99, and 300–14; *ZS* 7 (1929) 68–85.

———. "Der Spiegel Salomons. Ein abessinisches Amulett." *ZDMG* 91 (1937) 162–74.

———. "Die Binde der Rechtfertigung (Lefâfa ṣedek)." *Or* NS 9 (1940) 76–99 and 244–59.

———. "Übersetzung der ‚Preces officii matutini' in Dillmann's ‚Chrestomathia Aethiopica.'" *Or* NS 11 (1942) 333–66.

Fries, Karl. "Weddâsê Mârjâm: Ein äthiopischer Lobgesang an Maria." Dissertation Uppsala, 1892.

Fuhs, Hans Ferdinand. *Die Äthiopische Übersetzung des Propheten Micha*. BBB 28. Bonn: Hanstein, 1968.

———. *Die Äthiopische Übersetzung des Propheten Hosea*. BBB 38. Bonn: Hanstein, 1971.

Gervers, Michael. 2004. "The Portuguese Import of Luxury Textiles to Ethiopia in the 16th and 17th Centuries and Their Subsequent Artistic Influence." In *Indigenous and the Foreign in Christian Ethiopian Art: on Portuguese-Ethiopian Contacts in the 16th–17th Centuries: Papers from the Fifth International Conference on the History of Ethiopian Art (Arrabida, 26–30 November 1999)*, edited by Manuel João Ramos with Isabel Boavida, 121–34. Hants, UK: Ashgate, 2004.

Getatchew Haile. *The Different Collection of Nägś Hymns of the Ethiopic Literature*. Oikonomia 19. Erlangen, Germany: Lehrstuhl für Geschichte und Theologie des christlichen Ostens, 1983.

———. "Materials on the Theology of Qəb_at." In *Ethiopian Studies: Proceedings of the sixth international conference*, Tel-Aviv, 14–17 April 1980, edited by Gideon Goldenberg, 210–19. Boston: Balkema, 1986.

———. *The Epistle of Humanity of Emperor Zär'a Ya_ǝqob (Ṭomarä Təsbə't)*. CSCO, text 522, SA 95; tr. 523, SA 96 (1991).

———. *The Mariology of Emperor Zär'a Ya_ǝqob of Ethiopia*. OCA 242. Rome: Pontificium Institutum Studiorum Orientalium, 1992.

———. ጌታቸው ኃይሌ፣ ባሕረ ሐሳብ የዘመን ቤጠራ ቅርሳችን ከታሪክ ማስታወሻ ጋር ፣ Collegeville, MN, 1993 EC.

———. The *Mäṣḥafä Gǝnzät* as a Historical Source Regarding the Theology of the Ethiopian Orthodox Church." In *Scrinium. Revue de patrologie, d'hagiographie critique et d'histoire ecclésiastique. Tome 1: Varia Aethiopica in Memory of Sevir B. Chernetsov (1943–2005)*, 58–76. Saint Petersburg: Byzantinorossica, 2005.

———. *The Gǝ_ǝz Acts of Abba Ǝsṭifanos of G^wǝndag^{w}ǝnde*. CSCO 619/620 (= SA 110/111). Louvain: Peeters, 2006.

Getatchew Haile, and William F. Macomber. *A Catalogue of Ethiopian Mansucripts Microfilmed for the Ethiopian Manuscript Microfilm Library, Addis Ababa and for the Hill Monastic Manuscript Library*, volumes 1–10. Collegeville, 1973ff.

Giyorgis, L. W. G. *Tentawi ser'ata mahlet za-Abuna Yared (A study of the ancient musical system of Yared - In Amharic)*. Addis Ababa: Maison des Etudes Ethiopiennes & Institut Tigreen des Langues, 1997.

Grébaut, Sylvain. ―Le sixième jour de l'hexam r on d'Épiphane de Chypre." *ROC* 18 (1913) 432–41.

———. ―Les miracles de Jésus. Texte éthiopien publié et traduit." *PO* 12 (1919) 551–649 (I); 14 (1920) 767–840 (II); and 17 (1923) 783–854 (III). Paris: Firmin-Didot, 1919.

———. ―Prière pour conjurer les demons." *ROC* 23 (1922) 199–208.

———. *Les Paralipomènes, Livres I et II, Version Ethiopienne*. PO 23. Paris: Firmin-Didot, 1932.

———. ―Prière magique contre l'infection des plaies." *Aethiopica* (1933) 50ff.

——— and Eugenius Tisserant. ―Codices Aethiopici Vaticani et Borgiani, Barberinianus Orientalis 2, Rossianus 865, volumes I-II. In *Bybliotheca Vaticana* (1935–36).

———. ―La prière de Marie au Golgotha." *JA* 226 (1935) 273–86.

———. ―La prière *Sayfa malakot*." *Aethiopica* 4 (1936) 1–6.

———. ―L'Hymne-invocation *Lesâna sab'e*." *Aethiopica. Revue philologique* 3 (1936) 6–12.

———. ―La légend de Sousneyos et de Werzelyâ d'après de ms. Éthiopien Griaule n° 297." *Or* NS 6 (1937) 177–83.

———. *Catalogue des Manuscrits Éthiopiens de la Collection Griaule*. Volume I. Travaux et m m oires de l'Institut d'ethnologie 29. Paris: Université de Paris, 1938; Volume II, In *Miscellanea Africana*

Lebaudy. Paris, 1941; Volume III. Travaux et m m oires de l'Institut d'ethnologie 30. Paris: Universit de Paris, 1944.

———. "Petit Ḥaṣoura Masqal." *Æthiops* 6 (1938) 12–3.

Grohmann, Adolf. *Aethiopische Marienhymnen*. Abhandlungen der Philologisch-Historischen Klasse der Sächsischen Akademie der Wissenschaften 33,4. Leipzig: Teubner, 1919.

Hammerschmidt, Ernst. *Aethiopische liturgische Texte der Bodleian Library in Oxford*. Veröffentlichung 38. Berlin: Akademie, 1960.

———. *Studies in the Ethiopic Anaphoras*, 2nd ed. AF 25. Stuttgart: Steiner, 1987.

Hammerschmidt, Ernst and Veronika Six. *Äthiopische Handschriften, Teil 1: Die Handschriften der Staatsbibliothek Preussischer Kulturbesitz*. VOHD 20.4. Wiesbaden: Harrassowitz, 1983; *Teil 2: Die Handschriften der Bayerischen Staatsbibliothek*. VOHD 20.5. Wiesbaden: Harrassowitz, 1989; Veronika Six, *Äthiopische Handschriften, Teil 3: Handschriften deutscher Bibliotheken und Museen und aus Privatbesitz*. VOHD 20:6. Stuttgart: Steiner, 1994.

———. *Äthiopische Handschriften vom Tanasee, Teil 1: Reisebericht und Beschreibung der Handschriften in dem Kloster des heiligen Gabriel auf der Insel Kebran*. VOHD 20.1 (1973); *Teil 2: Die Handschriften von Dabra Maryam und von Rema*. VOHD 20.2 (1977). *Teil 3: Nebst einem Nachtrag zum Katalog der äthiopischen Handschriften deutscher Bibliotheken und Museen*. VOHD 20.3 (1999). Wiesbaden: Steiner.

Heldman, Marilyn Eiseman, S. C. Munro-Hay, and Roderick Grierson. *African Zion: The Sacred Art of Ethiopia*. New Haven: Yale University Press, 1993.

Hayoz, P. Chrysostome. "Portrait de Marie. Complainte de la Vierge. Deux poésies éthiopiennes inédites. Texte, traduction, commentaire." Dissertation Fribourg, Switzerland, 1956.

Irvine, Keith, and L. H. Ofosu-Appiah, eds. *The Encyclopaedia Africana Dictionary of African Biography, volume one: Ethiopia-Ghana*. New York: Reference, 1997.

Julian, John. *A Dictionary of Hymnology: Setting forth the Origin and History of Christian Hymns of all Ages and Nations*. New York: Scribner, 1892.

Knibb, Michael A. *Translating the Bible: The Ethiopic Version of the Old Testament*. The Schweich Lectures of the British Academy, 1995. Oxford: Published for The British Academy, 1999.

Lash, Christopher. "'Gate of Light': An Ethiopian Hymn to the Blessed Virgin." *Eastern Churches Review* 4 (1972) 36–46; and 5 (1973) 143–56.
Leander, Pontus. `*Arganona Ueddase*' *nach Handschriften in Uppsala, Berlin, Tübingen und Frankfurt a. M.* Göteborgs Högskolas Årsskrift 28. Leipzig, 1922.
Lepisa, Tito. "The Three Modes and the Signs of the Songs in the Ethiopian Liturgy." In, *Proceedings of The Third International Conference of Ethiopian Studies 1966*, edited by Richard Pankhurst, et. al., 162–87. Addis Ababa: Addis Ababa University Press, 1969–70.
Lifchitz, D bor ah, and Sylvain Gr ba ut. *Textes éthiopiens magico-religieux*. Paris: Institut d'ethnologie, 1940.
Littmann, Enno. "*Arde 'et*: The Magic Book of the Disciples." *JAOS* 25 (1904) 1–48.
Löfgren, Oscar. "Äthiopische Wandamulette." *OS* 11 (1962) 95–120.
Ludolf, Hiob. *Psalterium Davidis Aethiopice et Latine*. 1701.
Marcus Harold. *A History of Ethiopia*. Berkeley: University of California Press, 1994.
Marrassini, Paolo. *Vita Omelia Miracoli del Santo Gabra Manfas Qeddus*. CSCO 597 and 598 (= EA 107 and 108). Lovain: Peeters, 2003.
McVey, Kathleen. *Ephrem the Syrian: Hymns*. New York: Paulist, 1989.
Mekarios, A. *The Ethiopian Orthodox Tewahedo Church: Faith, Order of Worship and Ecumenical Relations*. Addis Ababa: Tensae, 1996.
Mercer, Samuel A. B. "The Anaphora of Our Lord in the Ethiopic Liturgy." *JSOR* 1 (1917) 24–40.
Mercier, Jacques. "Les peintures des rouleaux protecteurs éthiopiens." *JES* 12.2 (1974) 107–46.
———. "Les plus anciens rouleaux protecteurs éthiopiens de la Bibliothèque Nationale de Paris." *AE* 10 (1976) 227–42.
———. *Zauberrollen aus Äthiopien: Kultbilder magischer Riten*. Munich: Prestel, 1979.
———. *Ethiopian Magic Scrolls*. New York: Braziller, 1979.
———. *Art that Heals: The Image as Medicine in Ethiopia*. New York: Prestel, 1997.
Mercier, Jacques and Henri Marchal. *Le roi Salomon et les ma tres du regard. Art et médecine en thi opie, Musée National des Arts d Afrique et d Océanie, 20 Octobre 1992–25 Janvier 1993*. Paris: National Museum, 1992.

Mondon-Vidailhet, Casimir. "La Musique Ethiopienne." In *Encyclopedie de la Musique et Dictionnaire du Conservatoire, Premiere Partie: Histoire de la Musique*, edited by A. Lavignac and L. de la Laurence, 3178–3196. Paris, Libraire Delagrave, 1922.

Neugebauer, Otto. *Ethiopic Astronomy and Computus*. Vienna: Verlag der Österreichischen Akademie der Wissenschaften, 1979.

———. *Chronography in Ethiopic Sources*. Osterreichische Ak. der Wiss. Phil.–hist. Kl. Sitz. 512. Vienna: Österreichischen Akademie der Wissenschaften, 1989.

Niccum, Curt. "The Book of Acts in Ethiopic (with critical text and apparatus) and its relation to the Greek textual tradition." PhD dissertation Universtiy of Notre Dame, 2000.

O'Hanlon, Douglas. *Features of the Abyssinian Church*. London: SPCK, 1946.

Pankhurst, Richard. "A Serious Question of Ethiopian Studies: Five Thousand Ethiopian Manuscripts Abroad, and the International Community," *Addis Tribune*, 17 December 1999; available online at http://www.afromet.org/Archives/AddisTribune/17–12–99/Five.htm.

Pereira, Francisco Maria Esteves. *Le Livre d'Esther*, PO 9 (1913) 1–56.

———. *O livro do profeta Amós e a sua versão etiópica*. Separata de Boletin do Segunda Classe 11. Lisbon: Academia das sciêncas de Lisboa, 1917.

———. *Le troisième livre de Ezrâ (Esdras et Néhémie canoniques): version éthiopienne*. PO 13.5. Paris: Firmin-Didot, 1919.

———. *Acta Martyrum I*. CSCO 37 ; SA 20 (reprint, 1962) 259–75.

Perruchon, J. "Le livre des mysteres du ciel et de la terre." PO 1 (1947) 1–96.

Säbattu Kidanat, Qəddase Maryam, Mälkə'a Guba'e. Addis Ababa: Täsfa 1959 EC.

Shelemay, Kay Kaufman. "Zemā: A Concept of Sacred Music in Ethiopia." *The World of Music* 24 (1982): 52–64.

———. "The Musician and Transmission of Religious Tradition: The Multiple Roles of the Ethiopian Däbtära. *JRA* 22 (1992) 242–60.

Shelemay, Kay Kaufman, and Peter Jeffery, eds. *Ethiopian Christian Religious Chant: An Anthology. Introduction*, Volume I (1993); *Performance*, Volume 2 (1994); and *History of Ethiopian Chant*, Volume 3 (1997). Madison WI: A-R Editions, 1993–1997

Six, Veronika. "Kategorien der äthiopischen Zaubertexte." *ZDMG* 139 (1989) 310–17.

———. *Äthiopische Handschriften, Teil 3: Handschriften Deutscher Bibliotheken, Museen und Privatbesitz*. Stuttgart: Steiner, 1994.

———. "Die äthiopischen Handschriften des Völkerkundemuseums der Universität Zürich." Part I *OC* 80 (1996) 116–152; Part II *OC* 81 (1997) 127–47.

———. "Kategorien der äthiopischen Zaubertexte." *ZDMG* 139 (1989) 310–17.

Stoffregen Pedersen, Kirsten. *Traditional Ethiopian Exegesis of the Book of Psalms*. Wiesbaden: Harrassowitz, 1995.

Strelcyn, Stefan. *Catalogue des Manuscrits Éthiopiens de la Collection Griaule, volume IV*, Ethiopien 373 (Griaule 69); Ethiopien 674 (Griaule 366); Nouvelles acquisitions: Ethiopiens 301–304. Paris: Institut d'Ethnologie, 1954.

———. *Prières magique éthiopiens pour délier les charmes (maftəḥ šəray)*. Rocznik orientalistyczny 18. Warsaw: Panstwowe Wydawnictwo Naukowe, 1955.

———. *Catalogue of Ethiopic Manuscripts in the John Rylands University Library of Manchester*. Manchester: Manchester University Press, 1974.

———. *Catalogue des manuscrits éthiopiens de l'Accademia Nazionale dei Lincei: Fonds Conti Rossini et Fonds Caetani 209, 375, 376, 377, 378*. ISBB 9. Rome: Accademia Nazionale dei Lincei, 1976.

———. *Catalogue of Ethiopian Manuscripts in the British Library Acquired since the Year 1877*. London: British Museum, 1978.

———. "Catalogue of Ethiopic Manuscripts of the Wellcome Institute of the History of Medicine in London." *BSOAS* 35 (1972) 27–55.

———. *Médicine et plantes d' thiopie [I]: Les traits médicaux éthiopiens*. Zakład orientalistyki Polskiej Akademii Nauk. Prace orientalistyczny 14 Warsaw, 1968; *[II]: Enquête sur les noms et emploi des plantes en Éthiopie*. Naples: Istituto Universitario orientale, 1973.

Uhlig, Siegbert. *Introduction to Ethiopian Palaeography*. AF 28. Stuttgart: Steiner, 1990.

Uhlig, Siegbert, and Helge Maehlum. *Novum Testamentum aethiopice: die Gefangenschaftsbriefe*. AF 33. Stuttgart: Steiner, 1993.

Ullendorff, Edward. *Ethiopia and the Bible*. The Schweich Lectures, 1967. London: Oxford University Press, 1968.

VanderKam, James C. *The Book of Jubilees*. 2 volumes. CSCO 510/511; SA 87/88; Louvain: Peeters, 1989.

———. "The Manuscript Tradition of Jubilees." In *Enoch and the Mosaic Torah*, ed. Gabriele Boccaccini and Giovanni Ibba, 3–21. Grand Rapids: Eerdmans, 2009.

Velat, Bernard. *Me̱erāf. Commun del'office divin éthiopien pour toute l'année*. *PO* 34 (1966) I–XV and 1–413. Paris: Firmin-Didot, 1966.

———. *Étude sur le Me̱erāf. Commun del'office divin éthiopien. Introduction, traduction française, commentaire litugique et musica*. *PO* 33 (1966). Paris: Didot, 1966.

———. *Ṣom Deggua. Antiphonaire du carême. Quatre premières semaines*. PO 32.1–2 (1966) and 32.3–4 (1969).

Wechsler, M. G. *Evangelium Iohannis Aethiopicum*. CSCO SA 109. Louvain: Peeters, 2005.

Weischer, Bernd Manuel. "Die äthiopischen Psalmen- und Qerlosfragmente in Erevan/Armenien." *OC* 53 (1969) 142–143.

———. *Qerellos I. Afrikanische Forschungen* 7. Hamburg 1973.

———. *Qerellos III: Der Dialog "Dass Christus einer ist" des Kyrillos von Alexandrien*. AF 2 Wiesbaden: Steiner, 1977.

———. *Qerellos IV. 1: Homilien und Briefe zum Konzil von Ephesos*. AF 4. Wiesbaden: Steiner, 1979.

———. *Qerellos IV 2: Traktate des Epiphanius von Zypern und des Proklos von Kyzikos*. AF 6. Wiesbaden: Steiner, 1979.

———. *Qerellos IV 3: Traktate des Severianos Von Gabala, Gregorios Thaumaturgus und Kyrillos von Alexandrien*. AF 7. Wiesbaden: Steiner, 1980.

Wendt, Kurt. *Das Maṣḥafa Milād (Liber Nativitatis) und Maṣḥafa Sellāsē (Liber Trinitatis) des Kaisers Zarʾa Yā̱qob*. CSCO 41. Louvain: Secr. du CSCO, 1962.

Weninger, Stefan. "Ephrem." In *Encyclopaedia Aethiopica*, 2:331–32. Wiesbaden: Harrassowitz, 2005.

Wright, William. *Catalogue of Ethiopic Manuscripts in the British Museum acquired since the Year 1847*. London: British Museum, 1877.

Zotenberg, Hermann. *Catalogue des manuscrits éthiopiens (gheez et amharique) de la Bibliothèque Nationale*. Paris, 1877.

Zuurmond, Rochus. *Novum Testamentum Aethiopice: The Synoptic Gospels*. I. General Introduction and II. Gospel of Mark. AF 27. Wiesbaden: Harrassowitz, 1989. III. Gospel of Matthew. AF 55. Wiesbaden: Harrassowitz, 2001.

Index of Works in the Codices

Absolution of the Son, 77
Acts
  of Gäbrä Krestos, 85
  of Gälawədewos, 174
  of Gäbrä Mänfäs Qəddus, 104
  of George, 187
  of Krestos Samra, 204
  of Märqorewos, 181
Acts of
  Gäbrä Mänfäs Qəddus, 233
Alphabet
  Amharic, 185
  Gə_əz (rejected leaf), 135
Amharic Language and Math Exercises, 202
Anaphora
  List, 143
  of Athanasius, 129
    commentary on, 140
  of Basil, 130
    commentary on, 141
  of Cyril, 129
    commentary on, 142
  of Dioscorus, 129
    commentary on, 142
  of Epiphanius, 129
    commentary on, 141
  of Gregory
    commentary on, 141
  of Gregory, brother of Basil, 129
  of Gregory, the second, 129
  of Gregory, the Wonder Worker, 129
    commentary on, 143
  of Jacob of Serugh, 129
    commentary on, 142
  of John Chrysostom, 129
    commentary on, 142
  of John, Son of Thunder, 129
    commentary on, 139
  of Mary attributed to Cyriacus of Bəhənsa, 82, 113, 129
    commentary on, 140
  of Our Lady Mary, 117
  of Our Lord, 114, 129
    commentary on, 139
  of the 318 Orthodox Fathers, 129
    commentary on, 140
  of the Apostles, 129
    commentary on, 139
Anathemas of the Fathers, 148
Antiphonary for the Fast of Lent excerpt, 166
Antiphonary for the year, $Dəgg^wa$, 92, 97
Arabic Phrases with Amharic Translation, 185
Ardə't, 74
Asmat Prayer, 163, 164
  against a demon, 81
  against an enemy, 81
  against evil spirit, evil eye, epilepsy and Legewon, 79
  against Hail, 158
  against the devil, 185
  against the evil eye, 82
  of John, Son of Thunder, 162
  of Solomon against demons and witch doctors, 81
  of the Archangel Mika'el, 64
  of the prophet Moses, 209
  of the Seven Archangels, 78, 162
  of the Trinity, 72
  to Fanu'el the archabel against disease, miscarriage, bleeding and the evil eye, 79

to protect shinbone and against a witch doctor who killed a person before his time, 80
Bandlet of Righteousness, 116
Beauty of the News, 169
Bible
  1 Chronicles (in Amharic), 42
  1 Corinthians, 44, 134
    commentary on, 197
  1 John, 44
  1 Kings, 42
  1 Kings (in Amharic), 42
  1 Peter, 44
  1 Samuel (in Amharic), 42
  1 Thessalonians, 44, 135
    commentary on, 199
  1 Timothy, 44, 135
    commentary on, 200
  2 Chronicles (in Amharic), 42
  2 Corinthians, 44, 134
  2 John, 45
  2 Kings, 42
  2 Kings (in Amharic), 42
  2 Parileipomenon, 42
  2 Peter, 44
  2 Samuel (in Amharic), 42
  2 Thessalonians, 44, 135
    commentary on, 199
  2 Timothy, 44, 135
    commentary on, 200
  3 John, 45
  3 Kings, 42
  4 Kings, 42
  Acts, 132
  Acts of the Apostles, 43
  Acts of the Apostles chapter 17, 88
  Baruch, 47
  Colossians, 44, 135
  Deuteronomy, 41, 111
  Ecclesiasticus, 47
  Enoch, 47
  Ephesians, 44, 135
    commentary on, 198
  Esther, 42
  Exodus, 41, 110
  Ezra, 42, 47
  Galatians, 44, 135
    commentary on, 198
  Genesis, 41, 110
    Introduction, 110
  Gospel
    excerpt, 185
  Gospel of John, 43
    excerpt, 91
  Gospel of John 3
    excerpt, 209
  Gospel of Luke, 43
    excerpt, 90
  Gospel of Mark, 43
    excerpt, 90
  Gospel of Matthew, 43
    commentary by John Chrysostom, 213
    excerpt, 90
  Hebrews, 44, 135
    commentary on, 201
  I Maccabbees, 46
  II Ezra, 47
  II Maccabbees, 46
  III Maccabbees, 46
  James, 45
  Jeremiah chapter 17, 88
  Joshua, 42
  Jubilees, 46
  Jude, 45
  Judges, 42
  Judith, 47
  Leviticus, 41, 110
  Leviticus chapter 23, 88
  Nehemiah, 42
  Numbers, 41, 110
  Paraleipomenon of Daniel, 48
  Paraleipomenon of Jeremiah, 47
  Parileipomenon, 42
  Pauline Epistles
    Introductions, 132

Philemon, 44, 135
   commentary on, 201
Philippians, 44, 135
Psalm 26, 72
Psalms
   excerpt, 72
Psalms excerpt, 163
Psalms of David, 43
Revelation, 45
   excerpt, 135
Romans, 44, 134
   commentary on, 196, 197, 198, 199, 200, 201
Ruth, 42
Susanna, 47
Titus, 44, 135
   commentary on, 200
Tobit, 47
Wisdom of Solomon, 47
Bible-(besides Psalter)
   Gospel of John, 236
Blessings for the one who follows this faith and consequences for the one who rejects this faith with a testimony to its power, 185
Book of Confession, 75
Book of Disciples, *Ardə't*, 74
Book of Penance, 75
Calendar
   Instructions about the measurement of shadows for the telling of time, 114, 185
   of the Weevily and Unweevily Months, 53
Calendar Tables, 152, 211
   of the Epact and Solar Cycle fo the year, 212
Canticle of the Flower, 53
   excerpt, 53
Chants
   Halleluiatic Chants Index, 155
   Mäwaśət, 166
   Məraf, 86, 97

School Chants, 97
Ziq, 55, 57, 59
Chart
   Measurements of the shadows of the hours, 211
   of käntəros, cycle of a quarter of a year, 211
   Orbit and Windows of the Stars, 210
Commentary, 171
   on Anaphora of
      Athanasius, 140
      Basil, 141
      Cyril, 142
      Dioscorus, 142
      Epiphanius, 141
      Gregory, 141
      Gregory, the Wonder Worker, 143
      Jacob of Serugh, 142
      John Chrysostom, 142
      John, Son of Thunder, 139
      Mary attributed to Cyriacus of Bəhənsa, 140
      Our Lord, 139
      the 318 Orthodox Fathers, 140
      the Apostles, 139
   on Litanical Prayer, 138
   on Matthew by John Chrysostom
      excerpt, 213
   on Missal (in Amharic), 137
   on Mystagogia, 138
   on Prayer of the Covenant, 138
   on Supplications, 138
   on the Farewell Speech of Moses (in Amharic), 111
   on the Mystery of the Trinity, 183
   on the Ordinary of the Mass, 139
   on the Orit, 110
   on the Pauline Epistles, 196

on the Tabernacle (in Amharic), 111
on the Ten Commandments (in Amharic), 184
Thirteen Stations of the Cross (in Amharic), 184
Computus
  Abušahər
    excerpt, 151
  Bahərä Hasab, 152, 213
  Bahərä Hasab (in Amharic), 151
  story of its revelation, 151
Confession of Faith, 170
Curse
  on anyone who erases from the book, 135
  on anyone who steals the book, 158
Days on which the heavens are open to receive prayer, 102
Didascalia, 147
Epistle
  of Cyril of Alexandria to John of Antioch, 170
  of John of Antioch to Cyril of Alexandria, 170
  of the Synod of Ephesus to John of Antioch, 170
Explanation of the Islamic Teaching on Jesus and Mary (in Amharic), 185
Faith of Gregory Thaumaturgus, 170
Faith of Jacob Al Baradai, 148, 213
Faith of the Fathers, 147
Five Pillars of Mystery, 183, 213
God of the Luminaries, 77, 113
God Reigns, 71
Grammar
  Gə_əz, 173
Greetings for the Saints
  excerpt, 158
Harp of Praise, 158
Homiliary in Honor of the Monthly Feast of the Archangel Michael, 62, 67, 100
Homily
  by a Sage on Melchisedec, 170
  by Acacius of Melitene, 169
  by Cyril of Alexandria, 169, 170
    on Melchisedec, 170
  by Epiphanius of Cyprus, 170
    on the Trinity, 170
  by Eusiebius of Heraclea, 169
  by Firmus of Caesarea, 170
  by Juvenalius of Jerusalem, 169
  by Proclus of Cyzicus, 170
  by Rheginus of Constantinople, 169
  by Severianus of Gabala, 170
  by Severus of Synnada, 169
  by Theodotus of Ancyra, 169
  by Theodotus of Ancyra,, 170
Horologium
  for Daytime Hours, 88
Hymn to Saint George (and Mary)
  O who is quick for help, 51
Hymn to Sebastian, 79
Hymns
  during communion, 114
  for the Lent Season, 155
  God Reigns, 71
  to Mary, Angels Praise Her, 135
Image
  of Fanu'el, 82
  of Gälawədewos, 174
  of Gäbrä Mänfas Qəddus, 71
  of Gabriel, 51, 64, 71
  of George, 51, 71
  of John the Baptist, 70
  of Krestos Samra, 204
  of Märqorewos, 181
  of Mary, 51

of Michael, 51, 64, 71
of Michael, second, 64
of Raguel, 161
of the Guardian Angel, 163
of the Suffering of Our Lord
   excerpt, 118
of the Trinity, 118, 207
Introductory Rite from Muˍallaqa, 190
Lamentations of the Virgin, 114
Lamentations of the Virgin, Addendum, 114
Liṭon, 128
List
   of Alexandrian Popes, 213
Litanies, 83
Litany
   for the evening prayer, 128
Liturgy
   for the Dedication of a Church, 120
   on the history of, 138
Miracles
   of Gälawədewos, 174
   of Gäbrä Mänfas Qəddus, 104
   of George, 188
   of Jesus, 49, 89, 195
   of Krestos Samra, 204
   of Märqorewos, 181
   of Mary, 1, 39, 88, 189
     Introduction, 213
   of Mary, Introductory Rite, 1
Missal, 128, 137
Mystagogia, 78, 113, 138, 147
Mystery of Baptism, 184
Mystery of Heaven and Earth, 212
Mystery of Holy Communion, 184
Mystery of the Baptism, 184
Mystery of the Incarnation, 183
   excerpt, 185
Mystery of the Resurrection of the Dead, 184, 213

Mystery of the Trinity, 183
Name
   of *Abba*, 114, 118
   of Abuna, 130
   of archbishop, 45, 130
   of bishop, 45, 83, 130, 166
   of emperor, 45, 143
   of empress, 45
   of king, 123, 166, 205
   of Minister of Pen, 46
   of owner, 48, 54, 65, 72, 74, 83, 89, 94, 98, 102, 107, 114, 118, 119, 148, 158, 164, 202, 205, 209
   of owner's mother, 98
   of owner's wife, 83
   of scribe, 39, 65, 72, 74, 85, 98, 107, 114, 118, 143, 205, 207
   of the months, 152
   of translators, 46
Net of Solomon, 80
Nicaean Creed
   History and Commentary, 140
Note
   on the Italian Language, 202
   on the Prophet Mohammad and his wives, 185
   on the year of enthronement of Ethiopian Kings, 202
On the 318 Orthodox Fathers, 170
On the Life of Jesus, 202
On the Nativity and Life of Our Lord, 170
On the Orthodox Faith, 168
Ordinary of the Mass
   commentary on, 139
Petition, 157
Prayer
   against the tongue of people, 78
   Explanation of Eucharistic Prayer, 143
   for the Gospel Readings during the Night, 129

for the owner and the scribe, 114
For the sake of the peaceful holy things, 113
Litanical, 138
of Mary at Golgotha, 81
of Petition collected from Coptic Songs by *Abba* Athanasius, archbishop of Alexandria, 158
of Petition collected from Saint John, 158
of Petition of *Abba* Sinoda, 158
of Petition of Basil of Caearea, 157
of Petition of Cyril, archbishop of Alexandria, 158
of Petition of Ephrem the Syrian, 157, 158
of the Covenant, 77, 113, 128, 138
Office Prayers, 128
Scribal Prayer, 39
to Jesus
  Guard Me, 81
  I Take Refuge, 80
to Mary
  I Take Refuge, 80
Prayer of the Covenant, 128
Prescription
  for diarrhea, 72
  for stubborn bull, 72
Qerəlos, 168
  biography, 170
Record
  Colophon, 72, 94, 143, 181, 205, 207
  Copied by, 65, 72, 143, 207
  Deposition, 72
  Graduation Certificate, 167
  Letter of application, 202
  Note (illegible), 72

Note of attribution, 171
Note of authorship, 153
Note of donation, 185
Note of items lent, 213
Note of ownership, 48, 60, 65, 72, 98, 202, 213
Note of presentation, 65
Note of purchase, 48, 202
Note of translation, 42, 48
Notice of Royal Commission, 46
of baptismal name, 45, 65, 94, 119, 207
of birthday, 118, 119, 205
of gift, 119
Scholars of Gondar, 60
Säwasəw, 173
Säwasəw
  excerpt, 65
Supplication, 77, 128, 129
  commentary on, 138
  for Saint Mary, 129
  for the Cross, 129
  for the Departed, 128
Susənyos
  Collection of poems to, 158
Sword of Divinity, 82
Sword of the Trinity, 73, 116, 206, 209
  excerpt, 74
  variant form, 209
Synaxarium, 122, 126
Synaxarium, Concluding Prayer, 64
Ten Commandments, 213
  commentary on (in Amharic), 184
Testimonies of the Fathers, 147
That Christ is One, 169
Tomar, 148
Trinitarian Formula, 54, 65, 107

Index of Names and Places in the Codices

NB: Western names are put in the form: lastname, firstname. Ethiopian names are put in the traditional form: firstname, fathername.

Ab Śəlus, 98
Abäbä Čärənät, 119
Abäbä Čärənät, *Ləj*, 119
Abäbä of Gʷoha Ṣəyon, 46
Abäbä Täklä Ṣadəq, 118
Abära, 118, 119
Abraham, *Abba*, 45
Abreham, Bishop, 83
Agafari Täkläyäs, 48
Agafari Täkläyäs Wolde Mika'el, 48
Alämayähu Ṭäna, *Ləj*, 72
Amätä Śəllase, 83
Amhara Sayənt, 45
Aratä Maryam, 46
Arero Bedegon, 119
Arsanəyos, 158
Arusi, 130
Azänäč Aba Šawəl, 48
Basələyos, Bishop *Abba*, 166
Basəlyos, *Abuna*, 130
Basəlyos, *Abuna*, 128, 223
Bäyänägobaw, 83
Bəluy Täkle of Gondar, *Aläqa*, 45
Bərəhanä Mäsqäl, 74
Bərəhane Asäfa, 65
Betä Leḥem, 94
Betä Säyda Hospital, 46
Bəyä Giyorgis, 98
Bishop Abreham, 77
Bishop Qerəlos III, 77
Bulga, 46
Däbrä Libanos, 46
Dañe, 72

Efrata in Mänzih, 94
Əntoto Maryam, 45
Estifanos, 98
Fəsəḥ Ḥä Ṣəyon, 148
Gäbrä Qiros, *Abunä*, 39
Gäbrä Giyorgis, *Ačäge*, 45
Gäbrä Ḥəywät, *Abba*, 205
Gäbrä Ḥəywät, *Abba*, 205
Gäbrä Iyasus, 65, 107
Gäbrä Mädḫən, 72
Gäbrä Maryam, 209
Gäbrä Maryam, *Märige(ta)*, 143
Gäbrä Maryam of Efrata in Mänzih, 94
Gäbrä Mika'el, 65
Gäbrä Sänbät, 89
Gäbrä Śəllase, 83
Gäbrä Ṣəyon, 74
Gäbrä Yoḥannəs, 114
Giyorgis, 207
Gojjam, 56
Gondar, 45, 56, 60, 83
Gʷoha Ṣəyon, 46
Habtä Maryam of Däbrä Libanos, 46
Habtä Mik'ael of Sälale, 46
Hadis Täkle, 45
Ḥaylä Maryam, 164
Ḥaylä Maryam
 Hayla Maryam, 164
Ḥaylä Mäsqäl Kəbrät, *Märigeta*, 65
Ḥaylä Śəllase, 45, 48, 143, 205
Ḥaylä Śəllase, 166

243

Hayle, 45
Hayle Wäldä Rufe, 46
Həruy of Gondar, *Aläqa*, 45
Həruy Ṭəbäbu, 48
Həruy, *Aläqa*, 213
Hirutä Śəllase, 205
Isaac, *Abba*, 45
Iyasu, *Ləj*, 205
Kidanä Maryam, 65, 213
Lamma of Mäkanä Śəlasse, *Aläqa*, 45
Ləsanä Wärq of Däbrä Libanos, 46
Lə_ul Wäldä Rufa'el, 143
Luqas, Archbishop of Arusi Province, 130
Luqas, Bishop, 130
Mäfəqäre Ǝgzi'abḫer, 123
Mägabe Gʷangul Mäkonän, 167
Mäkanä Śəlasse, 45
Mäkʷonən Mäqʷuriya, 207
Mälakä Gänät Ṭərunäh, 60
Mälə'akä Gänät Kəfle, 45
Mänagäša Maryam, 45
Mänän, Empress, 45
Mänkər Fänta, 202
Mänz, 94, 207
Masfen Hayla Maryam, *Qäň*, 94
Matewos, 112, 114, 223
Mälə'akä Bərhan Ṣəge, 45
Mika'el, *Abba*, 45
Mikael, 205
Niqodimos, 148
Peṭros IV, *Abba*, 45, 112, 114, 223
Peṭros, Bishop, 130
Qäṣäla of Ǝntoto Maryam, *Aläqa*, 45
Qerəlos III, bishop, 83
Qerəlos, *Abba*, 45, 117, 118
Ras Makonnen, 45, 46
Sägäle, 205
Śahəle of Bulga, 46
Sälale, 46
Ṣata Mika'el Church, 185
Saynt (in Wollo), 143
Səbḥat Gäbrä Maryam, *Märigeta*, 167
Šəfäraw, *Gərazəmač*, 72
Shoa, 205
Sunət, 98
Susənyos, 211
Taddäsä, *Fitawərari*, 72
Takälä Täfäma, 202
Täklä Haymanot, 118
Täklä. Haymanot, 45
Täklä Maryam, 107
Täkle of Mänagäša Maryam, *Mäməhər*, 45
Täklä Ṣadəq, 119, 207
Täklä Śəllase, 65
Täkle, *Nəburä_əd*, 45
Täkle Ṣadəq of Däbrä Libanos, 46
Tamänä of Amhara Sayənt, *Aläqa*, 45
Täsäma of Bulga, 46
Wälätä Bərhan, 205
Wälätä Giyorgis, 45
Wälätä Iyäsus, 205
Wälätä Ṣadəq, 205
Wälättä Maryam, 102
Wäldä Amlak, 45
Wäldä Dawit Ṭəqä Ḥer, 98
Wäldä Giyorgis, 83
Wäldä Maryam, 107
Wäldä Maryam of Däbrä Libanos, 46
Wäldä Maryam of Saynt, 143
Wäldä Rufä_el, 102
Wäldä Ṣadəq, 52
Wäldä Säma_ət, 114
Wäldä Sändät Däsəta, 54
Wäldä Tənsa'e, 65
Wäldä Yoḥannəs, 72
Wäldä Yoḥannəs Dəl Näṣahu, 72
Wändəmagäñähu of Sälale, 46

Yäsäwawärq of Aratä Maryam, 46
Yohannes XV, bishop, 83

Zur Aba Ṣərḥa Arəyam, 167

Index of Miniatures in Codices

Aaron, 111
Angel, 164
  Afnin, 164
  Fanuel, 164
  Gabriel, 164
  Michael, 164
  Raguel, 164
    holding sun and moon, 164
  Rufael, 164
  Saquel, 164
    with sword and scabbard standing with his foot on a demon, 71
Box containing asmat prayers, 163, 164
Cardinal Points of the Compass, 213
Crude Drawing
  figure, 53, 158, 185
David and Solomon, 163
Gälawədewos, the Martyr as Equestrian Saint, 175
Gäbrä Mänfäs Qəddus, 164
Gäbrä Mänfäs Qəddus, 71
George and the Dragon, 38, 185
Holy Family
  printed card, 118
Holy Trinity, 185
  surrounded by the Four Living Creatures, 163
Jesus
  Crucifixion, 49, 164, 185
    printed card, 118
  Heart of Jesus, 205
  Last Supper
    printed card, 118
  Striking of the Head, 164
    printed card, 118
John, Son of Thunder, 164

Krestos Samra
  on way to Debre Libanos monastery, 205
  when she prayed in the middle of the river, 205
Lamb holding Cross, 164
Madonna and Child, 38, 71, 164, 185
  printed card, 118
Map of the Ocean, 152
Mary
  Crowned by the Trinity, 38
  Gave garment and chair to Saint Hildefonsus, 38
  The Assumption, 38
Nativity
  printed card, 118
Parting of the Red Sea, 111
Path of the Zodiak, 152, 153
Printed Card
  Crucifixion, 118
  Holy Family, 118
  Last Supper, 118
  Madonna and Child, 118
  Nativity, 118
  Striking of the Head, 118
Qerubim, 163
Serpents, 163, 164
Talismanic Charts and Symbols, 83
Winged Creature, 163
Yarəd, 93, 164

Index of Scribal Practices

Arranged for reading
  days of the week, 53, 73, 74, 104, 117, 157, 158, 165, 206, 209
  festivals, xxvii, 90, 91
  hours of the day, 88
  months, 174, 187
Binding
  Two-ring binder, 176
Book rebound, 73
Case (*maḥdär*)
  Double slip, 53, 55, 86, 112, 173, 183, 204
  Single slip, 77, 154
Cover
  Fabric double-pouch, 46, 53, 92, 99, 112
  Leather quarter bound, 96
  Leather tooled, 48, 50, 61, 67, 86, 92, 99, 110, 112, 116, 117, 125, 128, 137, 146, 154, 161
  Leather untooled, 120, 204
  Particle board, 204
  Plywood, 196
  Sawed boards, 75, 122, 132
Enumeration of types of chants, 93
Fabric
  Visible between turn ins, 85, 86, 116, 120, 128, 146, 154
Foliated
  Arabic numbers on each page, 207
  Gə_əz numbers, 118
Government scriptorium, 119, 143, 165, 207

Headband and tailband, 1, 48, 50, 61, 86, 137, 146, 157, 161, 204
Homoeoteleuton, 39
Leather cover, tooled, 1
Marginal notes
  Mnemonics, 171
Mirror niche, 209
Navigation system, 53, 55, 57, 59, 86, 92, 96, 110, 146, 154, 166, 183
Pastedowns, 38, 148
Pen trials, 52, 54, 65, 83, 98, 107, 213
Quire numbers, 49, 58, 60, 65, 76, 83, 87, 91, 102, 108, 111, 121, 123, 130, 148, 156, 159, 171, 173, 175, 182, 186, 188, 202, 209
Repair
  Cover board, 213
  Spliced folio, 167
Rubrication
  Alternating red and black letters, 121, 130, 165
  of God, and Mary, 207
  of God, Jesus, Mary and saints, 107, 116, 121, 205, 209
  of God, Mary and saints, 72, 85
  of Jesus and Mary, 49, 91, 195, 202
  of Jesus, Mary, and saints, 114
  of Mary, 38, 54, 58, 60, 74, 76, 83, 94, 98, 119, 130, 148, 159, 171, 173, 186, 213
  of Mary and saints, 52, 69, 87, 89, 102, 165, 182
  of saints, 175, 188
Scoring of lines ignored, 96

Scribal intervention, 39, 49, 52, 54, 56, 58, 60, 65, 69, 72, 74, 76, 83, 85, 87, 89, 91, 94, 98, 102, 108, 111, 115, 119, 123, 126, 130, 136, 144, 148, 153, 156, 159, 165, 167, 171, 173, 175, 182, 186, 188, 203, 205, 207, 214, 217

Seal, 43, 46, 54

Section division
  Ḥarāgs, 38, 43, 46, 52, 54, 65, 72, 74, 93, 119, 143, 165, 181, 202, 205, 207
  Line of alternating red and black dots, 38, 54, 56, 58, 60, 65, 69, 87, 89, 91, 94, 98, 102, 107, 114, 119, 126, 136, 143, 148, 153, 159, 167, 171, 181, 186, 195, 202, 213
  Line of black dots, 155
  Line of red dots, 130, 155, 188
  Multiple full stops, 38, 46, 48, 49, 54, 65, 69, 72, 74, 83, 85, 87, 89, 91, 94, 98, 102, 107, 111, 114, 116, 119, 121, 123, 126, 130, 136, 143, 148, 155, 159, 165, 167, 171, 175, 181, 195, 202, 207, 209, 213
  Pre-sixteenth-century system, 217

Spine strap, 135

Table of contents, 48

Textblock
  edges dyed red, 93